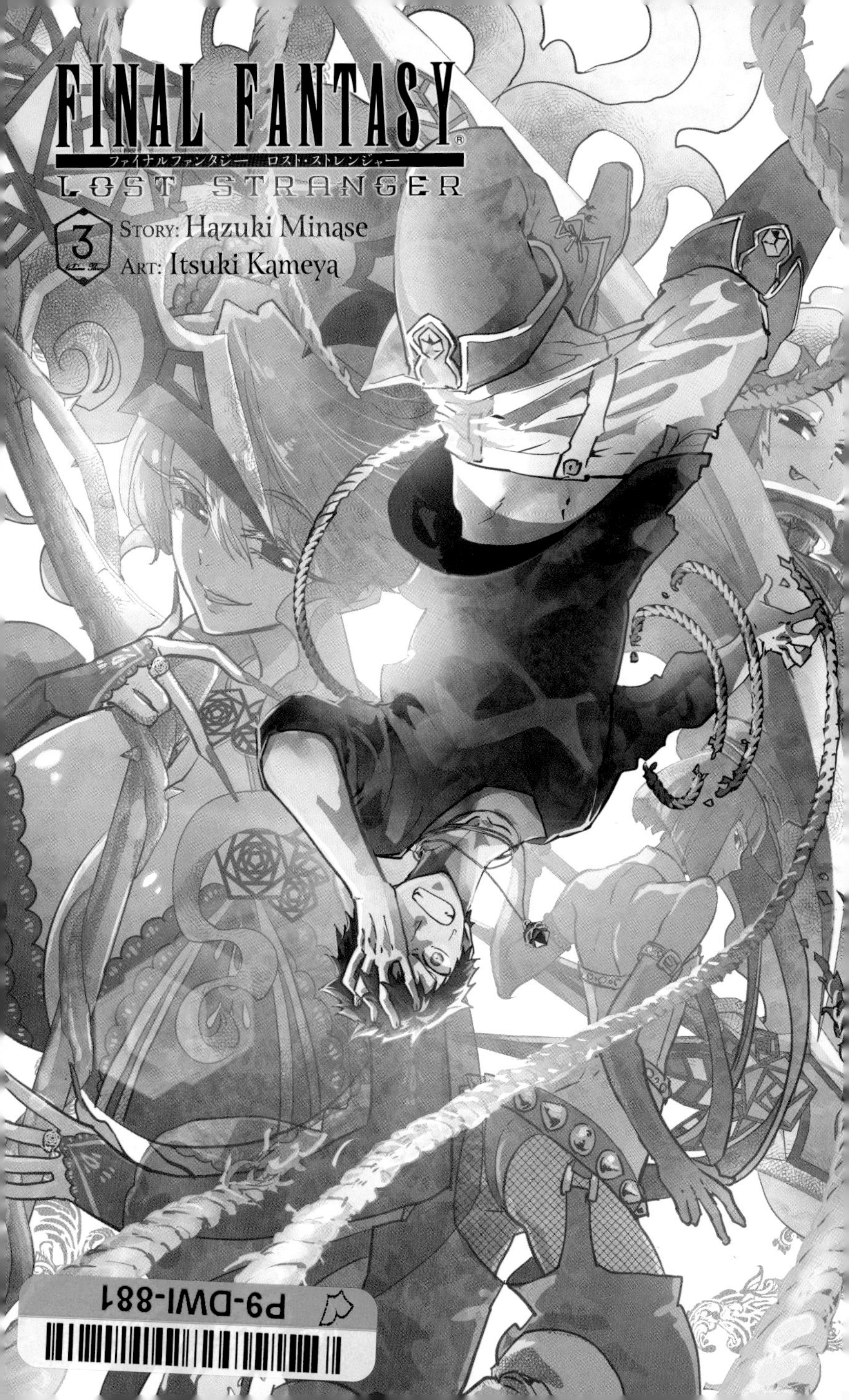
FINAL FANTASY®
ファイナルファンタジー　ロスト・ストレンジャー
LOST STRANGER
3
STORY: Hazuki Minase
ART: Itsuki Kameya

Contents

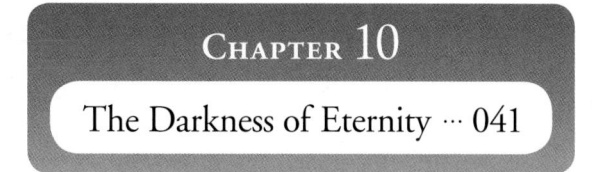
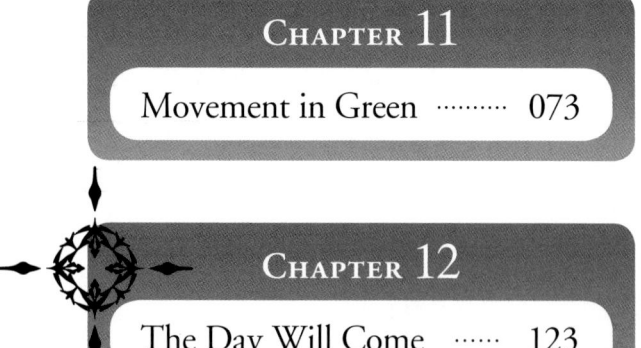

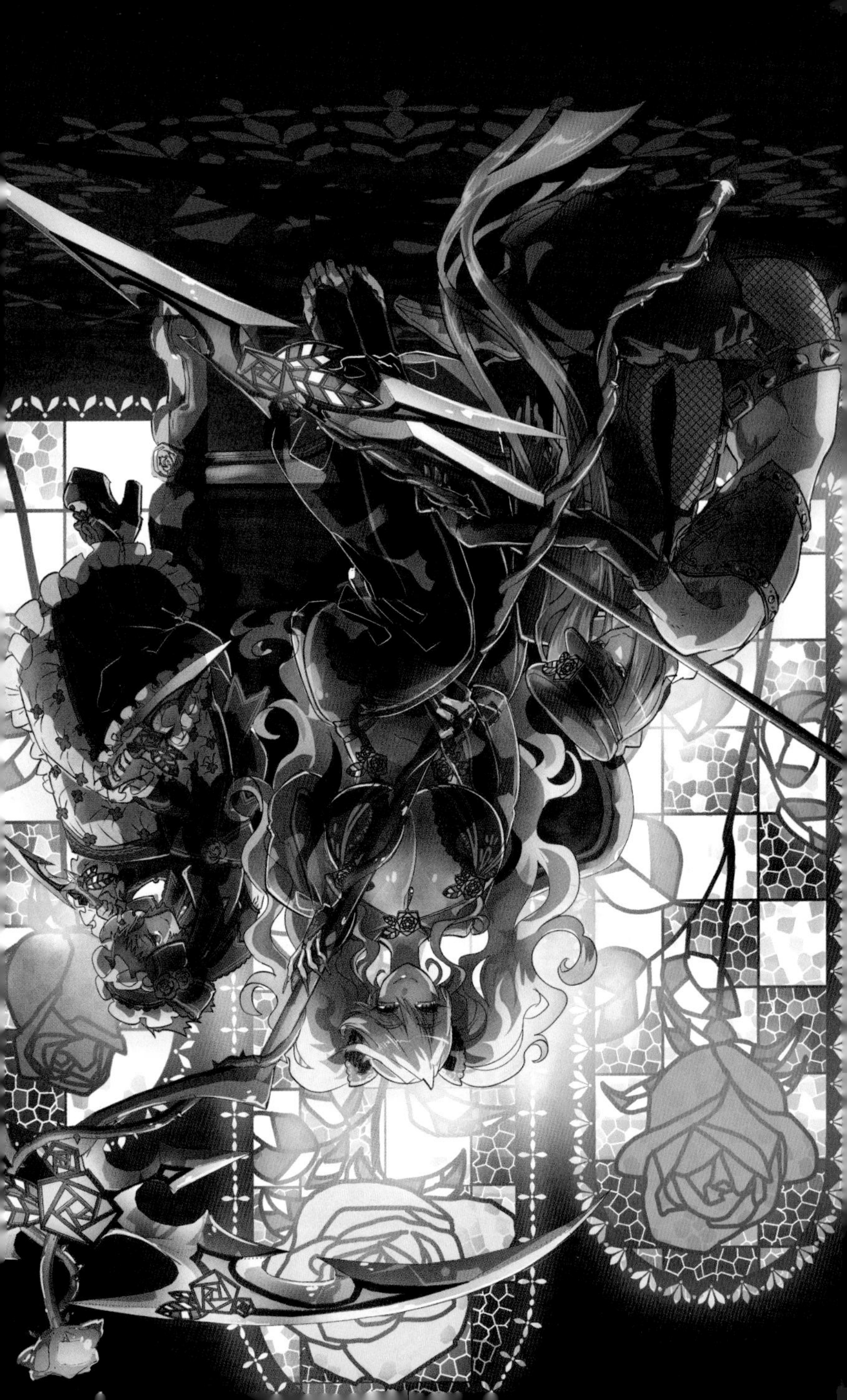

FINAL FANTASY®

ファイナルファンタジー　ロスト・ストレンジャー

LOST STRANGER

STORY & CHARACTERS

Shogo and his little sister, Yuko, are SE employees. After awakening from their run-in with a truck, they found themselves in the *FF* world they'd always longed for...! Much like in the games, Shogo and Yuko have fun exploring the area, but tragedy would soon befall them. The ultimate fantasy awaits—a forbidden tale of reincarnation in another world with an *FF* twist!!

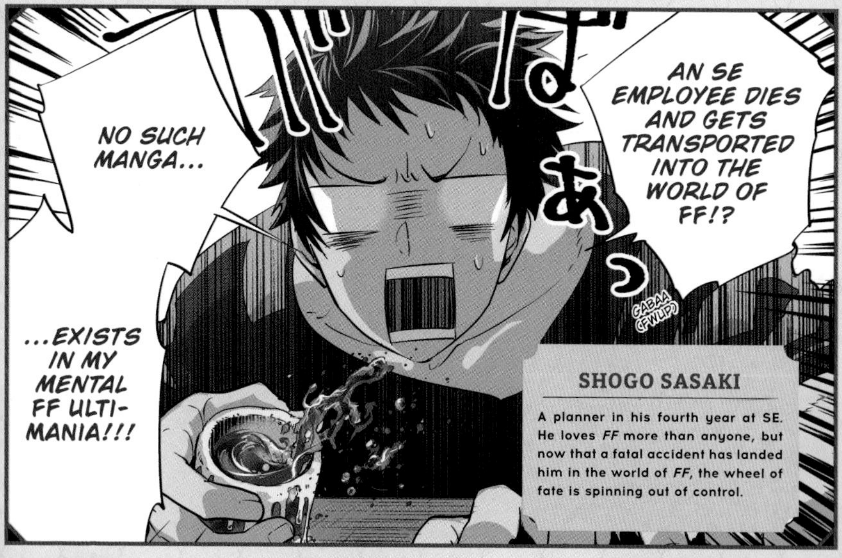
AN SE EMPLOYEE DIES AND GETS TRANSPORTED INTO THE WORLD OF FF!?
ばあっ
GABAA (FWUP)
NO SUCH MANGA...
...EXISTS IN MY MENTAL FF ULTI-MANIA!!!

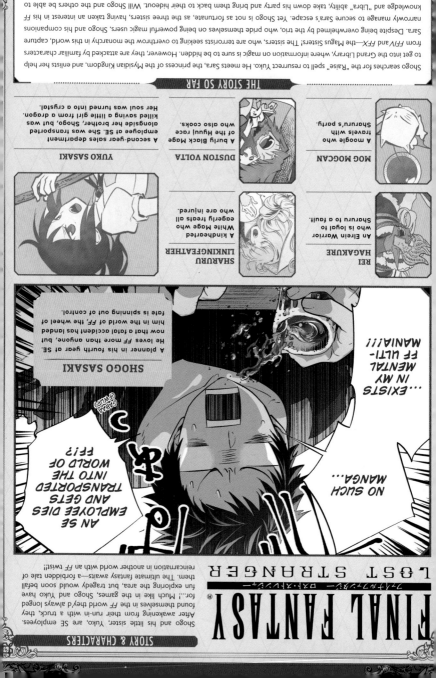

SHOGO SASAKI

A planner in his fourth year at SE. He loves *FF* more than anyone, but now that a fatal accident has landed him in the world of *FF*, the wheel of fate is spinning out of control.

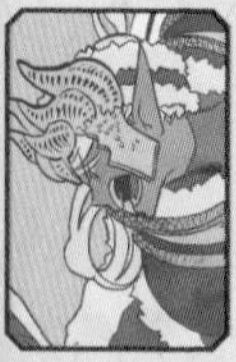

REI HAGAKURE

An Elrein Warrior who is loyal to Sharuru to a fault.

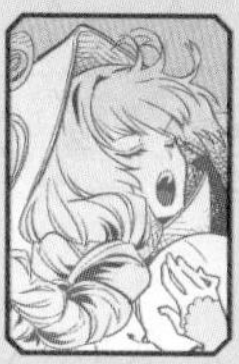

SHARURU LINKINGFEATHER

A kindhearted White Mage who eagerly treats all who are injured.

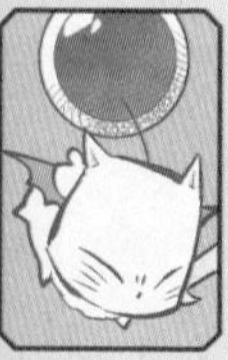

MOG MOGCAN

A moogle who travels with Sharuru's party.

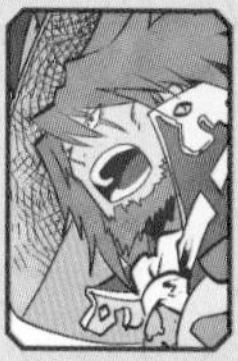

DUSTON VOLTA

A burly Black Mage of the Hyuuj race who also cooks.

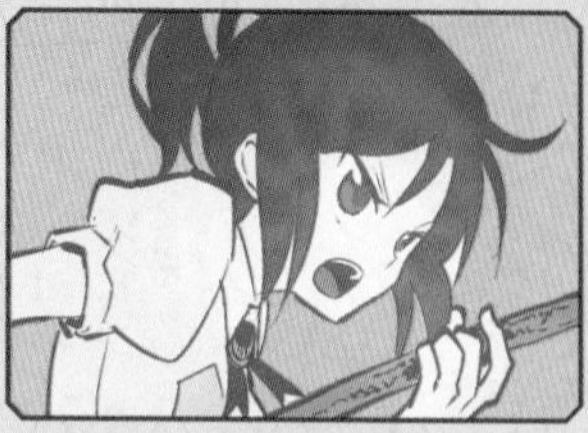

YUKO SASAKI

A second-year sales department employee at SE. She was transported alongside her brother, Shogo, but was killed saving a little girl from a dragon. Her soul was turned into a crystal.

THE STORY SO FAR

Shogo searches for the "Raise" spell to resurrect Yuko. He meets Sara, the princess of the Mysidian Kingdom, and enlists her help to get into the Grand Library, where information on magic is sure to be hidden. However, they are attacked by familiar characters from *FFIV* and *FFX*—the Magus Sisters! The sisters, who are terrorists seeking to overthrow the monarchy in this world, capture Sara. Despite being overwhelmed by the trio, who pride themselves on being powerful magic users, Shogo and his companions narrowly manage to secure Sara's escape. Yet Shogo is not as fortunate, as the three sisters, having taken an interest in his *FF* knowledge and "Libra" ability, take down his party and bring them back to their hideout. Will Shogo and the others be able to escape the clutches of these terrorists who possess an unusual affinity for magic?

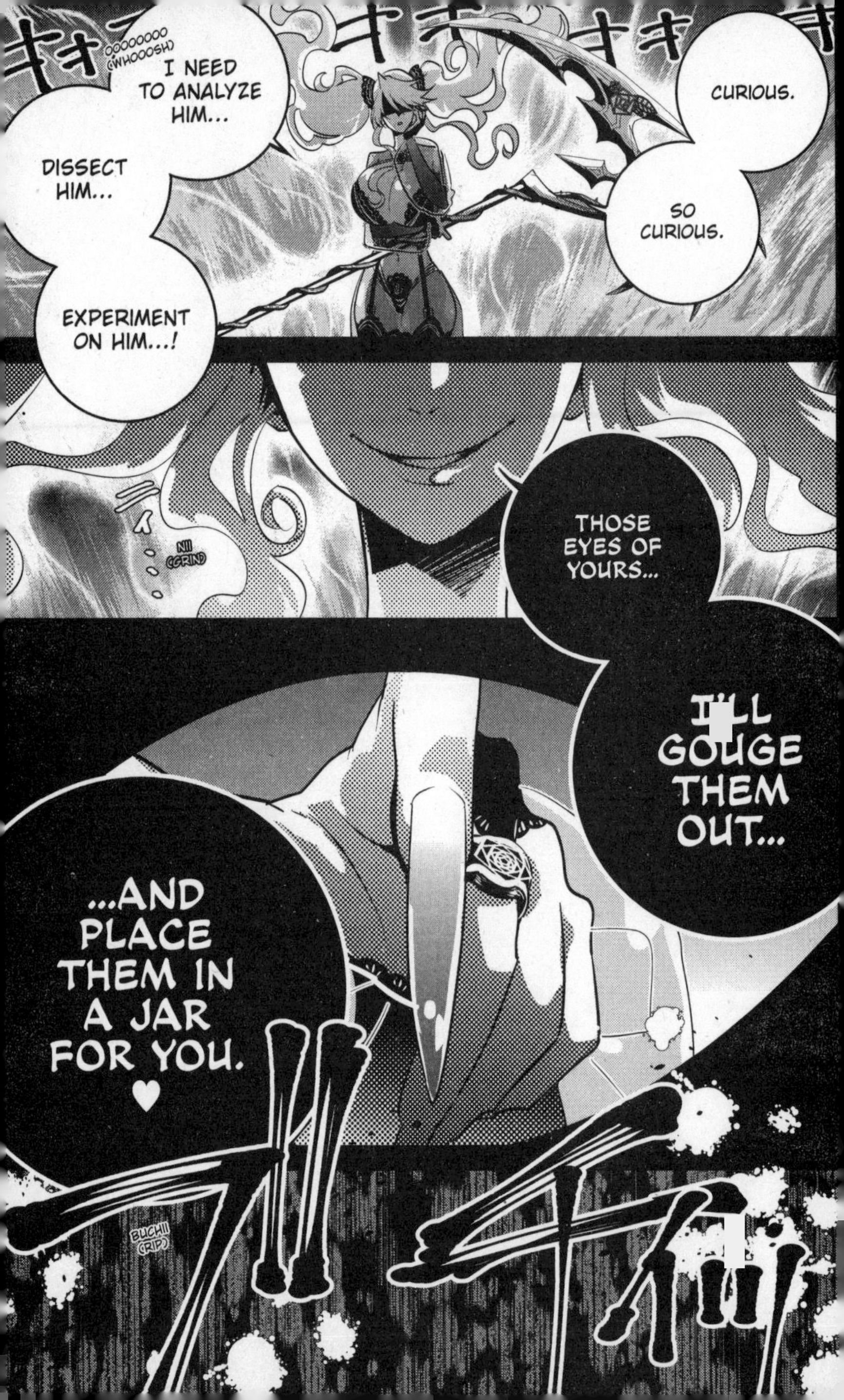
CURIOUS.
SO CURIOUS.
OOOOOOOO (WHOOOSH)
I NEED TO ANALYZE HIM...
DISSECT HIM...
EXPERIMENT ON HIM...!
NII (GRIN)
THOSE EYES OF YOURS...
I'LL GOUGE THEM OUT...
...AND PLACE THEM IN A JAR FOR YOU. ♥
BUCHII (RIP)

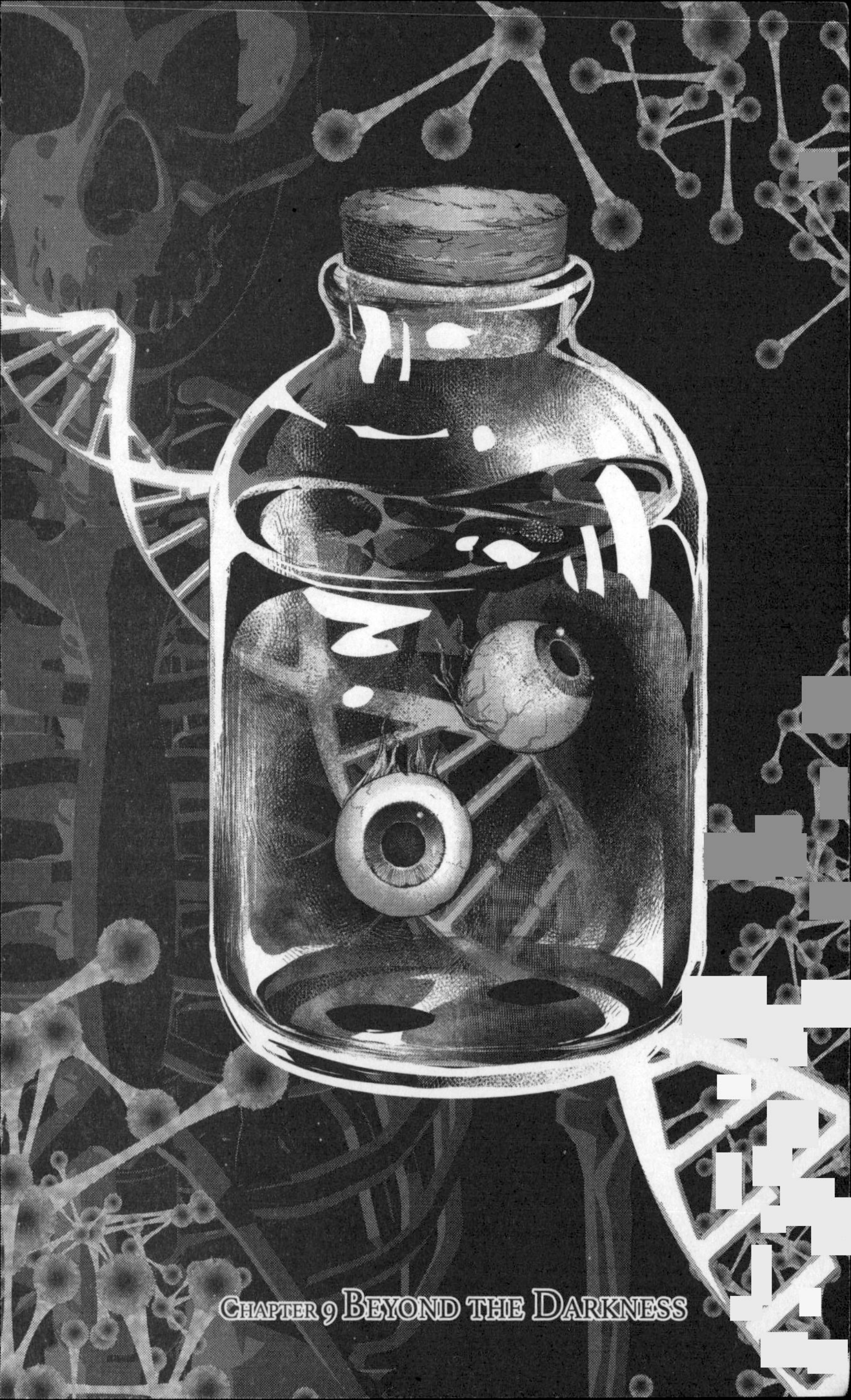

Chapter 9 Beyond the Darkness

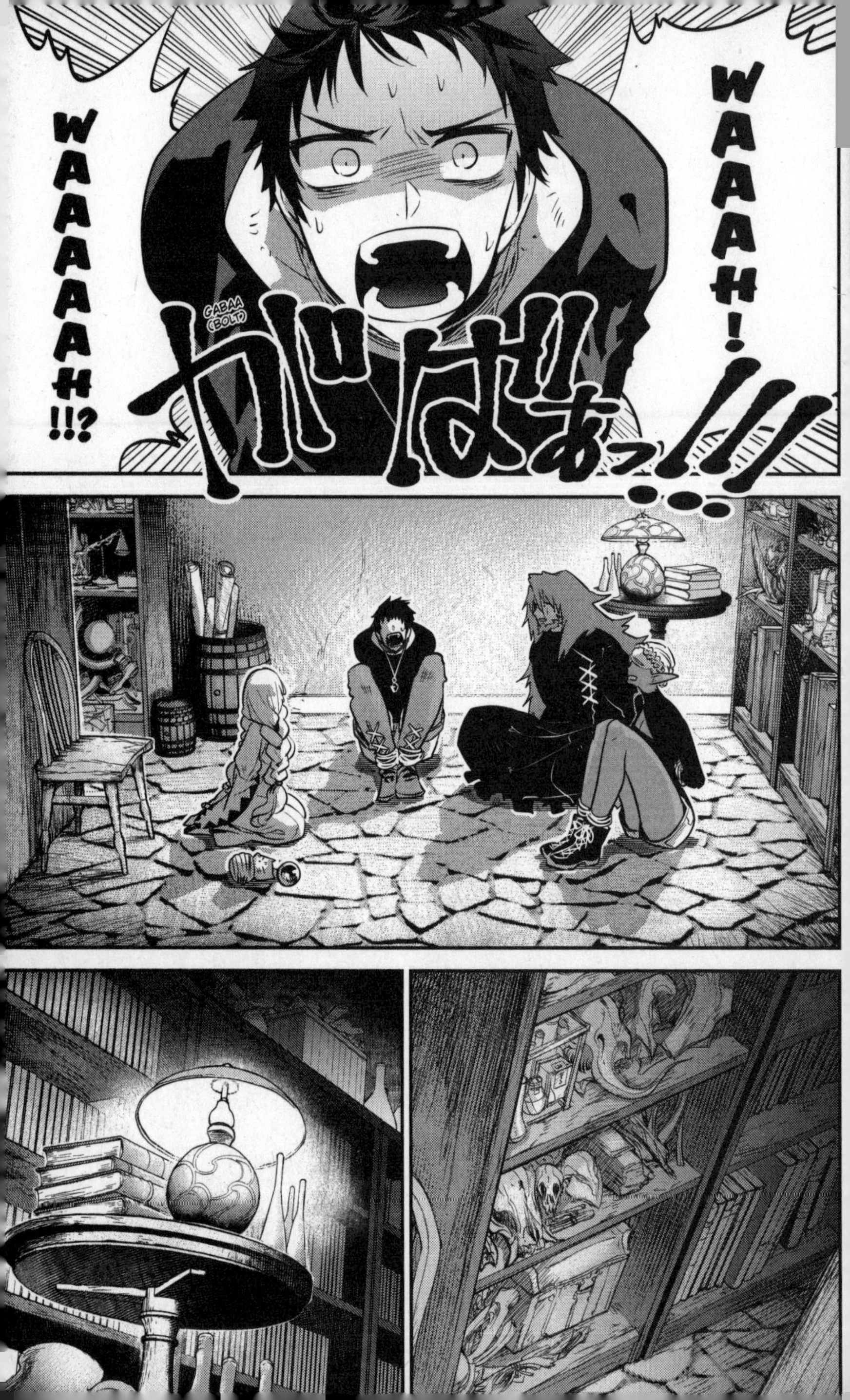
WAAAAH!
GABAA (BOLT)
がばっ!!!
WAAAAAAH!!?

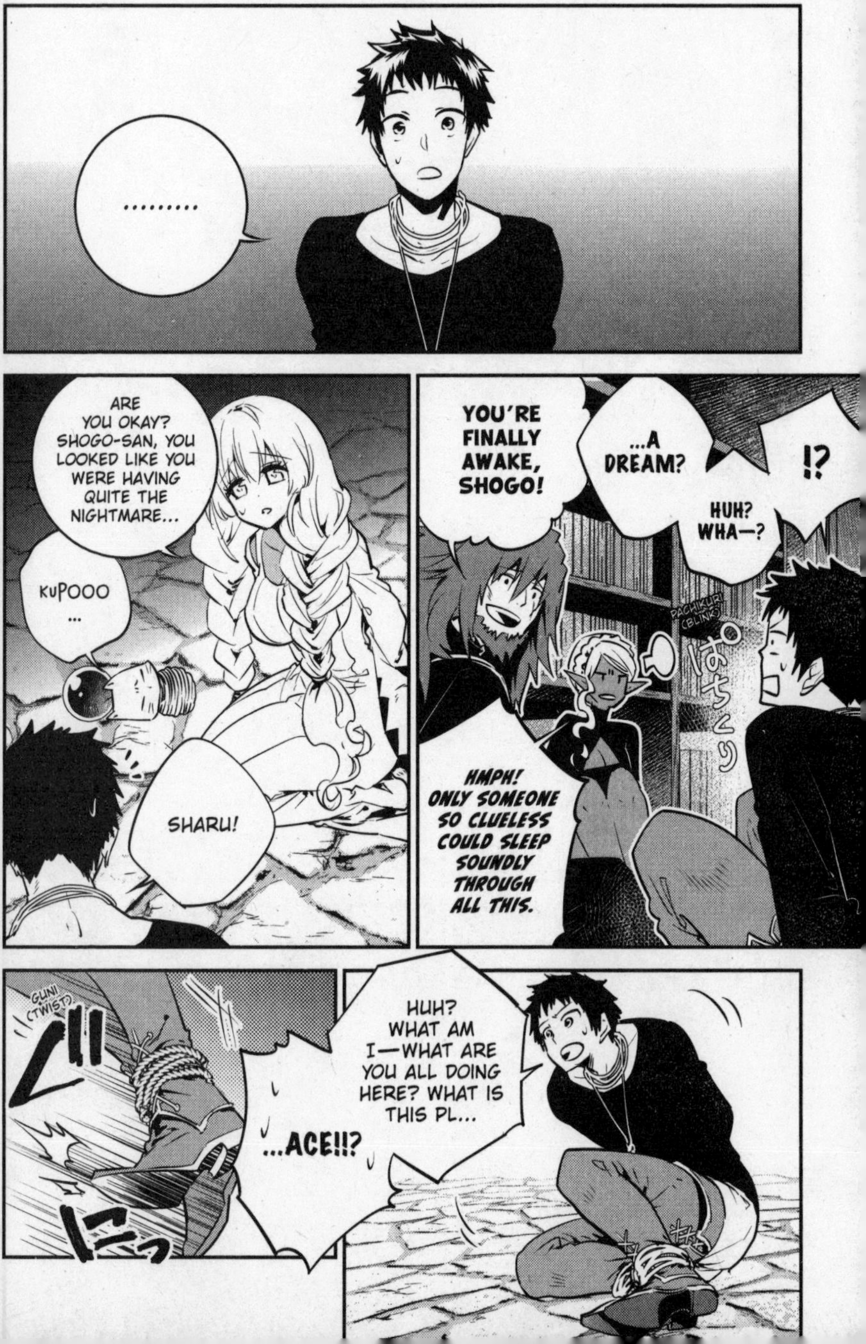
....
!?
HUH? WHA—?
...A DREAM?
YOU'RE FINALLY AWAKE, SHOGO!
PACHIKURI (BLINK)
HMPH! ONLY SOMEONE SO CLUELESS COULD SLEEP SOUNDLY THROUGH ALL THIS.
ARE YOU OKAY? SHOGO-SAN, YOU LOOKED LIKE YOU WERE HAVING QUITE THE NIGHTMARE...
KUPOOO ...
SHARU!
HUH? WHAT AM I—WHAT ARE YOU ALL DOING HERE? WHAT IS THIS PL...
...ACE!!?
GUNI (TWIST)

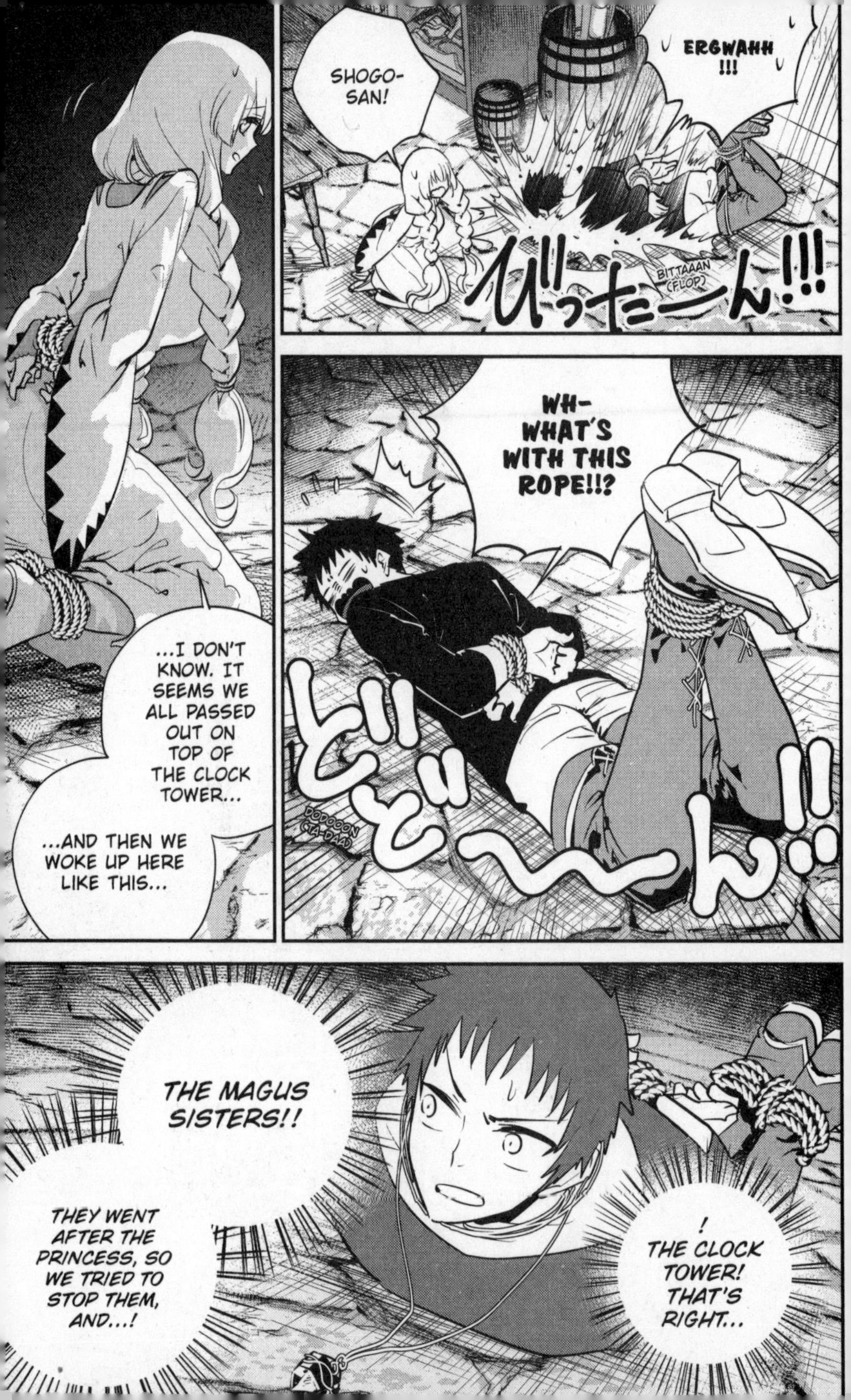
ERGWAHH!!!
SHOGO-SAN!
びったーん!!!
BITTAAN (FLOP)
WH- WHAT'S WITH THIS ROPE!!?
どど〜〜ん!!
DODOOON (TA-DAA)
...I DON'T KNOW. IT SEEMS WE ALL PASSED OUT ON TOP OF THE CLOCK TOWER...
...AND THEN WE WOKE UP HERE LIKE THIS...
! THE CLOCK TOWER! THAT'S RIGHT...
THE MAGUS SISTERS!!
THEY WENT AFTER THE PRINCESS, SO WE TRIED TO STOP THEM, AND...!

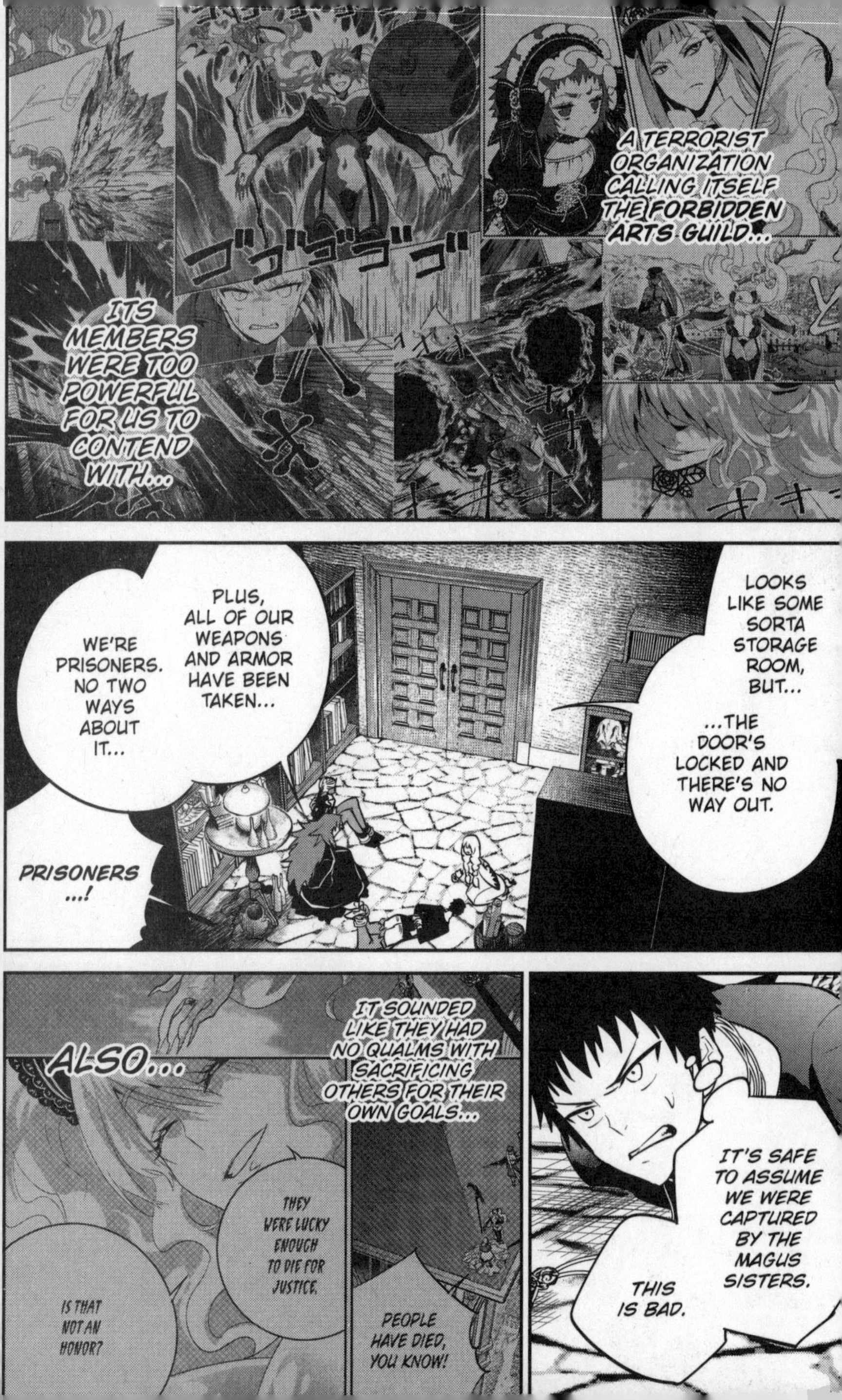
A TERRORIST ORGANIZATION CALLING ITSELF THE FORBIDDEN ARTS GUILD...
ITS MEMBERS WERE TOO POWERFUL FOR US TO CONTEND WITH...
LOOKS LIKE SOME SORTA STORAGE ROOM, BUT...
...THE DOOR'S LOCKED AND THERE'S NO WAY OUT.
PLUS, ALL OF OUR WEAPONS AND ARMOR HAVE BEEN TAKEN...
WE'RE PRISONERS. NO TWO WAYS ABOUT IT...
PRISONERS ...!
IT'S SAFE TO ASSUME WE WERE CAPTURED BY THE MAGUS SISTERS.
THIS IS BAD.
IT SOUNDED LIKE THEY HAD NO QUALMS WITH SACRIFICING OTHERS FOR THEIR OWN GOALS...
PEOPLE HAVE DIED, YOU KNOW!
ALSO...
THEY WERE LUCKY ENOUGH TO DIE FOR JUSTICE.
IS THAT NOT AN HONOR?

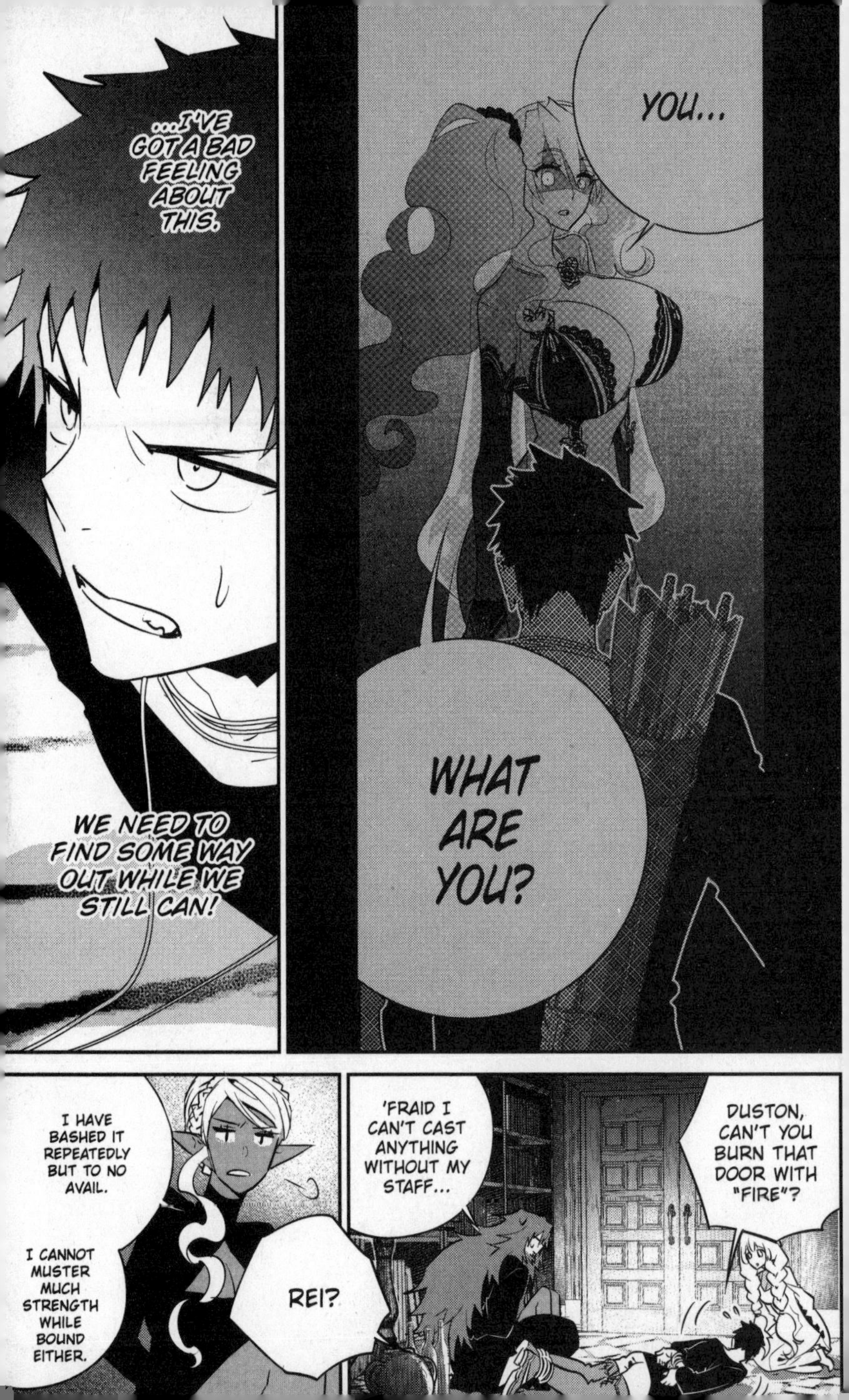
YOU...
WHAT ARE YOU?
...I'VE GOT A BAD FEELING ABOUT THIS.
WE NEED TO FIND SOME WAY OUT WHILE WE STILL CAN!
DUSTON, CAN'T YOU BURN THAT DOOR WITH "FIRE"?
'FRAID I CAN'T CAST ANYTHING WITHOUT MY STAFF...
REI?
I HAVE BASHED IT REPEATEDLY BUT TO NO AVAIL.
I CANNOT MUSTER MUCH STRENGTH WHILE BOUND EITHER.

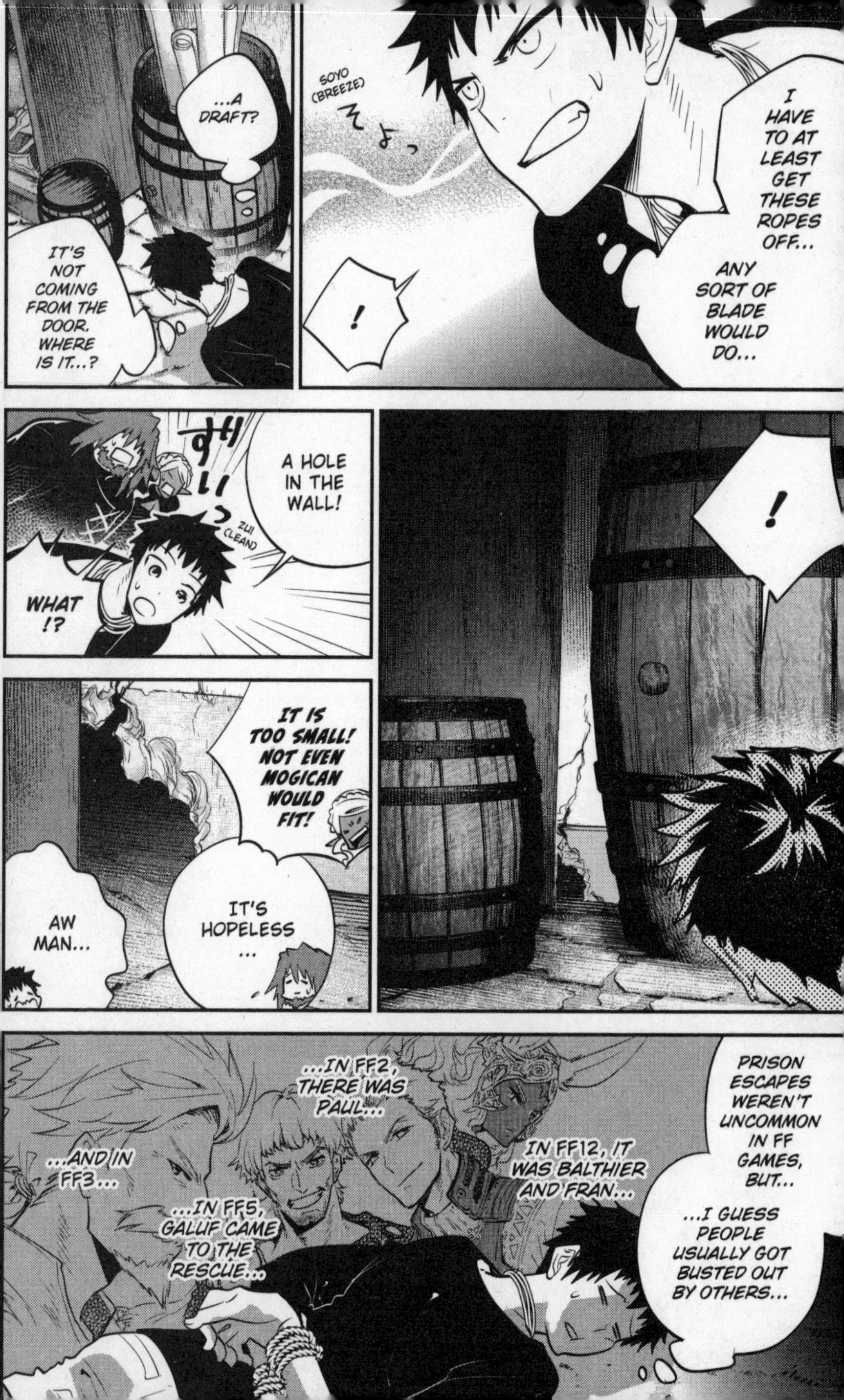
I HAVE TO AT LEAST GET THESE ROPES OFF...
ANY SORT OF BLADE WOULD DO...
SOYO (BREEZE)
!
...A DRAFT?
IT'S NOT COMING FROM THE DOOR. WHERE IS IT...?
!
A HOLE IN THE WALL!
ZUI (LEAN)
WHAT!?
IT IS TOO SMALL! NOT EVEN MOGICAN WOULD FIT!
IT'S HOPELESS...
AW MAN...
PRISON ESCAPES WEREN'T UNCOMMON IN FF GAMES, BUT...
...I GUESS PEOPLE USUALLY GOT BUSTED OUT BY OTHERS...
IN FF12, IT WAS BALTHIER AND FRAN...
...IN FF2, THERE WAS PAUL...
...IN FF5, GALUF CAME TO THE RESCUE...
...AND IN FF3...

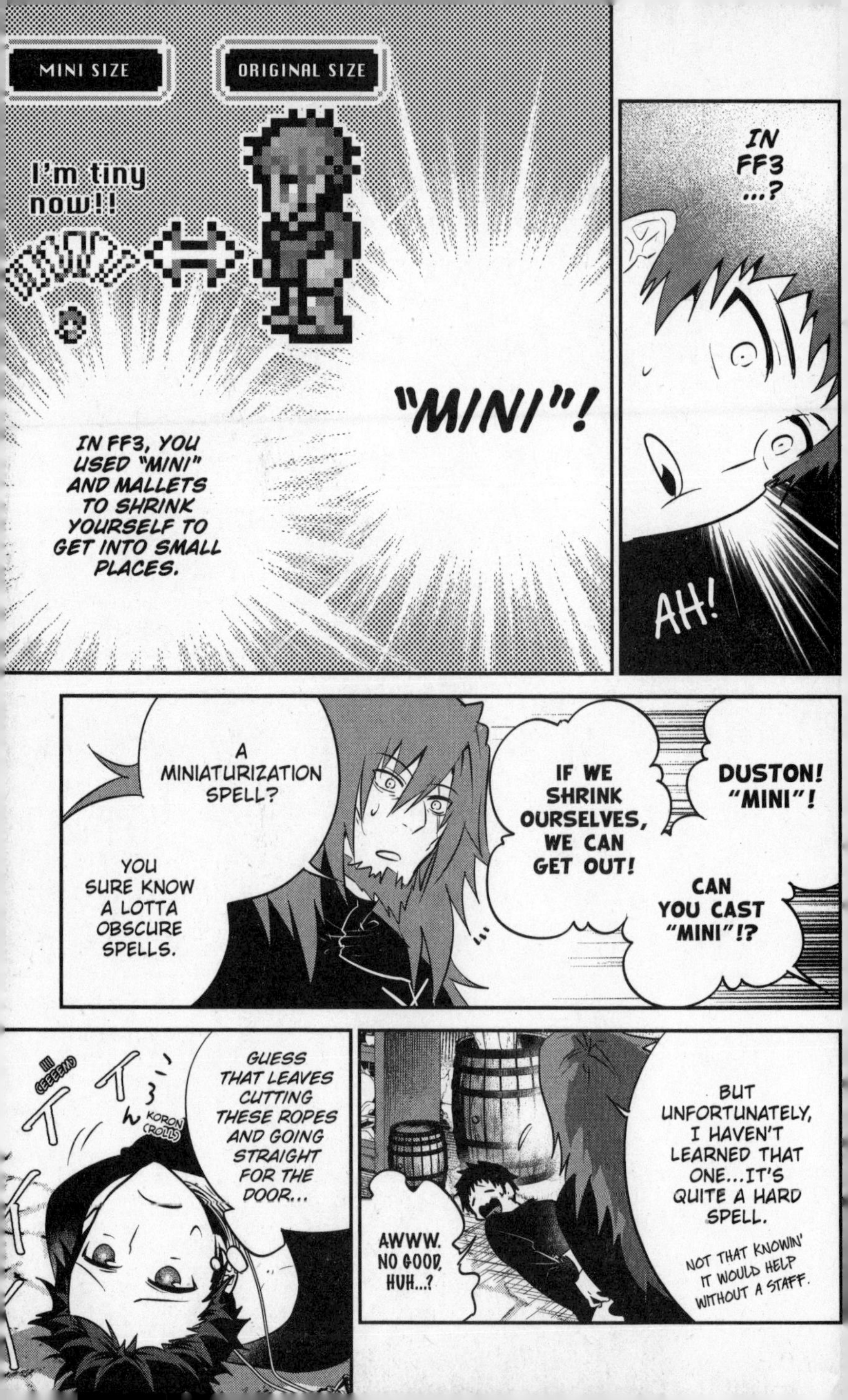
IN FF3 ...?
AH!
"MINI"!
IN FF3, YOU USED "MINI" AND MALLETS TO SHRINK YOURSELF TO GET INTO SMALL PLACES.
ORIGINAL SIZE
MINI SIZE
I'm tiny now!!
DUSTON! "MINI"!
CAN YOU CAST "MINI"!?
IF WE SHRINK OURSELVES, WE CAN GET OUT!
A MINIATURIZATION SPELL?
YOU SURE KNOW A LOTTA OBSCURE SPELLS.
BUT UNFORTUNATELY, I HAVEN'T LEARNED THAT ONE...IT'S QUITE A HARD SPELL.
NOT THAT KNOWIN' IT WOULD HELP WITHOUT A STAFF.
AWWW. NO GOOD, HUH...?
GUESS THAT LEAVES CUTTING THESE ROPES AND GOING STRAIGHT FOR THE DOOR...
KORON (ROLLS)
GEEEEMD

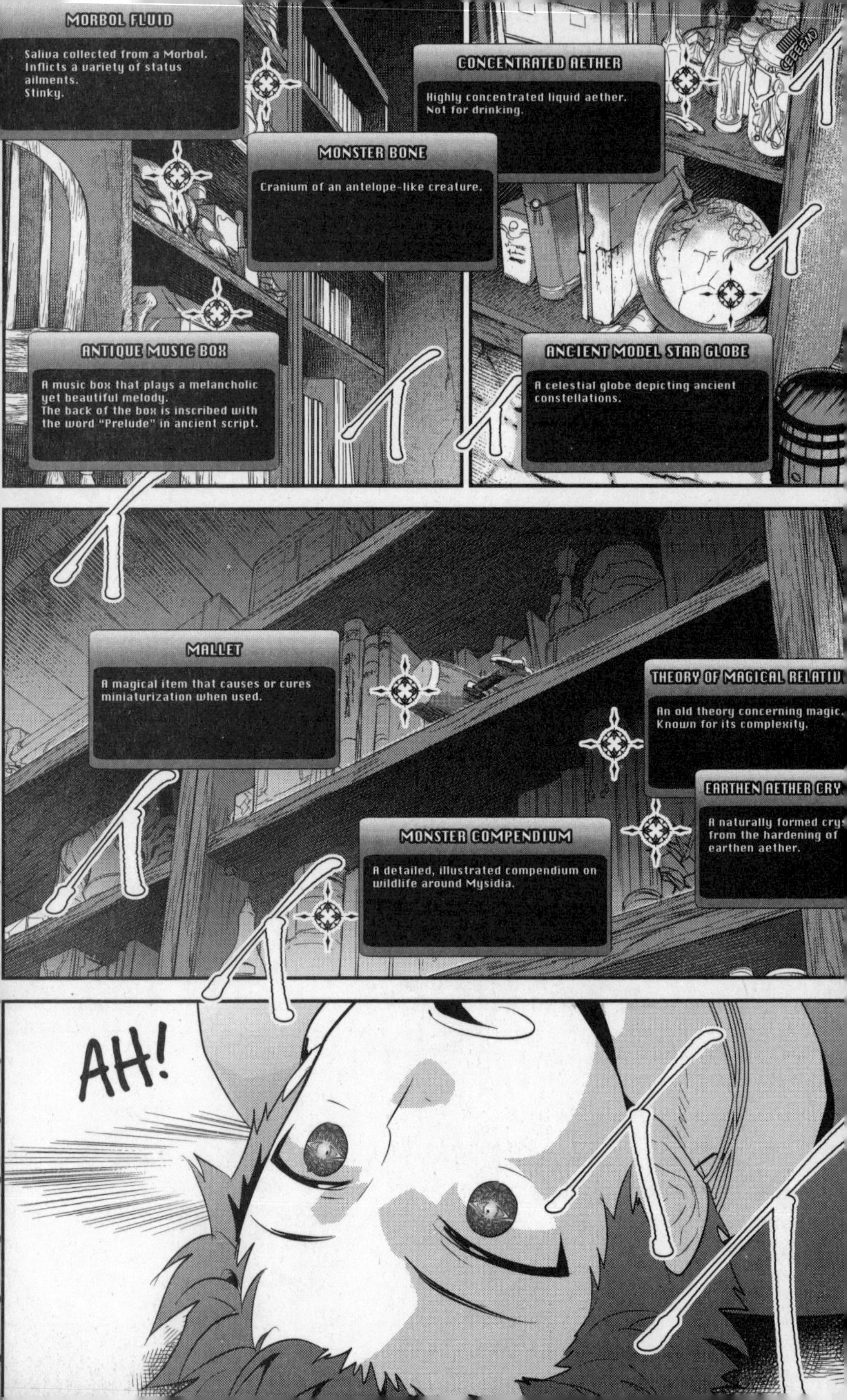
CONCENTRATED AETHER
Highly concentrated liquid aether.
Not for drinking.
ANCIENT MODEL STAR GLOBE
A celestial globe depicting ancient constellations.
MONSTER BONE
Cranium of an antelope-like creature.
MORBOL FLUID
Saliva collected from a Morbol.
Inflicts a variety of status ailments.
Stinky.
ANTIQUE MUSIC BOX
A music box that plays a melancholic yet beautiful melody.
The back of the box is inscribed with the word "Prelude" in ancient script.
THEORY OF MAGICAL RELATIV
An old theory concerning magic.
Known for its complexity.
EARTHEN AETHER CRY
A naturally formed crys from the hardening of earthen aether.
MALLET
A magical item that causes or cures miniaturization when used.
MONSTER COMPENDIUM
A detailed, illustrated compendium on wildlife around Mysidia.
AH!

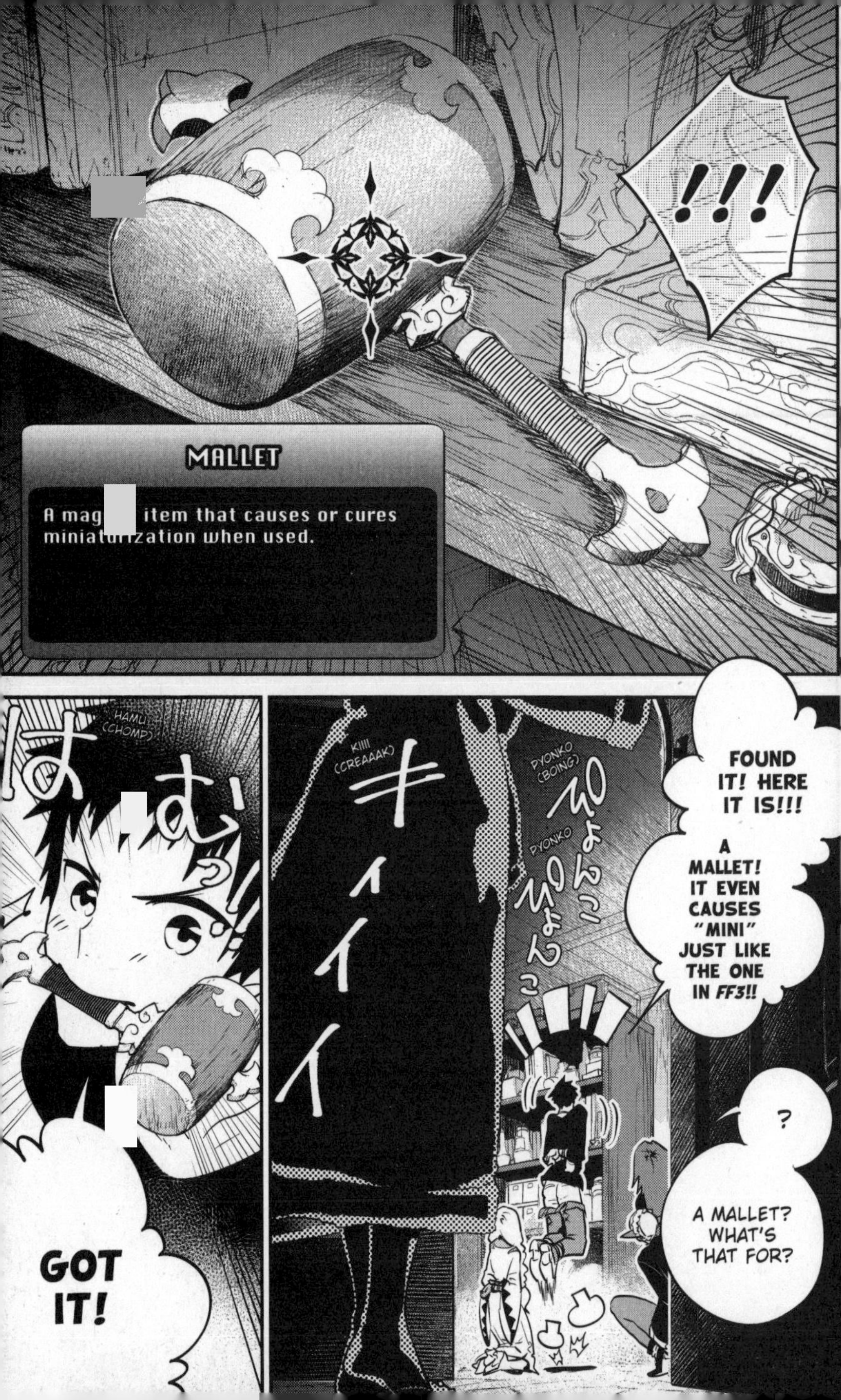
!!!
MALLET
A mag item that causes or cures miniaturization when used.
FOUND IT! HERE IT IS!!!
PYONKO (BOING)
ぴょんこ
PYONKO
ぴょんこ
A MALLET! IT EVEN CAUSES "MINI" JUST LIKE THE ONE IN *FF3*!!
?
A MALLET? WHAT'S THAT FOR?
KIIII (CREAAAK)
キィイイ
HAMU (CHOMP)
はむっ
GOT IT!

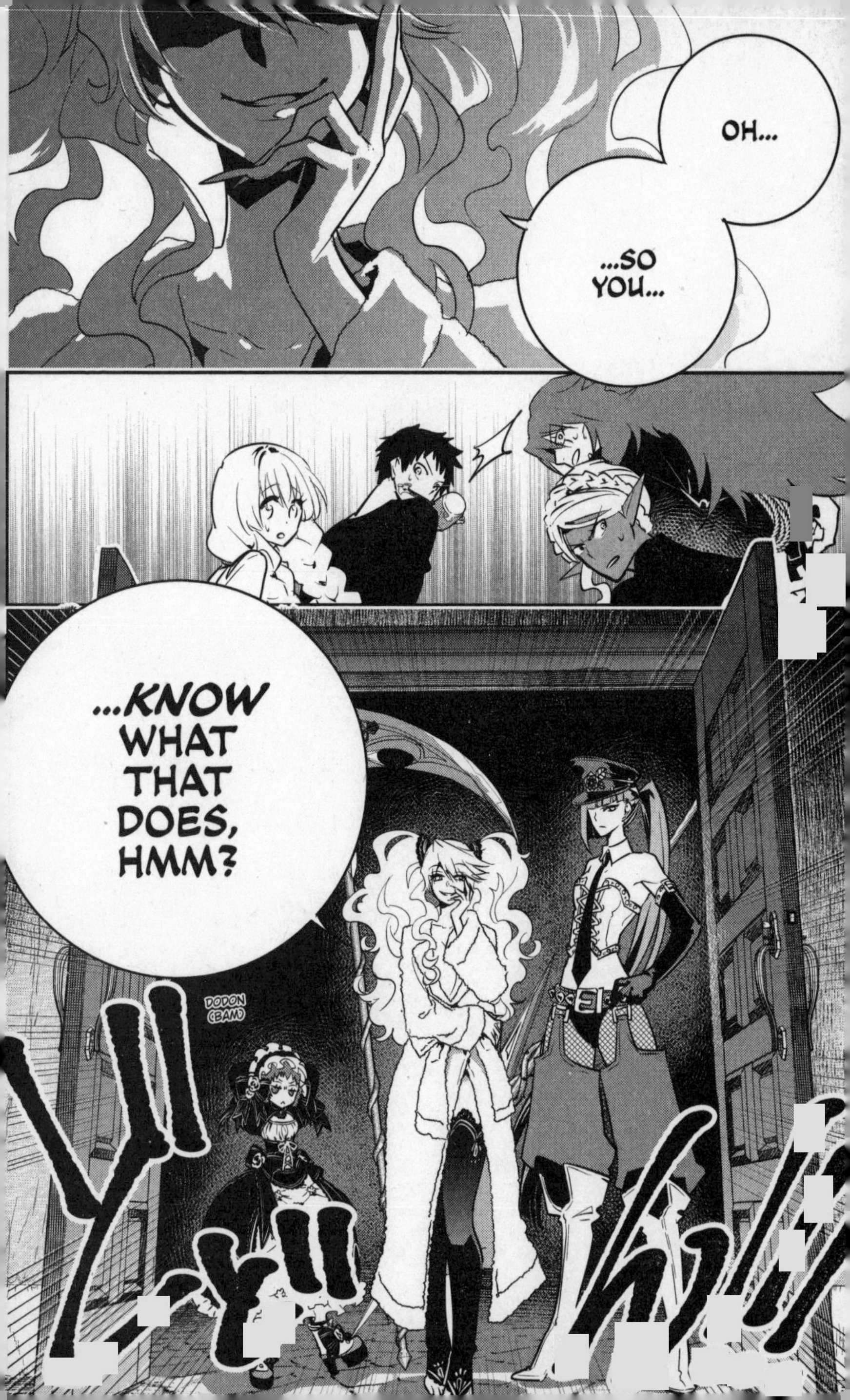
OH...
...SO YOU...
...KNOW WHAT THAT DOES, HMM?
DODON (BAM)

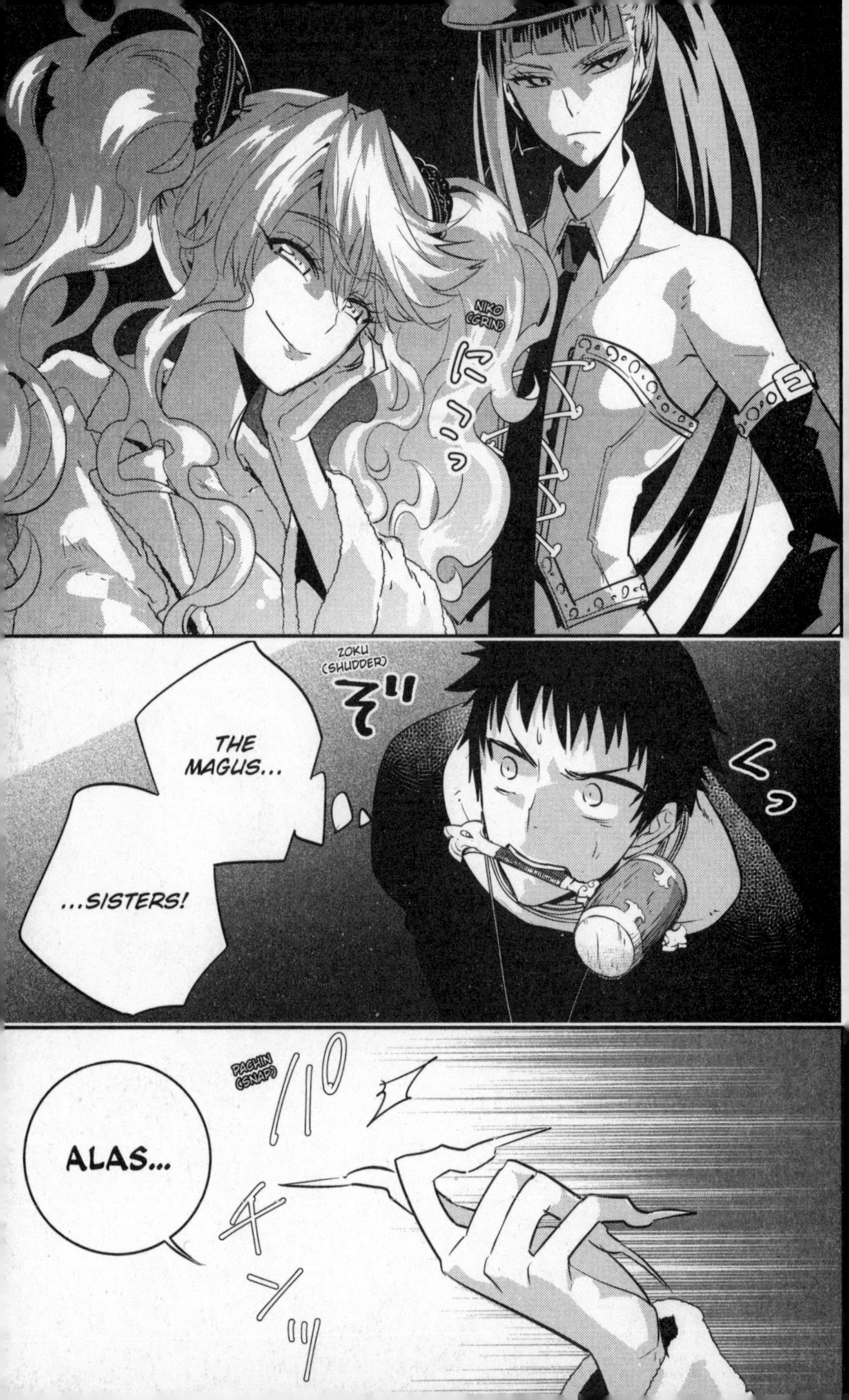
NIKO (GRIN)
ZOKU (SHUDDER)
THE MAGUS...
...SISTERS!
PACHIN (SNAP)
ALAS...

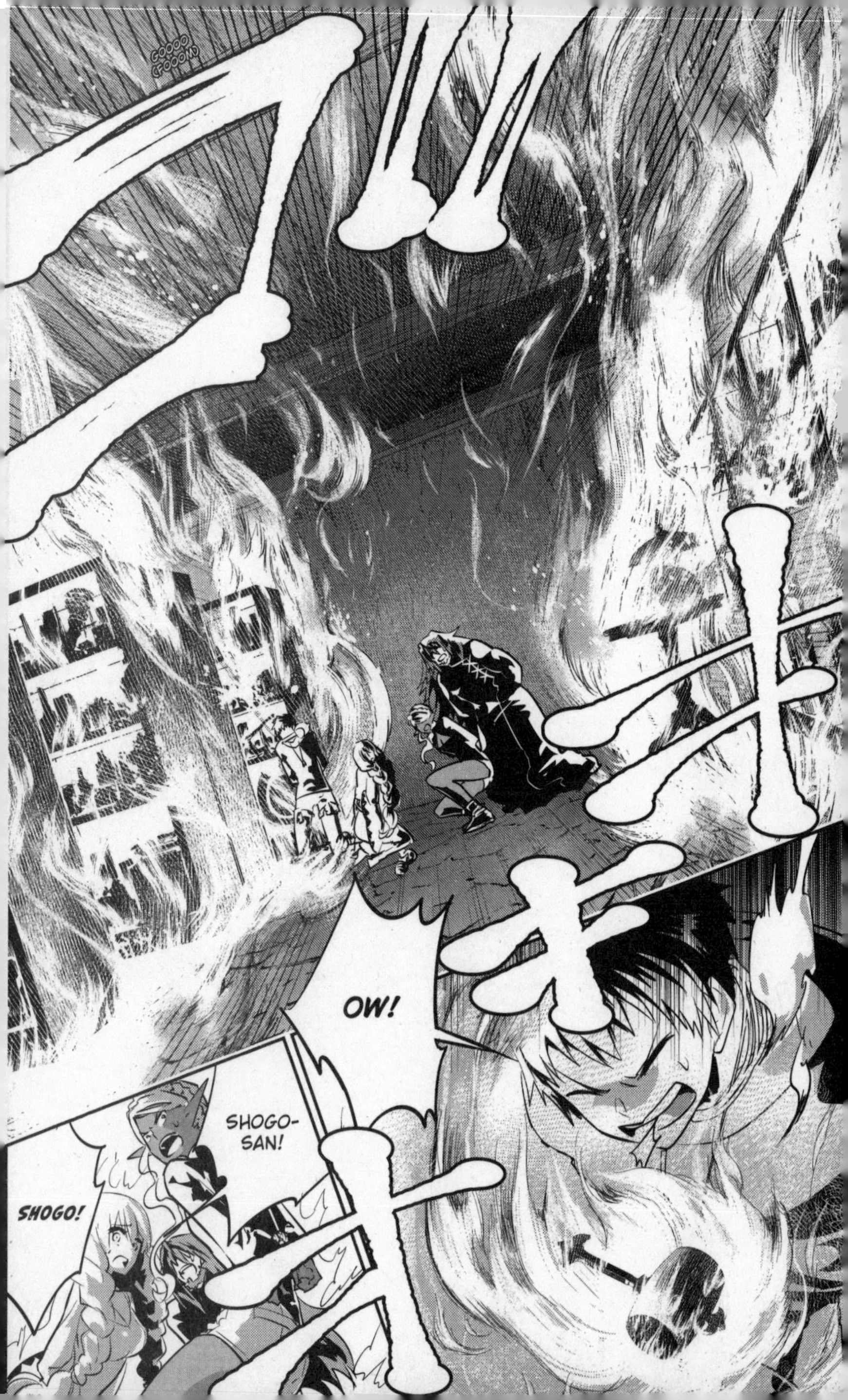
GOOOO (FOOOM)
OW!
SHOGO-SAN!
SHOGO!

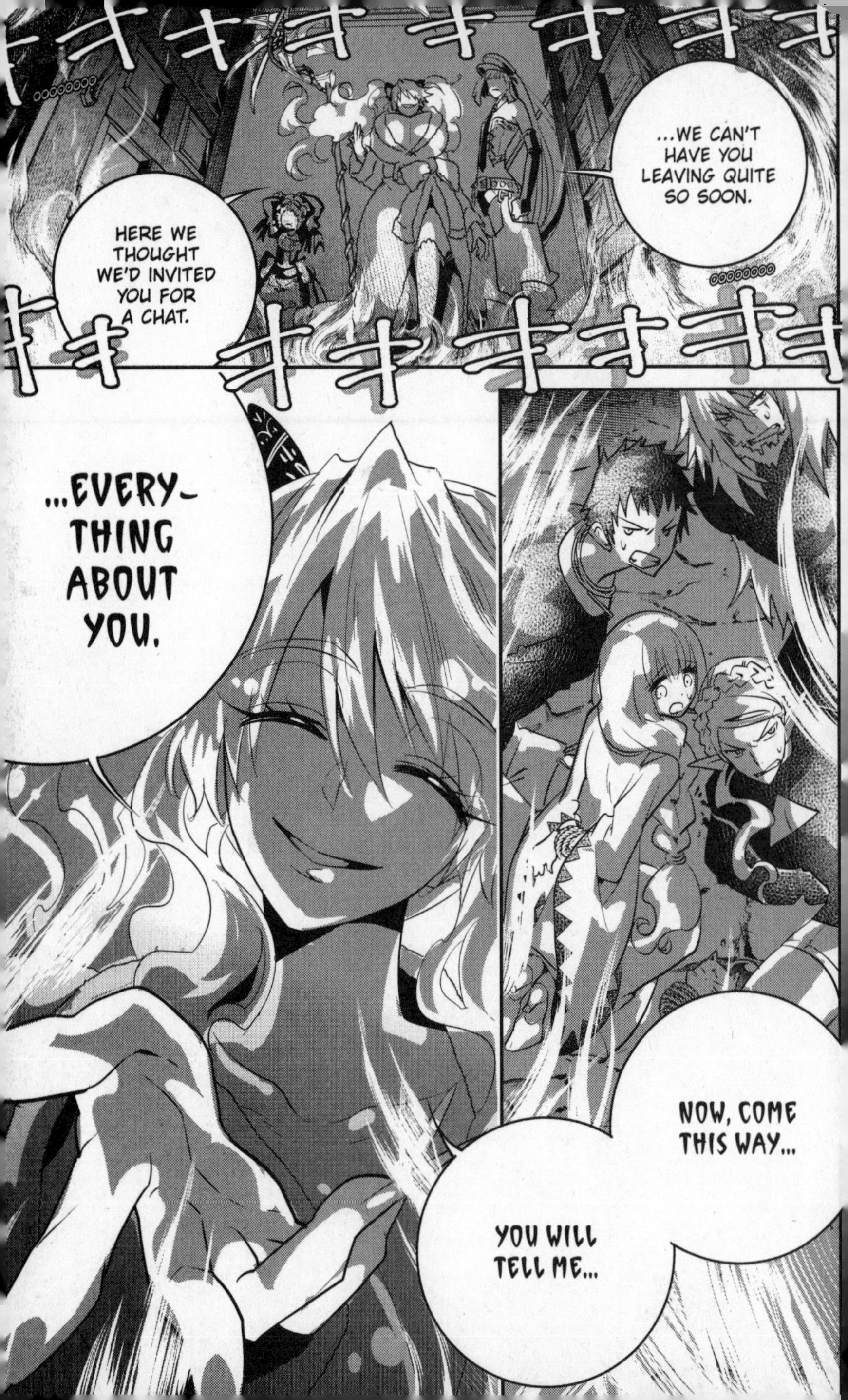
OOOOOOOO
...WE CAN'T HAVE YOU LEAVING QUITE SO SOON.
HERE WE THOUGHT WE'D INVITED YOU FOR A CHAT.
OOOOOOOO
NOW, COME THIS WAY...
YOU WILL TELL ME...
...EVERY-THING ABOUT YOU.

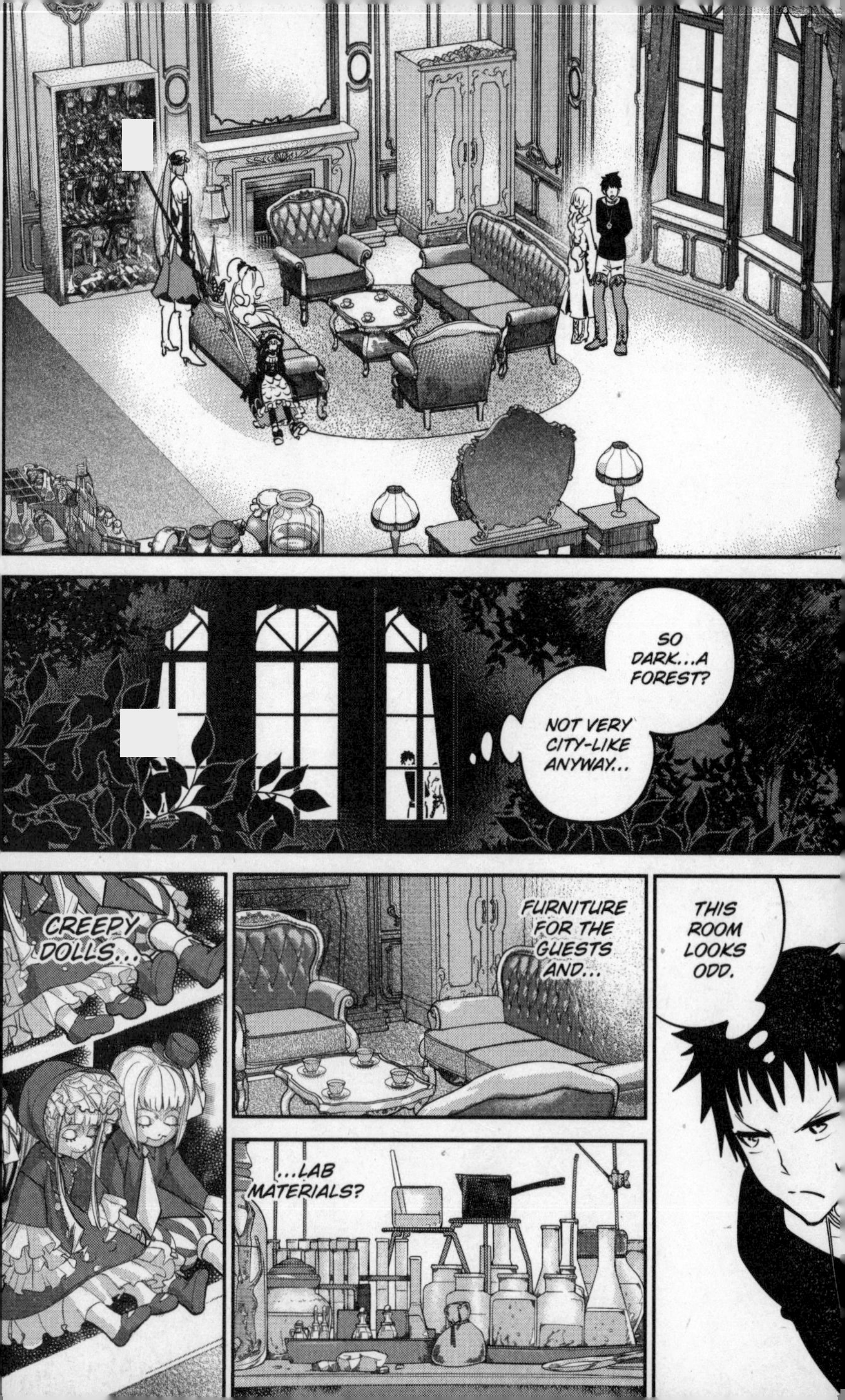
SO DARK...A FOREST?
NOT VERY CITY-LIKE ANYWAY...
THIS ROOM LOOKS ODD.
FURNITURE FOR THE GUESTS AND...
...LAB MATERIALS?
CREEPY DOLLS...

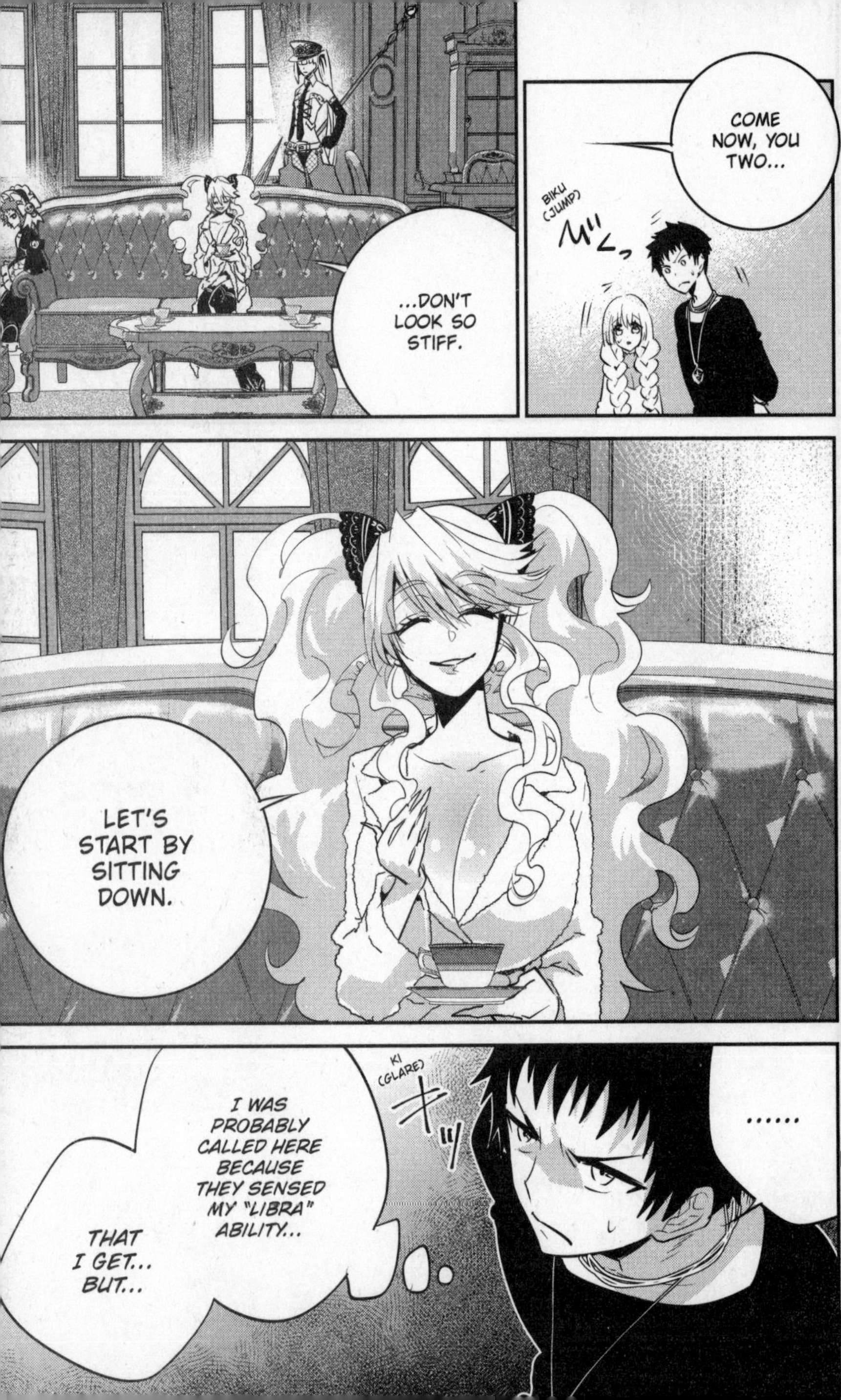
COME NOW, YOU TWO...
BIKU (JUMP)
...DON'T LOOK SO STIFF.
LET'S START BY SITTING DOWN.
......
KI (GLARE)
I WAS PROBABLY CALLED HERE BECAUSE THEY SENSED MY "LIBRA" ABILITY...
THAT I GET... BUT...

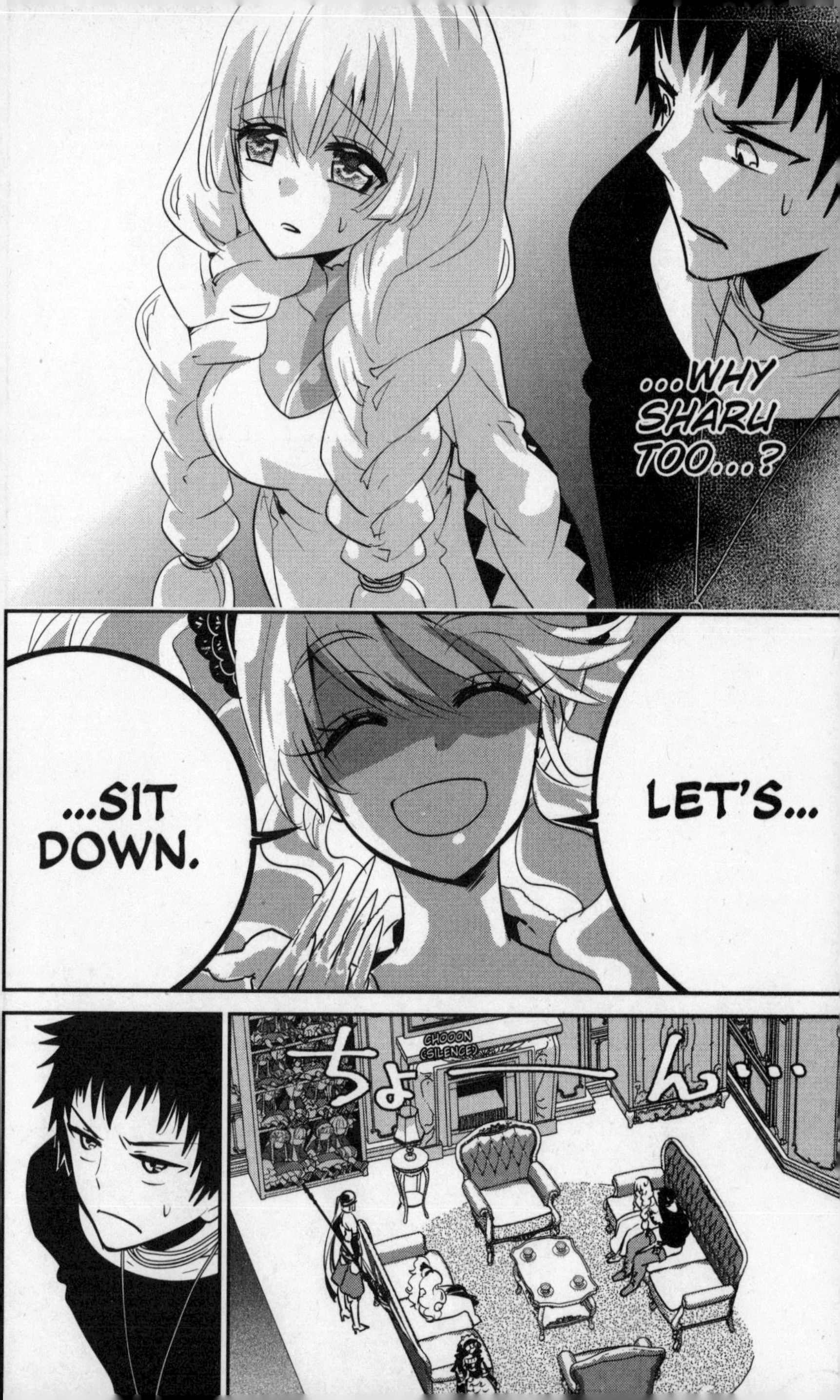
...WHY SHARU TOO...?
LET'S...
...SIT DOWN.
ちょーーーん...
CHOOON (SILENCED)

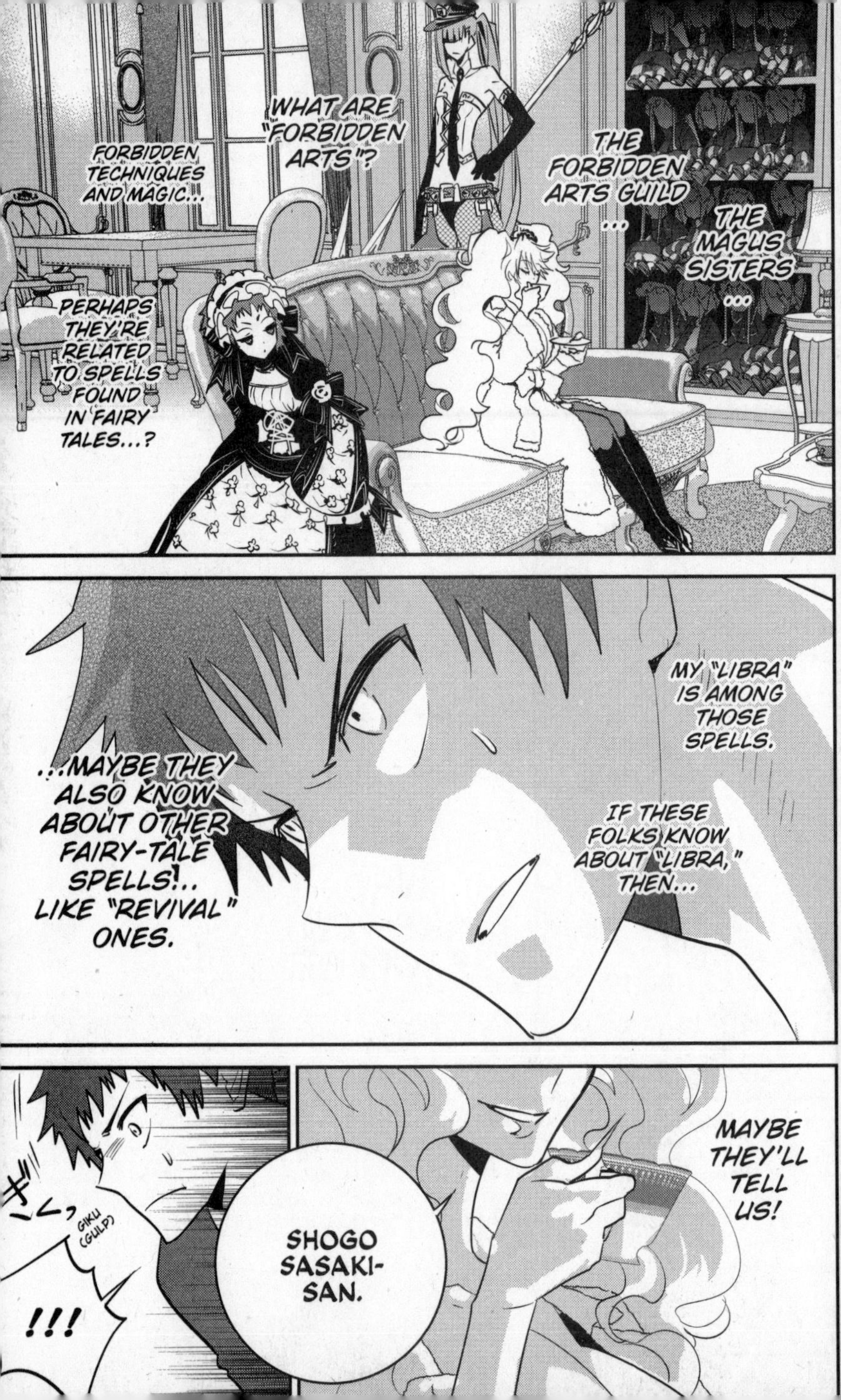
THE MAGUS SISTERS...
THE FORBIDDEN ARTS GUILD...
WHAT ARE "FORBIDDEN ARTS"?
FORBIDDEN TECHNIQUES AND MAGIC...
PERHAPS THEY'RE RELATED TO SPELLS FOUND IN FAIRY TALES...?
MY "LIBRA" IS AMONG THOSE SPELLS.
IF THESE FOLKS KNOW ABOUT "LIBRA," THEN...
...MAYBE THEY ALSO KNOW ABOUT OTHER FAIRY-TALE SPELLS!... LIKE "REVIVAL" ONES.
MAYBE THEY'LL TELL US!
SHOGO SASAKI-SAN.
GIKU (GULP)
!!!

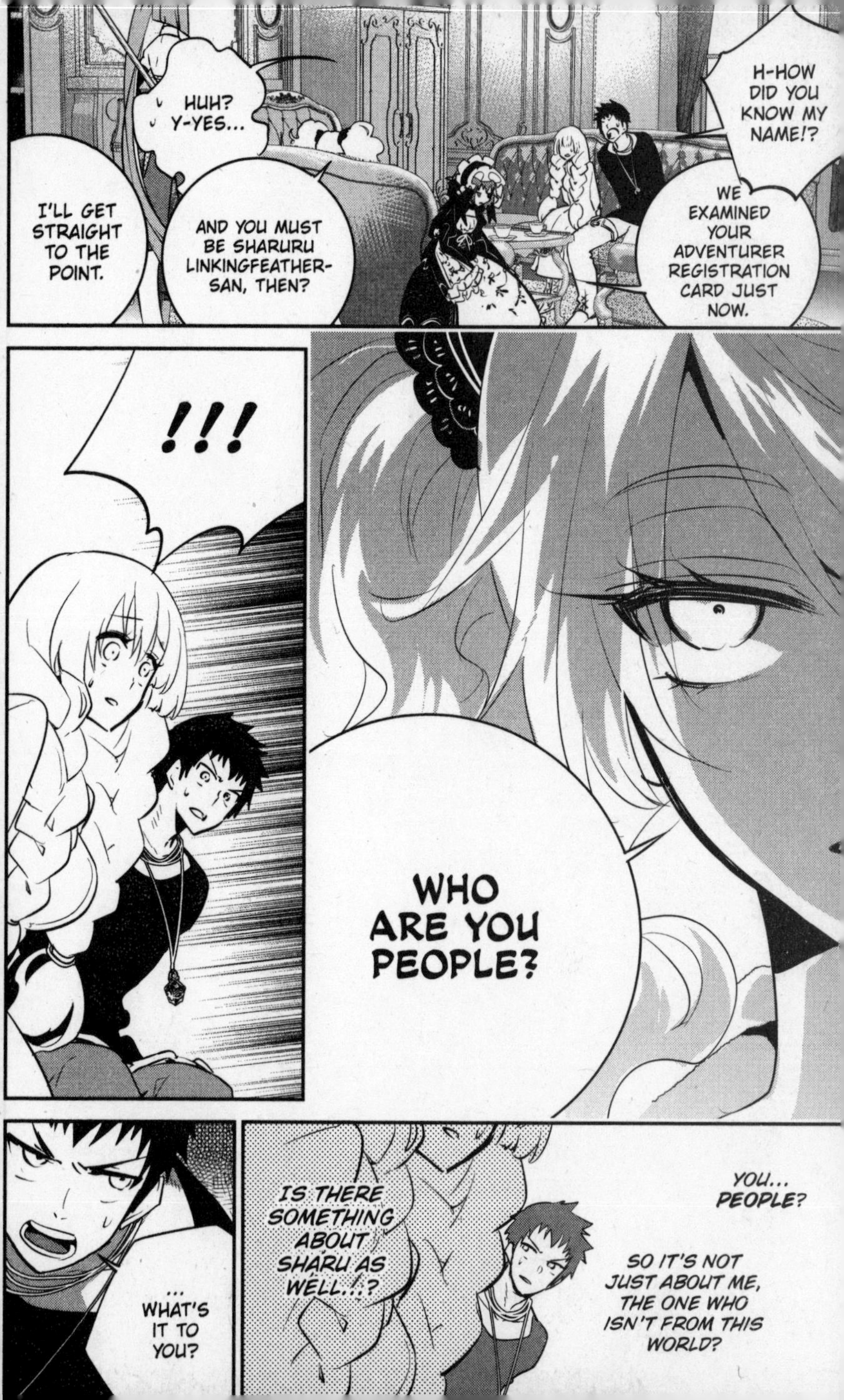
H-HOW DID YOU KNOW MY NAME!?
WE EXAMINED YOUR ADVENTURER REGISTRATION CARD JUST NOW.
HUH? Y-YES...
AND YOU MUST BE SHARURU LINKINGFEATHER-SAN, THEN?
I'LL GET STRAIGHT TO THE POINT.
WHO ARE YOU PEOPLE?
!!!
YOU... PEOPLE?
SO IT'S NOT JUST ABOUT ME, THE ONE WHO ISN'T FROM THIS WORLD?
IS THERE SOMETHING ABOUT SHARU AS WELL...?
...WHAT'S IT TO YOU?

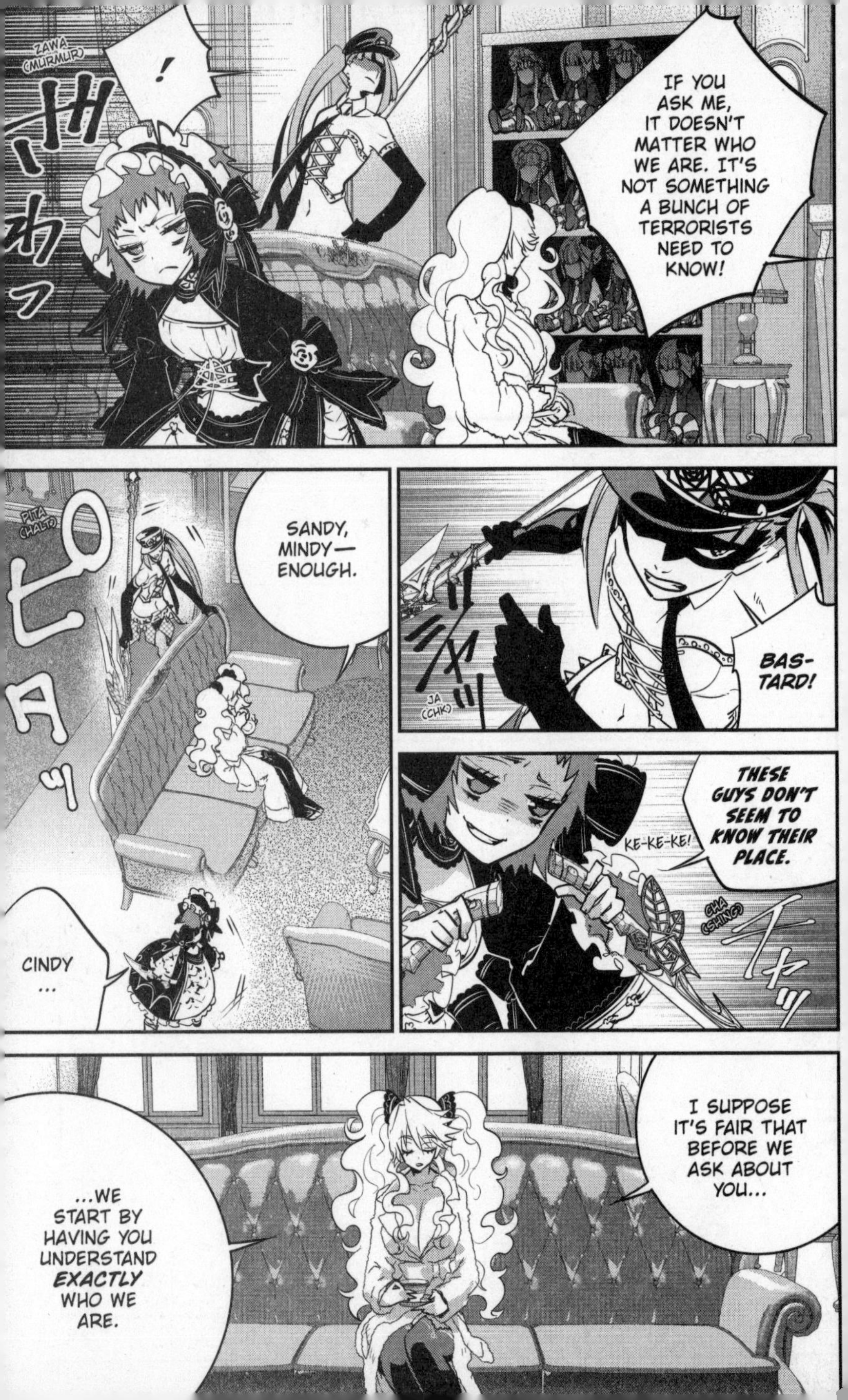
IF YOU ASK ME, IT DOESN'T MATTER WHO WE ARE. IT'S NOT SOMETHING A BUNCH OF TERRORISTS NEED TO KNOW!
!
ZAWA (MURMUR)
BAS-TARD!
JA (CHK)
THESE GUYS DON'T SEEM TO KNOW THEIR PLACE.
KE-KE-KE!
GHA (SHING)
SANDY, MINDY— ENOUGH.
PITA (HALT)
CINDY ...
I SUPPOSE IT'S FAIR THAT BEFORE WE ASK ABOUT YOU...
...WE START BY HAVING YOU UNDERSTAND EXACTLY WHO WE ARE.

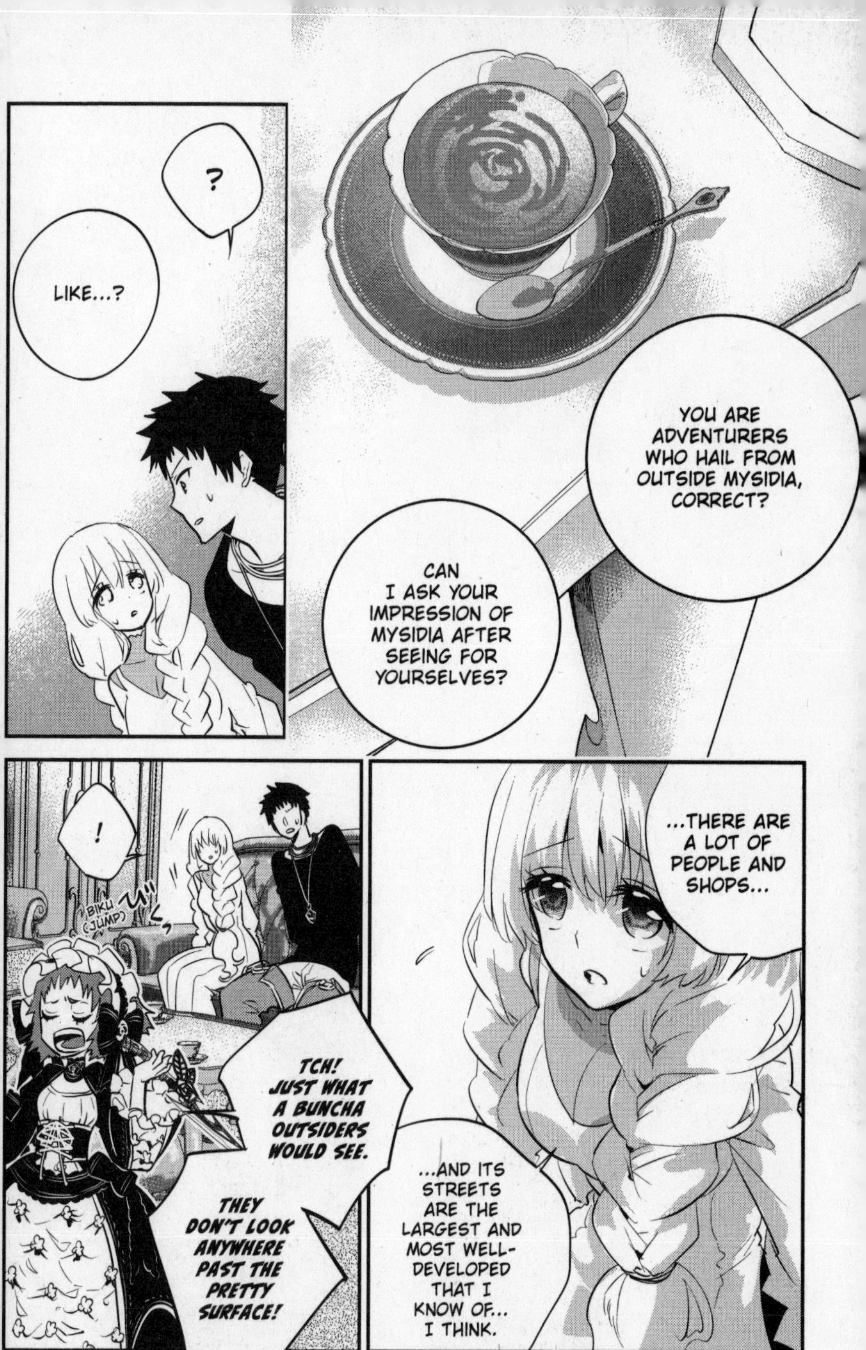
YOU ARE ADVENTURERS WHO HAIL FROM OUTSIDE MYSIDIA, CORRECT?
CAN I ASK YOUR IMPRESSION OF MYSIDIA AFTER SEEING FOR YOURSELVES?
?
LIKE...?
...THERE ARE A LOT OF PEOPLE AND SHOPS...
...AND ITS STREETS ARE THE LARGEST AND MOST WELL-DEVELOPED THAT I KNOW OF... I THINK.
!
BIKU (JUMP)
TCH! JUST WHAT A BUNCHA OUTSIDERS WOULD SEE.
THEY DON'T LOOK ANYWHERE PAST THE PRETTY SURFACE!

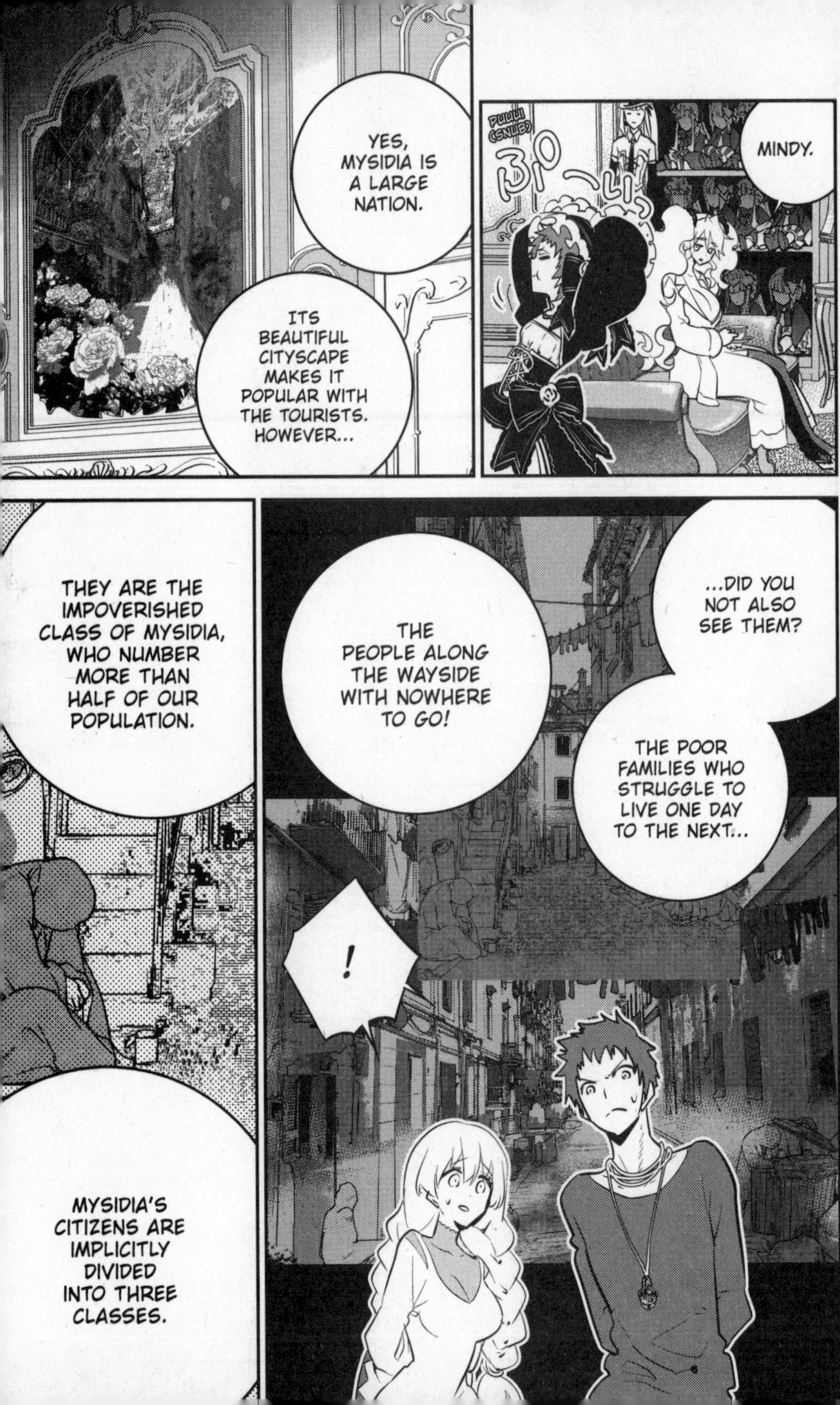
MINDY.
PUUUI (SNUB)
YES, MYSIDIA IS A LARGE NATION.
ITS BEAUTIFUL CITYSCAPE MAKES IT POPULAR WITH THE TOURISTS. HOWEVER...
...DID YOU NOT ALSO SEE THEM?
THE POOR FAMILIES WHO STRUGGLE TO LIVE ONE DAY TO THE NEXT...
THE PEOPLE ALONG THE WAYSIDE WITH NOWHERE TO GO!
!
THEY ARE THE IMPOVERISHED CLASS OF MYSIDIA, WHO NUMBER MORE THAN HALF OF OUR POPULATION.
MYSIDIA'S CITIZENS ARE IMPLICITLY DIVIDED INTO THREE CLASSES.

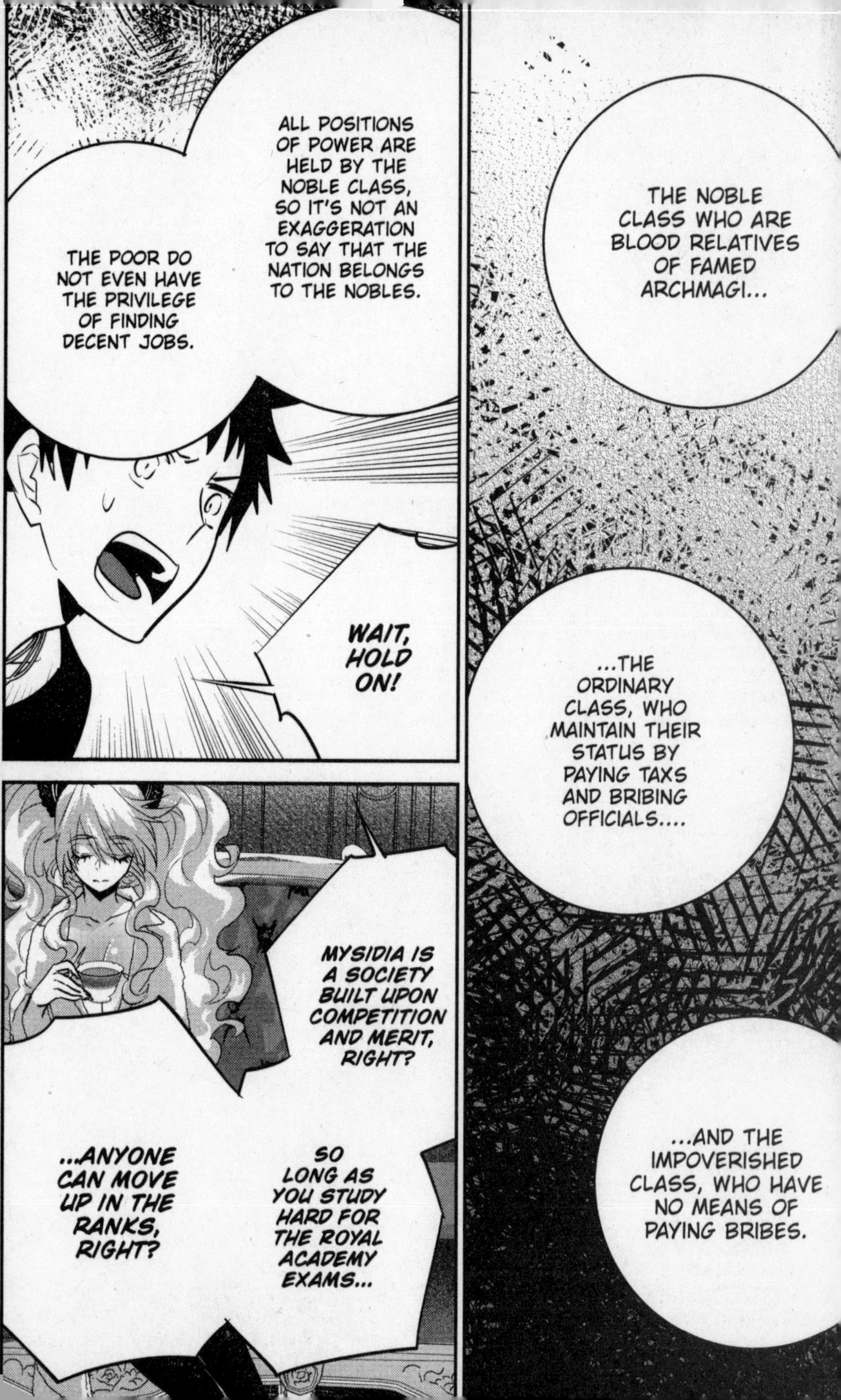
THE NOBLE CLASS WHO ARE BLOOD RELATIVES OF FAMED ARCHMAGI...
...THE ORDINARY CLASS, WHO MAINTAIN THEIR STATUS BY PAYING TAXS AND BRIBING OFFICIALS....
...AND THE IMPOVERISHED CLASS, WHO HAVE NO MEANS OF PAYING BRIBES.
ALL POSITIONS OF POWER ARE HELD BY THE NOBLE CLASS, SO IT'S NOT AN EXAGGERATION TO SAY THAT THE NATION BELONGS TO THE NOBLES.
THE POOR DO NOT EVEN HAVE THE PRIVILEGE OF FINDING DECENT JOBS.
WAIT, HOLD ON!
MYSIDIA IS A SOCIETY BUILT UPON COMPETITION AND MERIT, RIGHT?
SO LONG AS YOU STUDY HARD FOR THE ROYAL ACADEMY EXAMS...
...ANYONE CAN MOVE UP IN THE RANKS, RIGHT?

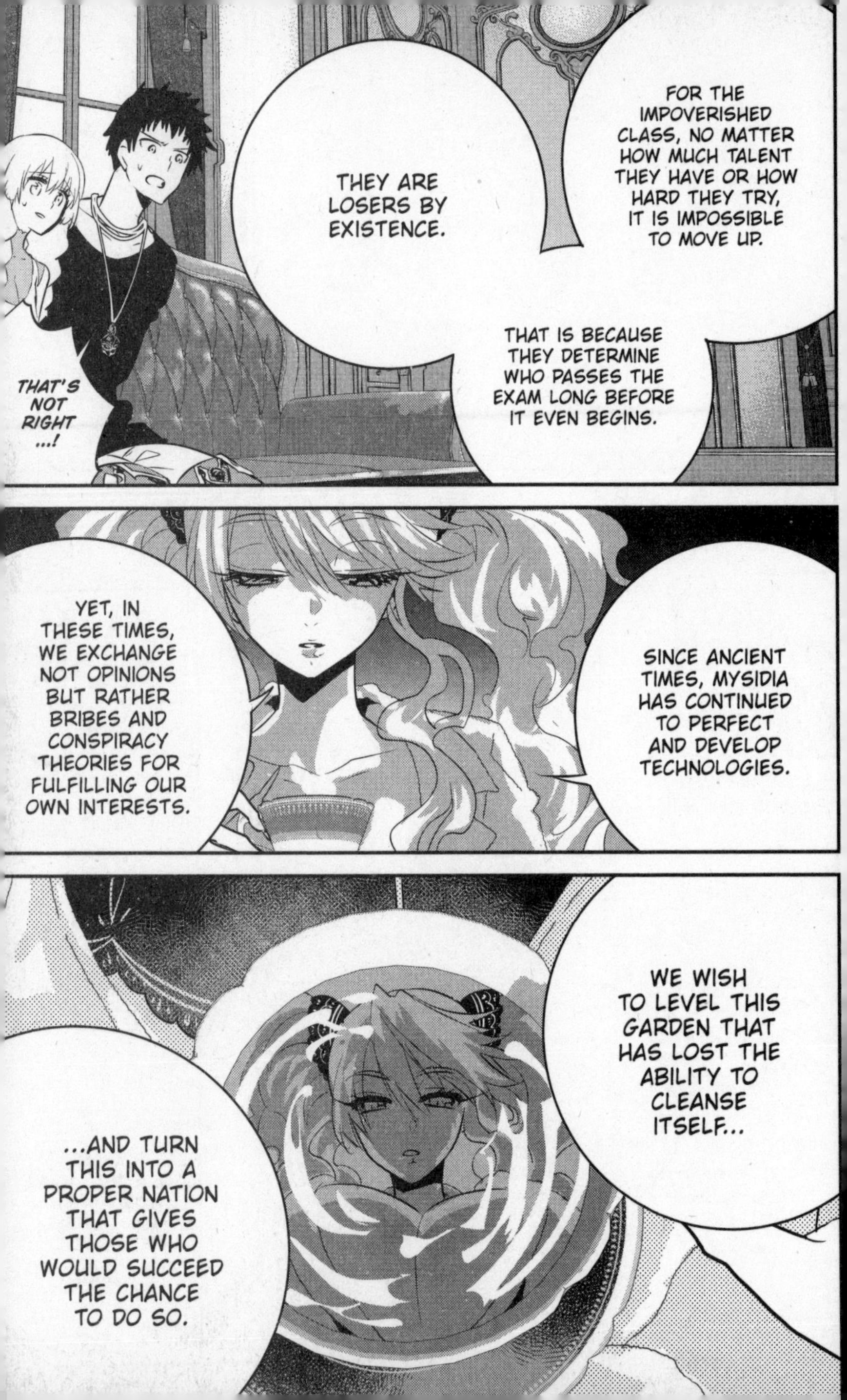
FOR THE IMPOVERISHED CLASS, NO MATTER HOW MUCH TALENT THEY HAVE OR HOW HARD THEY TRY, IT IS IMPOSSIBLE TO MOVE UP.
THEY ARE LOSERS BY EXISTENCE.
THAT IS BECAUSE THEY DETERMINE WHO PASSES THE EXAM LONG BEFORE IT EVEN BEGINS.
THAT'S NOT RIGHT ...!
SINCE ANCIENT TIMES, MYSIDIA HAS CONTINUED TO PERFECT AND DEVELOP TECHNOLOGIES.
YET, IN THESE TIMES, WE EXCHANGE NOT OPINIONS BUT RATHER BRIBES AND CONSPIRACY THEORIES FOR FULFILLING OUR OWN INTERESTS.
WE WISH TO LEVEL THIS GARDEN THAT HAS LOST THE ABILITY TO CLEANSE ITSELF...
...AND TURN THIS INTO A PROPER NATION THAT GIVES THOSE WHO WOULD SUCCEED THE CHANCE TO DO SO.

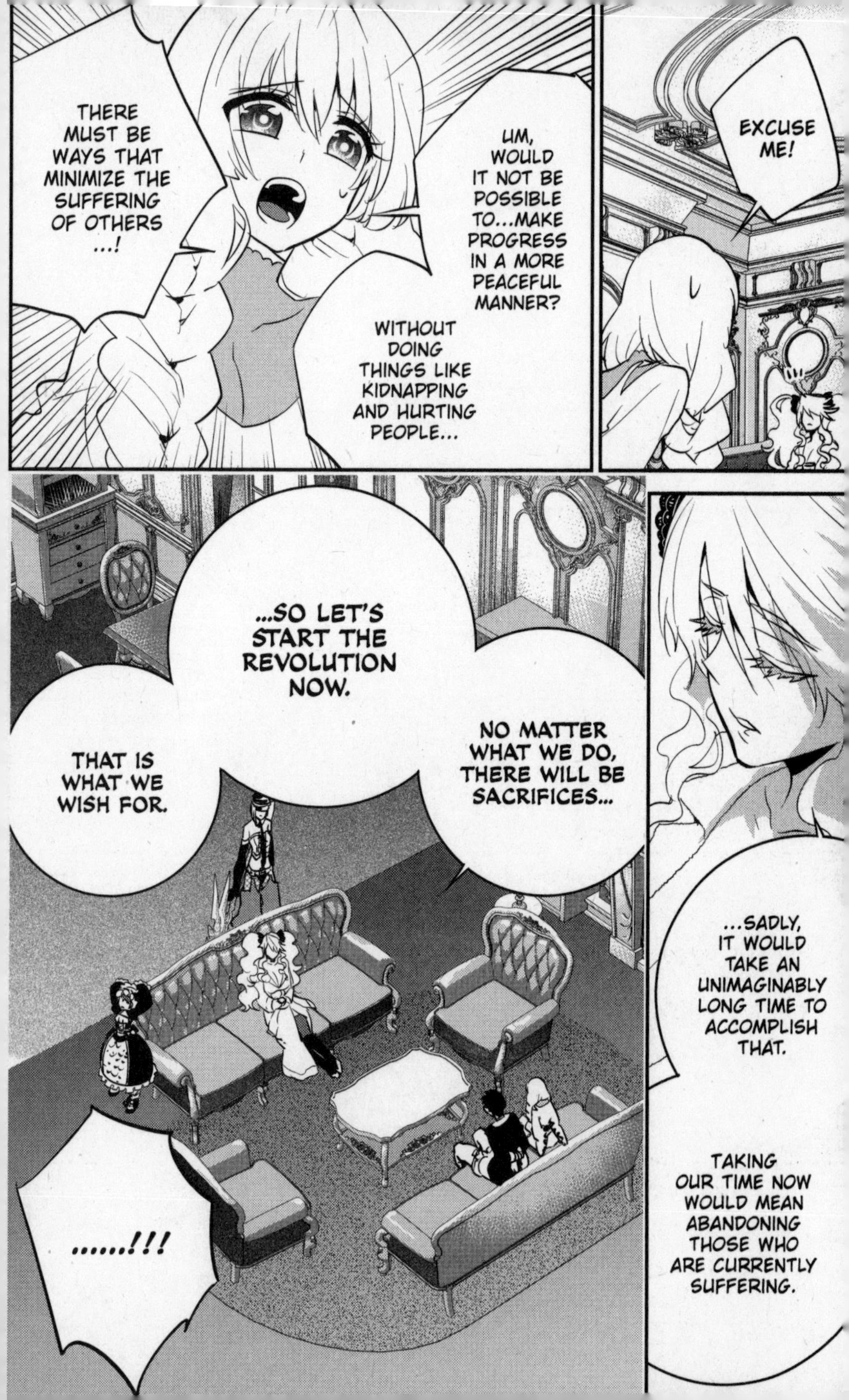
EXCUSE ME!
THERE MUST BE WAYS THAT MINIMIZE THE SUFFERING OF OTHERS ...!
UM, WOULD IT NOT BE POSSIBLE TO...MAKE PROGRESS IN A MORE PEACEFUL MANNER?
WITHOUT DOING THINGS LIKE KIDNAPPING AND HURTING PEOPLE...
...SADLY, IT WOULD TAKE AN UNIMAGINABLY LONG TIME TO ACCOMPLISH THAT.
TAKING OUR TIME NOW WOULD MEAN ABANDONING THOSE WHO ARE CURRENTLY SUFFERING.
NO MATTER WHAT WE DO, THERE WILL BE SACRIFICES...
...SO LET'S START THE REVOLUTION NOW.
THAT IS WHAT WE WISH FOR.
......!!!

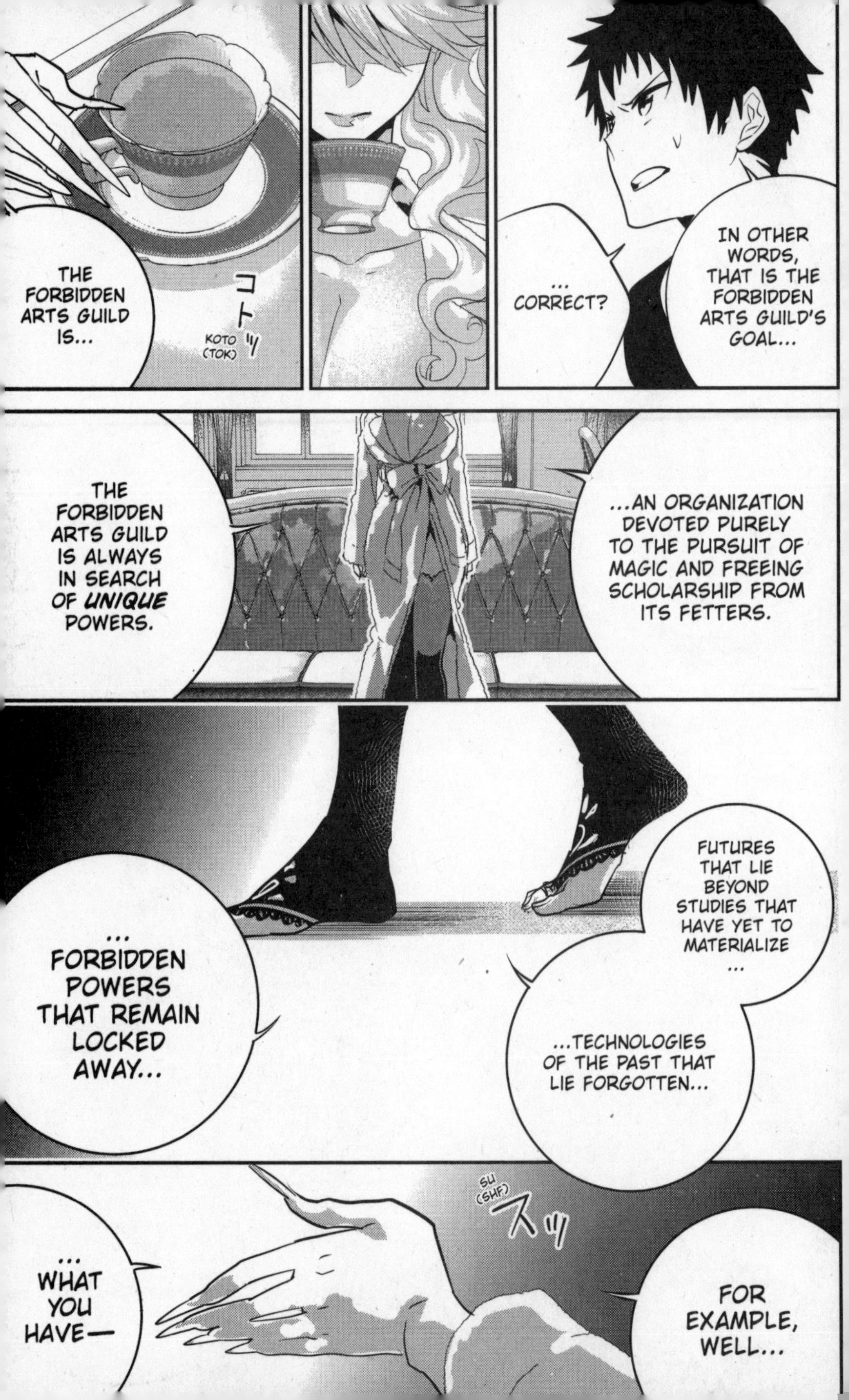
IN OTHER WORDS, THAT IS THE FORBIDDEN ARTS GUILD'S GOAL...
...CORRECT?
コトッ KOTO (TOK)
THE FORBIDDEN ARTS GUILD IS...
...AN ORGANIZATION DEVOTED PURELY TO THE PURSUIT OF MAGIC AND FREEING SCHOLARSHIP FROM ITS FETTERS.
THE FORBIDDEN ARTS GUILD IS ALWAYS IN SEARCH OF UNIQUE POWERS.
FUTURES THAT LIE BEYOND STUDIES THAT HAVE YET TO MATERIALIZE...
...TECHNOLOGIES OF THE PAST THAT LIE FORGOTTEN...
...FORBIDDEN POWERS THAT REMAIN LOCKED AWAY...
スッ SU (SHF)
FOR EXAMPLE, WELL...
...WHAT YOU HAVE—

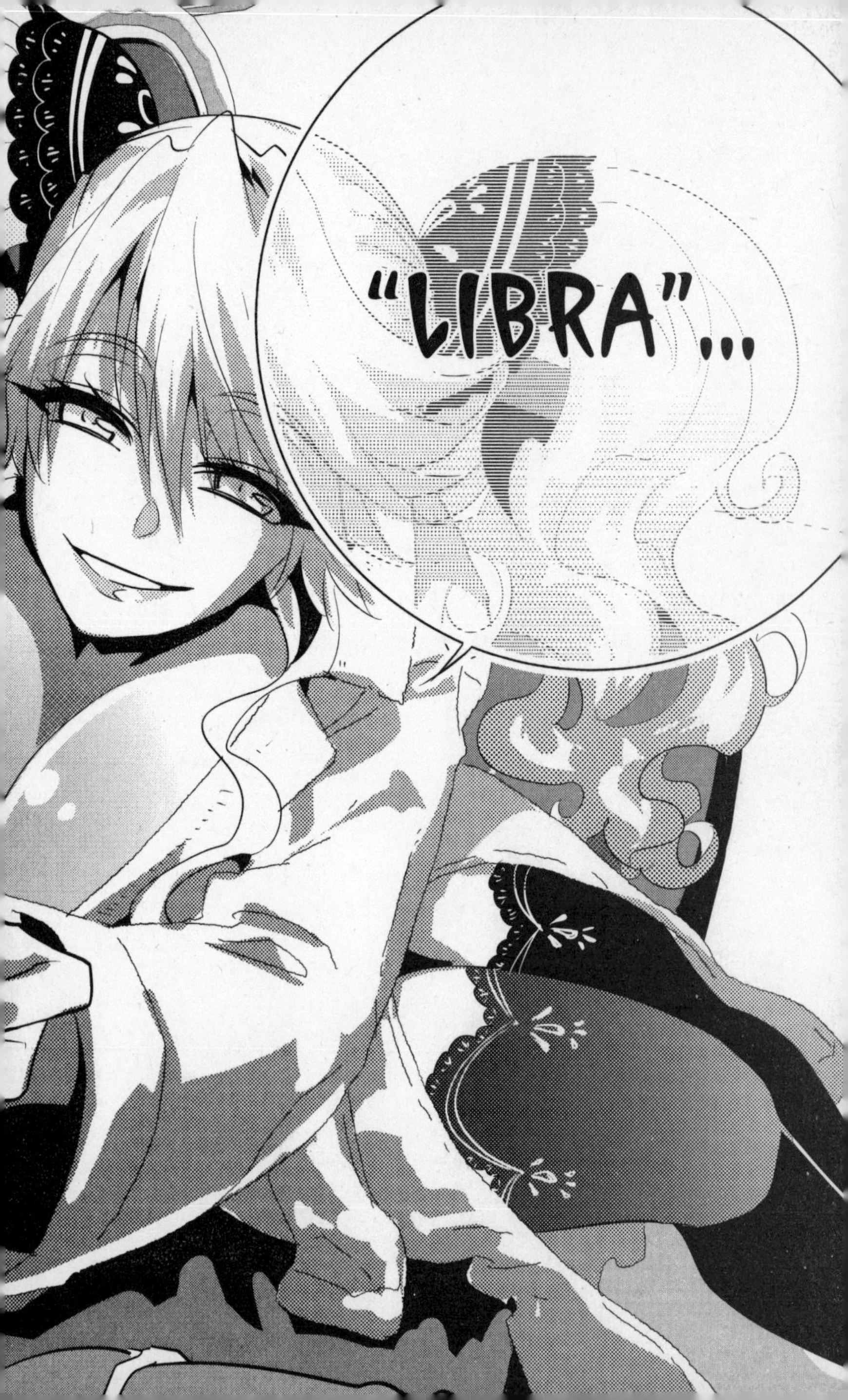
"LIBRA"...

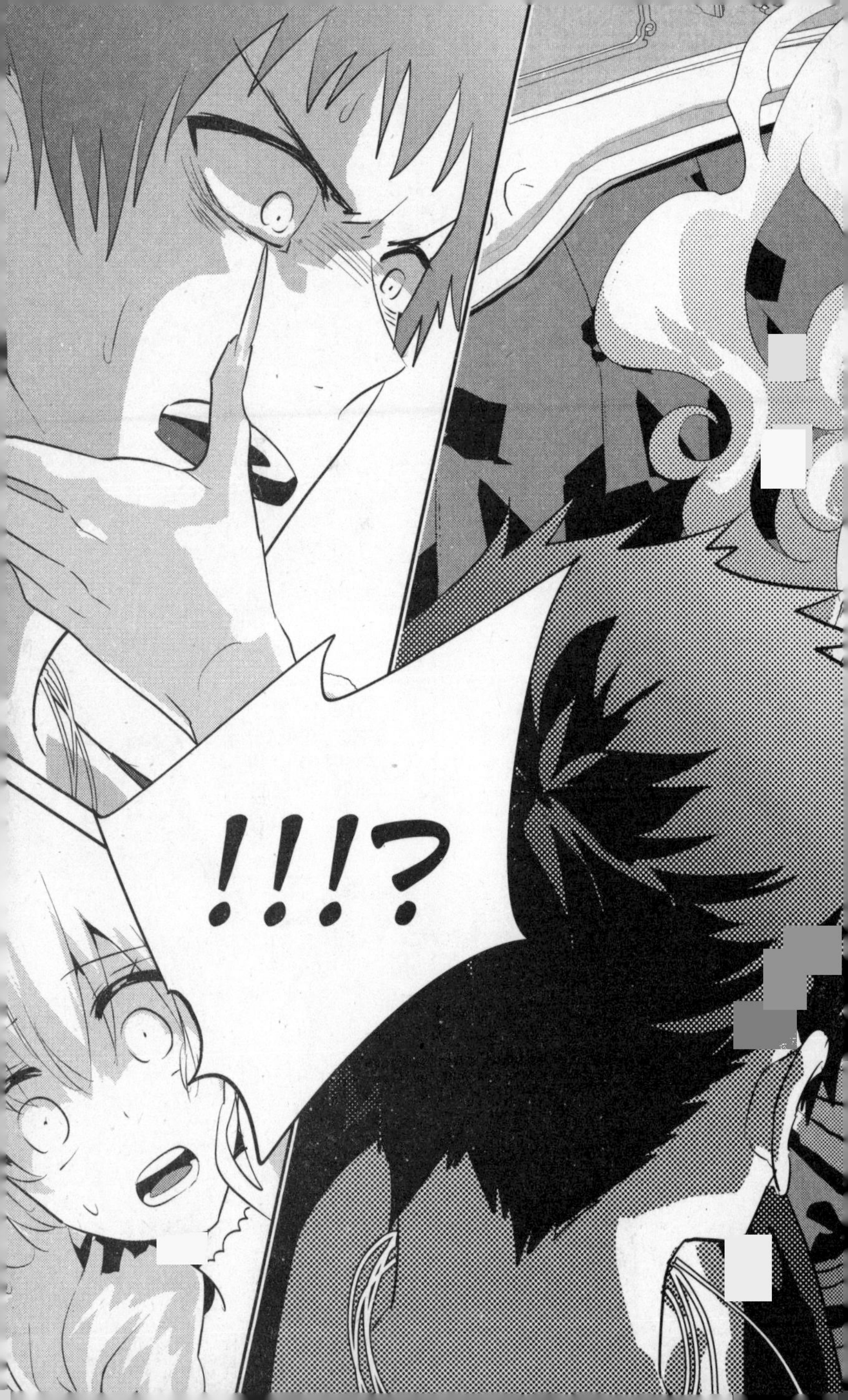
!!!?

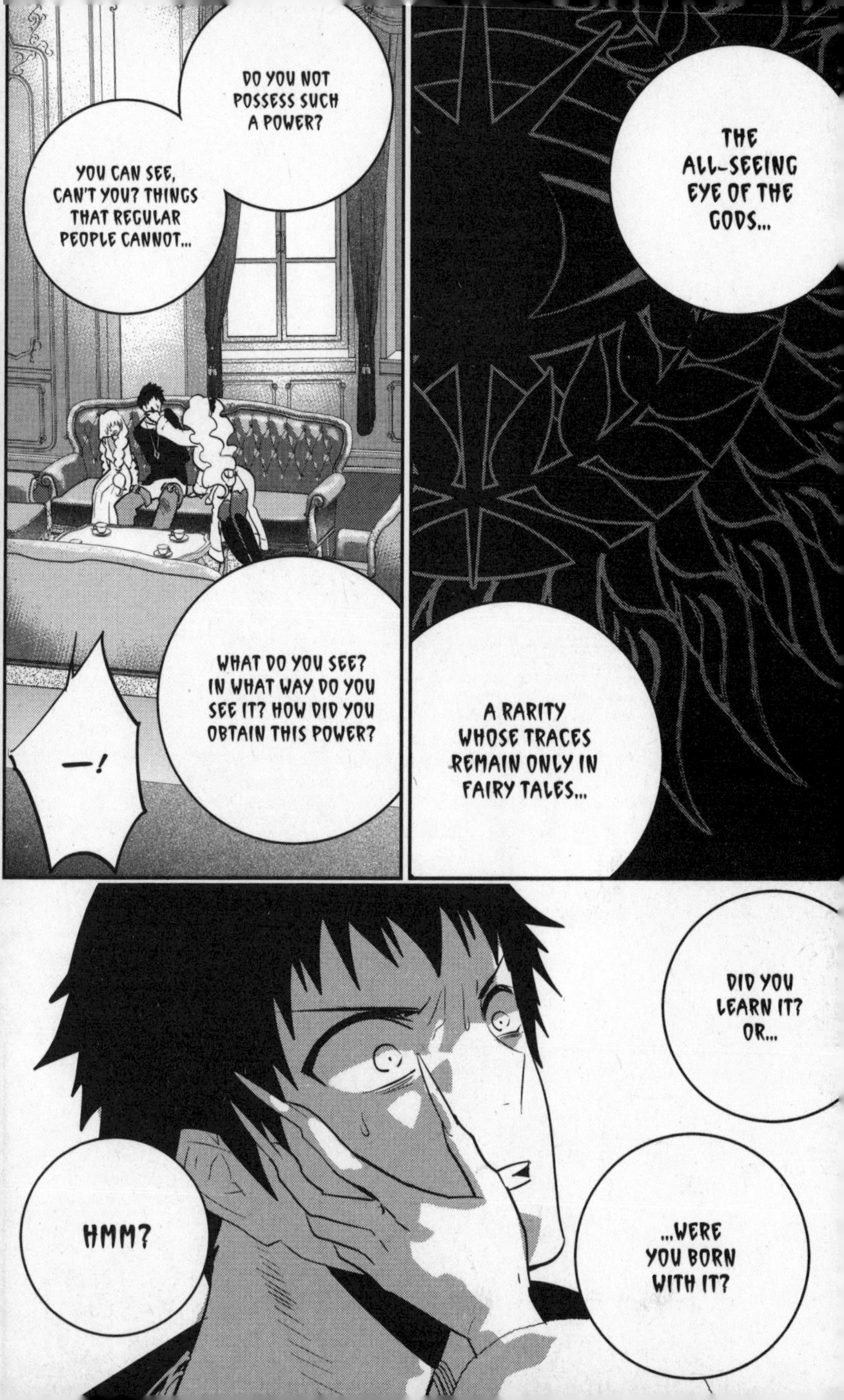
THE ALL-SEEING EYE OF THE GODS...
A RARITY WHOSE TRACES REMAIN ONLY IN FAIRY TALES...
DO YOU NOT POSSESS SUCH A POWER?
YOU CAN SEE, CAN'T YOU? THINGS THAT REGULAR PEOPLE CANNOT...
WHAT DO YOU SEE? IN WHAT WAY DO YOU SEE IT? HOW DID YOU OBTAIN THIS POWER?
—!
DID YOU LEARN IT? OR...
...WERE YOU BORN WITH IT?
HMM?

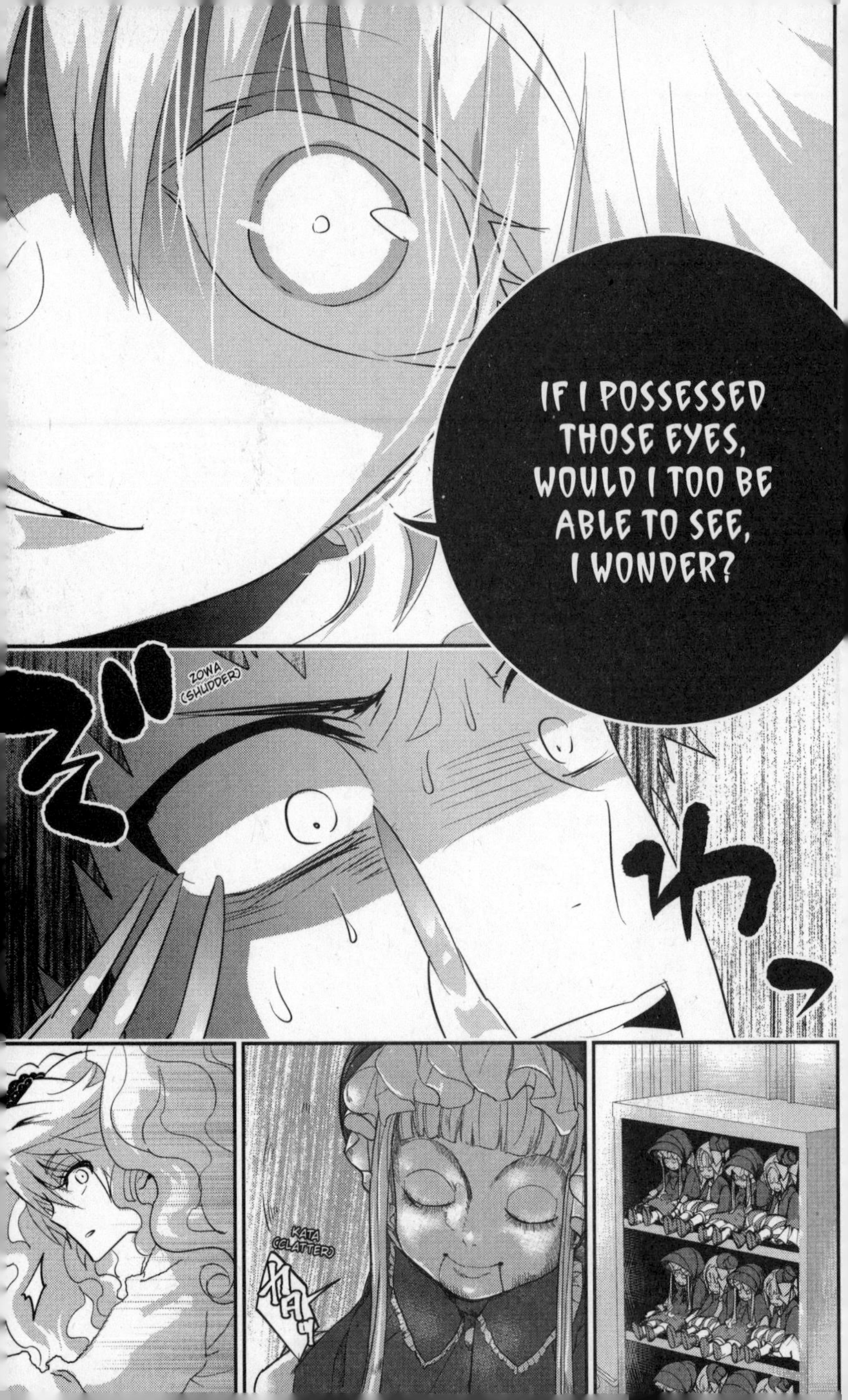
IF I POSSESSED THOSE EYES, WOULD I TOO BE ABLE TO SEE, I WONDER?
ZOWA (SHUDDER)
KATA (CLATTER)

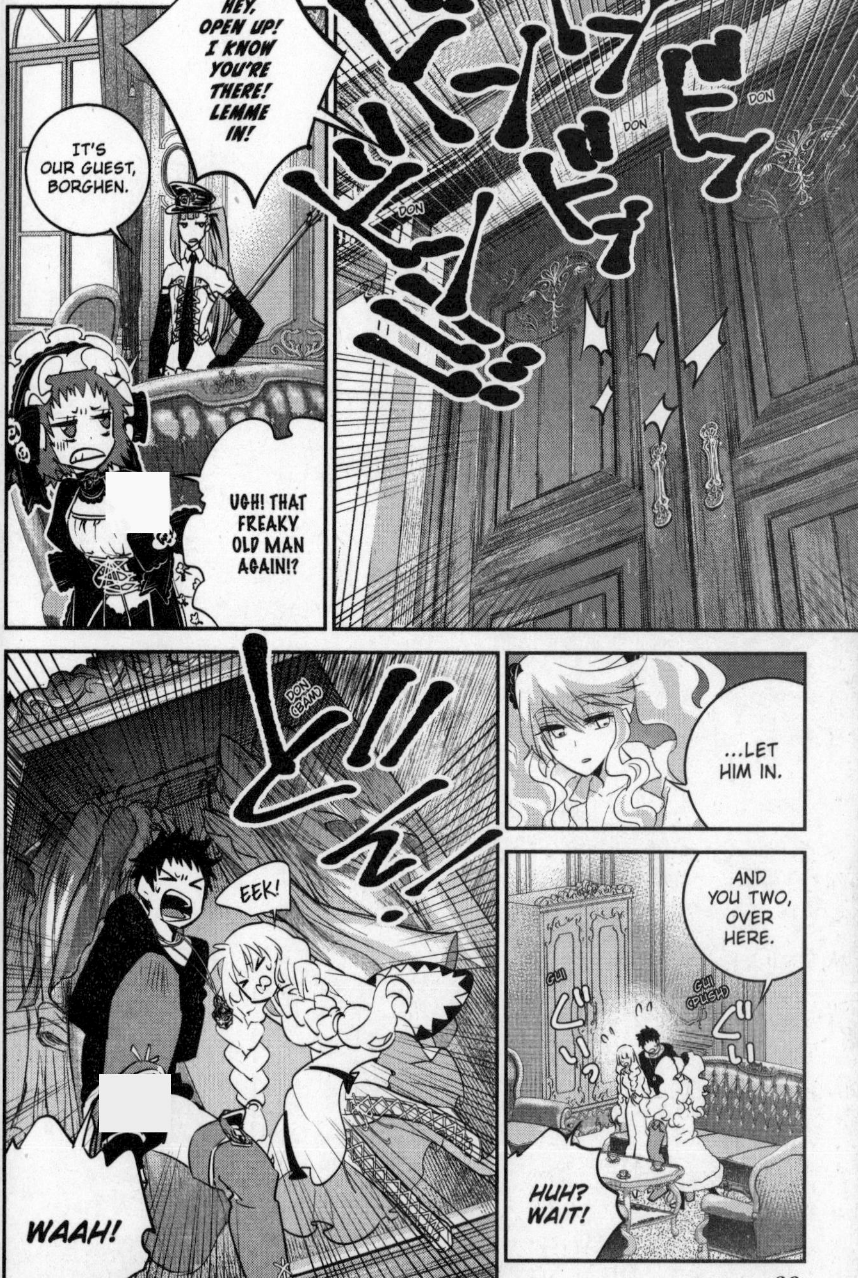
DON (KNOCK)
DON
DON
DON
DON
HEY, OPEN UP! I KNOW YOU'RE THERE! LEMME IN!
IT'S OUR GUEST, BORGHEN.
UGH! THAT FREAKY OLD MAN AGAIN!?
...LET HIM IN.
AND YOU TWO, OVER HERE.
GUI (PUSH)
GUI
HUH? WAIT!
DON (BAM)
EEK!
WAAH!

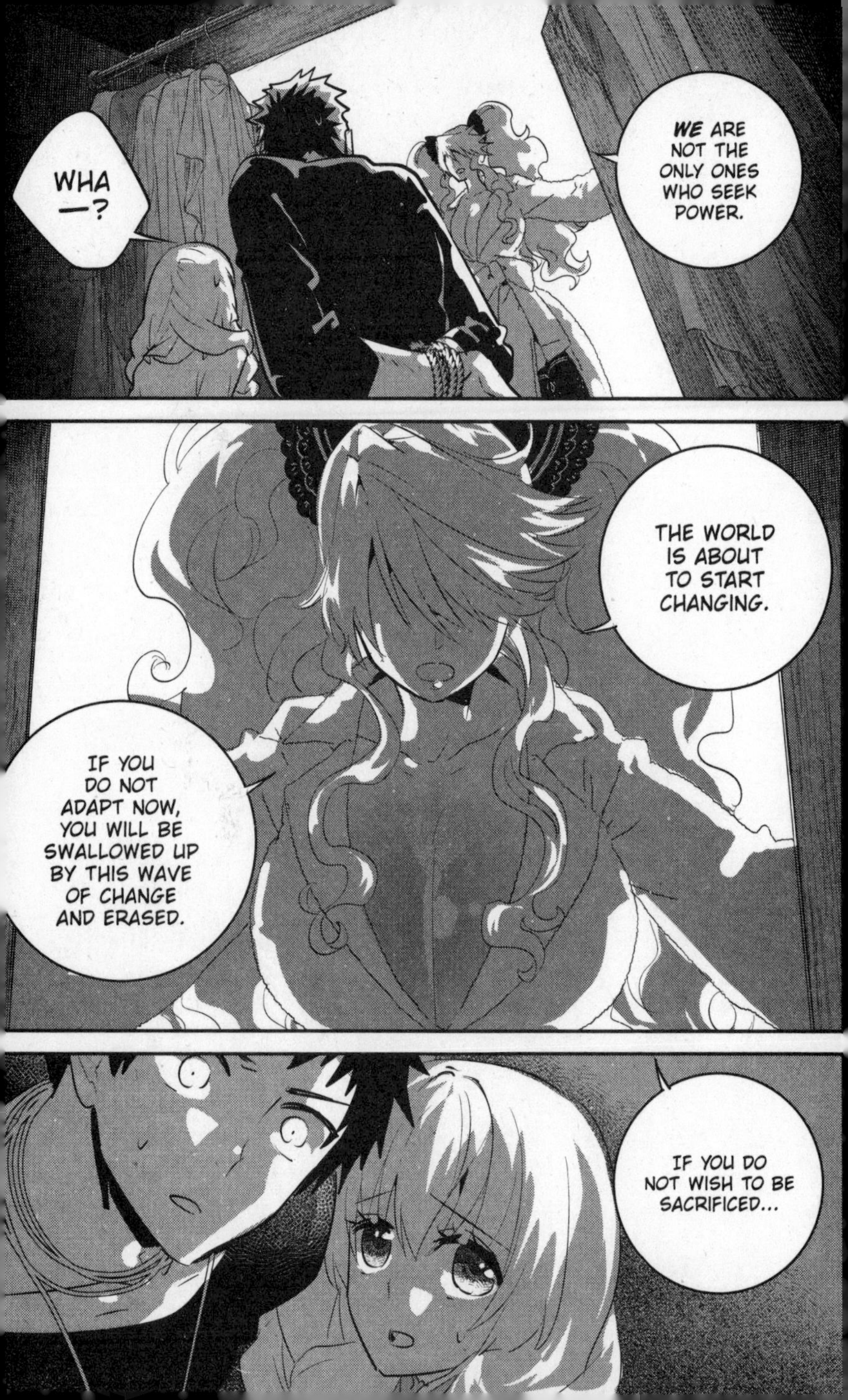
WE ARE NOT THE ONLY ONES WHO SEEK POWER.
WHA —?
THE WORLD IS ABOUT TO START CHANGING.
IF YOU DO NOT ADAPT NOW, YOU WILL BE SWALLOWED UP BY THIS WAVE OF CHANGE AND ERASED.
IF YOU DO NOT WISH TO BE SACRIFICED...

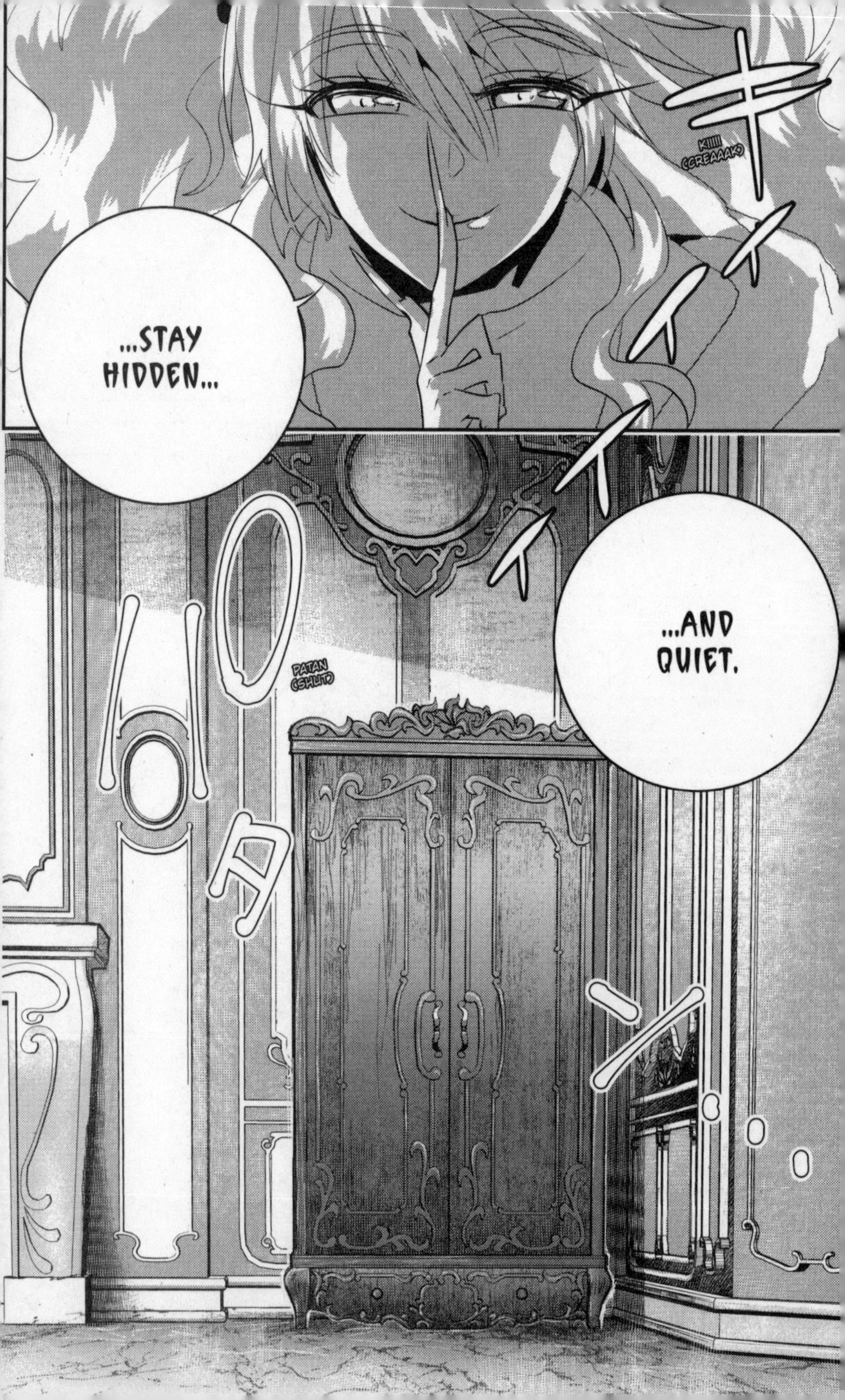
KIIII (CREAAAK)
...STAY HIDDEN...
...AND QUIET.
PATAN (SHUT)

FINAL FANTASY®

ファイナルファンタジー　ロスト・ストレンジャー

LOST STRANGER

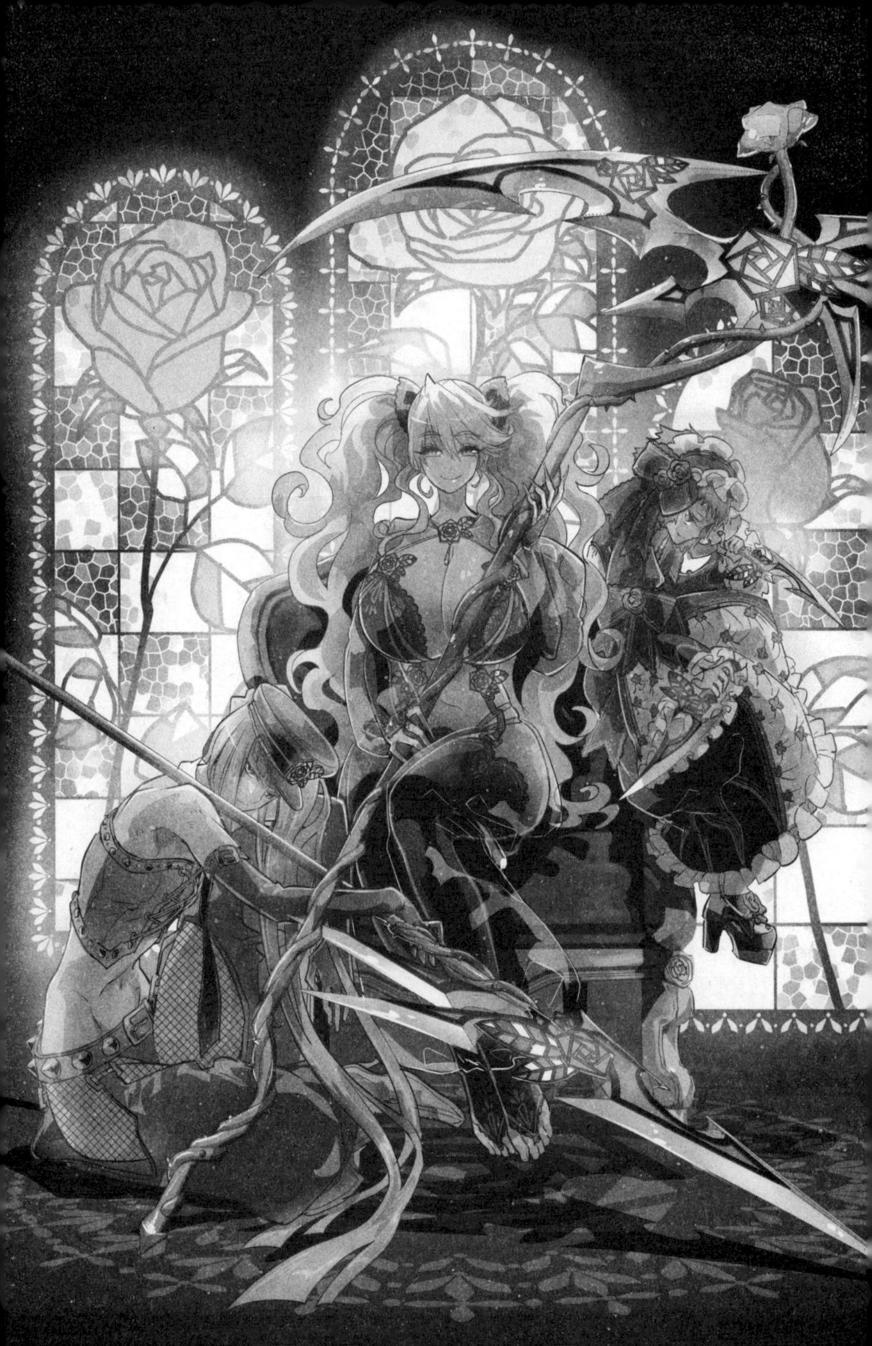

Chapter 10 The Darkness of Eternity

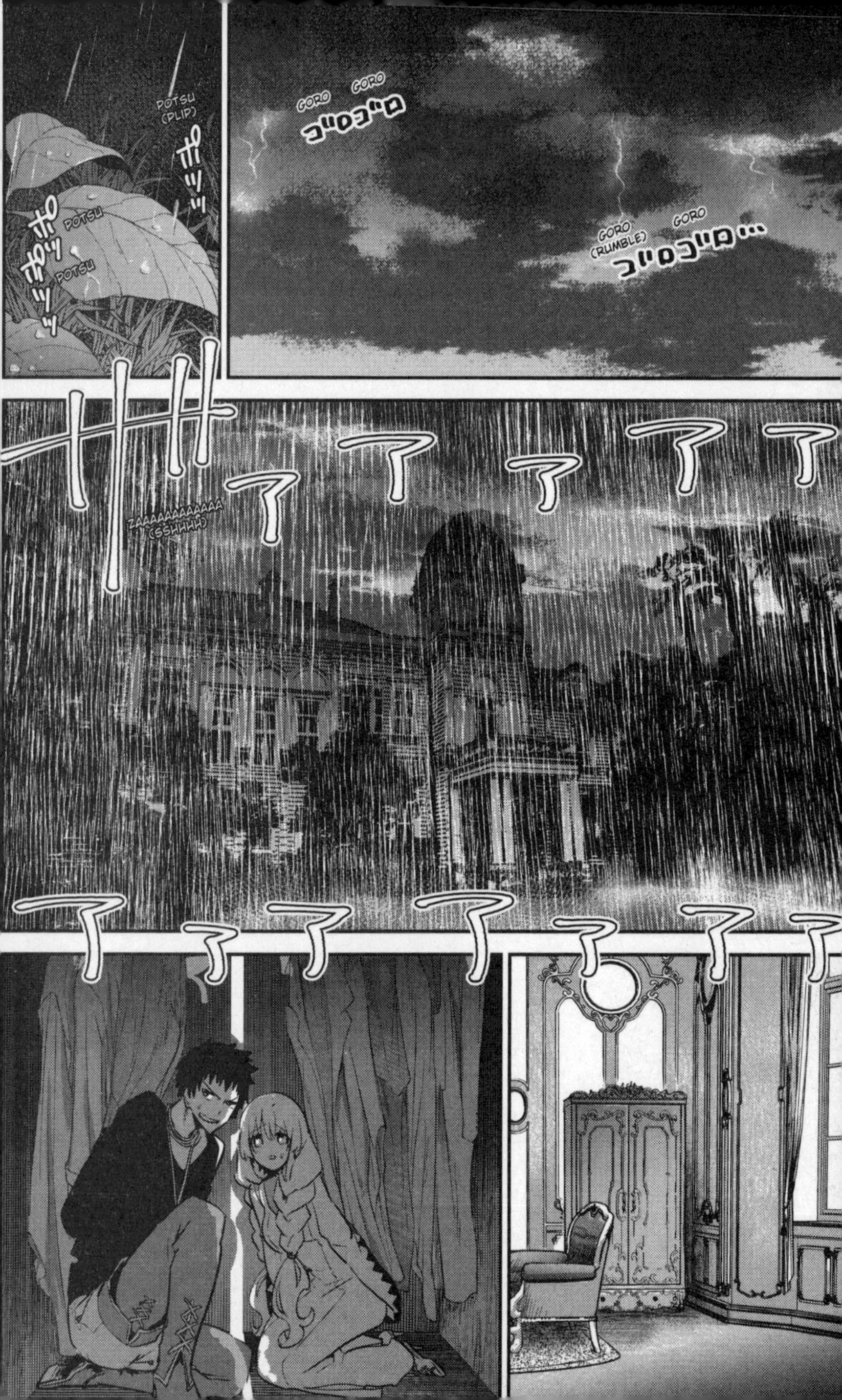

GORO GORO
ゴロゴロ
GORO (RUMBLE) GORO
ゴロゴロ…
POTSU (PLIP)
ポッッ
POTSU POTSU
ポッポッッ
ZAAAAAAAAAAAA (SSHHHH)
ザザザァァァァァァァァァァァ

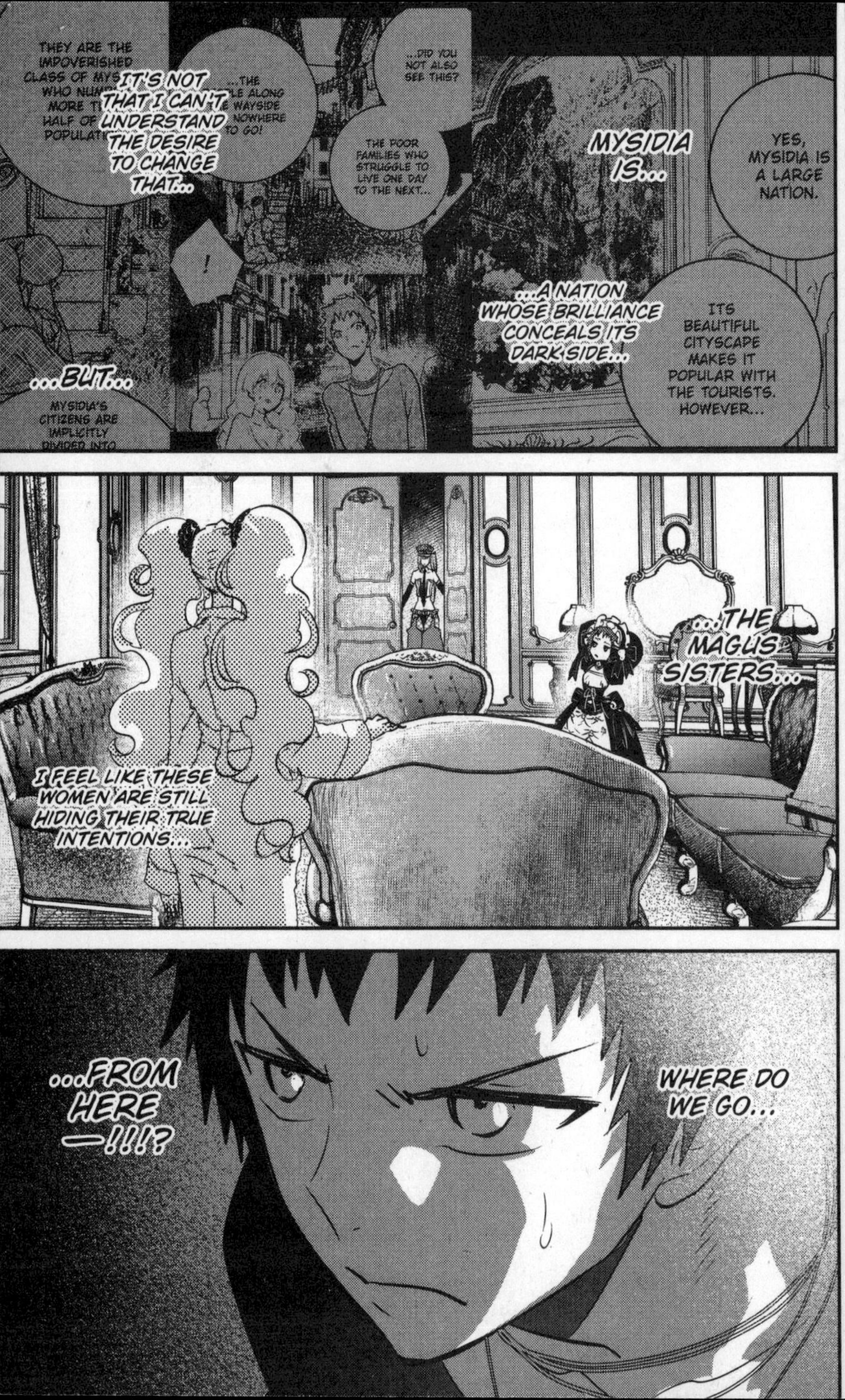
YES, MYSIDIA IS A LARGE NATION.
MYSIDIA IS...
ITS BEAUTIFUL CITYSCAPE MAKES IT POPULAR WITH THE TOURISTS. HOWEVER...
...A NATION WHOSE BRILLIANCE CONCEALS ITS DARK SIDE...
...DID YOU NOT ALSO SEE THIS?
THE POOR FAMILIES WHO STRUGGLE TO LIVE ONE DAY TO THE NEXT...
!
IT'S NOT THAT I CAN'T UNDERSTAND THE DESIRE TO CHANGE THAT...
...BUT...
MYSIDIA'S CITIZENS ARE IMPLICITLY DIVIDED INTO
...THE MAGUS SISTERS...
I FEEL LIKE THESE WOMEN ARE STILL HIDING THEIR TRUE INTENTIONS...
WHERE DO WE GO...
...FROM HERE—!!!?

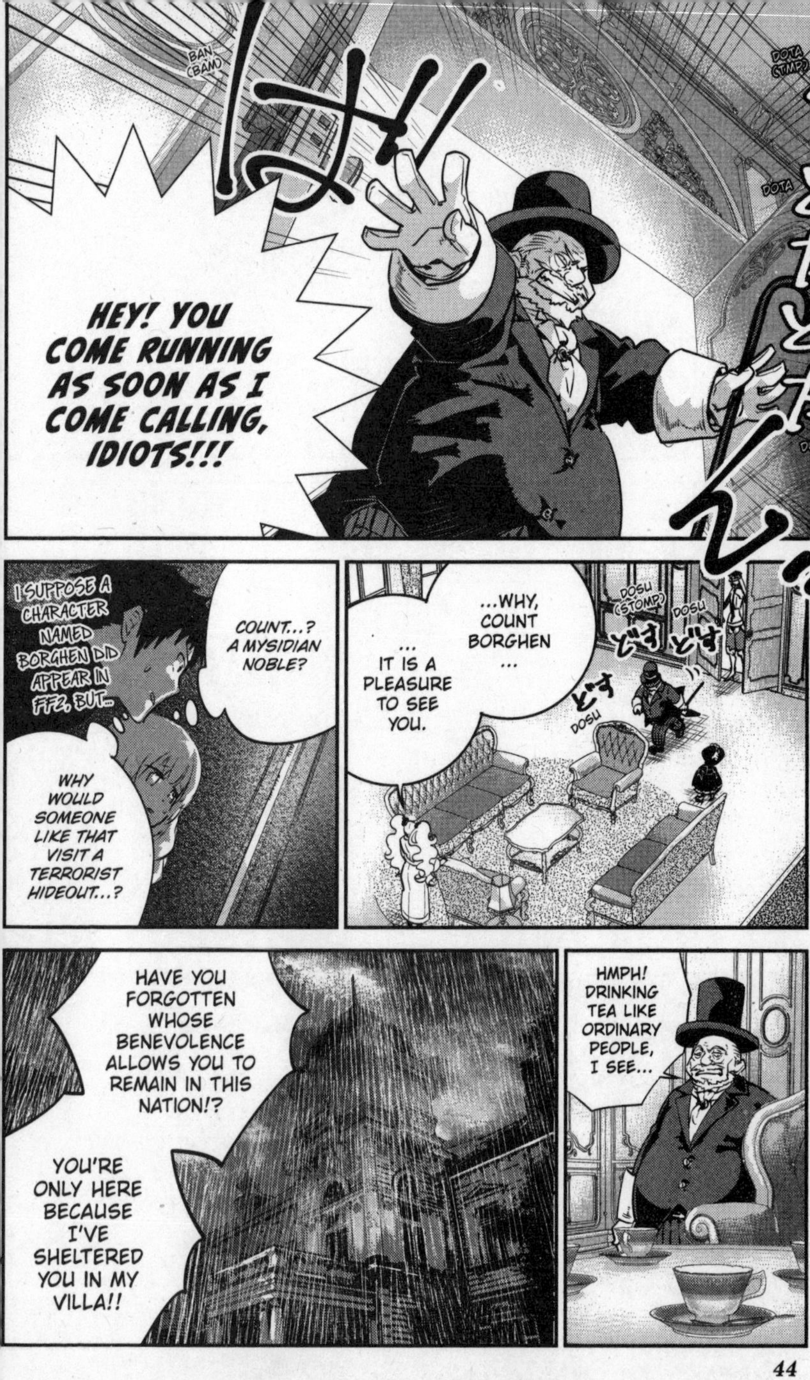
BAN (BAM)
DOTA (TMP)
DOTA
HEY! YOU COME RUNNING AS SOON AS I COME CALLING, IDIOTS!!!
DOTA
…WHY, COUNT BORGHEN …
… IT IS A PLEASURE TO SEE YOU.
DOSU (STOMP)
DOSU
DOSU
COUNT…? A MYSIDIAN NOBLE?
I SUPPOSE A CHARACTER NAMED BORGHEN DID APPEAR IN FF2, BUT…
WHY WOULD SOMEONE LIKE THAT VISIT A TERRORIST HIDEOUT…?
HMPH! DRINKING TEA LIKE ORDINARY PEOPLE, I SEE…
HAVE YOU FORGOTTEN WHOSE BENEVOLENCE ALLOWS YOU TO REMAIN IN THIS NATION!?
YOU'RE ONLY HERE BECAUSE I'VE SHELTERED YOU IN MY VILLA!!

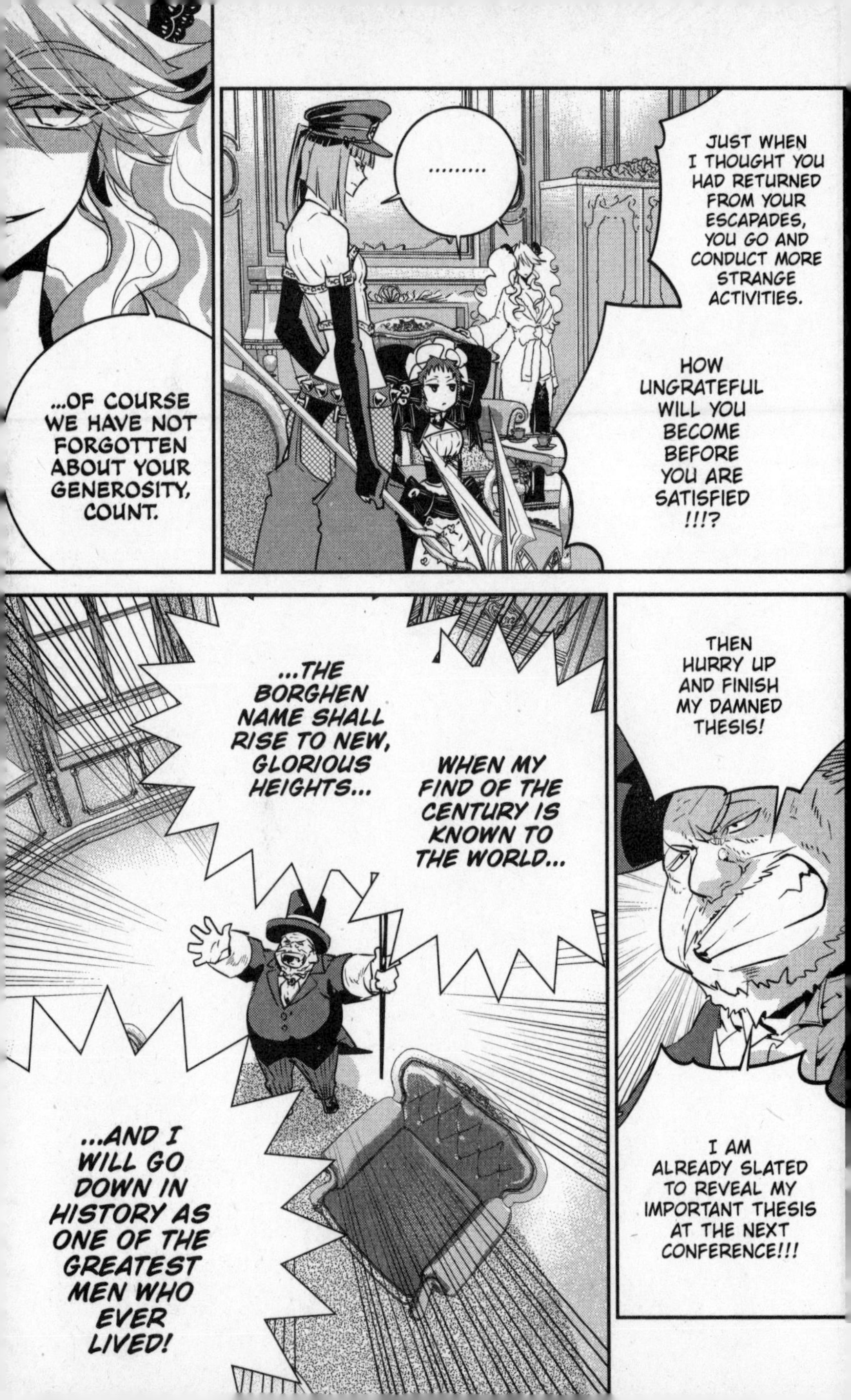
JUST WHEN I THOUGHT YOU HAD RETURNED FROM YOUR ESCAPADES, YOU GO AND CONDUCT MORE STRANGE ACTIVITIES.
HOW UNGRATEFUL WILL YOU BECOME BEFORE YOU ARE SATISFIED !!!?
....
...OF COURSE WE HAVE NOT FORGOTTEN ABOUT YOUR GENEROSITY, COUNT.
THEN HURRY UP AND FINISH MY DAMNED THESIS!
I AM ALREADY SLATED TO REVEAL MY IMPORTANT THESIS AT THE NEXT CONFERENCE!!!
WHEN MY FIND OF THE CENTURY IS KNOWN TO THE WORLD...
...THE BORGHEN NAME SHALL RISE TO NEW, GLORIOUS HEIGHTS...
...AND I WILL GO DOWN IN HISTORY AS ONE OF THE GREATEST MEN WHO EVER LIVED!

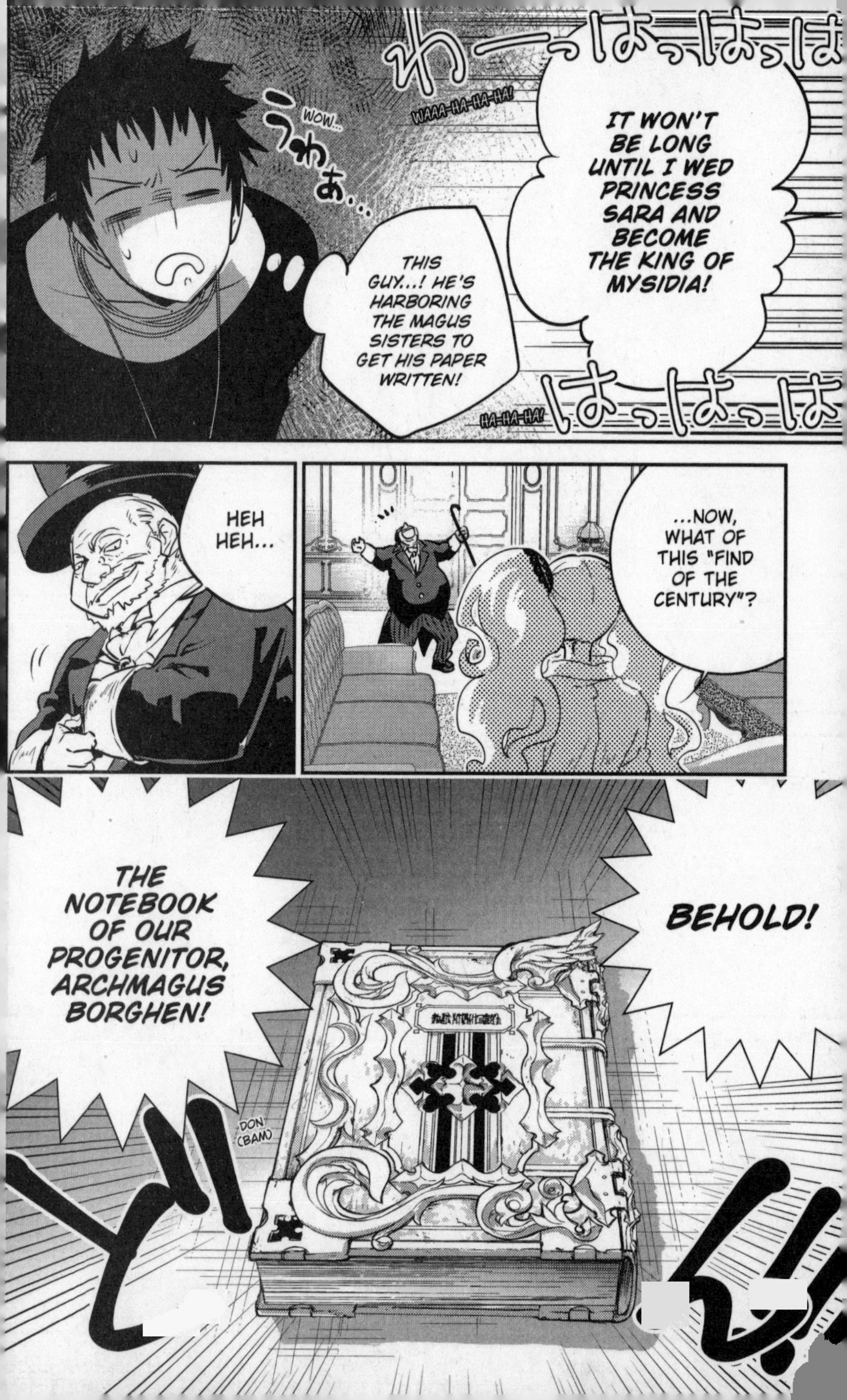
わーっはっはっは
WAAA-HA-HA-HA!
IT WON'T BE LONG UNTIL I WED PRINCESS SARA AND BECOME THE KING OF MYSIDIA!
はっはっは
HA-HA-HA!
THIS GUY...! HE'S HARBORING THE MAGUS SISTERS TO GET HIS PAPER WRITTEN!
うわあ...
WOW...
...NOW, WHAT OF THIS "FIND OF THE CENTURY"?
HEH HEH...
BEHOLD!
THE NOTEBOOK OF OUR PROGENITOR, ARCHMAGUS BORGHEN!
DON (BAM)

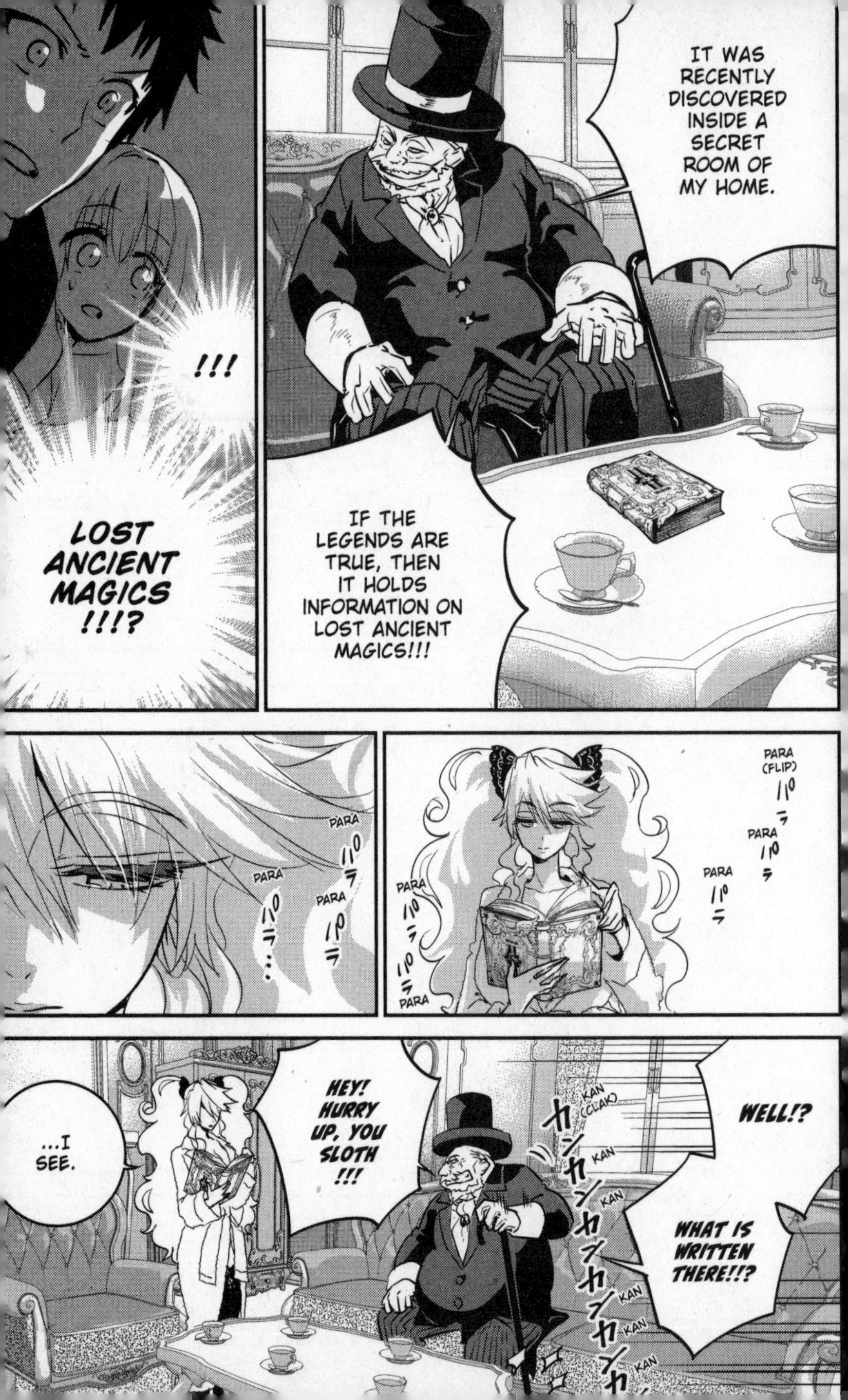
IT WAS RECENTLY DISCOVERED INSIDE A SECRET ROOM OF MY HOME.
IF THE LEGENDS ARE TRUE, THEN IT HOLDS INFORMATION ON LOST ANCIENT MAGICS!!!
!!!
LOST ANCIENT MAGICS !!!?
PARA (FLIP)
PARA
PARA
PARA
PARA
PARA
PARA
PARA
...
WELL!?
WHAT IS WRITTEN THERE!!?
KAN (CLAK)
KAN
KAN
KAN
KAN
KAN
HEY! HURRY UP, YOU SLOTH !!!
...I SEE.

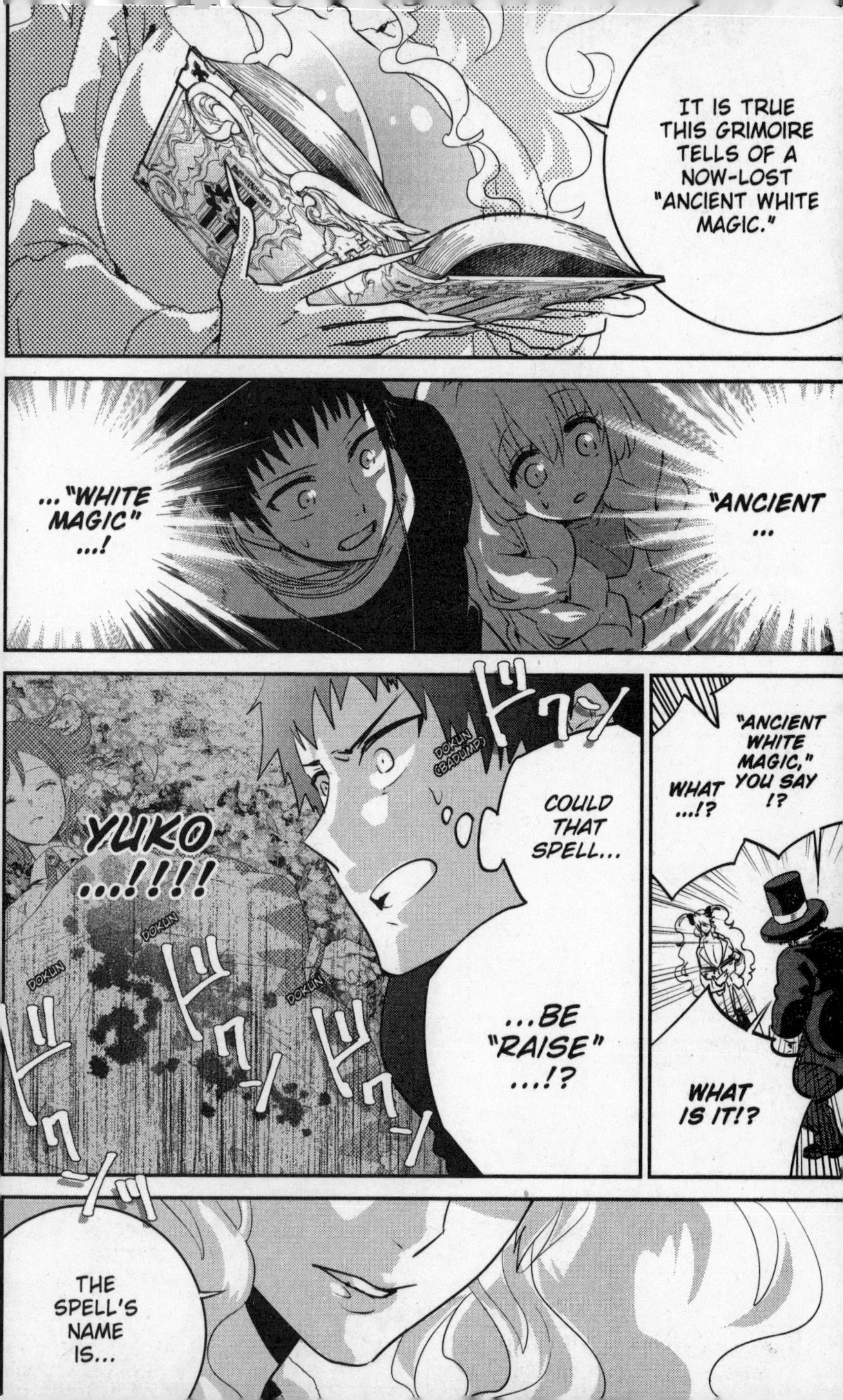
IT IS TRUE THIS GRIMOIRE TELLS OF A NOW-LOST "ANCIENT WHITE MAGIC."
"ANCIENT ...
..."WHITE MAGIC" ...!
"ANCIENT WHITE MAGIC," YOU SAY !?
WHAT ...!?
WHAT IS IT!?
DOKUN (BADUMP)
COULD THAT SPELL...
...BE "RAISE" ...!?
YUKO ...!!!!
DOKUN
DOKUN
DOKUN
THE SPELL'S NAME IS...

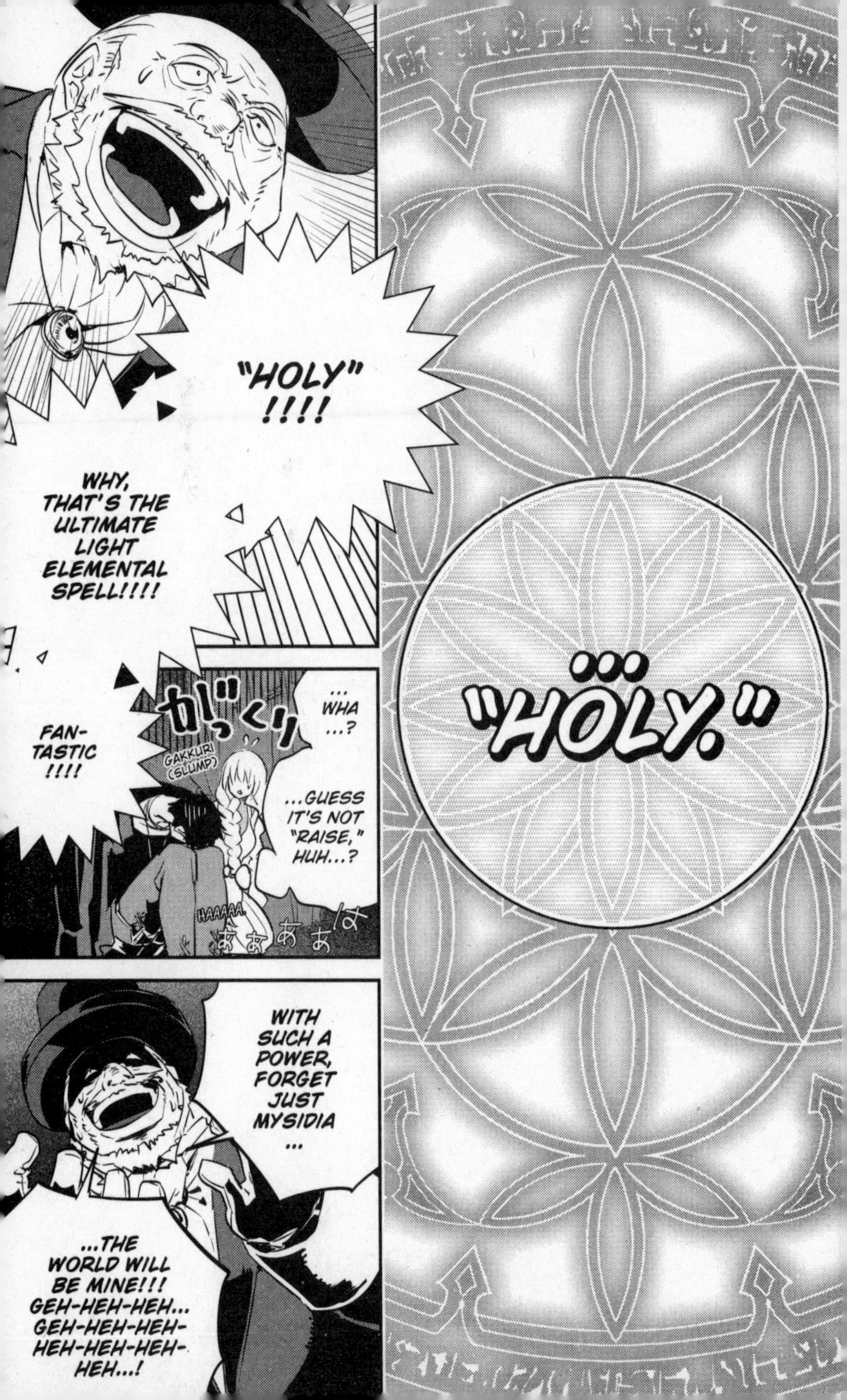
..."HOLY."
"HOLY" !!!!
WHY, THAT'S THE ULTIMATE LIGHT ELEMENTAL SPELL!!!!
FAN-TASTIC !!!!
...WHA ...?
GAKKURI (SLUMP)
...GUESS IT'S NOT "RAISE," HUH...?
HAAAAA.
WITH SUCH A POWER, FORGET JUST MYSIDIA ...
...THE WORLD WILL BE MINE!!! GEH-HEH-HEH... GEH-HEH-HEH-HEH-HEH-HEH-HEH...!

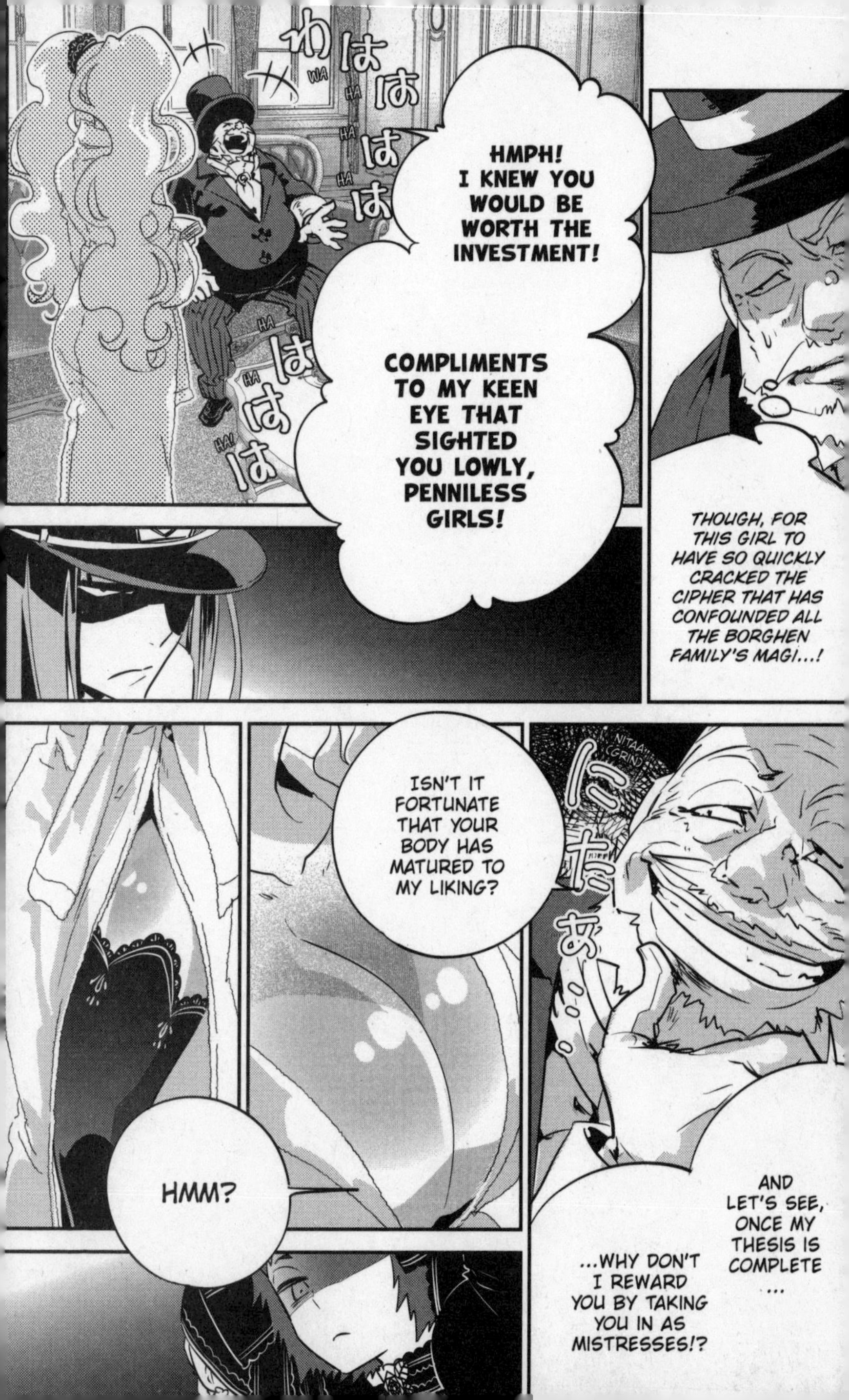
THOUGH, FOR THIS GIRL TO HAVE SO QUICKLY CRACKED THE CIPHER THAT HAS CONFOUNDED ALL THE BORGHEN FAMILY'S MAGI...!
わははははは
WA HA HA HA HA HA HA!
HMPH! I KNEW YOU WOULD BE WORTH THE INVESTMENT!
COMPLIMENTS TO MY KEEN EYE THAT SIGHTED YOU LOWLY, PENNILESS GIRLS!
にたぁ
NITAA (GRIN)
AND LET'S SEE, ONCE MY THESIS IS COMPLETE...
...WHY DON'T I REWARD YOU BY TAKING YOU IN AS MISTRESSES!?
ISN'T IT FORTUNATE THAT YOUR BODY HAS MATURED TO MY LIKING?
HMM?

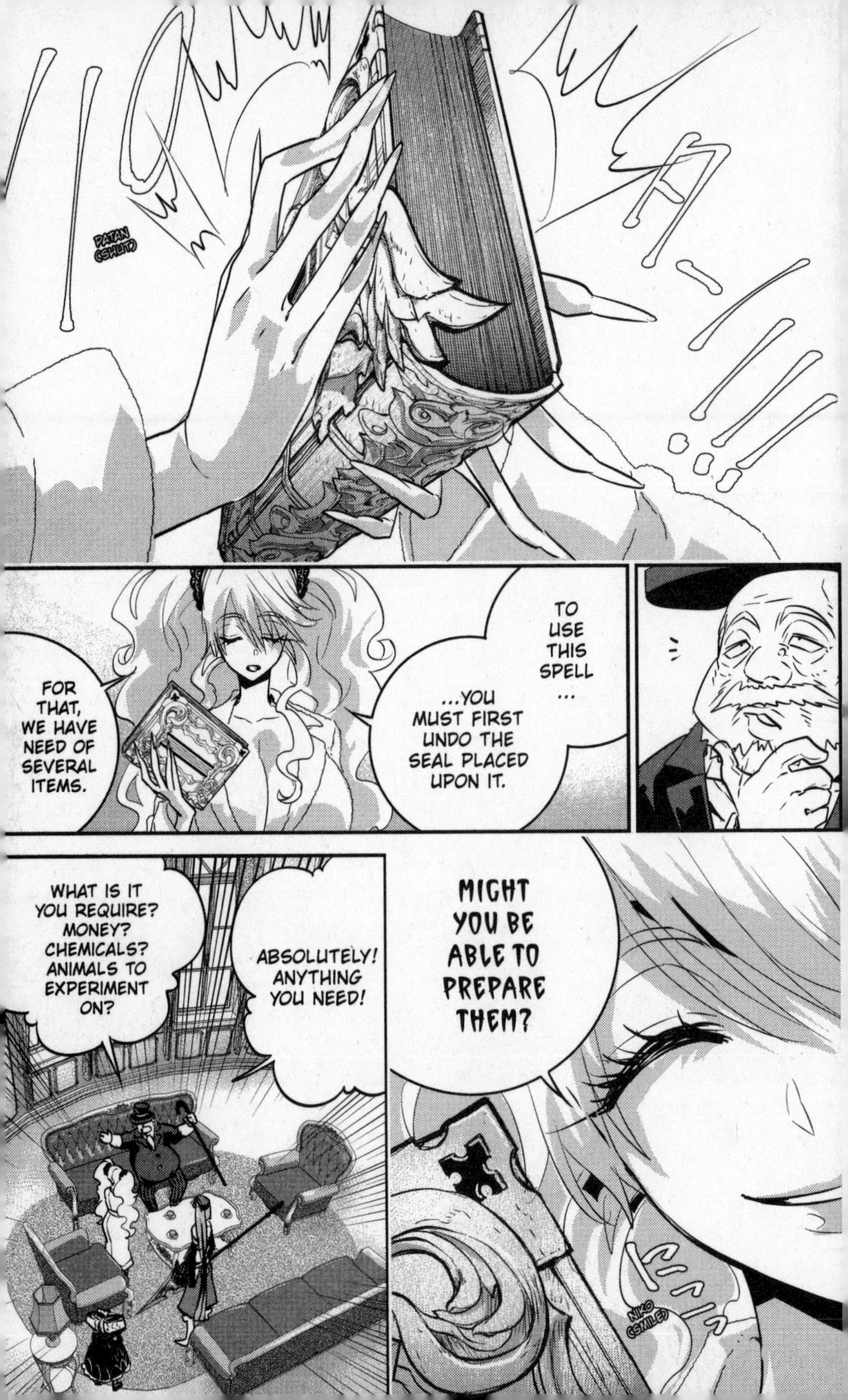
PATAN (SHUT)
TO USE THIS SPELL ...
...YOU MUST FIRST UNDO THE SEAL PLACED UPON IT.
FOR THAT, WE HAVE NEED OF SEVERAL ITEMS.
MIGHT YOU BE ABLE TO PREPARE THEM?
NIKO (SMILE)
WHAT IS IT YOU REQUIRE? MONEY? CHEMICALS? ANIMALS TO EXPERIMENT ON?
ABSOLUTELY! ANYTHING YOU NEED!

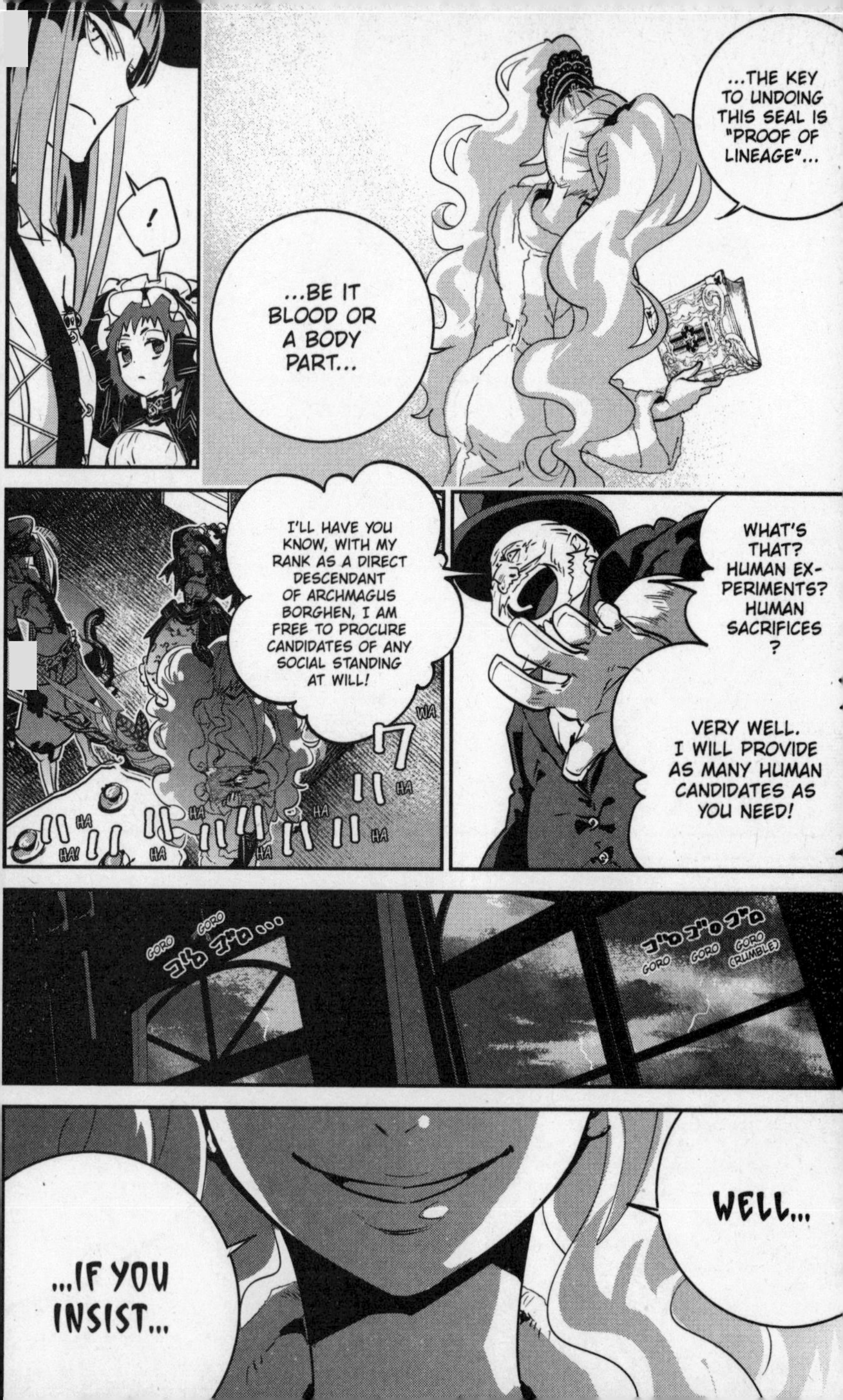
...THE KEY TO UNDOING THIS SEAL IS "PROOF OF LINEAGE"...
...BE IT BLOOD OR A BODY PART...
!
WHAT'S THAT? HUMAN EX-PERIMENTS? HUMAN SACRIFICES ?
VERY WELL. I WILL PROVIDE AS MANY HUMAN CANDIDATES AS YOU NEED!
I'LL HAVE YOU KNOW, WITH MY RANK AS A DIRECT DESCENDANT OF ARCHMAGUS BORGHEN, I AM FREE TO PROCURE CANDIDATES OF ANY SOCIAL STANDING AT WILL!
WA HA HA HA HA HA HA HA HA HA!
GORO GORO GORO (RUMBLE)
GORO GORO...
WELL...
...IF YOU INSIST...

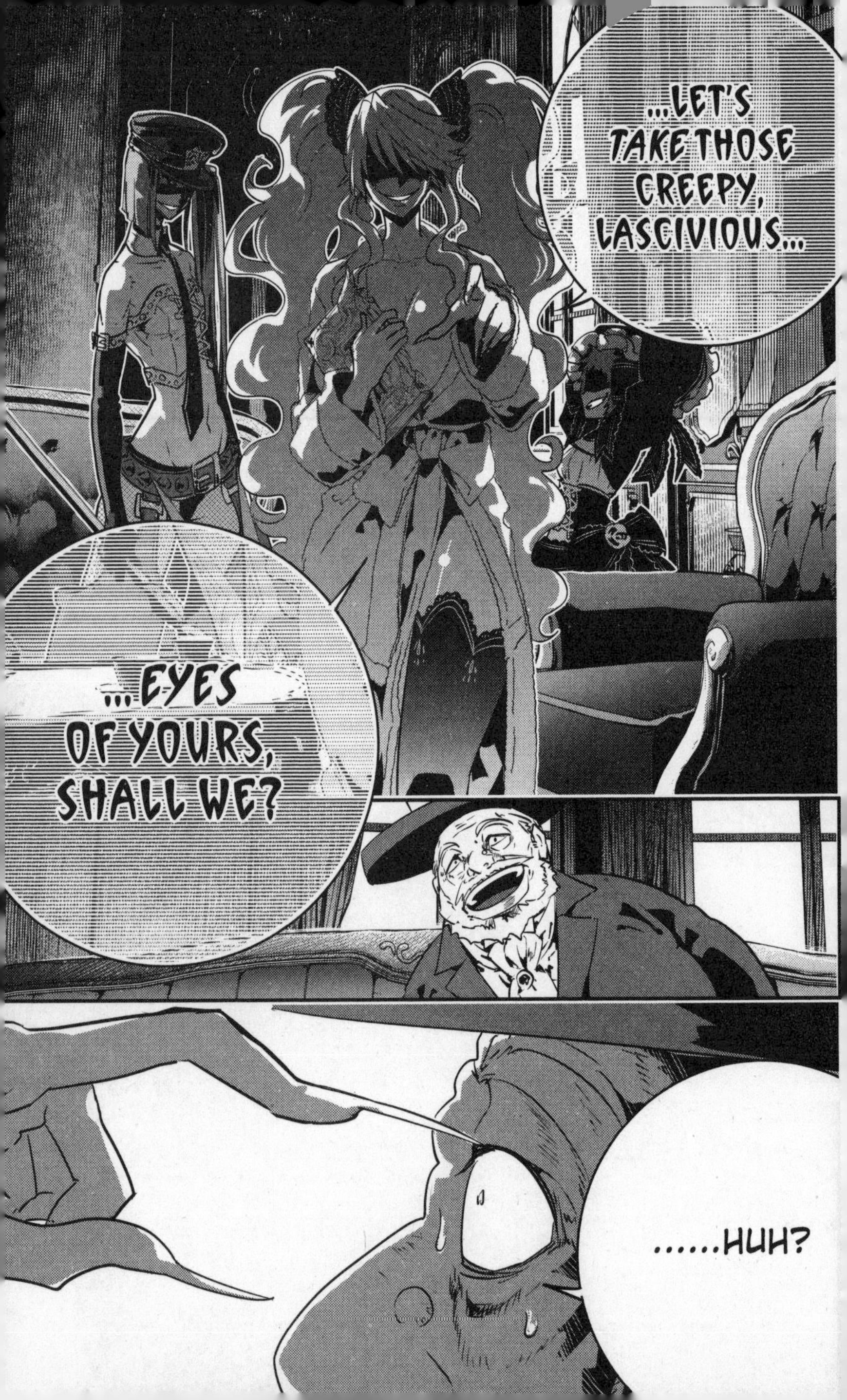
...LET'S TAKE THOSE CREEPY, LASCIVIOUS...
...EYES OF YOURS, SHALL WE?
......HUH?

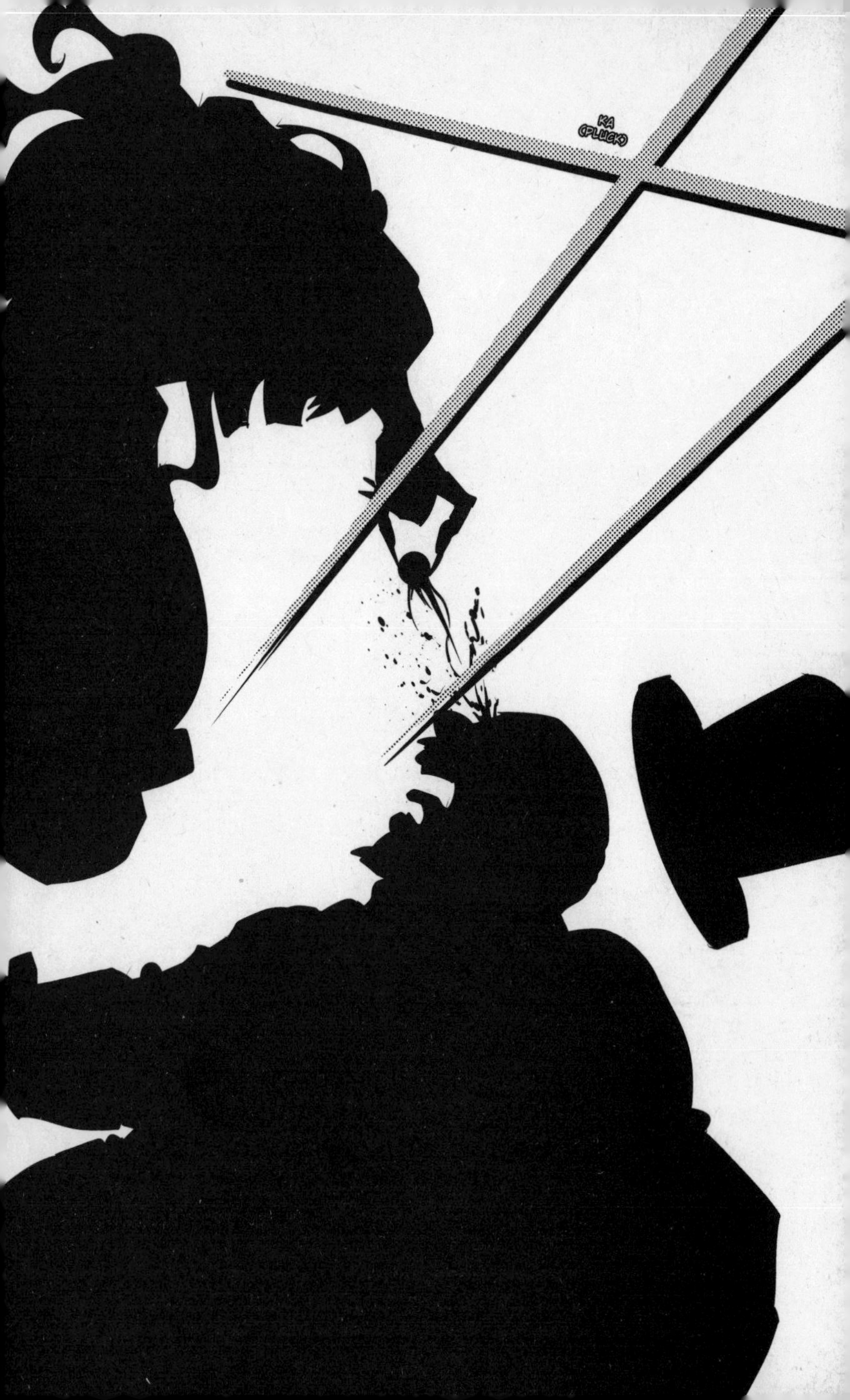
KA
(PLUCK)

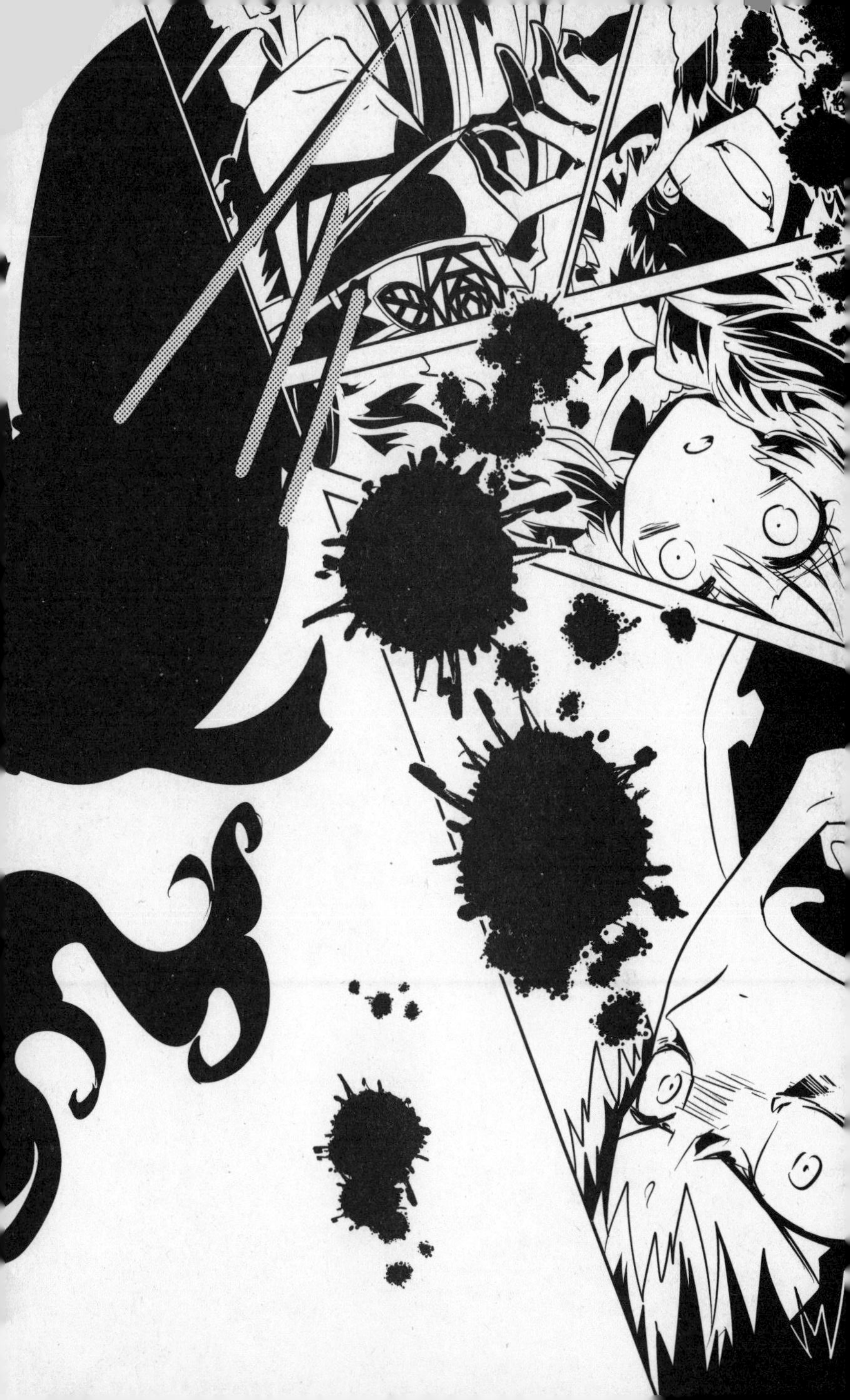

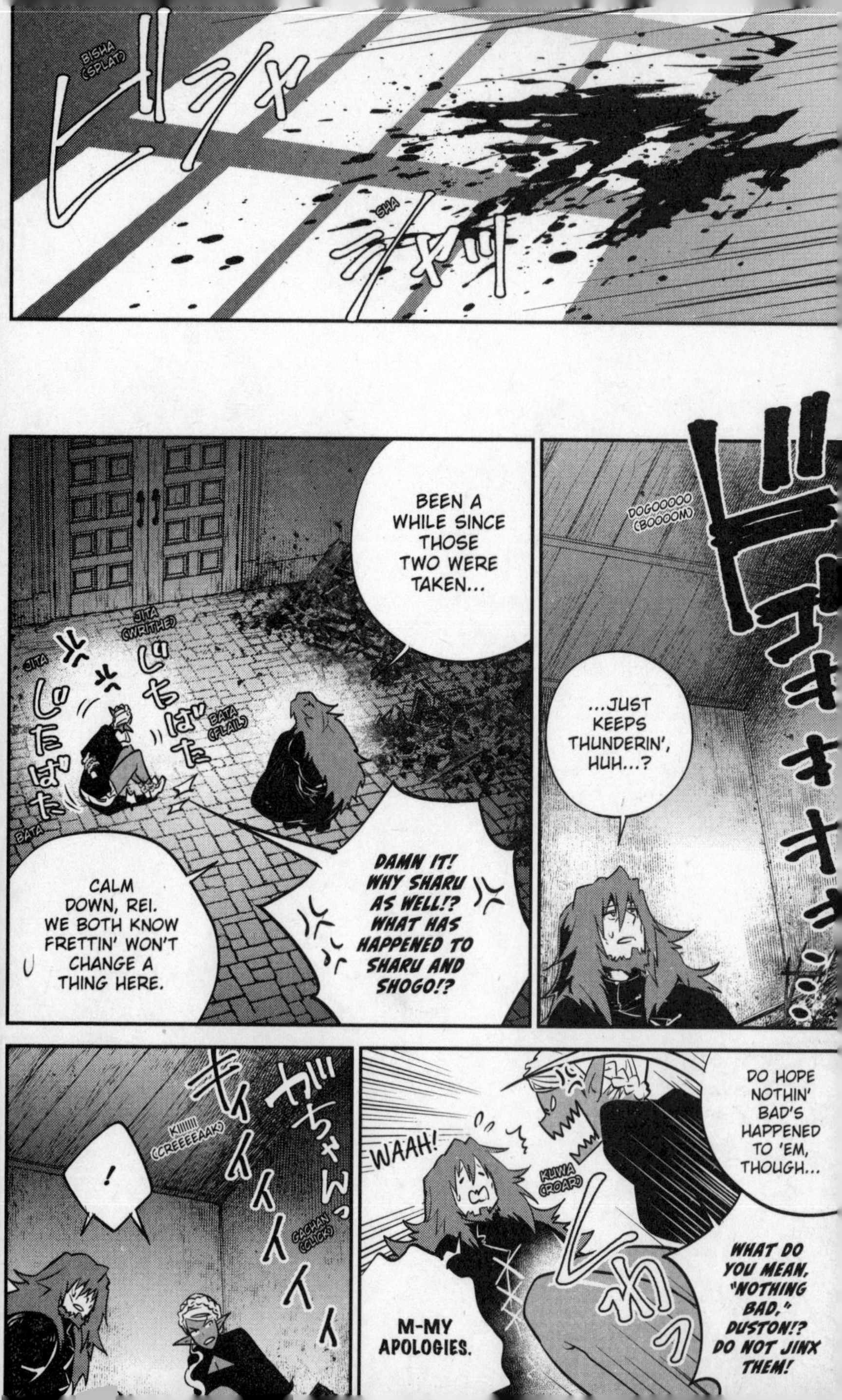

BISHA (SPLAT)
SHA
DOGOOOOO (BOOOOM)
...JUST KEEPS THUNDERIN', HUH...?
BEEN A WHILE SINCE THOSE TWO WERE TAKEN...
DAMN IT! WHY SHARU AS WELL!? WHAT HAS HAPPENED TO SHARU AND SHOGO!?
JITA (WRITHE)
BATA (FLAIL)
JITA
BATA
CALM DOWN, REI. WE BOTH KNOW FRETTIN' WON'T CHANGE A THING HERE.
DO HOPE NOTHIN' BAD'S HAPPENED TO 'EM, THOUGH...
WHAT DO YOU MEAN, "NOTHING BAD," DUSTON!? DO NOT JINX THEM!
KUWA (ROAR)
WAAH!
M-MY APOLOGIES.
GACHAN (CLICK)
KIIIIIII (CREEEEAAK)
!

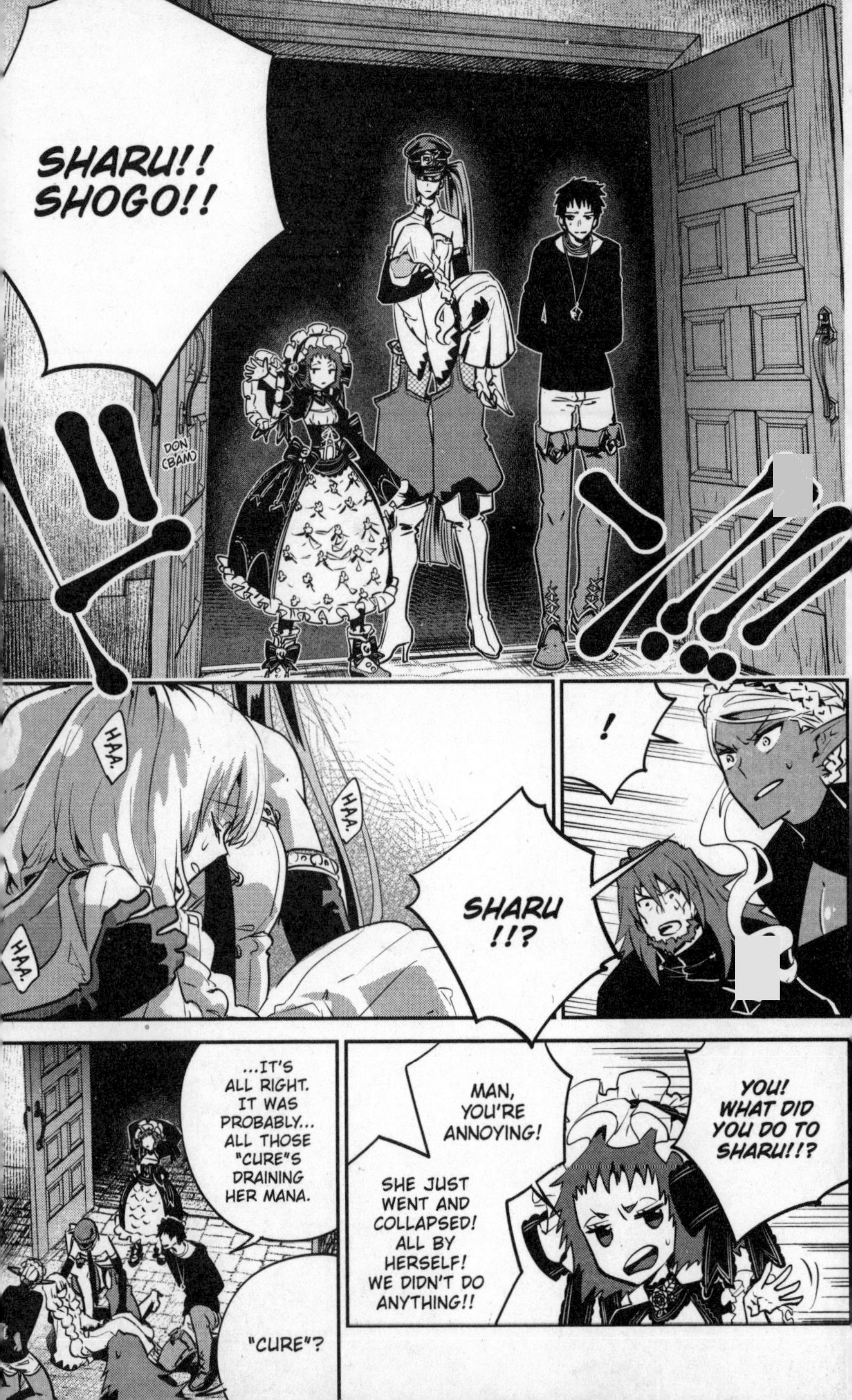
SHARU!! SHOGO!!
!!
DON (BAM)
...!!
!
SHARU !!?
HAA.
HAA.
HAA.
YOU! WHAT DID YOU DO TO SHARU!!?
MAN, YOU'RE ANNOYING!
SHE JUST WENT AND COLLAPSED! ALL BY HERSELF! WE DIDN'T DO ANYTHING!!
...IT'S ALL RIGHT. IT WAS PROBABLY... ALL THOSE "CURE"S DRAINING HER MANA.
"CURE"?

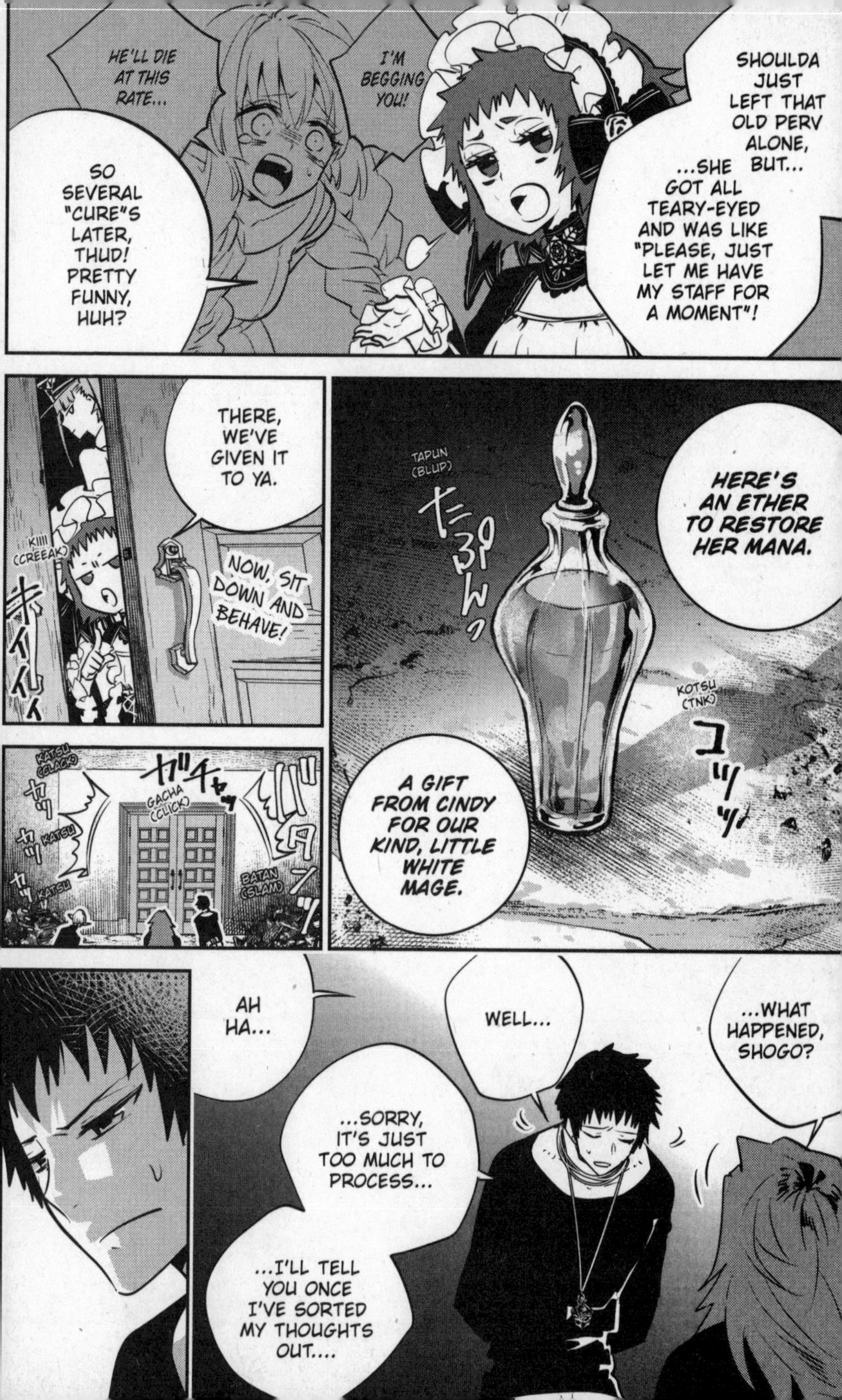
SHOULDA JUST LEFT THAT OLD PERV ALONE, BUT...
...SHE GOT ALL TEARY-EYED AND WAS LIKE "PLEASE, JUST LET ME HAVE MY STAFF FOR A MOMENT"!
I'M BEGGING YOU!
HE'LL DIE AT THIS RATE...
SO SEVERAL "CURE"S LATER, THUD! PRETTY FUNNY, HUH?
HERE'S AN ETHER TO RESTORE HER MANA.
TAPUN (BLUP)
KOTSU (TNK)
A GIFT FROM CINDY FOR OUR KIND, LITTLE WHITE MAGE.
THERE, WE'VE GIVEN IT TO YA.
KIIII (CREEAK)
NOW, SIT DOWN AND BEHAVE!
KATSU (CLACK)
KATSU
KATSU
GACHA (CLICK)
BATAN (SLAM)
...WHAT HAPPENED, SHOGO?
WELL...
...SORRY, IT'S JUST TOO MUCH TO PROCESS...
...I'LL TELL YOU ONCE I'VE SORTED MY THOUGHTS OUT....
AH HA...

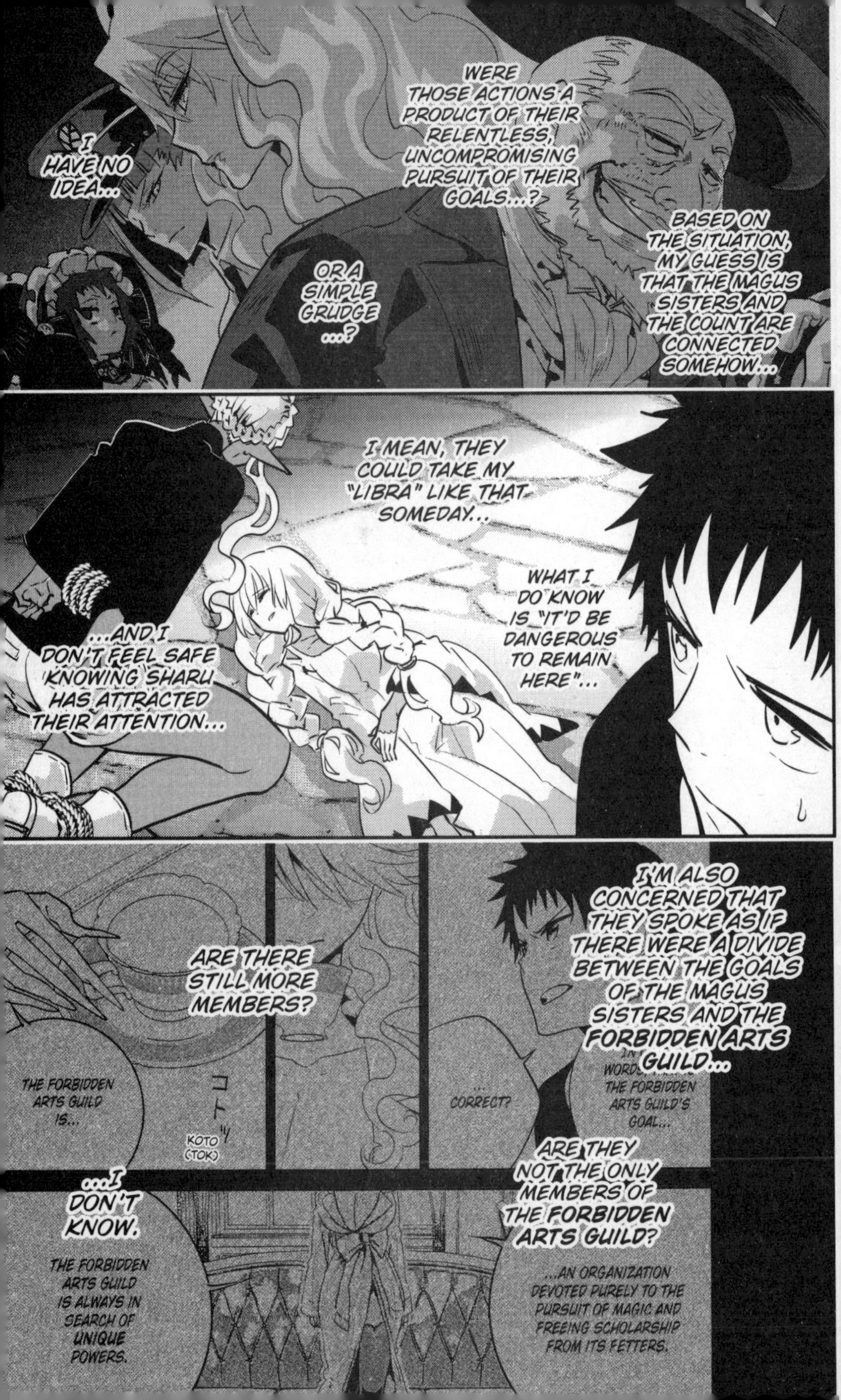
BASED ON THE SITUATION, MY GUESS IS THAT THE MAGUS SISTERS AND THE COUNT ARE CONNECTED SOMEHOW...
WERE THOSE ACTIONS A PRODUCT OF THEIR RELENTLESS, UNCOMPROMISING PURSUIT OF THEIR GOALS...?
OR A SIMPLE GRUDGE ...?
I HAVE NO IDEA...
I MEAN, THEY COULD TAKE MY "LIBRA" LIKE THAT SOMEDAY...
WHAT I DO KNOW IS "IT'D BE DANGEROUS TO REMAIN HERE"...
...AND I DON'T FEEL SAFE KNOWING SHARU HAS ATTRACTED THEIR ATTENTION...
I'M ALSO CONCERNED THAT THEY SPOKE AS IF THERE WERE A DIVIDE BETWEEN THE GOALS OF THE MAGUS SISTERS AND THE FORBIDDEN ARTS GUILD...
THE FORBIDDEN ARTS GUILD'S GOAL...
...CORRECT?
ARE THERE STILL MORE MEMBERS?
KOTO (TOK)
THE FORBIDDEN ARTS GUILD IS...
ARE THEY NOT THE ONLY MEMBERS OF THE FORBIDDEN ARTS GUILD?
...AN ORGANIZATION DEVOTED PURELY TO THE PURSUIT OF MAGIC AND FREEING SCHOLARSHIP FROM ITS FETTERS.
...I DON'T KNOW.
THE FORBIDDEN ARTS GUILD IS ALWAYS IN SEARCH OF UNIQUE POWERS.

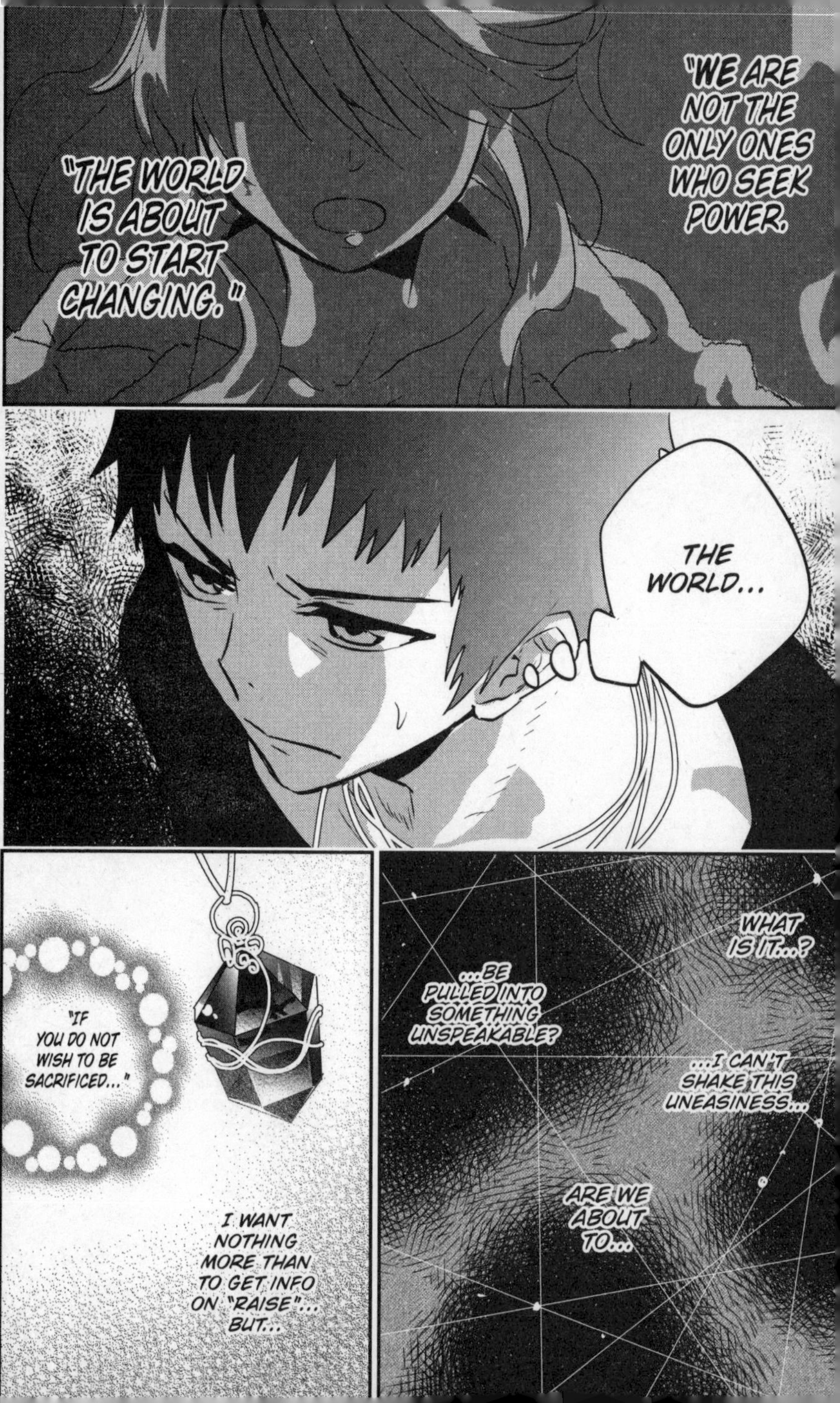
"WE ARE NOT THE ONLY ONES WHO SEEK POWER.
"THE WORLD IS ABOUT TO START CHANGING."
THE WORLD...
WHAT IS IT...?
...I CAN'T SHAKE THIS UNEASINESS...
ARE WE ABOUT TO...
...BE PULLED INTO SOMETHING UNSPEAKABLE?
"IF YOU DO NOT WISH TO BE SACRIFICED..."
I WANT NOTHING MORE THAN TO GET INFO ON "RAISE"... BUT...

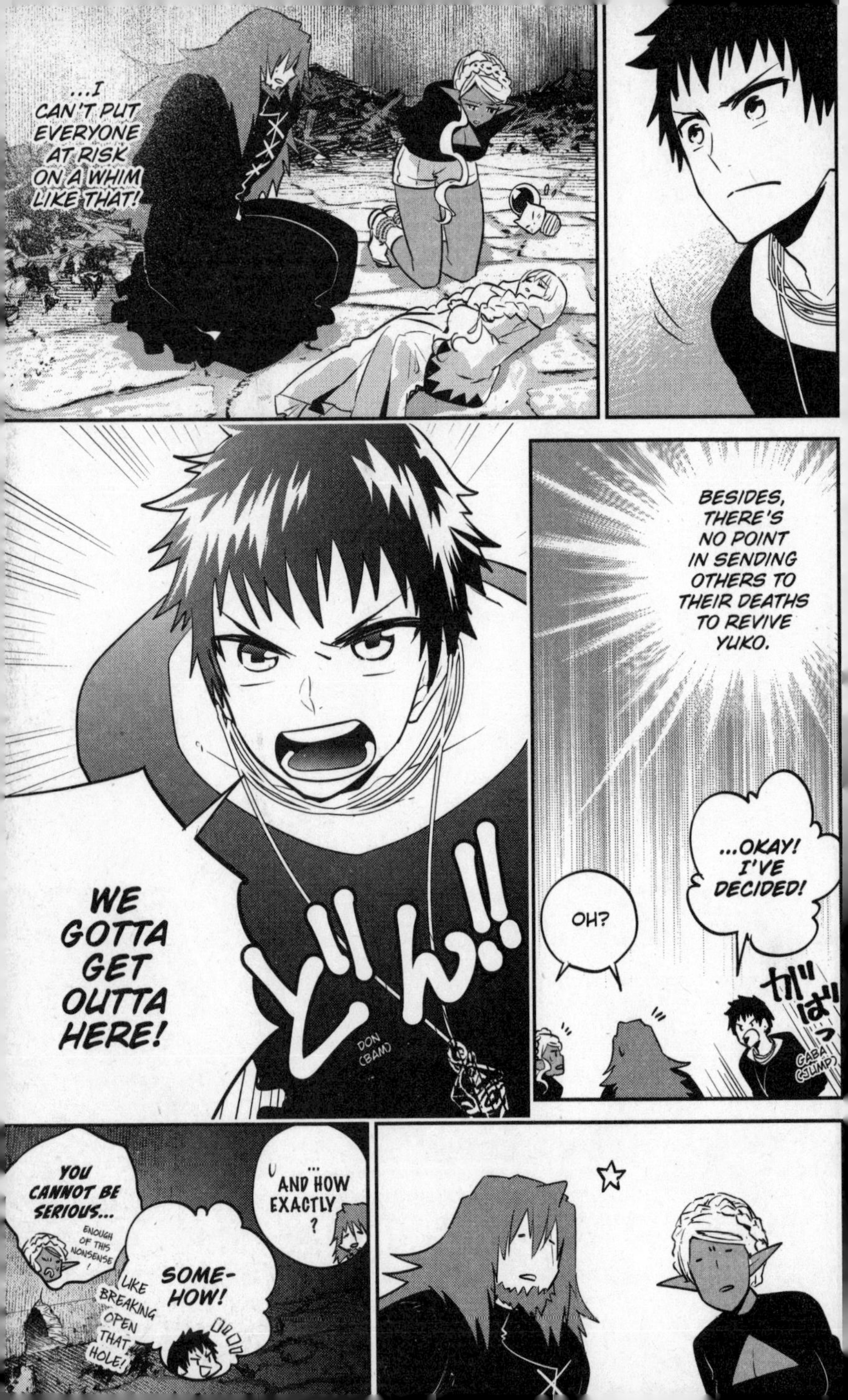
...I CAN'T PUT EVERYONE AT RISK ON A WHIM LIKE THAT!
BESIDES, THERE'S NO POINT IN SENDING OTHERS TO THEIR DEATHS TO REVIVE YUKO.
がばっ
GABA (JUMP)
...OKAY! I'VE DECIDED!
OH?
WE GOTTA GET OUTTA HERE!
どん!!
DON (BAM)
...AND HOW EXACTLY?
SOME-HOW!
LIKE BREAKING OPEN THAT HOLE!
YOU CANNOT BE SERIOUS...
ENOUGH OF THIS NONSENSE!

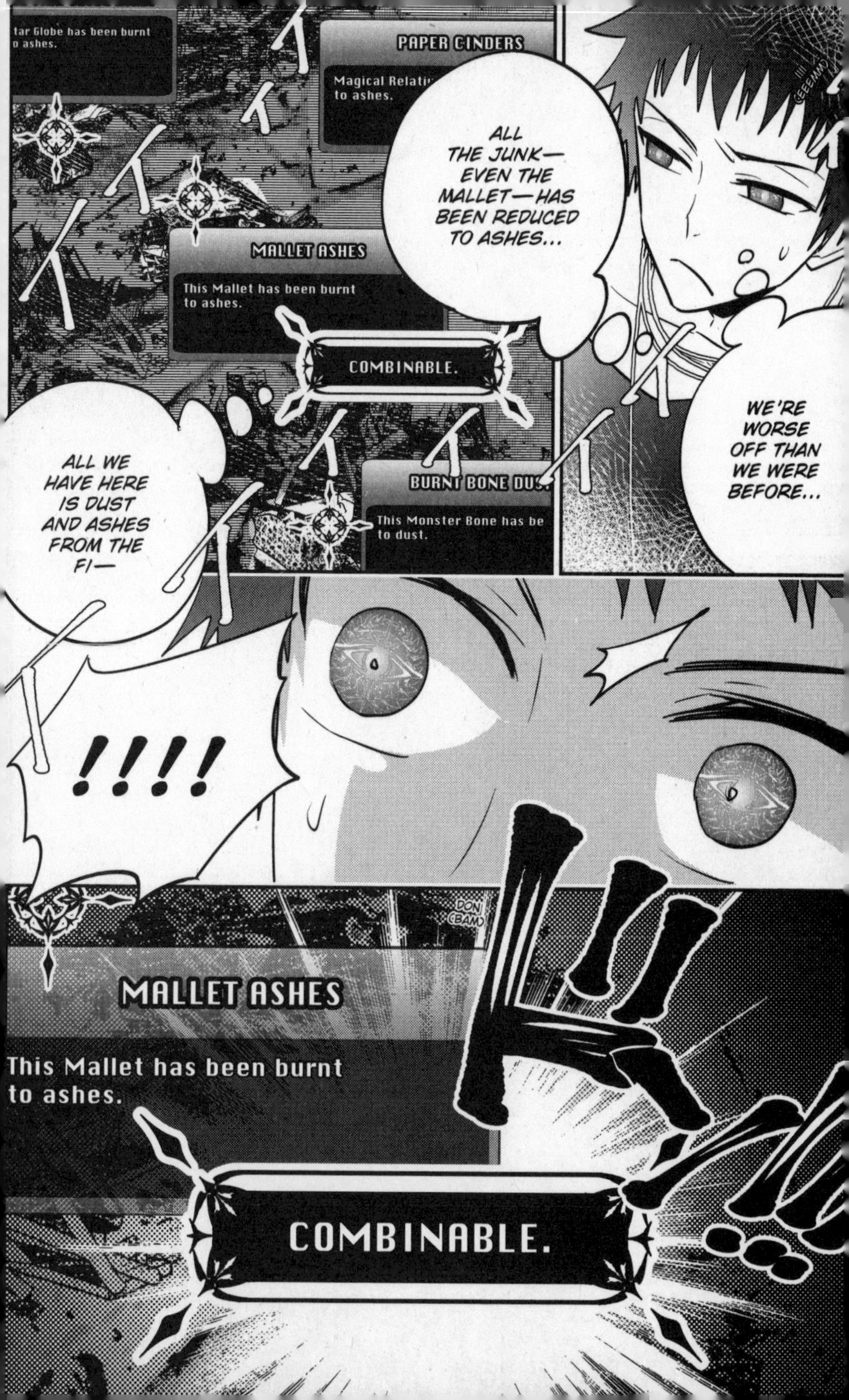
(EEEWW)
ALL THE JUNK—EVEN THE MALLET—HAS BEEN REDUCED TO ASHES...
WE'RE WORSE OFF THAN WE WERE BEFORE...
PAPER CINDERS
Magical Relati
to ashes.
tar Globe has been burnt
o ashes.
MALLET ASHES
This Mallet has been burnt
to ashes.
COMBINABLE.
BURNT BONE DUS
This Monster Bone has be
to dust.
ALL WE HAVE HERE IS DUST AND ASHES FROM THE FI—
!!!!
DON (BAM)
MALLET ASHES
This Mallet has been burnt
to ashes.
COMBINABLE.

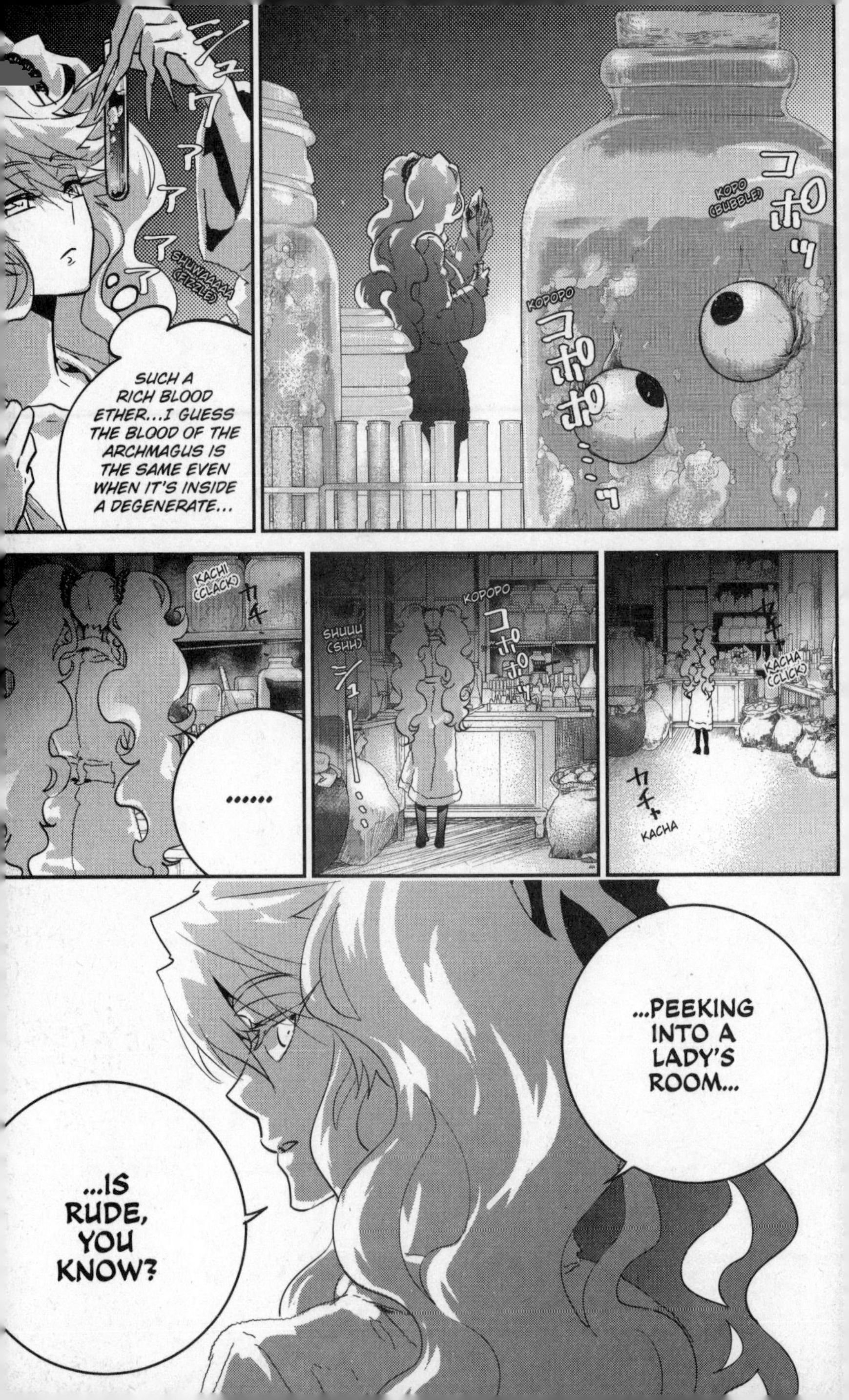
コポッ
KOPO (BUBBLE)
コポポ…ッ
KOPOPO
シュワァァァァ
SHUWAAAAA (FIZZLE)
SUCH A RICH BLOOD ETHER...I GUESS THE BLOOD OF THE ARCHMAGUS IS THE SAME EVEN WHEN IT'S INSIDE A DEGENERATE...
カチャ
KACHA (CLICK)
カチャ
KACHA
コポポ
KOPOPO
シュー
SHUUU (SHH)
カチ
KACHI (CLACK)
......
...PEEKING INTO A LADY'S ROOM...
...IS RUDE, YOU KNOW?

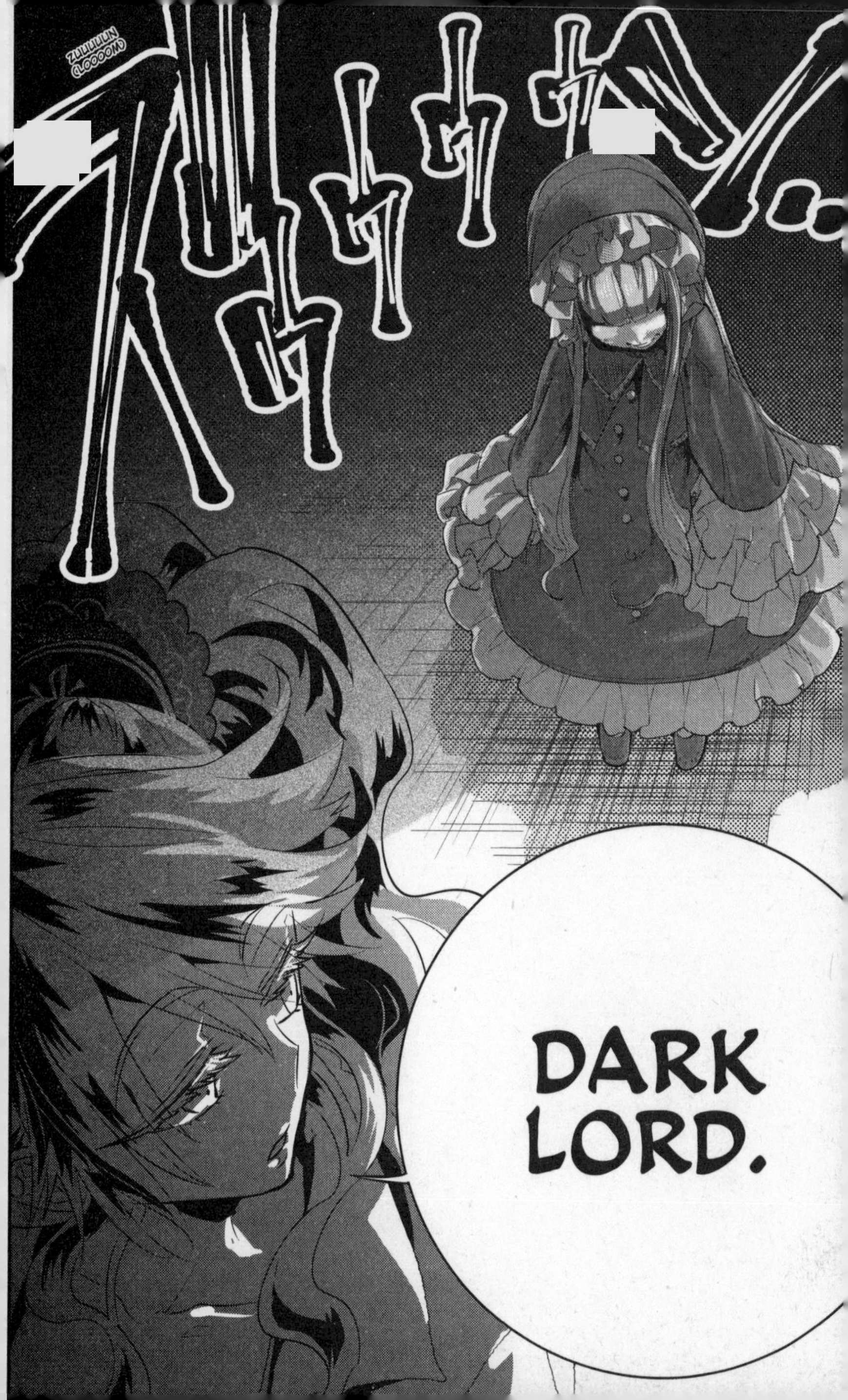
ZUNNNNN (GLOOOOM)
DARK LORD.

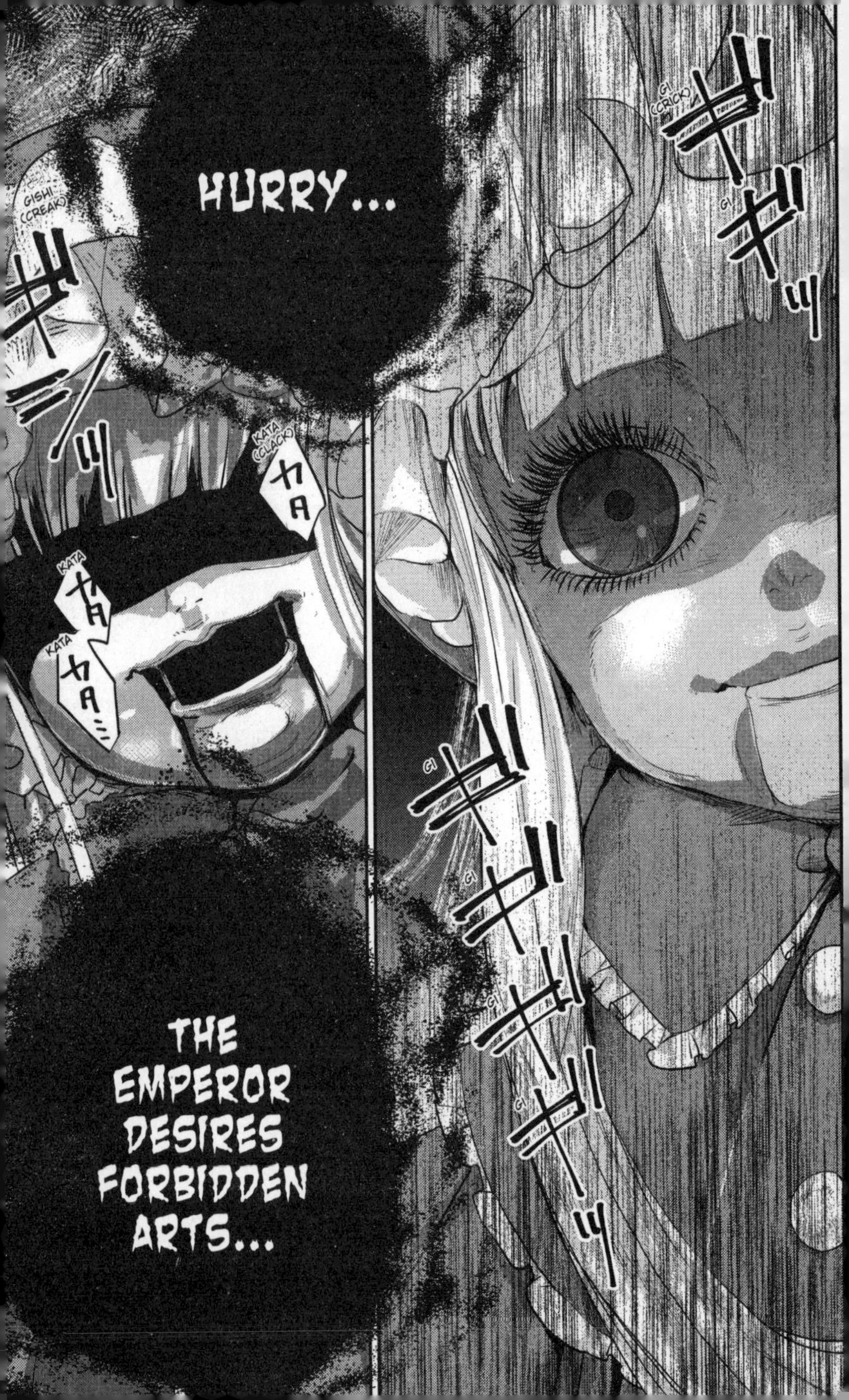
GI (CRICK)
GI
GI
GI
GI
GI
HURRY...
GISHI (CREAK)
KATA (CLACK)
KATA
KATA
THE EMPEROR DESIRES FORBIDDEN ARTS...

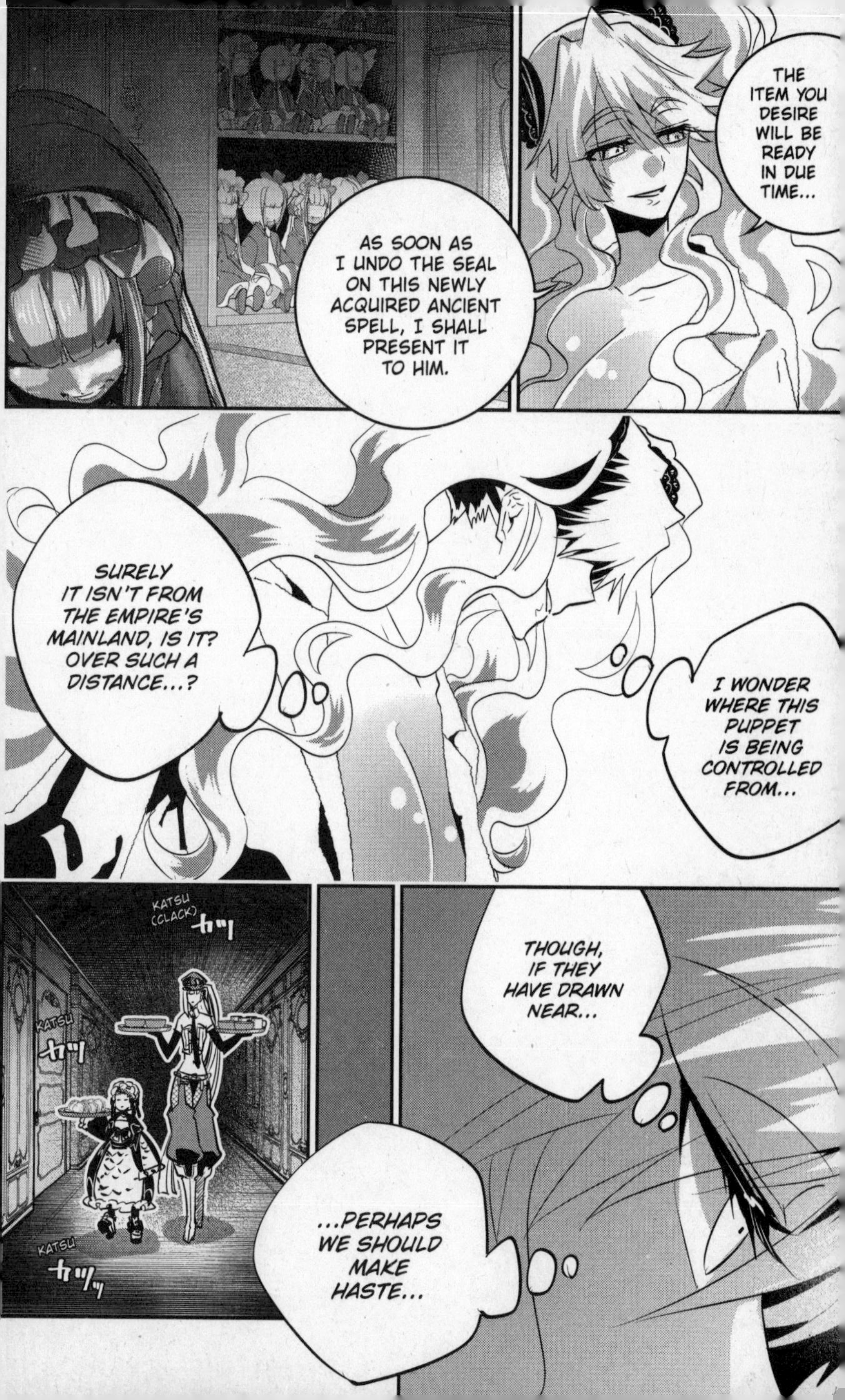
THE ITEM YOU DESIRE WILL BE READY IN DUE TIME...
AS SOON AS I UNDO THE SEAL ON THIS NEWLY ACQUIRED ANCIENT SPELL, I SHALL PRESENT IT TO HIM.
I WONDER WHERE THIS PUPPET IS BEING CONTROLLED FROM...
SURELY IT ISN'T FROM THE EMPIRE'S MAINLAND, IS IT? OVER SUCH A DISTANCE...?
THOUGH, IF THEY HAVE DRAWN NEAR...
...PERHAPS WE SHOULD MAKE HASTE...
KATSU (CLACK) カツ
KATSU カツ
KATSU カツッ

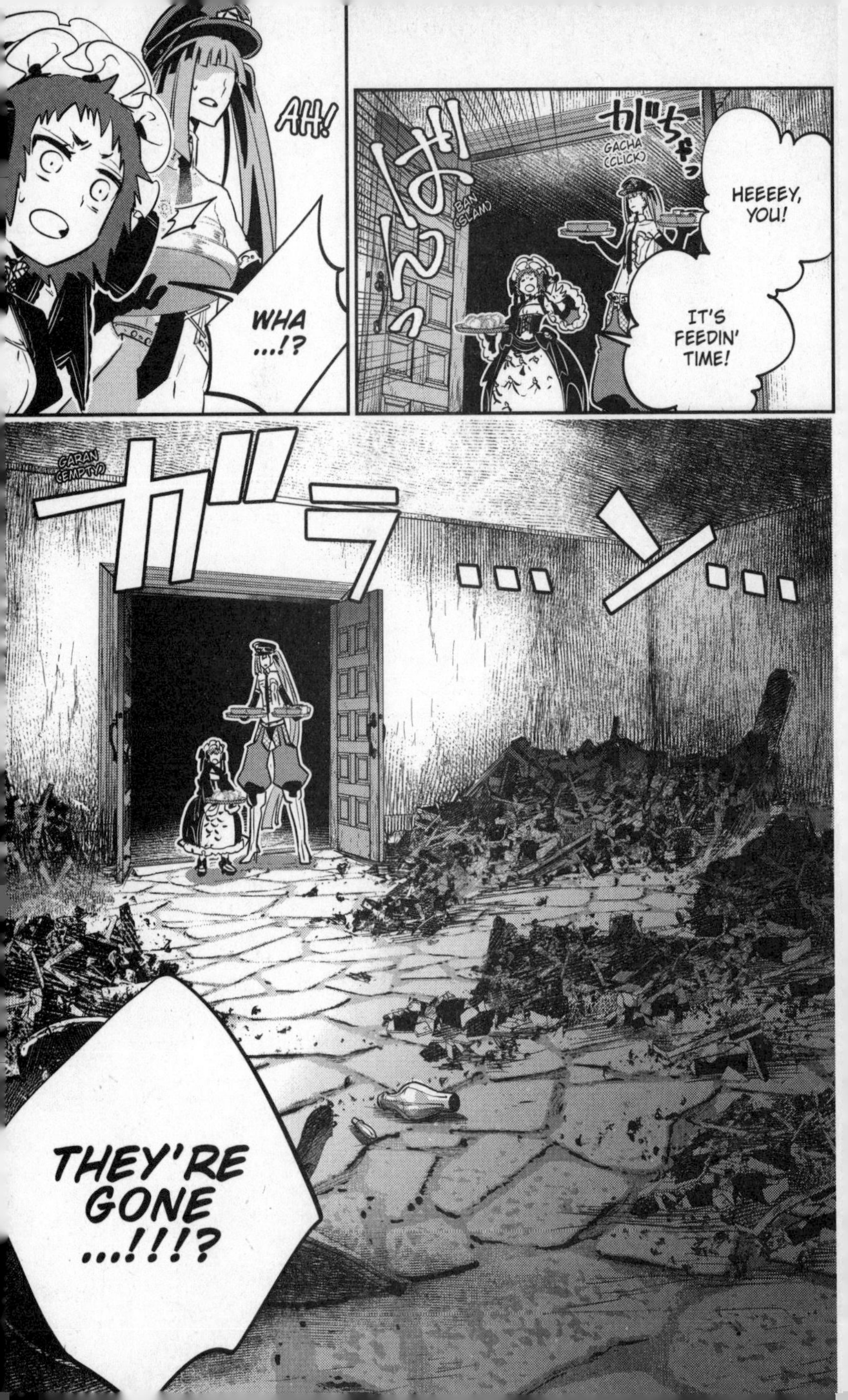
GACHA (CLICK)
HEEEEY, YOU!
IT'S FEEDIN' TIME!
BAN (SLAM)
AH!
WHA ...!?
GARAN (EMPTY)
THEY'RE GONE ...!!!?

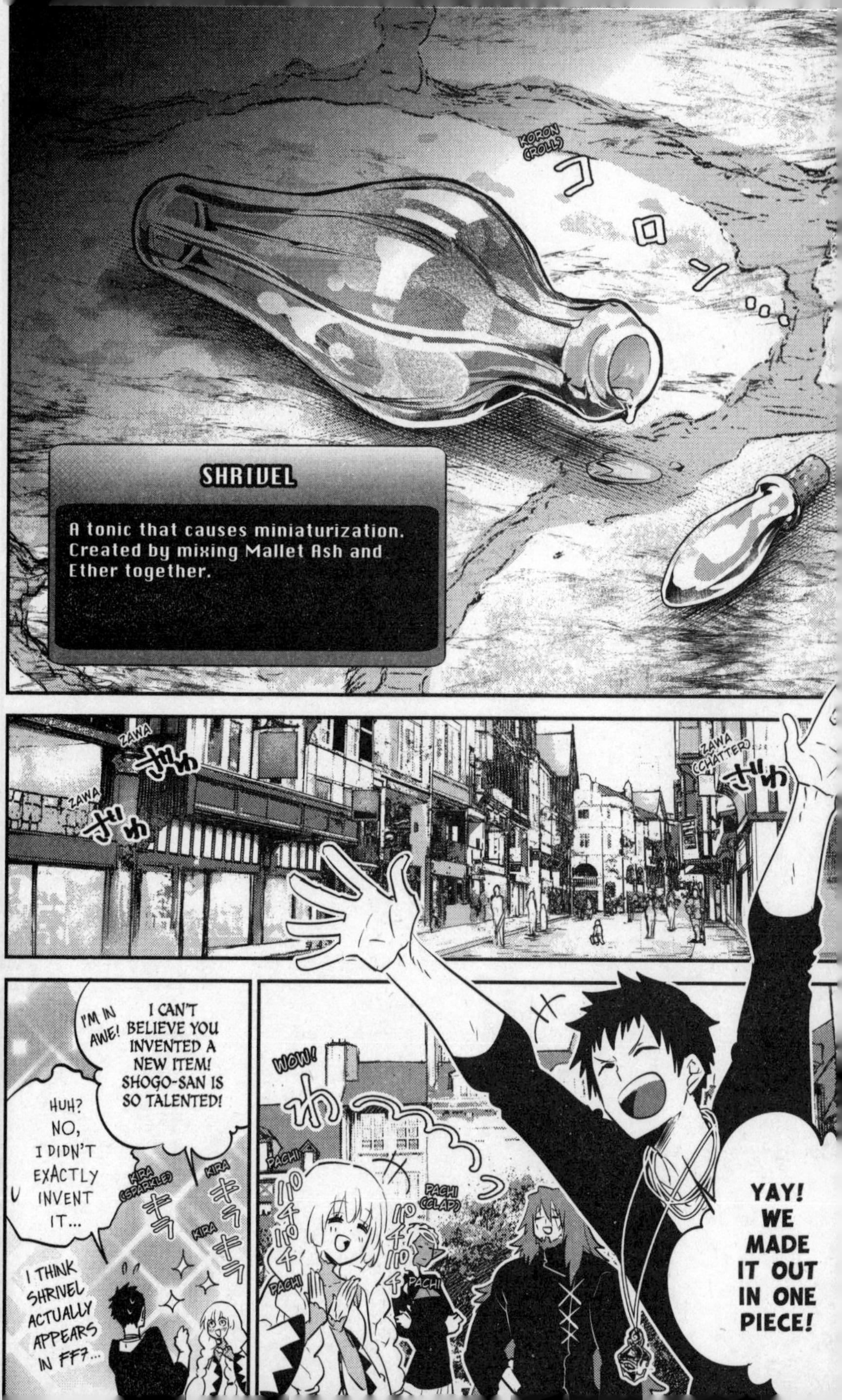
KORON (ROLL)
SHRIVEL
A tonic that causes miniaturization. Created by mixing Mallet Ash and Ether together.
ZAWA (CHATTER)
ZAWA
ZAWA
YAY! WE MADE IT OUT IN ONE PIECE!
WOW!
PACHI
PACHI (CLAP)
PACHI
PACHI
I'M IN AWE!
I CAN'T BELIEVE YOU INVENTED A NEW ITEM! SHOGO-SAN IS SO TALENTED!
KIRA
KIRA (SPARKLE)
KIRA
HUH? NO, I DIDN'T EXACTLY INVENT IT...
I THINK SHRIVEL ACTUALLY APPEARS IN FF7...

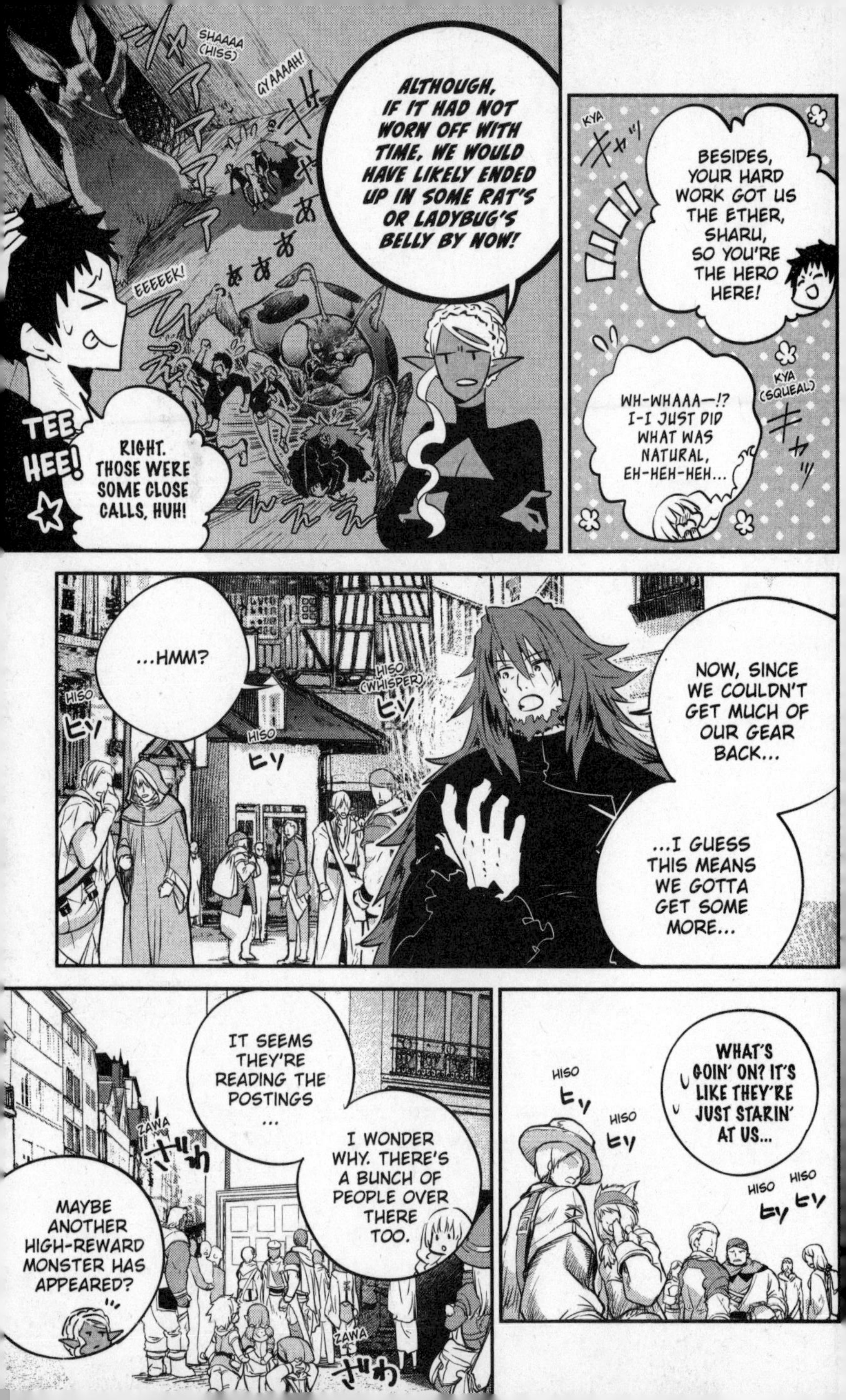
KYA
BESIDES, YOUR HARD WORK GOT US THE ETHER, SHARU, SO YOU'RE THE HERO HERE!
KYA (SQUEAL)
WH-WHAAA—!? I-I JUST DID WHAT WAS NATURAL, EH-HEH-HEH...
ALTHOUGH, IF IT HAD NOT WORN OFF WITH TIME, WE WOULD HAVE LIKELY ENDED UP IN SOME RAT'S OR LADYBUG'S BELLY BY NOW!
SHAAAA (HISS)
GYAAAAH!
EEEEEK!
TEE HEE!
RIGHT. THOSE WERE SOME CLOSE CALLS, HUH!
NOW, SINCE WE COULDN'T GET MUCH OF OUR GEAR BACK...
...I GUESS THIS MEANS WE GOTTA GET SOME MORE...
HISO (WHISPER)
HISO
HISO
...HMM?
WHAT'S GOIN' ON? IT'S LIKE THEY'RE JUST STARIN' AT US...
HISO
HISO
HISO
HISO
IT SEEMS THEY'RE READING THE POSTINGS...
I WONDER WHY. THERE'S A BUNCH OF PEOPLE OVER THERE TOO.
ZAWA
MAYBE ANOTHER HIGH-REWARD MONSTER HAS APPEARED?
ZAWA

...HUH?

HYOKO
(POOF)

THERE WAS THE THING WITH GREAD TREID TOO.

IF THE REWARD IS GOOD, MAYBE WE SHOULD GIVE IT A SHOT...

ZU ZU ZU ZU ZU ZU ZU (ZOOM)

WANTED WANTED WANTED WANTED
DEAD OR ALIVE DEAD OR ALIVE DEAD OR ALIVE DEAD OR ALIVE

ZU ZU ZU ZU ZU ZU

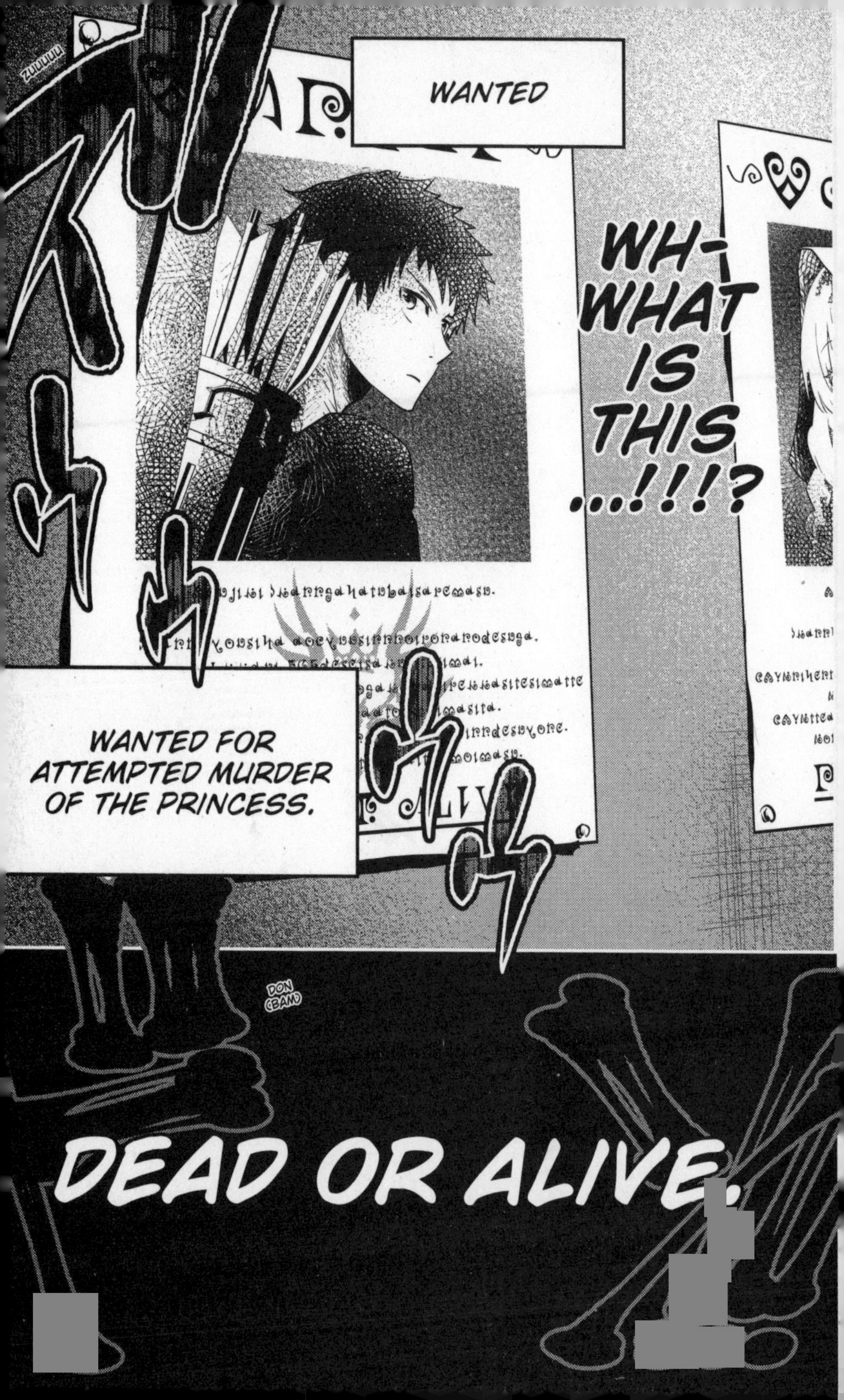
WANTED
WH-WHAT IS THIS...!!!?
ZUUUUU
WANTED FOR ATTEMPTED MURDER OF THE PRINCESS.
DON (BAM)
DEAD OR ALIVE.

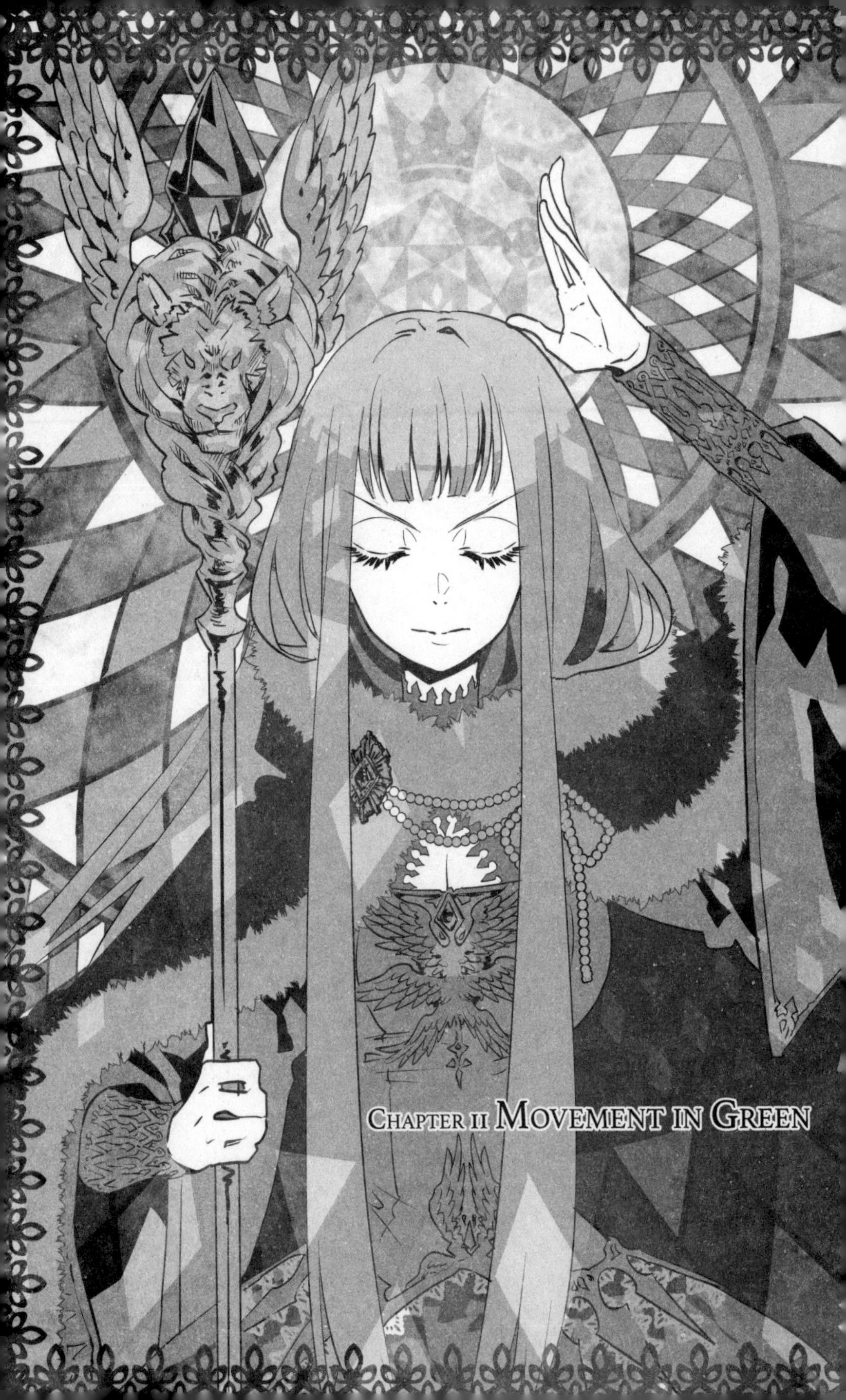
Chapter II Movement in Green

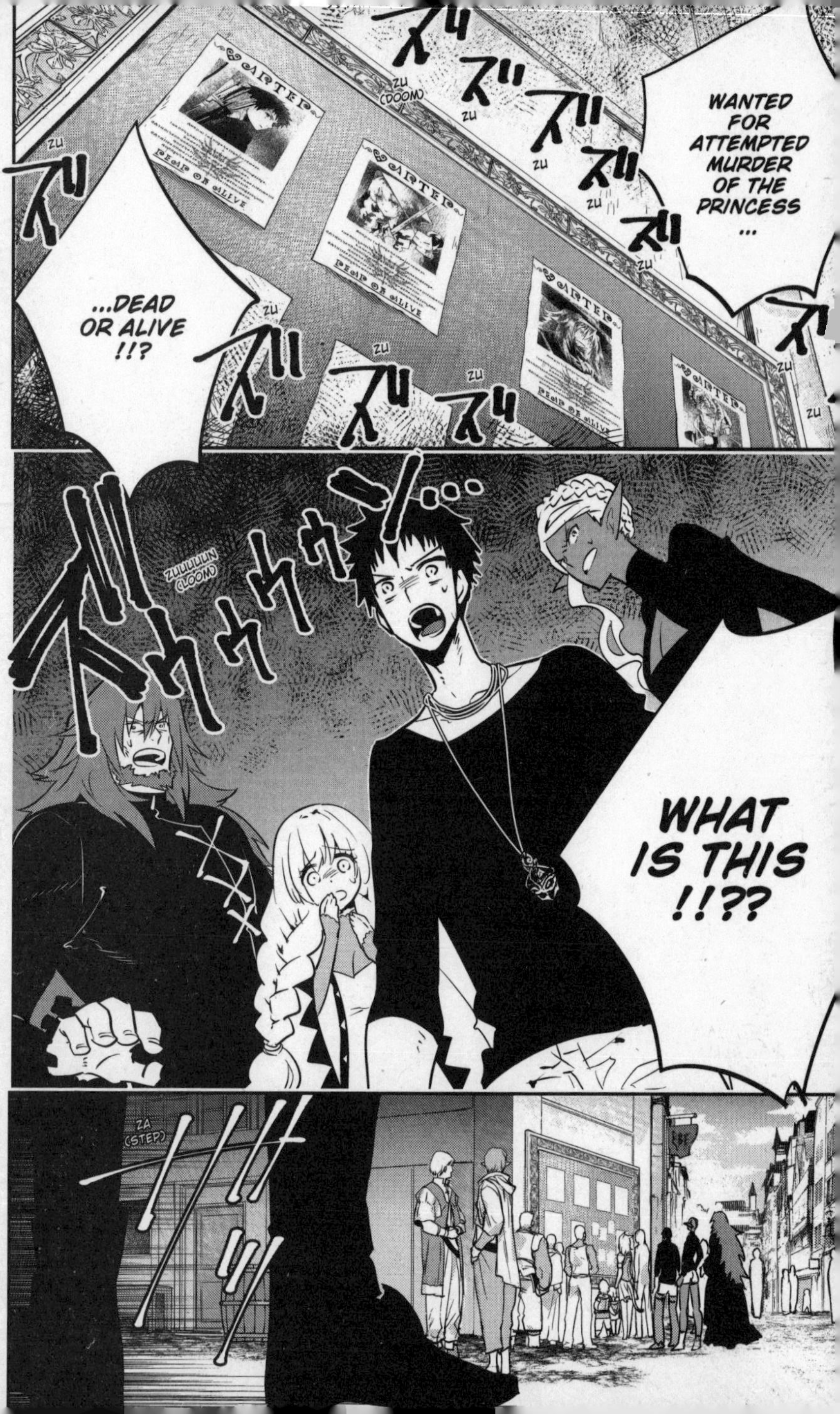
WANTED FOR ATTEMPTED MURDER OF THE PRINCESS ...
ZU (DOOM)
ZU
ZU
ZU
ZU
ZU
...DEAD OR ALIVE !!?
ZU
ZU
ZU
ZU
ZUUUUUN (GLOOM)
WHAT IS THIS !!??
ZA (STEP)

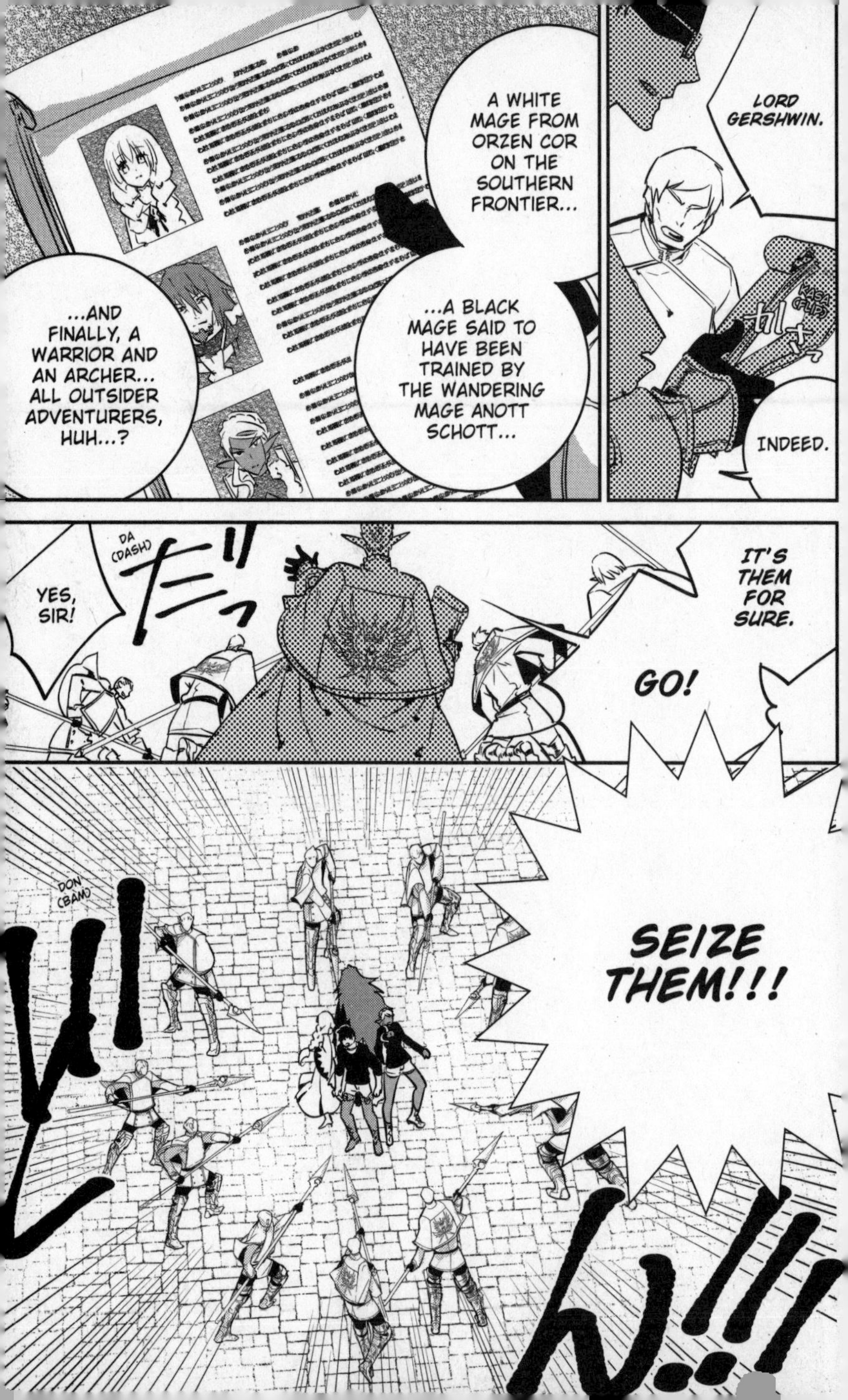
LORD GERSHWIN.
KASA (FLIP)
INDEED.
A WHITE MAGE FROM ORZEN COR ON THE SOUTHERN FRONTIER...
...A BLACK MAGE SAID TO HAVE BEEN TRAINED BY THE WANDERING MAGE ANOTT SCHOTT...
...AND FINALLY, A WARRIOR AND AN ARCHER... ALL OUTSIDER ADVENTURERS, HUH...?
IT'S THEM FOR SURE.
GO!
DA (DASH)
YES, SIR!
SEIZE THEM!!!
DON (BAM)

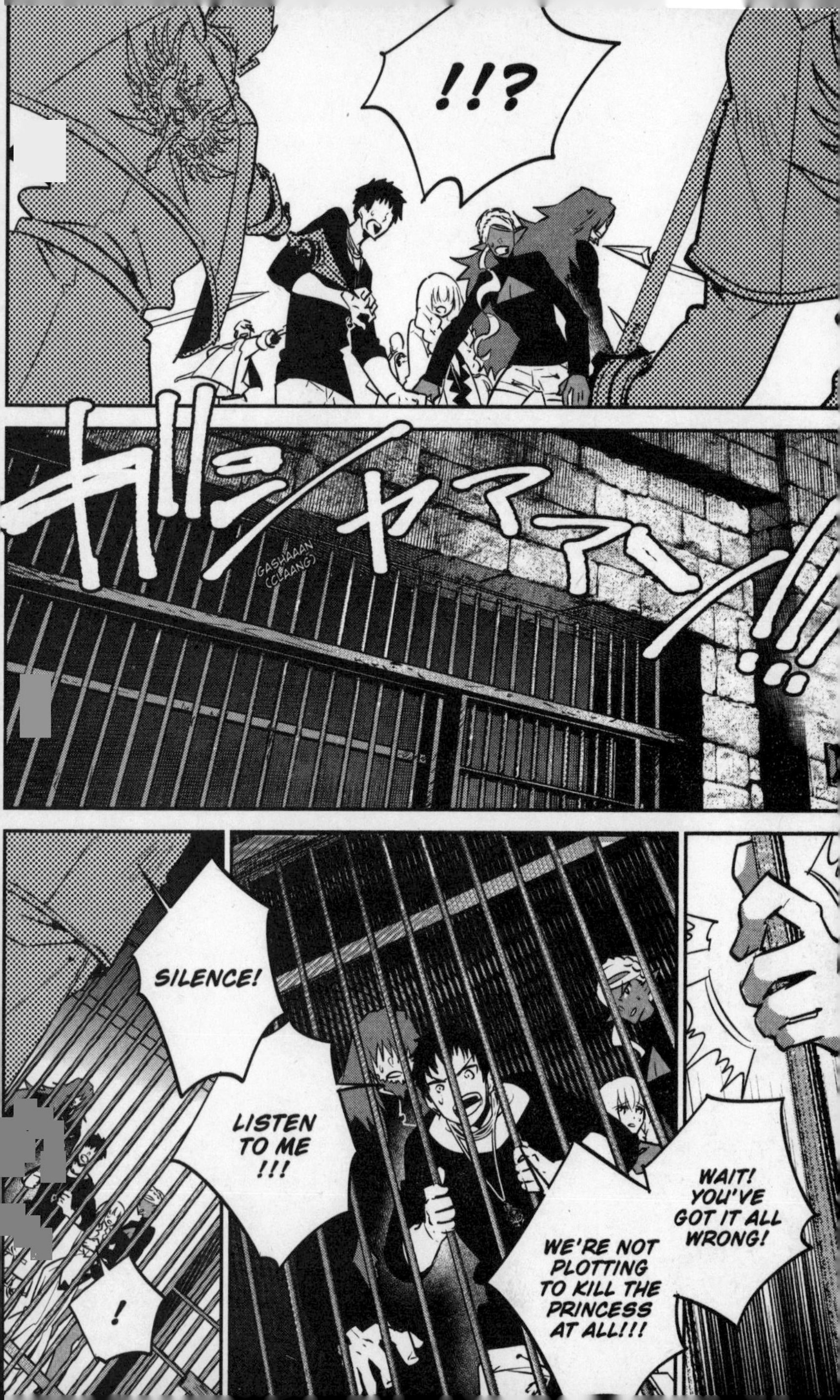
!!?
GASHAAAN (CLAANG)
WAIT! YOU'VE GOT IT ALL WRONG!
WE'RE NOT PLOTTING TO KILL THE PRINCESS AT ALL!!!
SILENCE!
LISTEN TO ME !!!
!

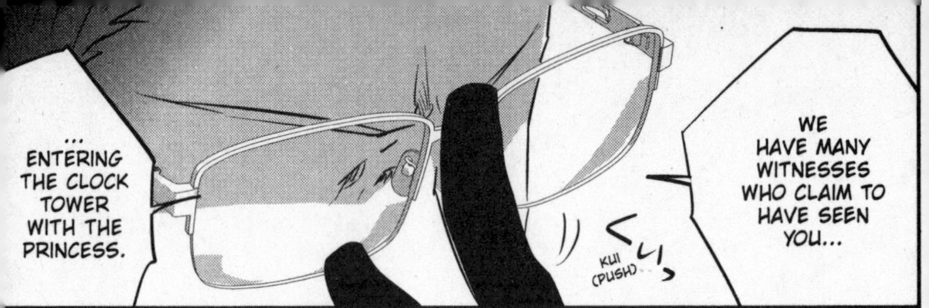
WE HAVE MANY WITNESSES WHO CLAIM TO HAVE SEEN YOU...
KUI (PUSH)
...ENTERING THE CLOCK TOWER WITH THE PRINCESS.
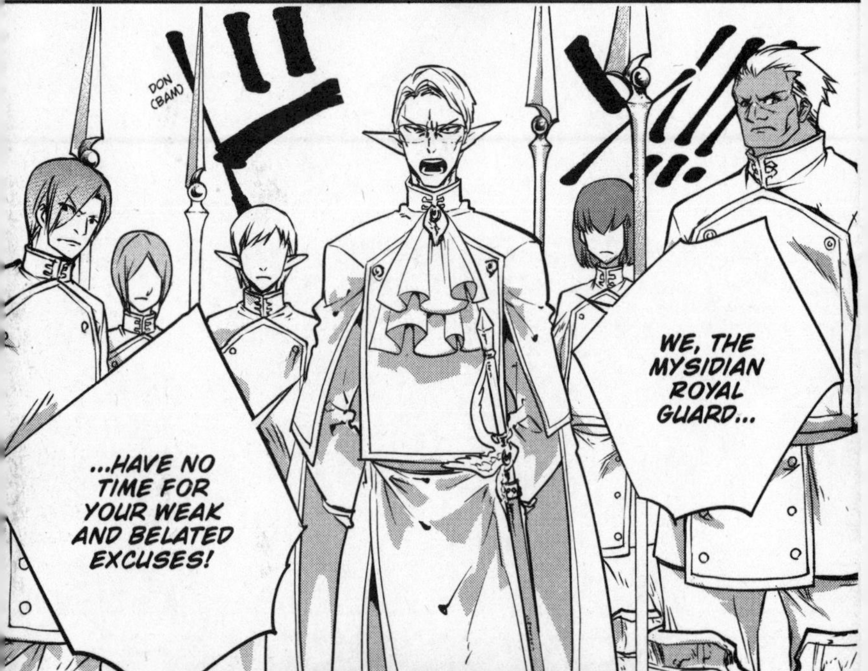
DON (BAM)
WE, THE MYSIDIAN ROYAL GUARD...
...HAVE NO TIME FOR YOUR WEAK AND BELATED EXCUSES!
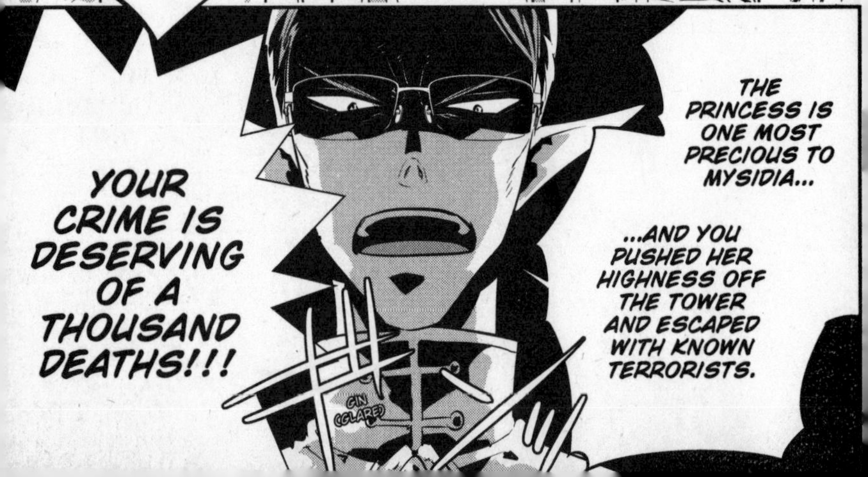
THE PRINCESS IS ONE MOST PRECIOUS TO MYSIDIA...
...AND YOU PUSHED HER HIGHNESS OFF THE TOWER AND ESCAPED WITH KNOWN TERRORISTS.
YOUR CRIME IS DESERVING OF A THOUSAND DEATHS!!!
GIN (GLARE)

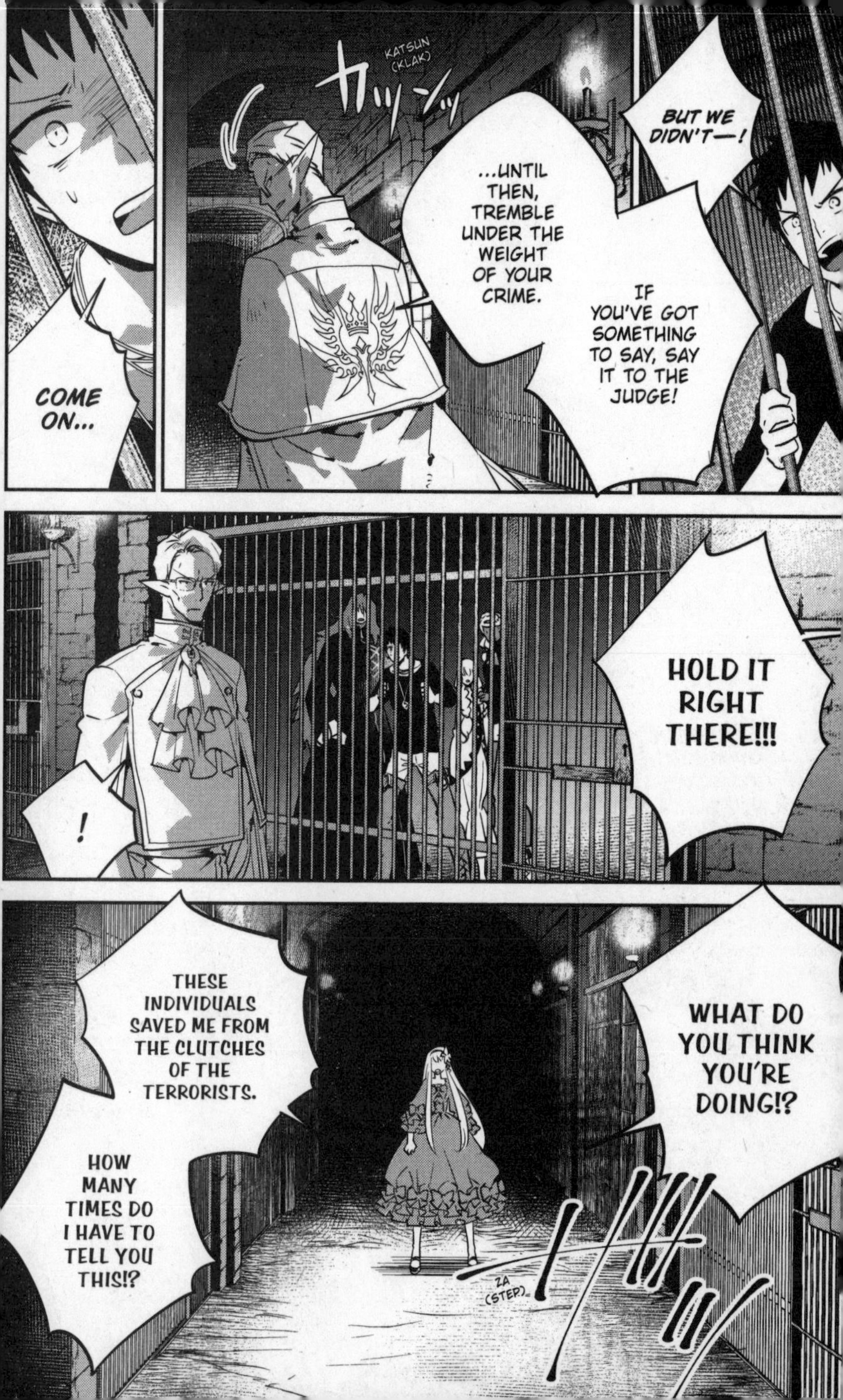
BUT WE DIDN'T—!
IF YOU'VE GOT SOMETHING TO SAY, SAY IT TO THE JUDGE!
...UNTIL THEN, TREMBLE UNDER THE WEIGHT OF YOUR CRIME.
KATSUN (KLAK)
COME ON...
HOLD IT RIGHT THERE!!!
!
WHAT DO YOU THINK YOU'RE DOING!?
ZA (STEP)
THESE INDIVIDUALS SAVED ME FROM THE CLUTCHES OF THE TERRORISTS.
HOW MANY TIMES DO I HAVE TO TELL YOU THIS!?

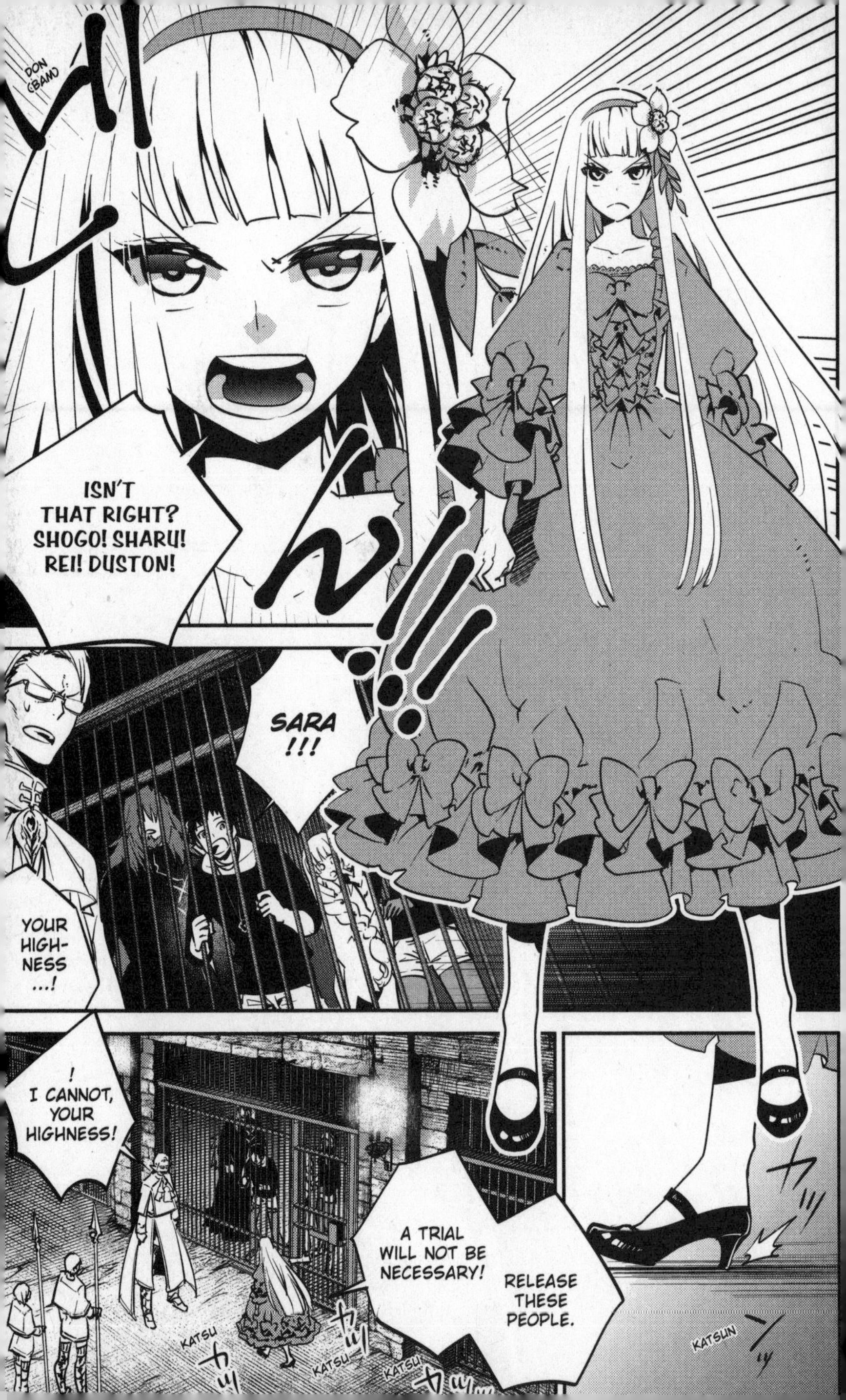
DON (BAM)
ISN'T THAT RIGHT? SHOGO! SHARU! REI! DUSTON!
SARA !!!
YOUR HIGH-NESS ...!
KATSUN
A TRIAL WILL NOT BE NECESSARY!
RELEASE THESE PEOPLE.
! I CANNOT, YOUR HIGHNESS!
KATSU
KATSU
KATSU

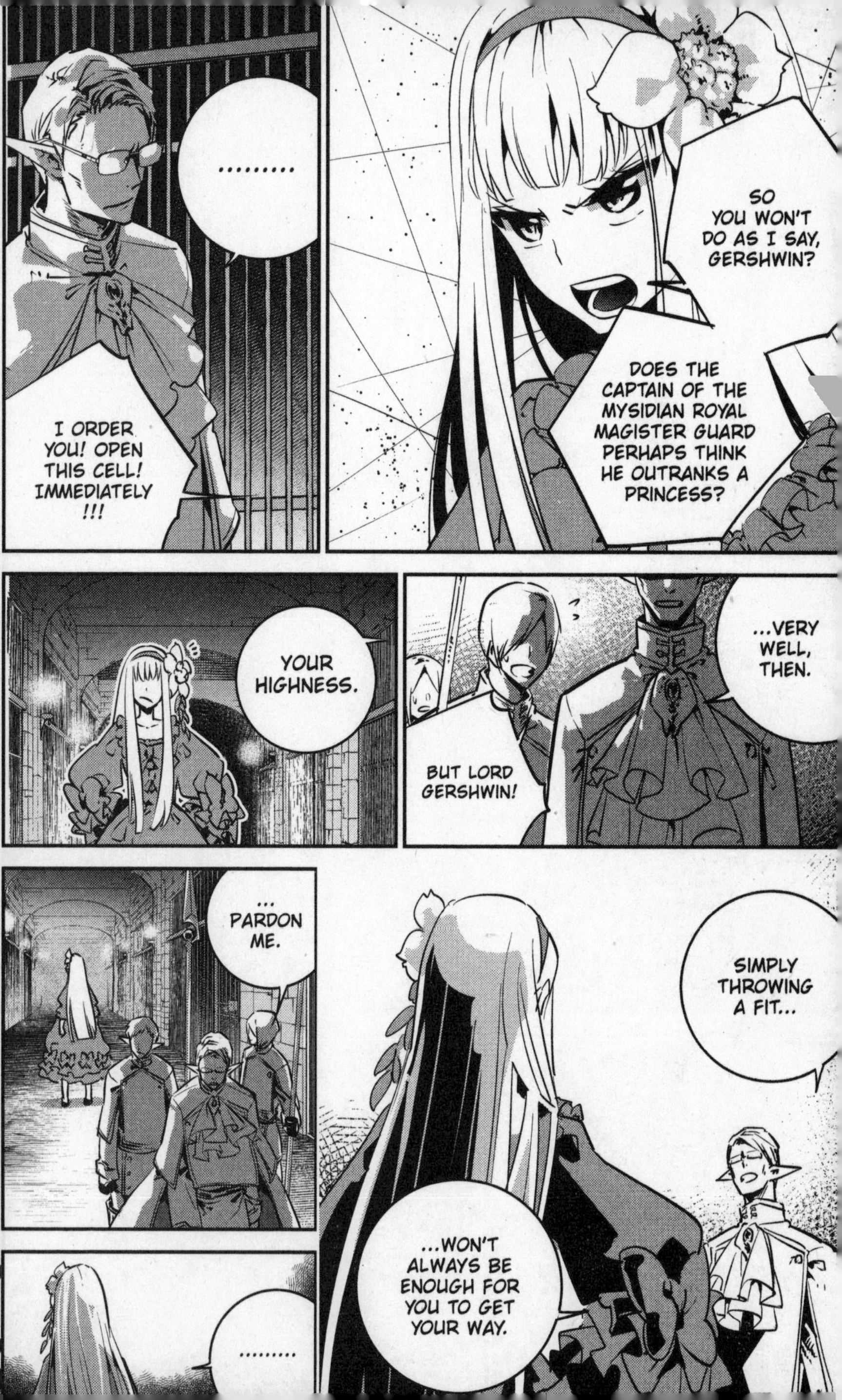
SO YOU WON'T DO AS I SAY, GERSHWIN?
DOES THE CAPTAIN OF THE MYSIDIAN ROYAL MAGISTER GUARD PERHAPS THINK HE OUTRANKS A PRINCESS?
....
I ORDER YOU! OPEN THIS CELL! IMMEDIATELY !!!
...VERY WELL, THEN.
BUT LORD GERSHWIN!
YOUR HIGHNESS.
SIMPLY THROWING A FIT...
...WON'T ALWAYS BE ENOUGH FOR YOU TO GET YOUR WAY.
... PARDON ME.
....

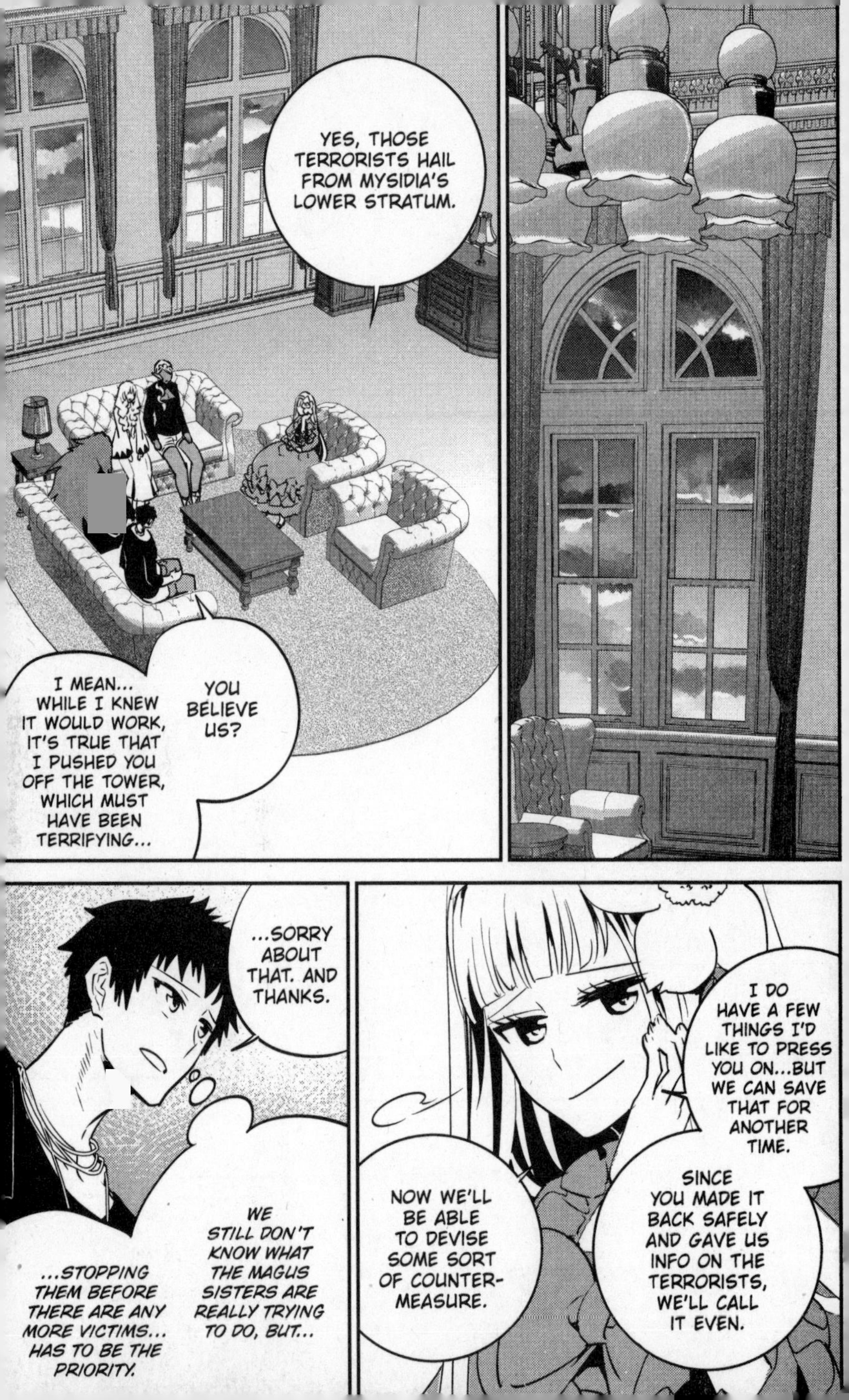
YES, THOSE TERRORISTS HAIL FROM MYSIDIA'S LOWER STRATUM.
YOU BELIEVE US?
I MEAN... WHILE I KNEW IT WOULD WORK, IT'S TRUE THAT I PUSHED YOU OFF THE TOWER, WHICH MUST HAVE BEEN TERRIFYING...
I DO HAVE A FEW THINGS I'D LIKE TO PRESS YOU ON...BUT WE CAN SAVE THAT FOR ANOTHER TIME.
SINCE YOU MADE IT BACK SAFELY AND GAVE US INFO ON THE TERRORISTS, WE'LL CALL IT EVEN.
NOW WE'LL BE ABLE TO DEVISE SOME SORT OF COUNTER-MEASURE.
...SORRY ABOUT THAT. AND THANKS.
WE STILL DON'T KNOW WHAT THE MAGUS SISTERS ARE REALLY TRYING TO DO, BUT...
...STOPPING THEM BEFORE THERE ARE ANY MORE VICTIMS... HAS TO BE THE PRIORITY.

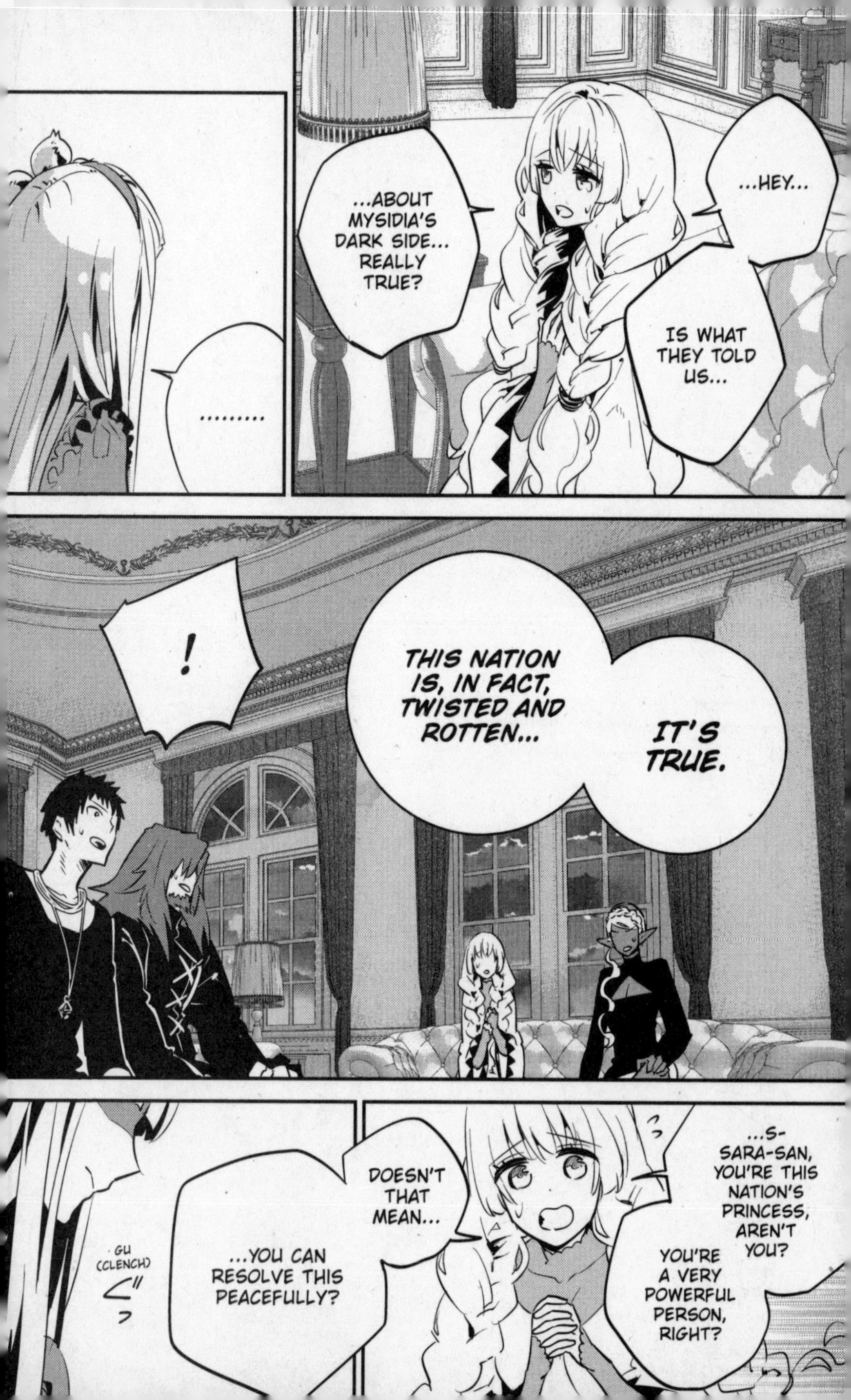
...HEY...
IS WHAT THEY TOLD US...
...ABOUT MYSIDIA'S DARK SIDE... REALLY TRUE?
....
THIS NATION IS, IN FACT, TWISTED AND ROTTEN...
IT'S TRUE.
!
...S-SARA-SAN, YOU'RE THIS NATION'S PRINCESS, AREN'T YOU?
YOU'RE A VERY POWERFUL PERSON, RIGHT?
DOESN'T THAT MEAN...
...YOU CAN RESOLVE THIS PEACEFULLY?
GU (CLENCH)

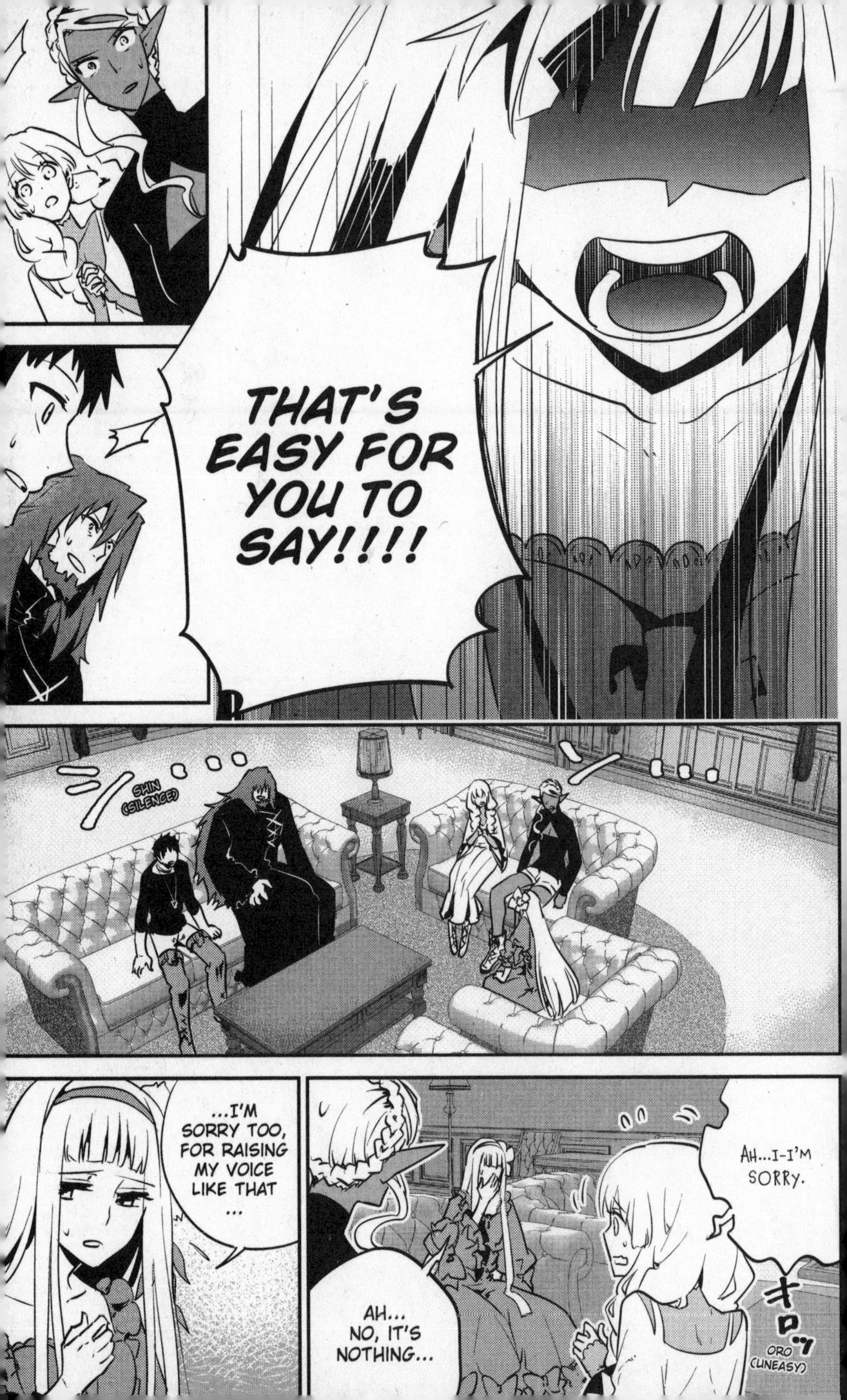
THAT'S EASY FOR YOU TO SAY!!!!
SHIN (SILENCED)
AH...I-I'M SORRY.
キロッ
ORO (UNEASY)
AH... NO, IT'S NOTHING...
...I'M SORRY TOO, FOR RAISING MY VOICE LIKE THAT ...

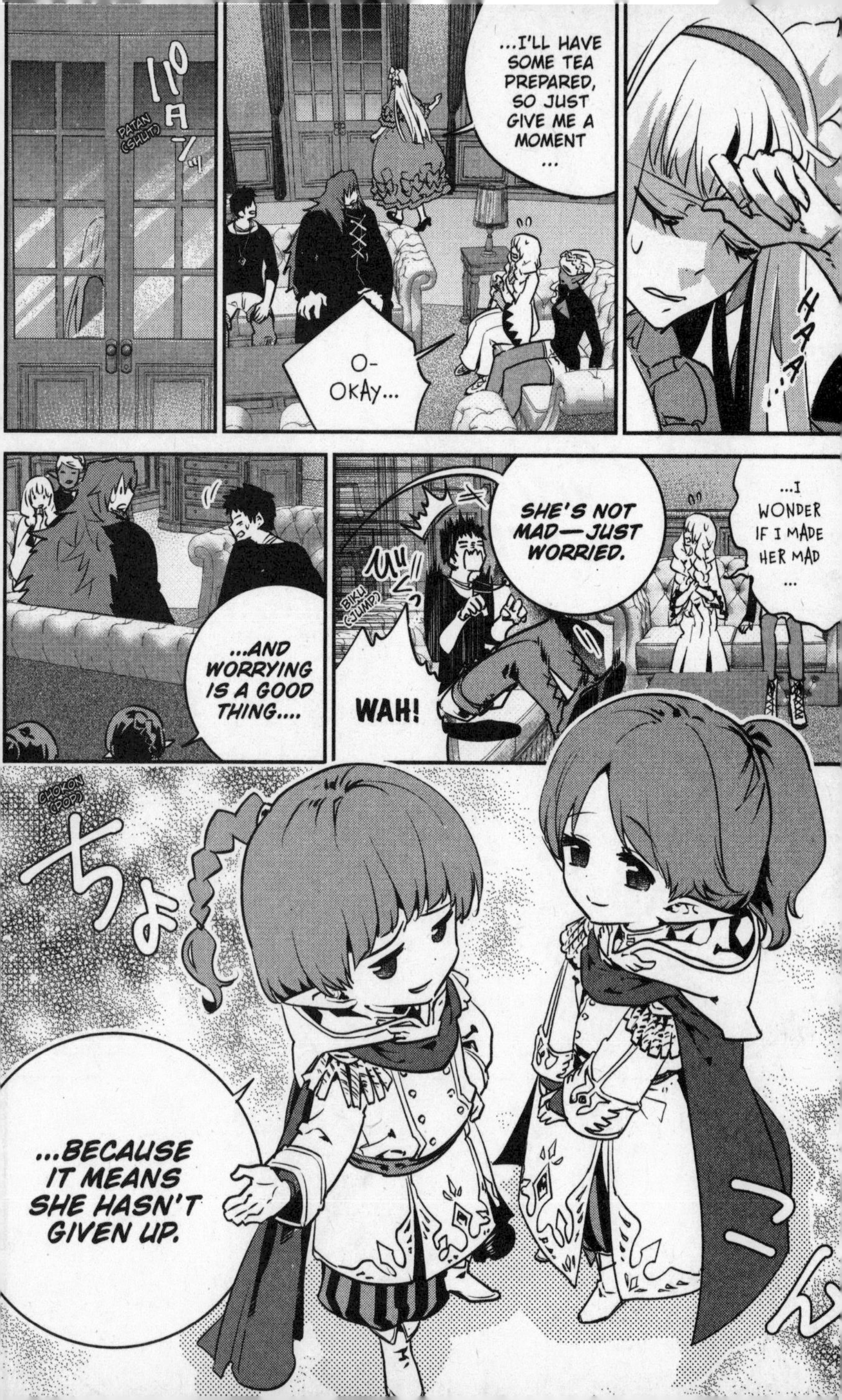
HAA...
...I'LL HAVE SOME TEA PREPARED, SO JUST GIVE ME A MOMENT ...
O-OKAY...
PATAN (SHUT)
...I WONDER IF I MADE HER MAD ...
SHE'S NOT MAD—JUST WORRIED.
BIKU (JUMP)
WAH!
...AND WORRYING IS A GOOD THING....
CHOKON (POP)
...BECAUSE IT MEANS SHE HASN'T GIVEN UP.

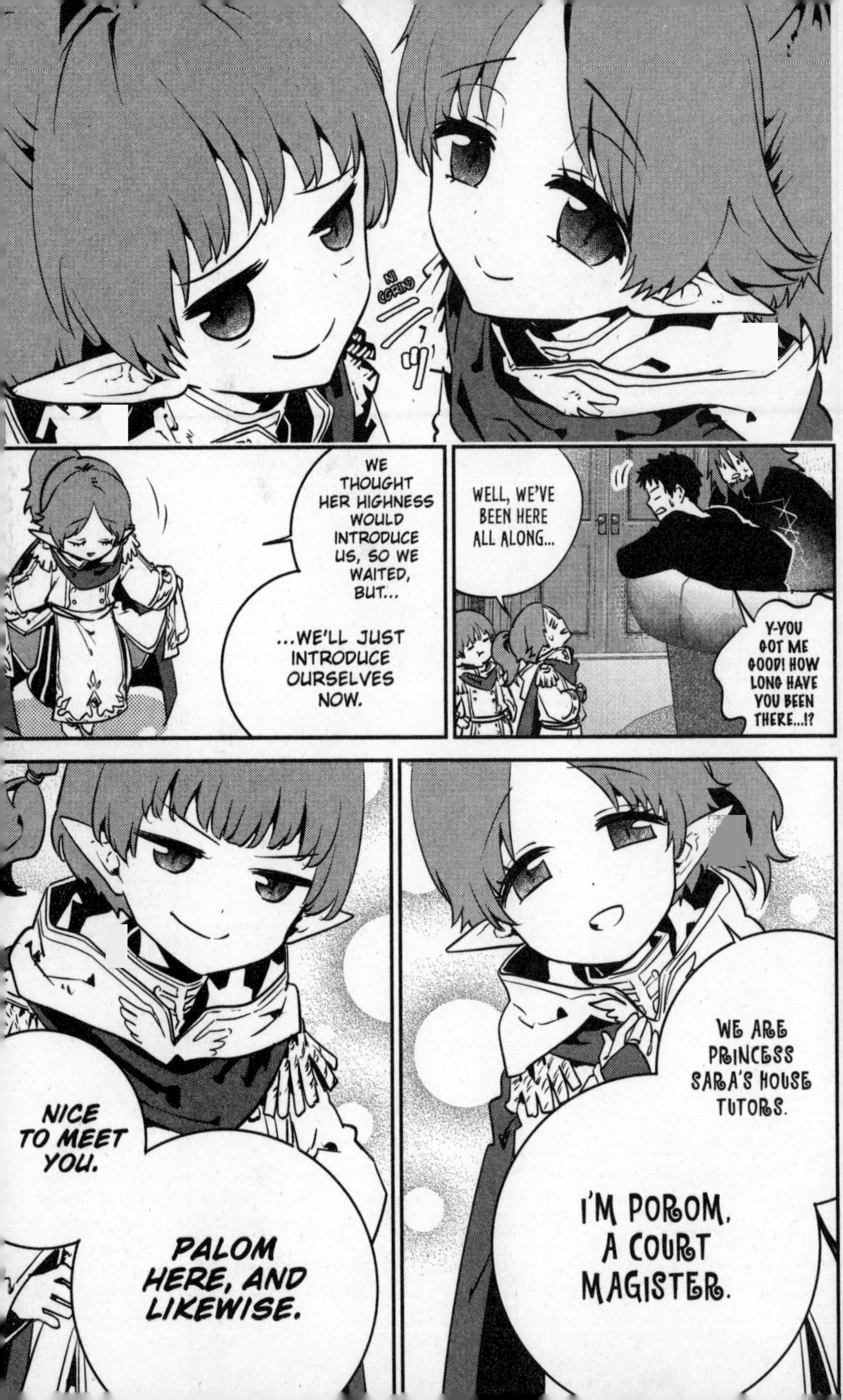
NI GGRIND
Y-YOU GOT ME GOOD! HOW LONG HAVE YOU BEEN THERE...!?
WELL, WE'VE BEEN HERE ALL ALONG...
WE THOUGHT HER HIGHNESS WOULD INTRODUCE US, SO WE WAITED, BUT...
...WE'LL JUST INTRODUCE OURSELVES NOW.
WE ARE PRINCESS SARA'S HOUSE TUTORS.
I'M POROM, A COURT MAGISTER.
NICE TO MEET YOU.
PALOM HERE, AND LIKEWISE.

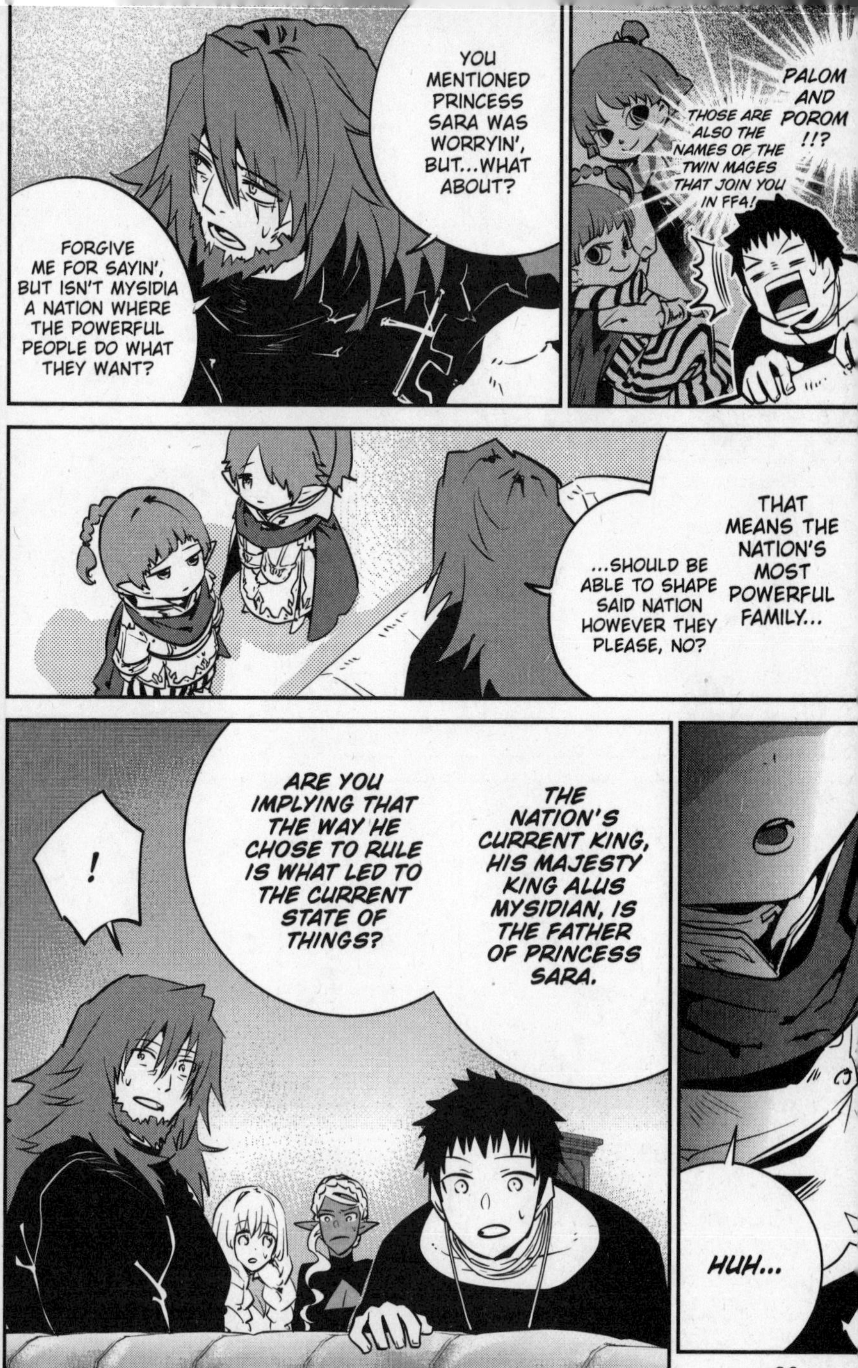
PALOM AND POROM !!?
THOSE ARE ALSO THE NAMES OF THE TWIN MAGES THAT JOIN YOU IN FF4!
YOU MENTIONED PRINCESS SARA WAS WORRYIN', BUT...WHAT ABOUT?
FORGIVE ME FOR SAYIN', BUT ISN'T MYSIDIA A NATION WHERE THE POWERFUL PEOPLE DO WHAT THEY WANT?
THAT MEANS THE NATION'S MOST POWERFUL FAMILY...
...SHOULD BE ABLE TO SHAPE SAID NATION HOWEVER THEY PLEASE, NO?
HUH...
THE NATION'S CURRENT KING, HIS MAJESTY KING ALUS MYSIDIAN, IS THE FATHER OF PRINCESS SARA.
ARE YOU IMPLYING THAT THE WAY HE CHOSE TO RULE IS WHAT LED TO THE CURRENT STATE OF THINGS?
!

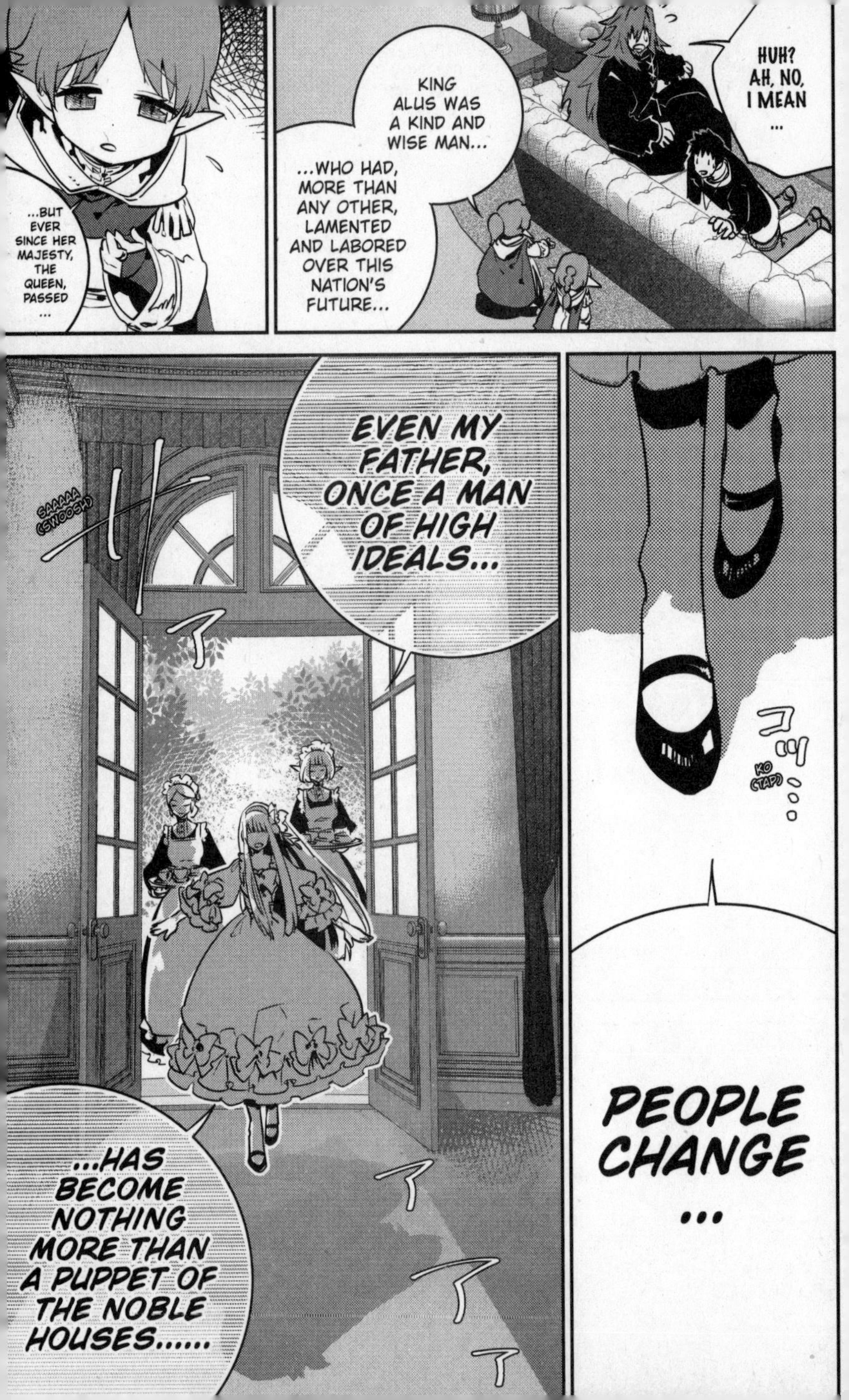
HUH? AH, NO, I MEAN ...
KING ALUS WAS A KIND AND WISE MAN...
...WHO HAD, MORE THAN ANY OTHER, LAMENTED AND LABORED OVER THIS NATION'S FUTURE...
...BUT EVER SINCE HER MAJESTY, THE QUEEN, PASSED ...
KO (TAP)
PEOPLE CHANGE ...
EVEN MY FATHER, ONCE A MAN OF HIGH IDEALS...
SAAAAA (SWOOSH)
...HAS BECOME NOTHING MORE THAN A PUPPET OF THE NOBLE HOUSES......

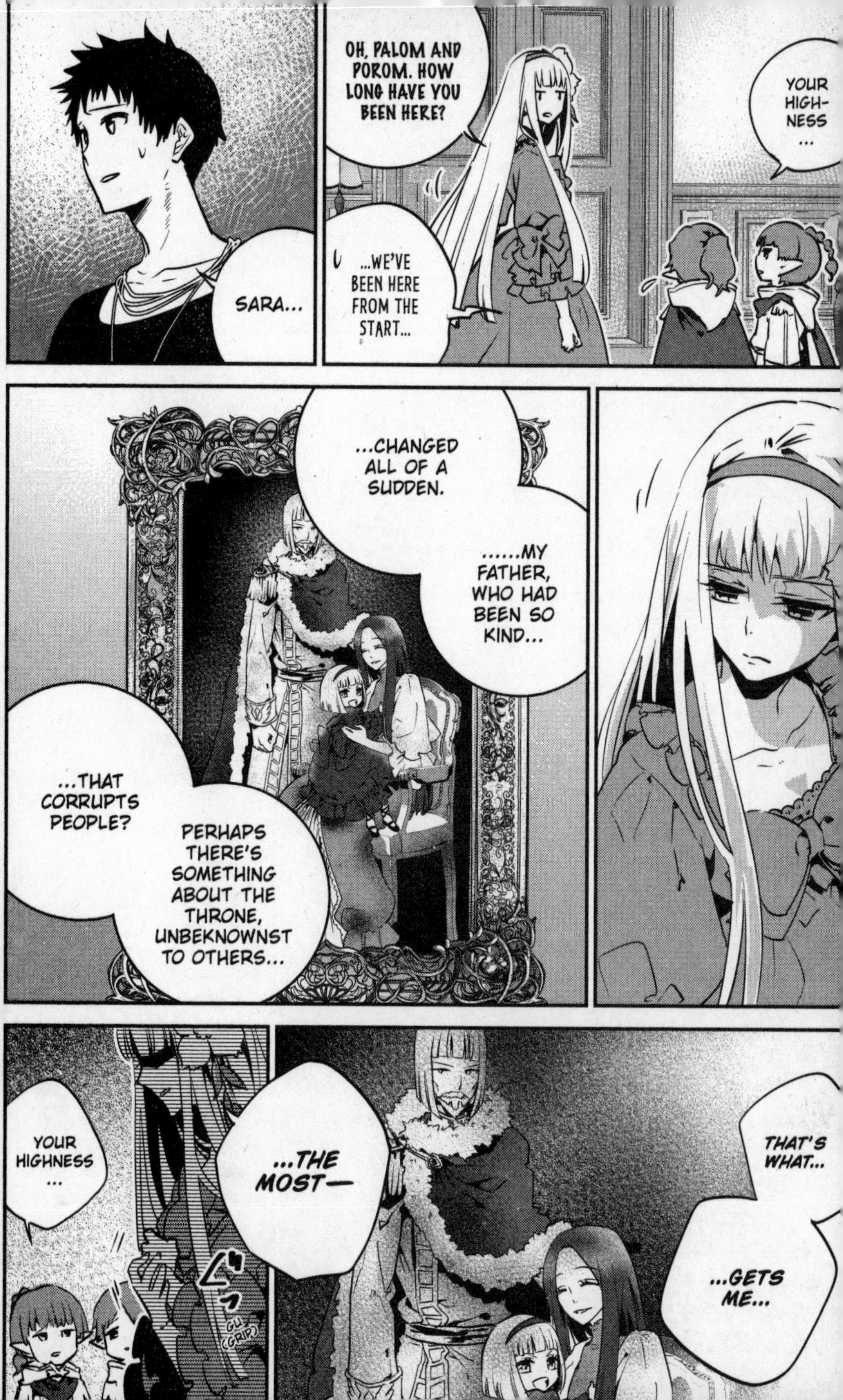
YOUR HIGH-NESS ...
OH, PALOM AND POROM. HOW LONG HAVE YOU BEEN HERE?
...WE'VE BEEN HERE FROM THE START...
SARA...
......MY FATHER, WHO HAD BEEN SO KIND...
...CHANGED ALL OF A SUDDEN.
PERHAPS THERE'S SOMETHING ABOUT THE THRONE, UNBEKNOWNST TO OTHERS...
...THAT CORRUPTS PEOPLE?
THAT'S WHAT...
...GETS ME...
...THE MOST—
GU (GRIP)
YOUR HIGHNESS ...

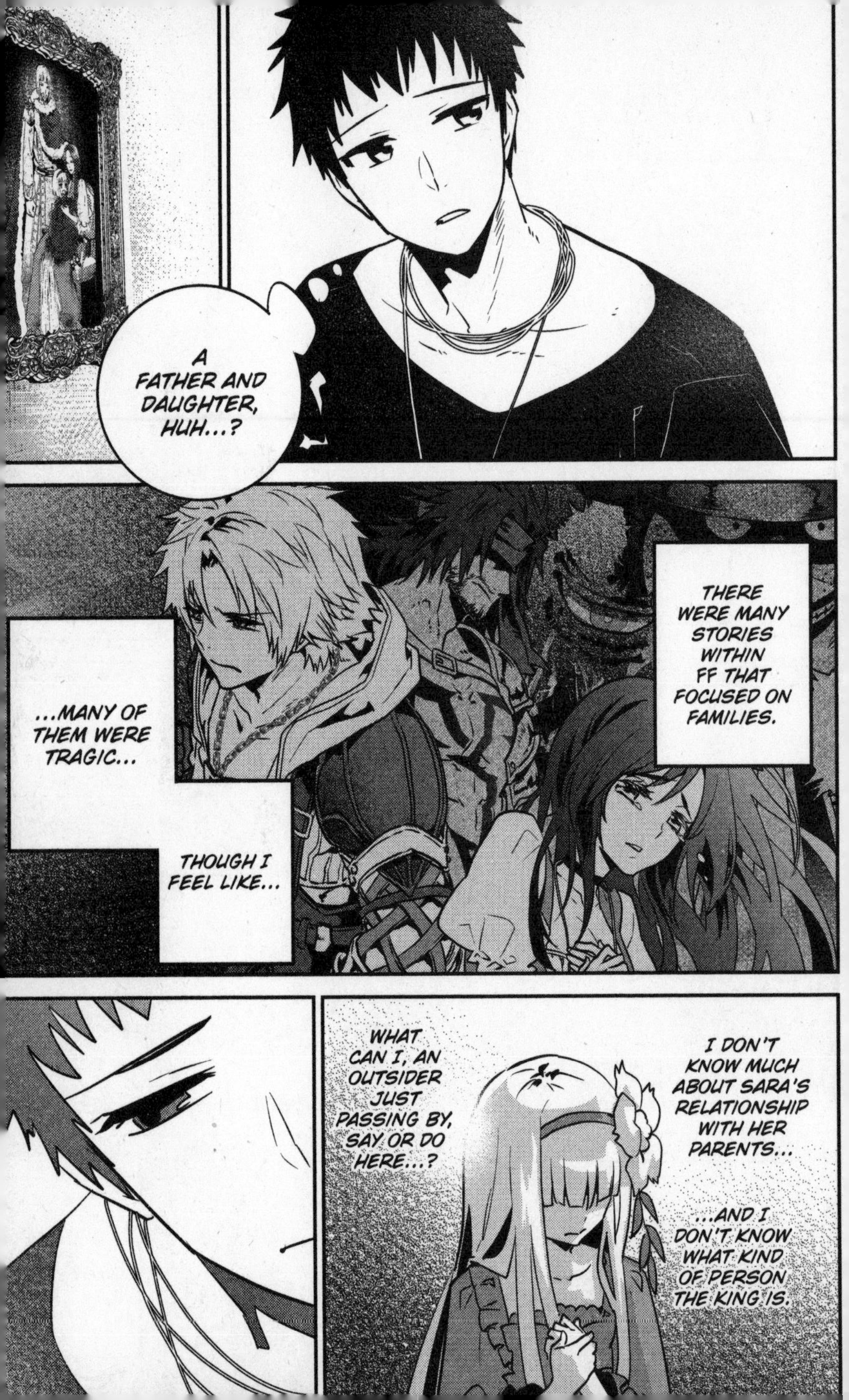
A FATHER AND DAUGHTER, HUH...?
THERE WERE MANY STORIES WITHIN FF THAT FOCUSED ON FAMILIES.
...MANY OF THEM WERE TRAGIC...
THOUGH I FEEL LIKE...
I DON'T KNOW MUCH ABOUT SARA'S RELATIONSHIP WITH HER PARENTS...
...AND I DON'T KNOW WHAT KIND OF PERSON THE KING IS.
WHAT CAN I, AN OUTSIDER JUST PASSING BY, SAY OR DO HERE...?

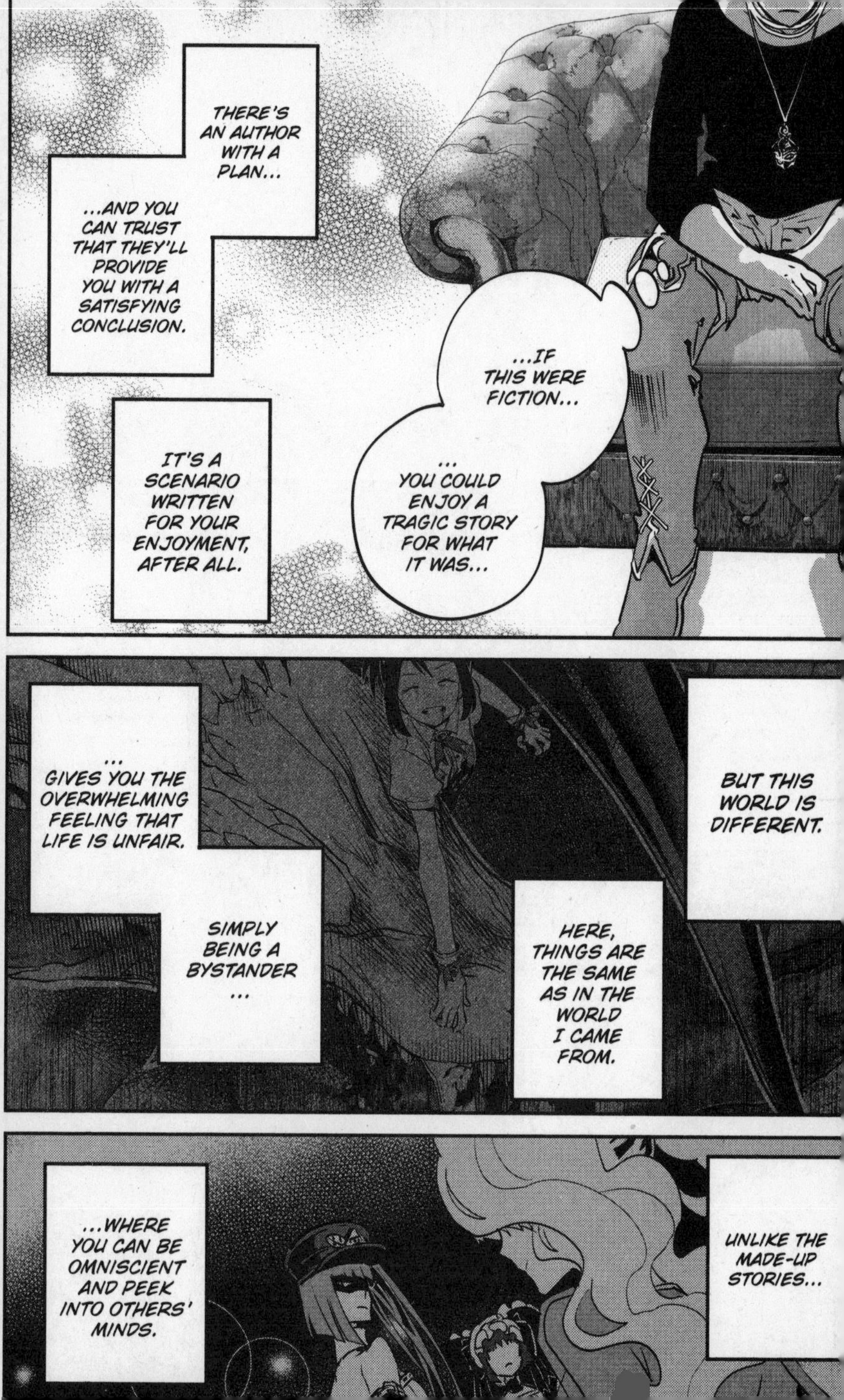
...IF THIS WERE FICTION...
...YOU COULD ENJOY A TRAGIC STORY FOR WHAT IT WAS...
THERE'S AN AUTHOR WITH A PLAN...
...AND YOU CAN TRUST THAT THEY'LL PROVIDE YOU WITH A SATISFYING CONCLUSION.
IT'S A SCENARIO WRITTEN FOR YOUR ENJOYMENT, AFTER ALL.
BUT THIS WORLD IS DIFFERENT.
HERE, THINGS ARE THE SAME AS IN THE WORLD I CAME FROM.
SIMPLY BEING A BYSTANDER...
...GIVES YOU THE OVERWHELMING FEELING THAT LIFE IS UNFAIR.
UNLIKE THE MADE-UP STORIES...
...WHERE YOU CAN BE OMNISCIENT AND PEEK INTO OTHERS' MINDS.

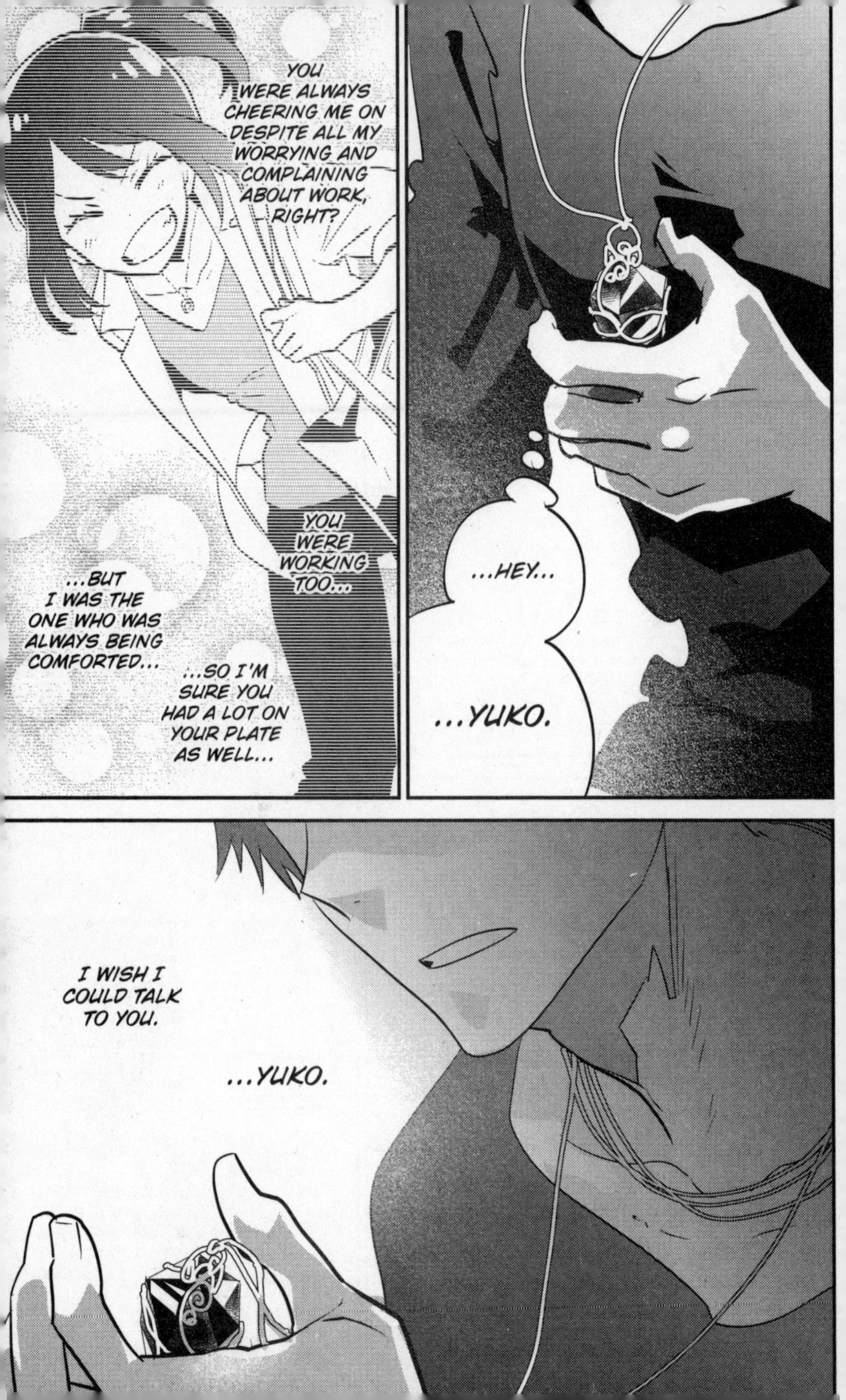
...HEY...
...YUKO.
YOU WERE ALWAYS CHEERING ME ON DESPITE ALL MY WORRYING AND COMPLAINING ABOUT WORK, RIGHT?
YOU WERE WORKING TOO...
...BUT I WAS THE ONE WHO WAS ALWAYS BEING COMFORTED...
...SO I'M SURE YOU HAD A LOT ON YOUR PLATE AS WELL...
I WISH I COULD TALK TO YOU.
...YUKO.

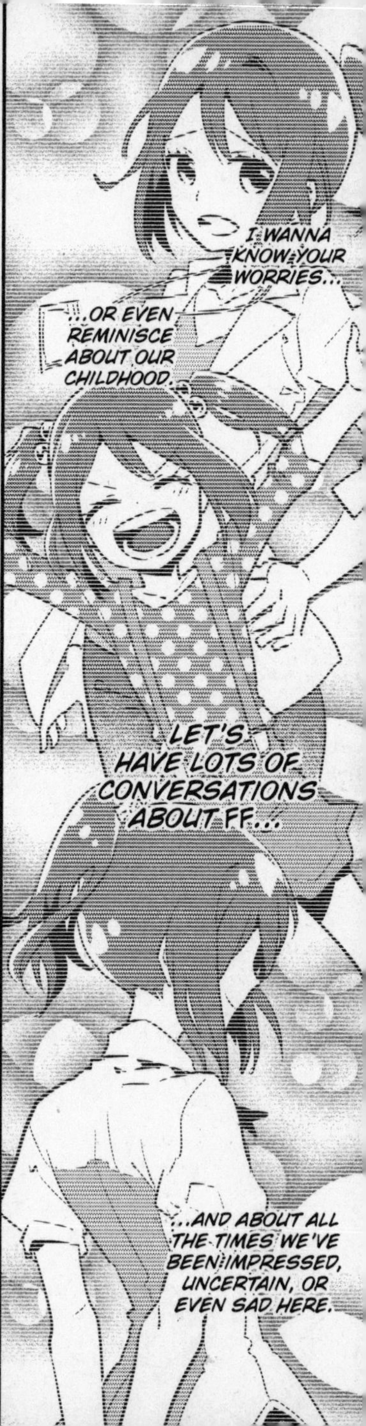
I WANNA KNOW YOUR WORRIES...
...OR EVEN REMINISCE ABOUT OUR CHILDHOOD.
LET'S HAVE LOTS OF CONVERSATIONS ABOUT FF...
...AND ABOUT ALL THE TIMES WE'VE BEEN IMPRESSED, UNCERTAIN, OR EVEN SAD HERE.
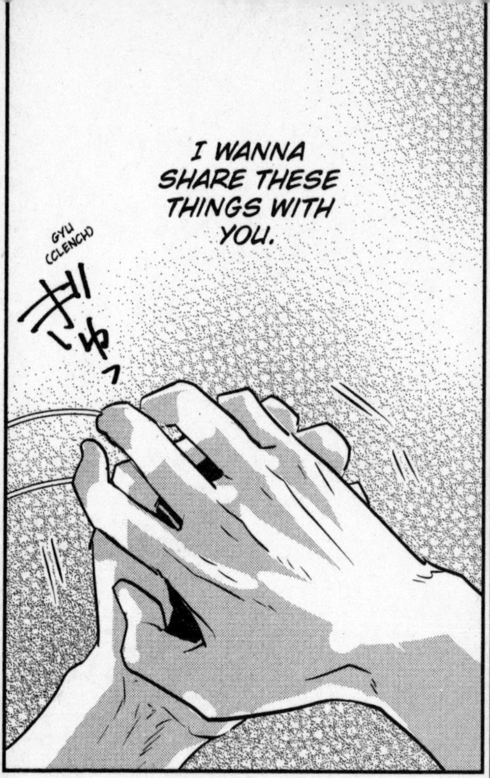
I WANNA SHARE THESE THINGS WITH YOU.
ぎゅっ
GYU (CLENCH)
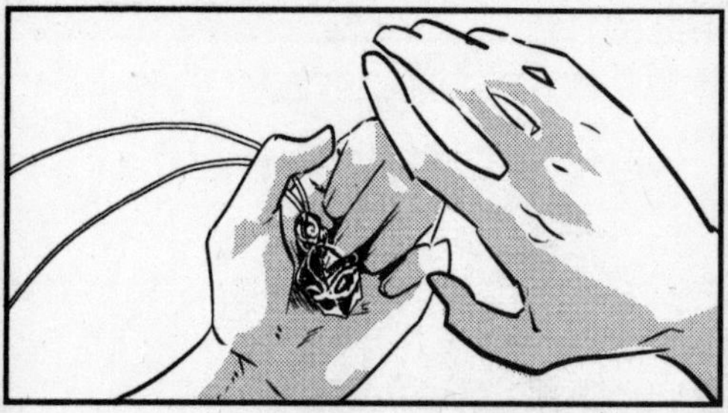
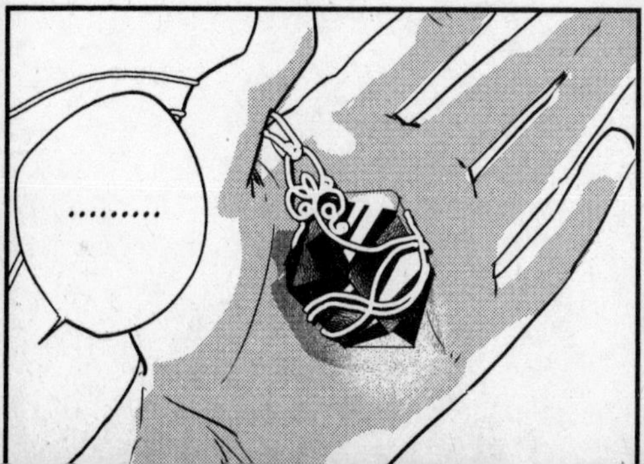
....

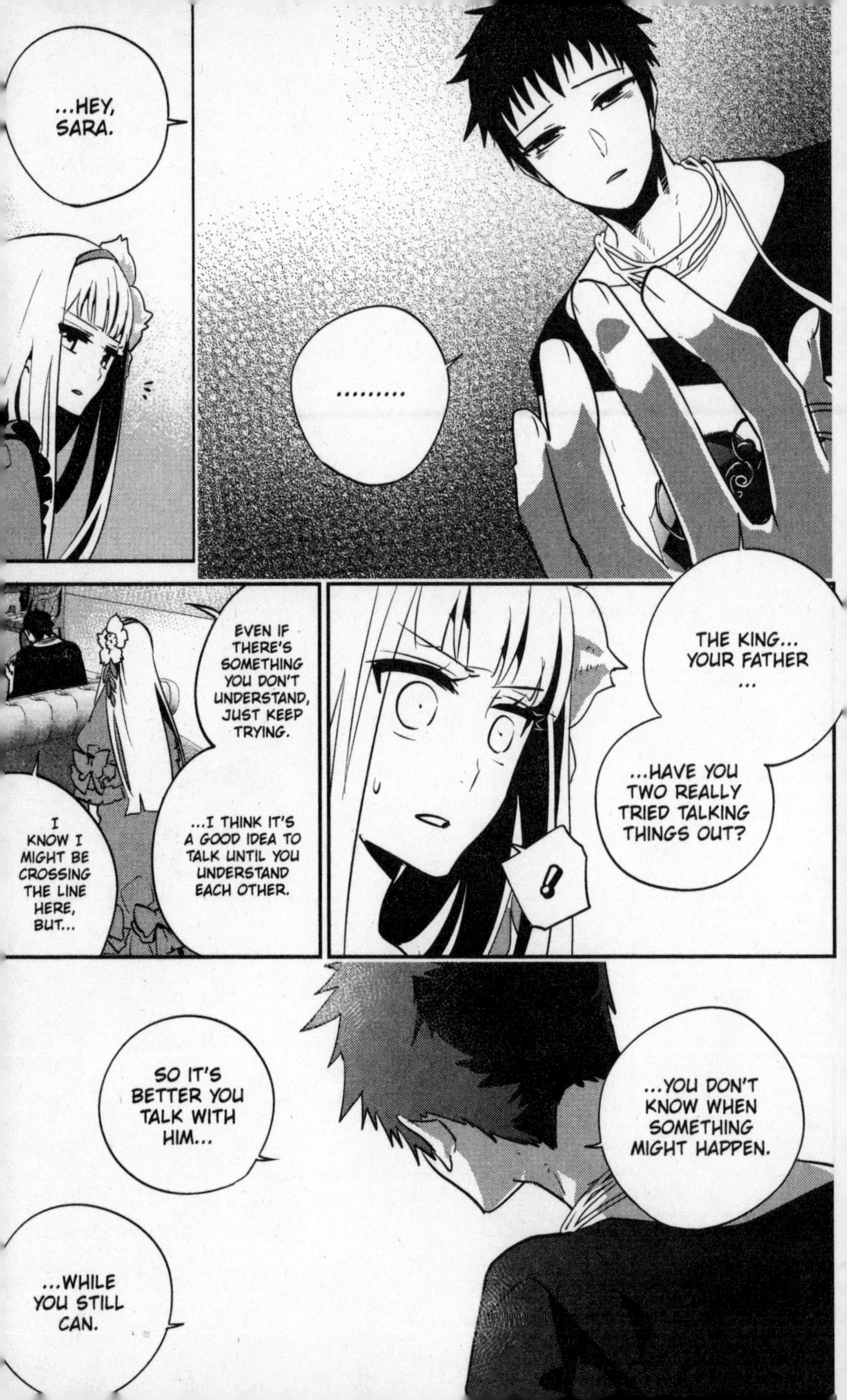
....
...HEY, SARA.
THE KING... YOUR FATHER ...
...HAVE YOU TWO REALLY TRIED TALKING THINGS OUT?
EVEN IF THERE'S SOMETHING YOU DON'T UNDERSTAND, JUST KEEP TRYING.
...I THINK IT'S A GOOD IDEA TO TALK UNTIL YOU UNDERSTAND EACH OTHER.
I KNOW I MIGHT BE CROSSING THE LINE HERE, BUT...
...YOU DON'T KNOW WHEN SOMETHING MIGHT HAPPEN.
SO IT'S BETTER YOU TALK WITH HIM...
...WHILE YOU STILL CAN.

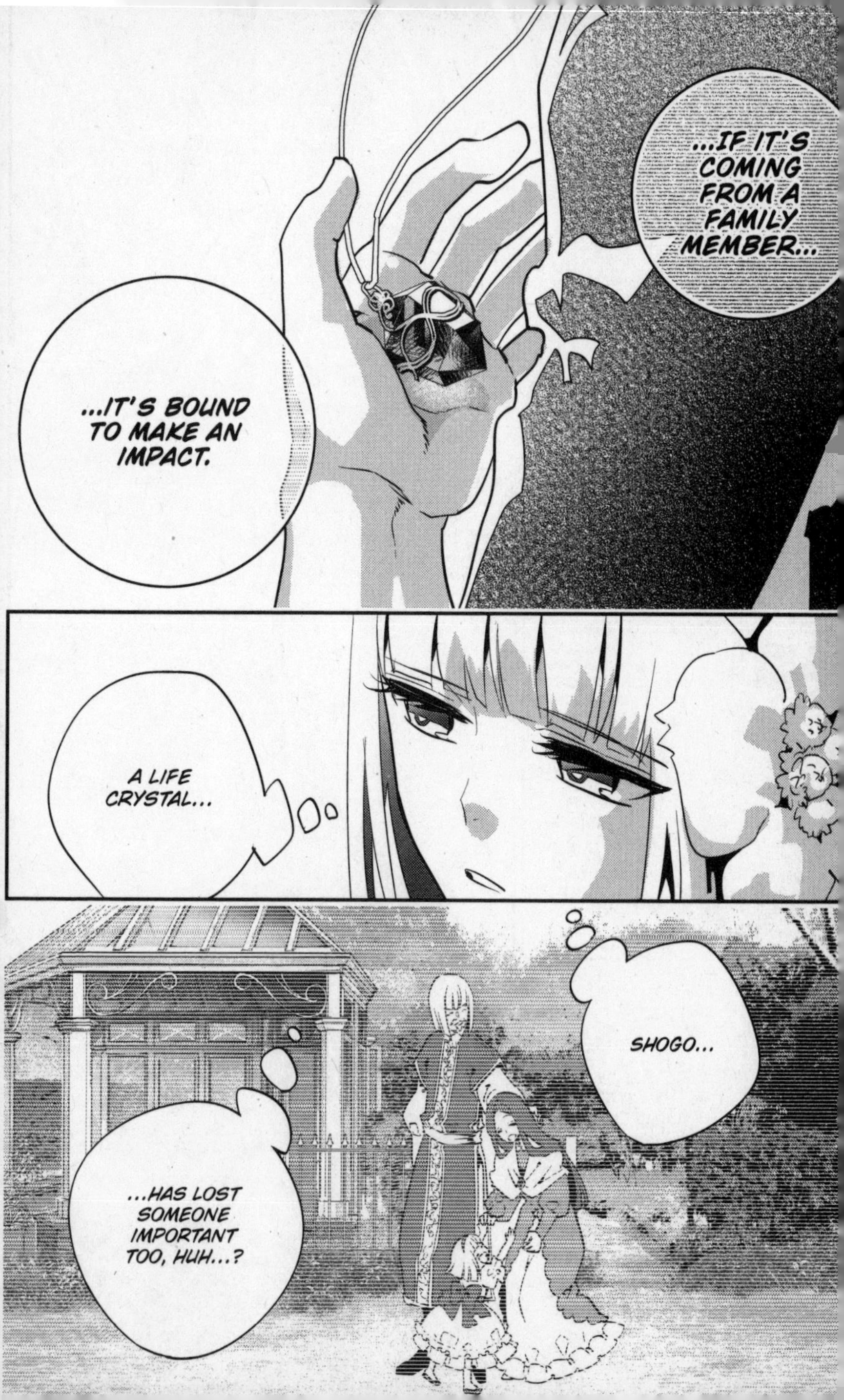
...IF IT'S COMING FROM A FAMILY MEMBER...
...IT'S BOUND TO MAKE AN IMPACT.
A LIFE CRYSTAL...
SHOGO...
...HAS LOST SOMEONE IMPORTANT TOO, HUH...?

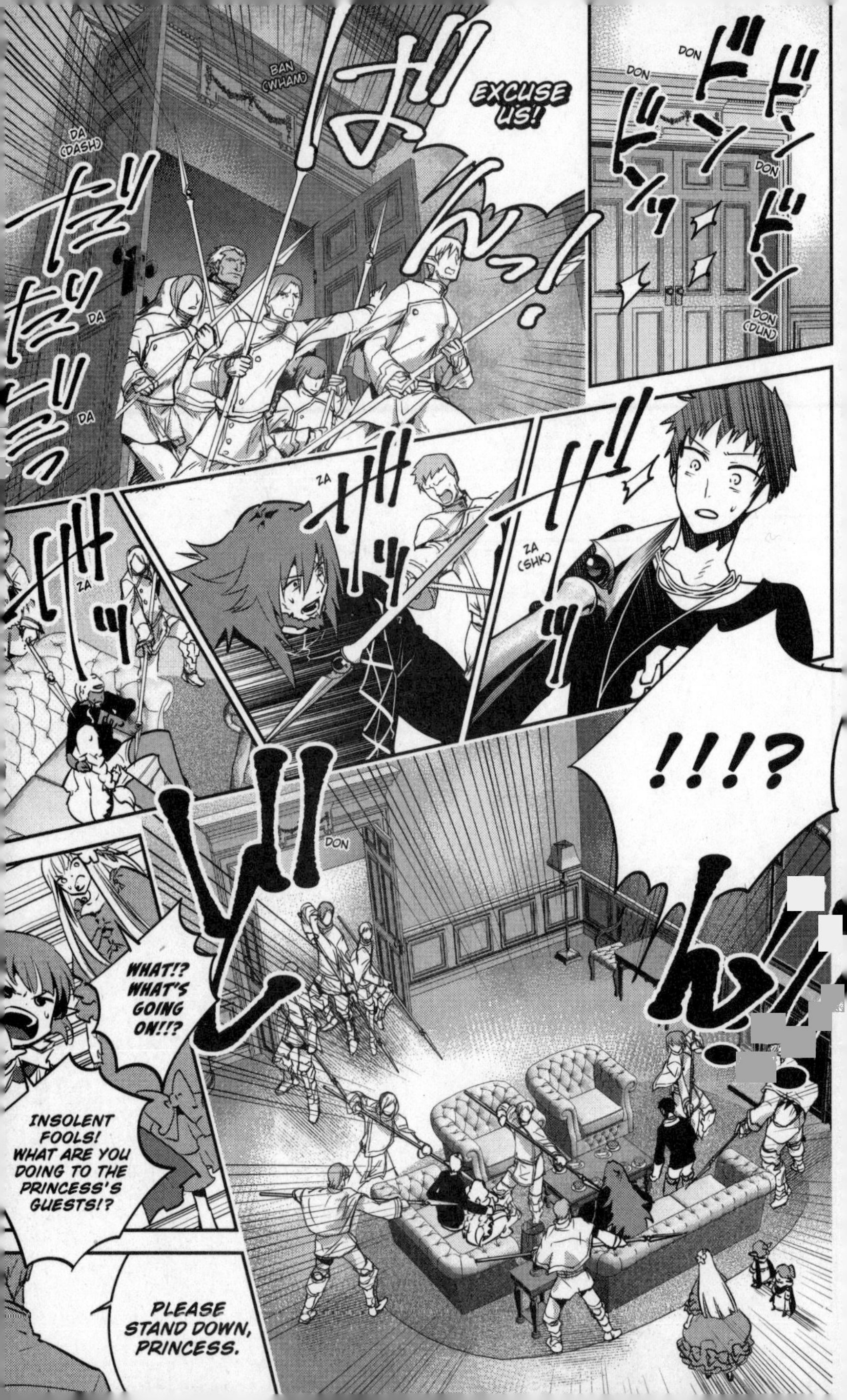
ドドン
DON
DON
ドンドン
DON
DON (DUN)
ばん
BAN (WHAM)
EXCUSE US!
だだだ
DA (DASH)
DA
DA
ザッ
ZA (SHK)
ザザ
ZA
ザッ
ZA
!!!?
ん
ドン
DON
WHAT!? WHAT'S GOING ON!!?
INSOLENT FOOLS! WHAT ARE YOU DOING TO THE PRINCESS'S GUESTS!?
PLEASE STAND DOWN, PRINCESS.

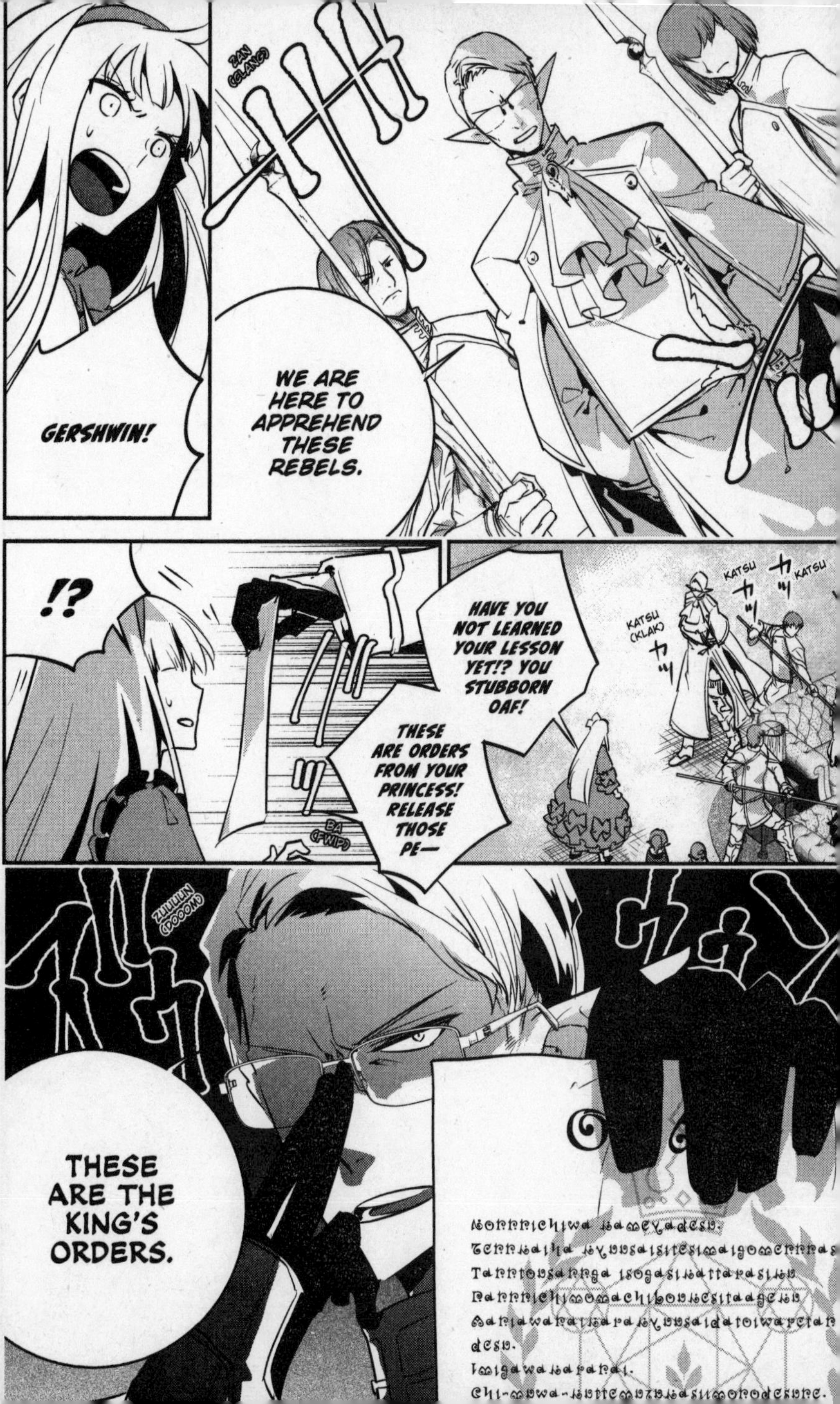
ZAN (CLANG)
WE ARE HERE TO APPREHEND THESE REBELS.
GERSHWIN!
KATSU
KATSU
KATSU (KLAK)
HAVE YOU NOT LEARNED YOUR LESSON YET!? YOU STUBBORN OAF!
THESE ARE ORDERS FROM YOUR PRINCESS! RELEASE THOSE PE—
BA (FWIP)
!?
ZUUUUN (DOOOOM)
THESE ARE THE KING'S ORDERS.

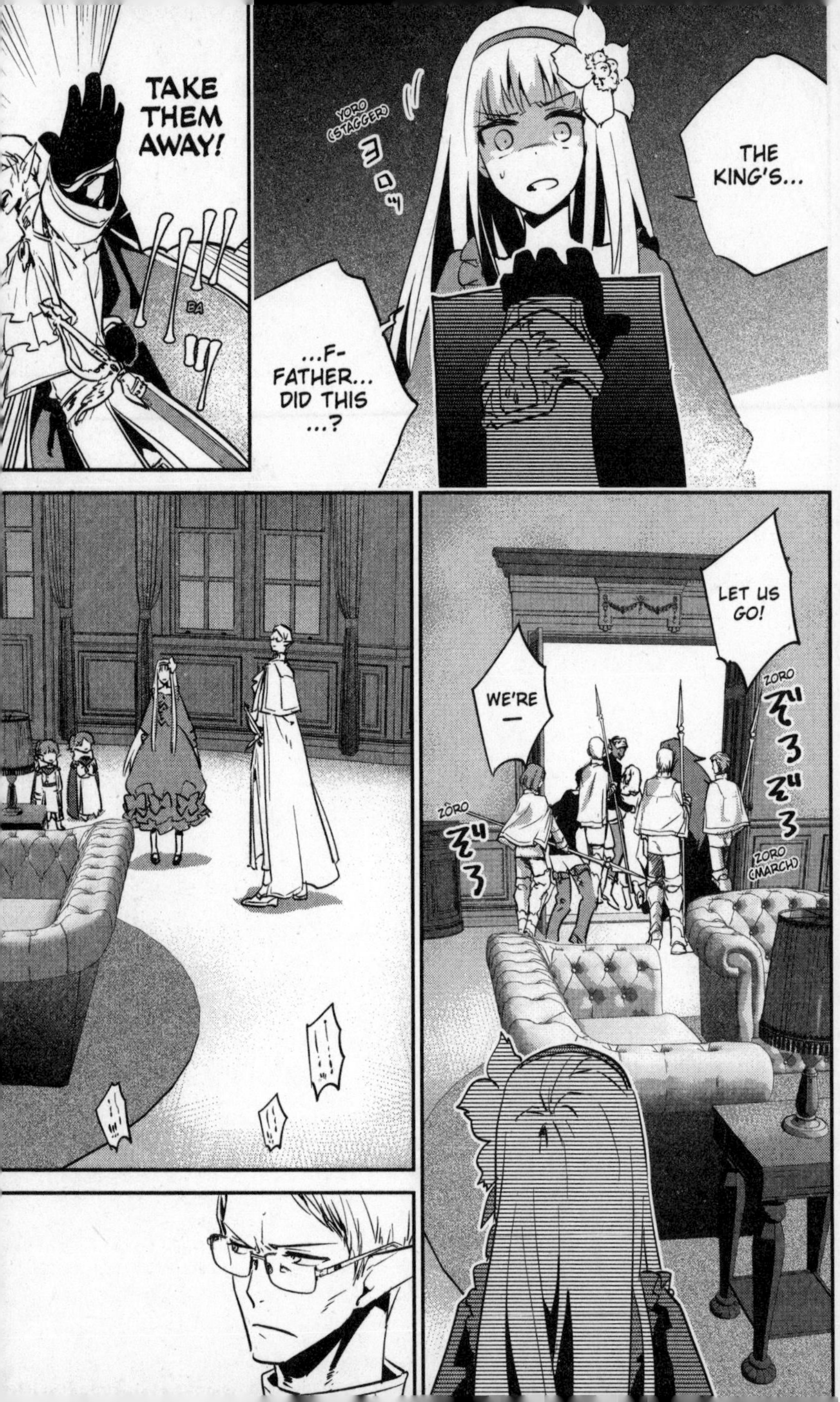
THE KING'S...
YORO (STAGGER)
...F-FATHER... DID THIS ...?
TAKE THEM AWAY!
BA
LET US GO!
WE'RE—
ZORO
ZORO (MARCH)
ZORO

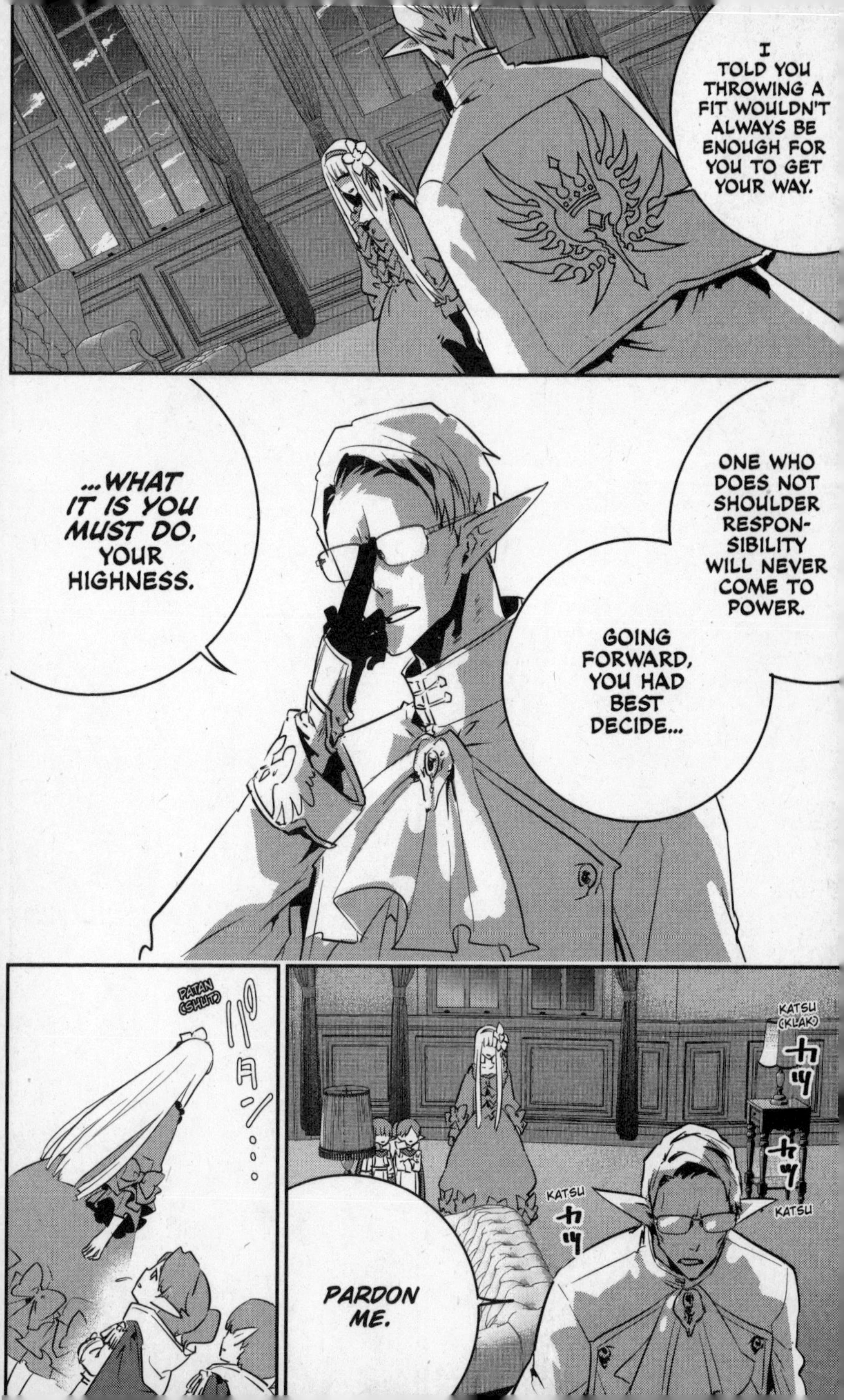
I TOLD YOU THROWING A FIT WOULDN'T ALWAYS BE ENOUGH FOR YOU TO GET YOUR WAY.
ONE WHO DOES NOT SHOULDER RESPON-SIBILITY WILL NEVER COME TO POWER.
GOING FORWARD, YOU HAD BEST DECIDE...
...WHAT IT IS YOU MUST DO, YOUR HIGHNESS.
KATSU (KLAK)
KATSU
KATSU
PARDON ME.
PATAN (SHUT)

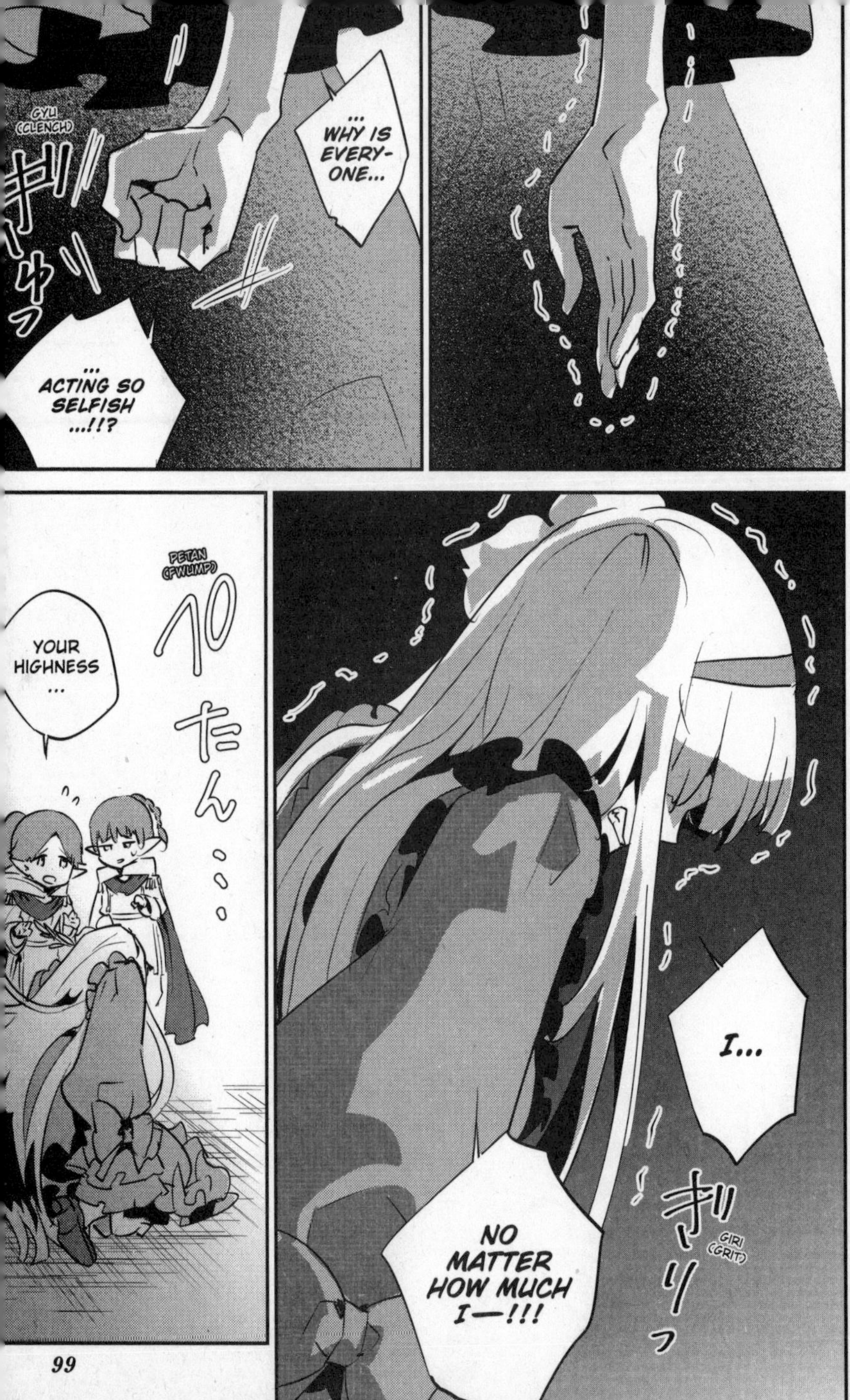
...WHY IS EVERY-ONE...
GYU (CLENCH)
ぎゅっ
...ACTING SO SELFISH ...!!?
I...
ぎりっ
GIRI (GRIT)
NO MATTER HOW MUCH I—!!!
ぺたん...
PETAN (FWUMP)
YOUR HIGHNESS ...

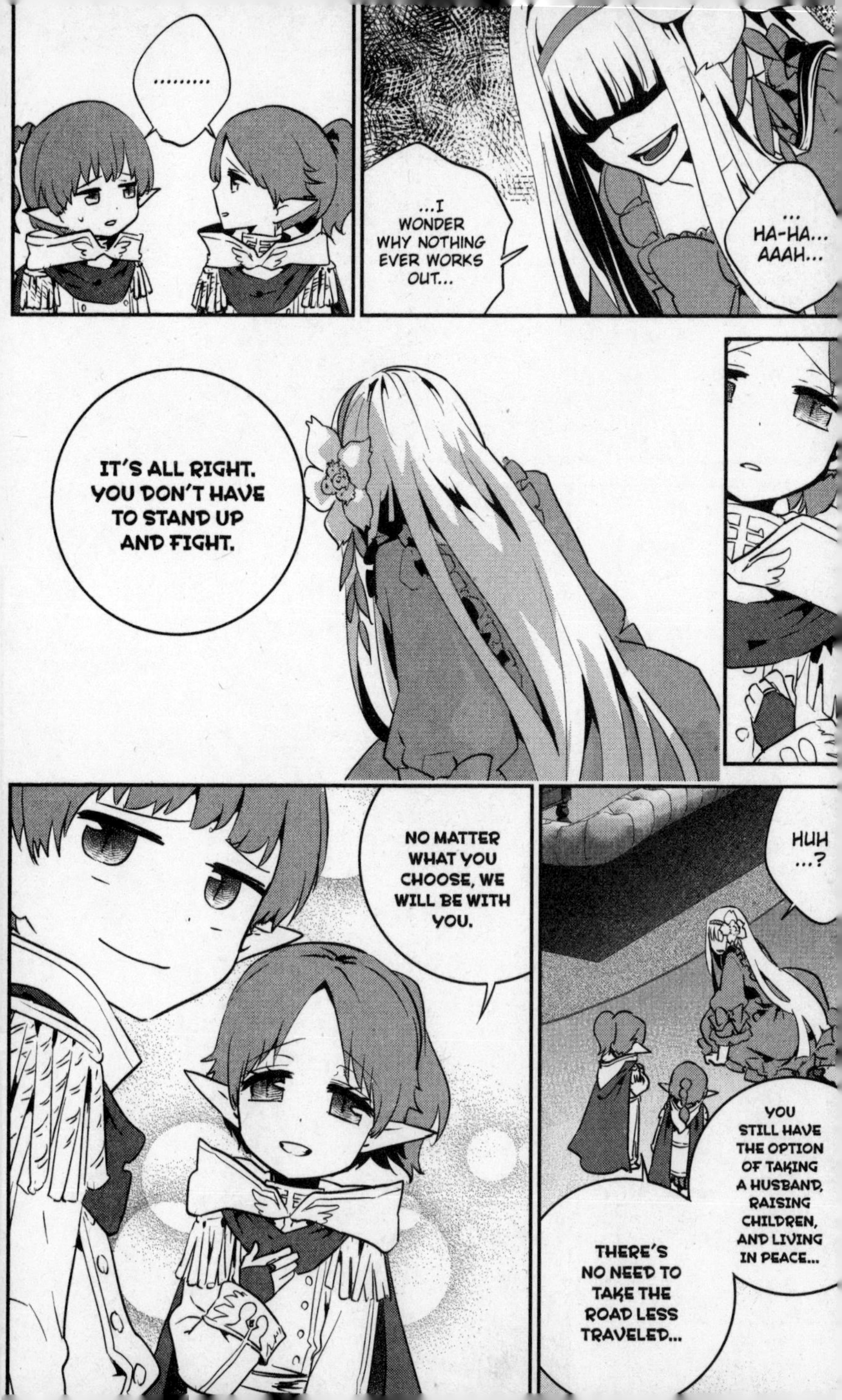
...
HA-HA...
AAAH...
...I WONDER WHY NOTHING EVER WORKS OUT...
....
IT'S ALL RIGHT. YOU DON'T HAVE TO STAND UP AND FIGHT.
HUH ...?
YOU STILL HAVE THE OPTION OF TAKING A HUSBAND, RAISING CHILDREN, AND LIVING IN PEACE...
THERE'S NO NEED TO TAKE THE ROAD LESS TRAVELED...
NO MATTER WHAT YOU CHOOSE, WE WILL BE WITH YOU.

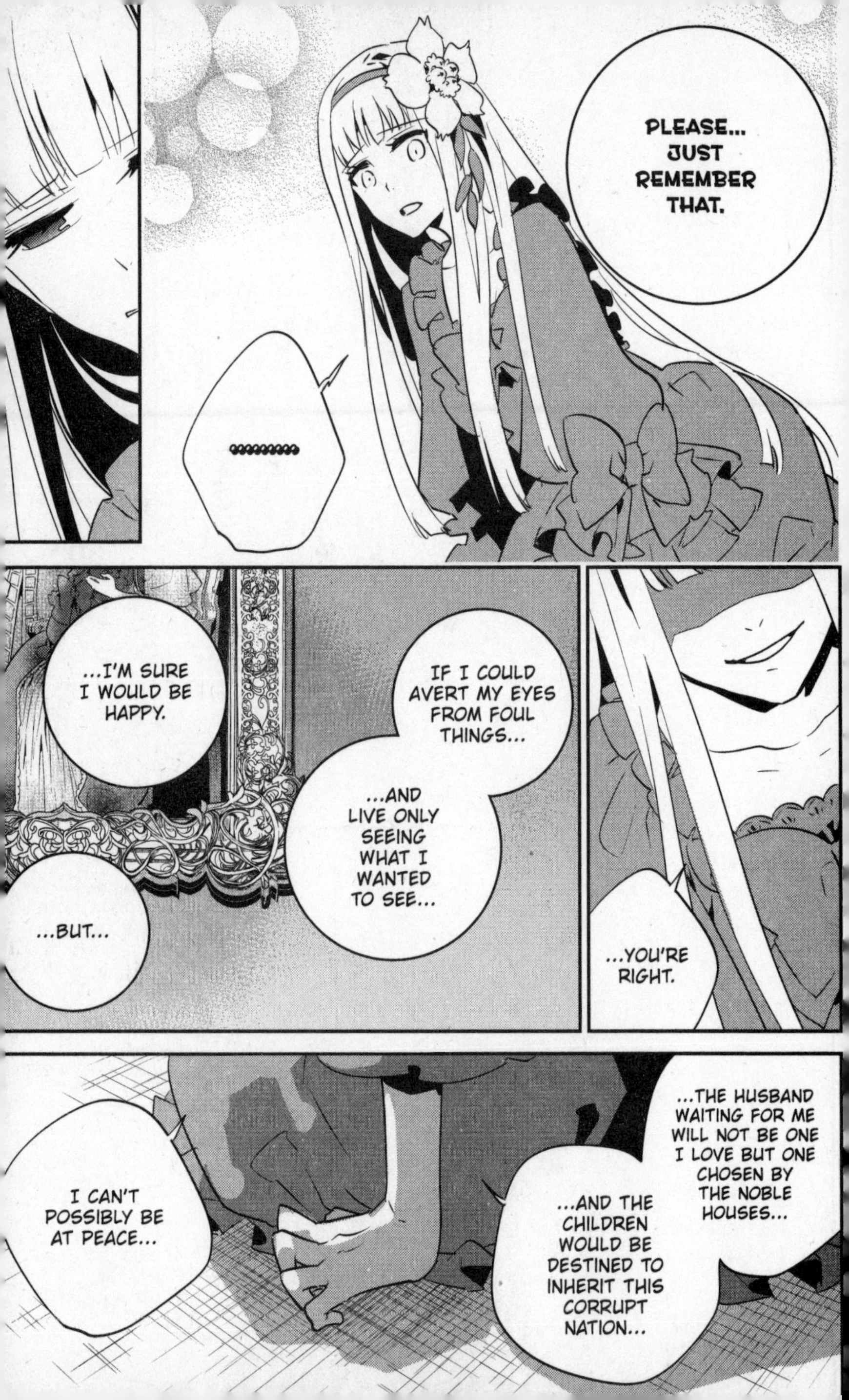
PLEASE... JUST REMEMBER THAT.
....
...YOU'RE RIGHT.
IF I COULD AVERT MY EYES FROM FOUL THINGS...
...AND LIVE ONLY SEEING WHAT I WANTED TO SEE...
...I'M SURE I WOULD BE HAPPY.
...BUT...
...THE HUSBAND WAITING FOR ME WILL NOT BE ONE I LOVE BUT ONE CHOSEN BY THE NOBLE HOUSES...
...AND THE CHILDREN WOULD BE DESTINED TO INHERIT THIS CORRUPT NATION...
I CAN'T POSSIBLY BE AT PEACE...

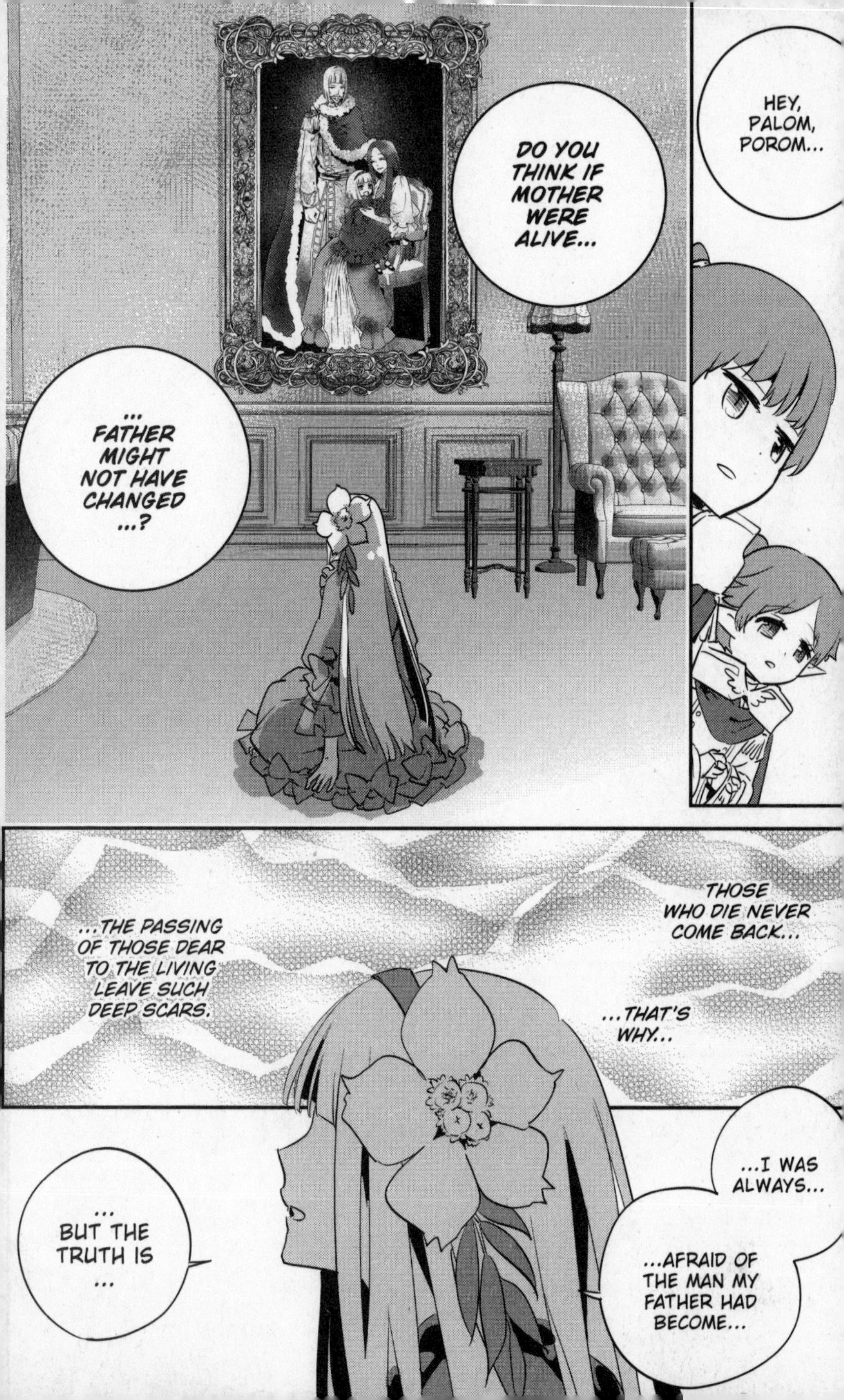
HEY, PALOM, POROM...
DO YOU THINK IF MOTHER WERE ALIVE...
... FATHER MIGHT NOT HAVE CHANGED ...?
THOSE WHO DIE NEVER COME BACK...
...THE PASSING OF THOSE DEAR TO THE LIVING LEAVE SUCH DEEP SCARS.
...THAT'S WHY...
...I WAS ALWAYS...
...AFRAID OF THE MAN MY FATHER HAD BECOME...
... BUT THE TRUTH IS ...

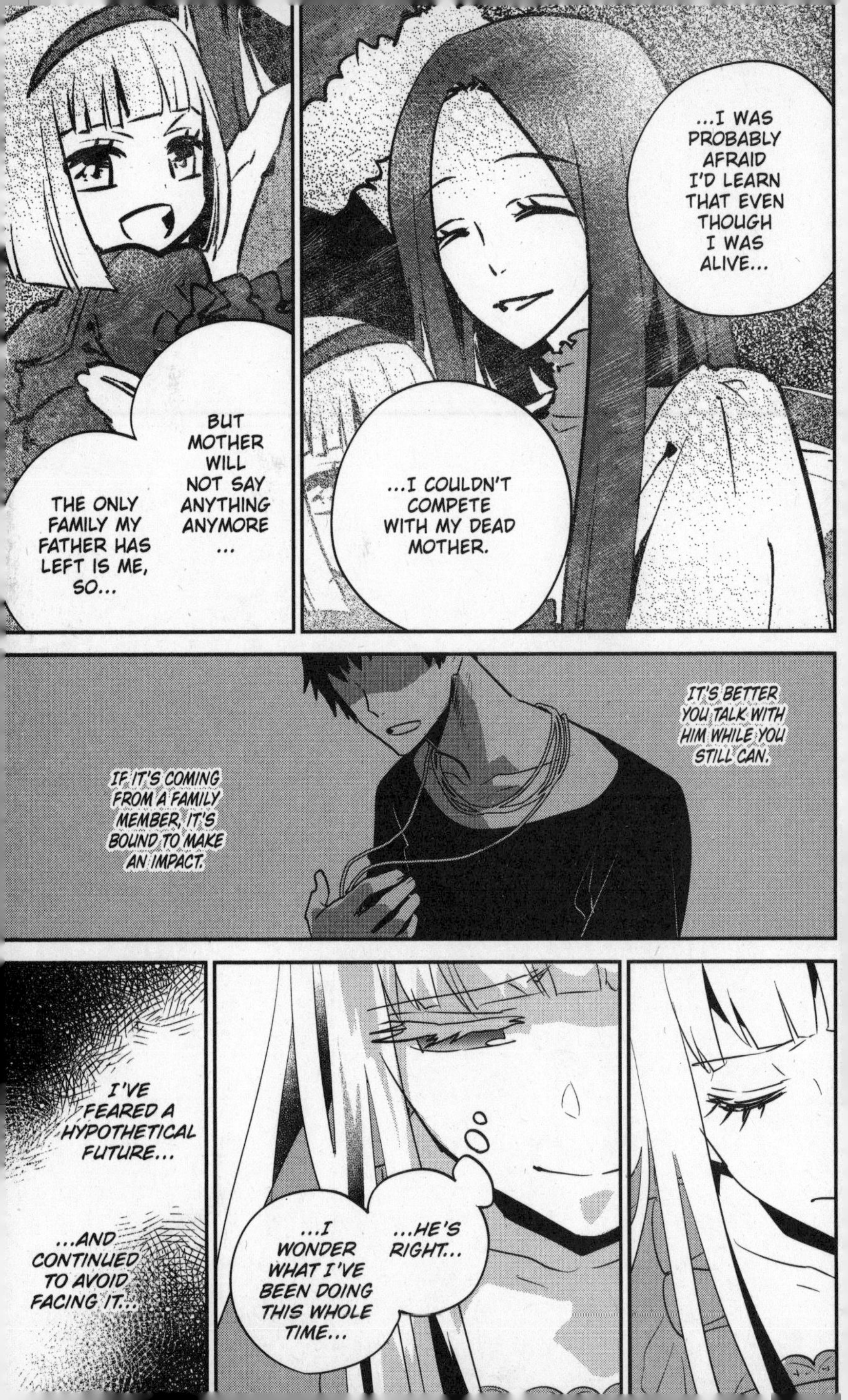
...I WAS PROBABLY AFRAID I'D LEARN THAT EVEN THOUGH I WAS ALIVE...
...I COULDN'T COMPETE WITH MY DEAD MOTHER.
BUT MOTHER WILL NOT SAY ANYTHING ANYMORE ...
THE ONLY FAMILY MY FATHER HAS LEFT IS ME, SO...
IT'S BETTER YOU TALK WITH HIM WHILE YOU STILL CAN.
IF IT'S COMING FROM A FAMILY MEMBER, IT'S BOUND TO MAKE AN IMPACT.
...HE'S RIGHT...
...I WONDER WHAT I'VE BEEN DOING THIS WHOLE TIME...
I'VE FEARED A HYPOTHETICAL FUTURE...
...AND CONTINUED TO AVOID FACING IT...

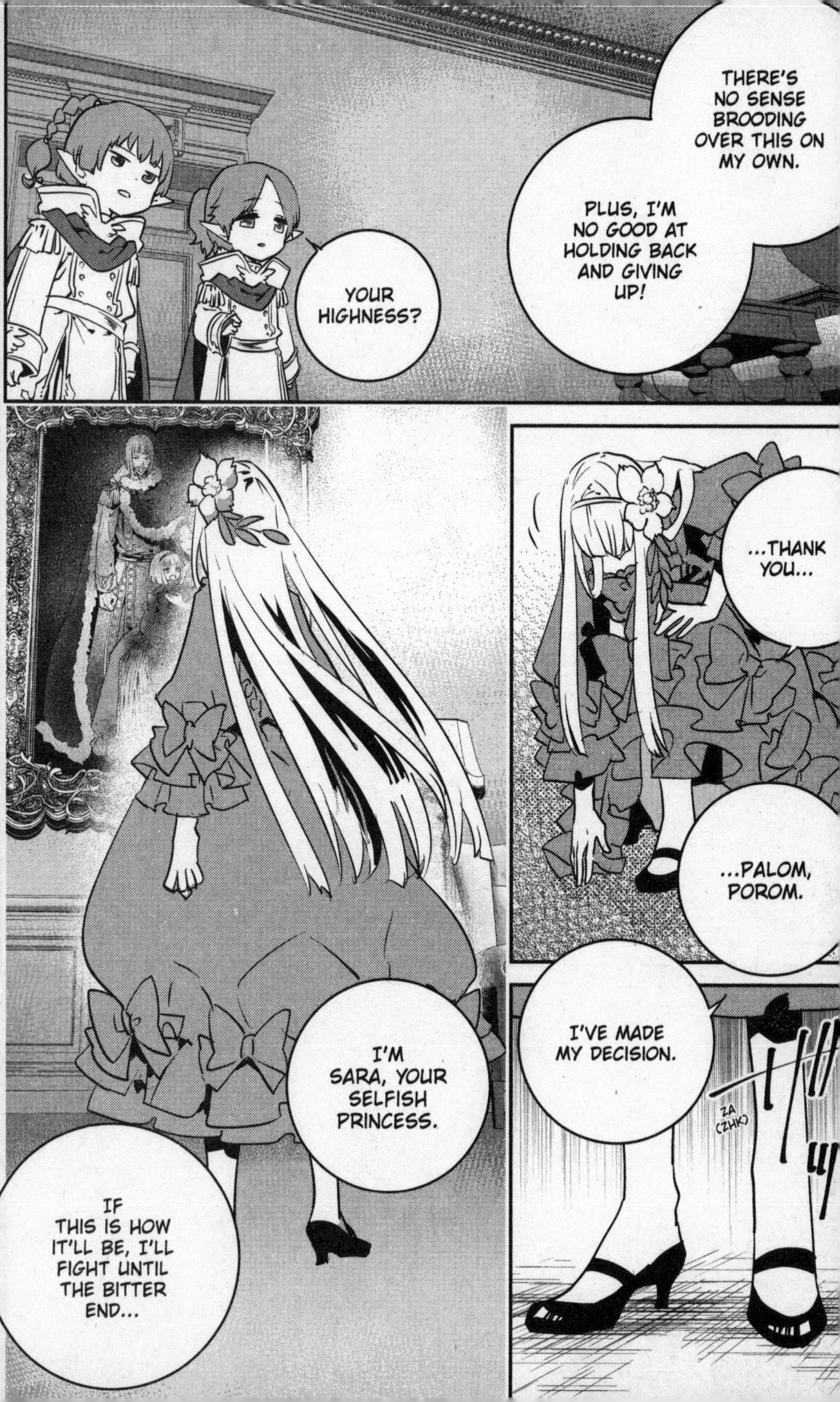
THERE'S NO SENSE BROODING OVER THIS ON MY OWN.
PLUS, I'M NO GOOD AT HOLDING BACK AND GIVING UP!
YOUR HIGHNESS?
...THANK YOU...
...PALOM, POROM.
I'VE MADE MY DECISION.
ZA (ZHK)
I'M SARA, YOUR SELFISH PRINCESS.
IF THIS IS HOW IT'LL BE, I'LL FIGHT UNTIL THE BITTER END...

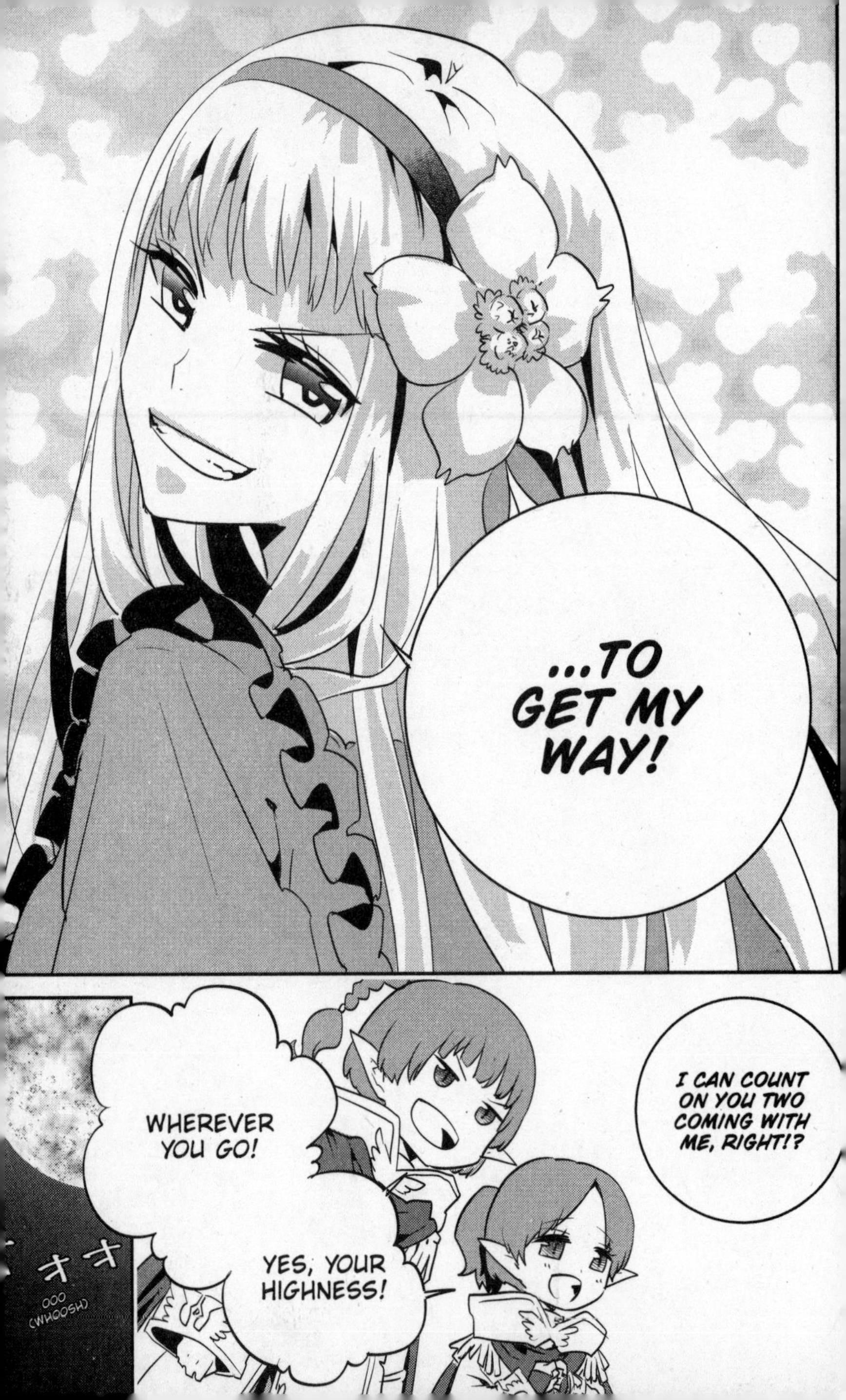
...TO GET MY WAY!
I CAN COUNT ON YOU TWO COMING WITH ME, RIGHT!?
WHEREVER YOU GO!
YES, YOUR HIGHNESS!
OOO (WHOOSH)

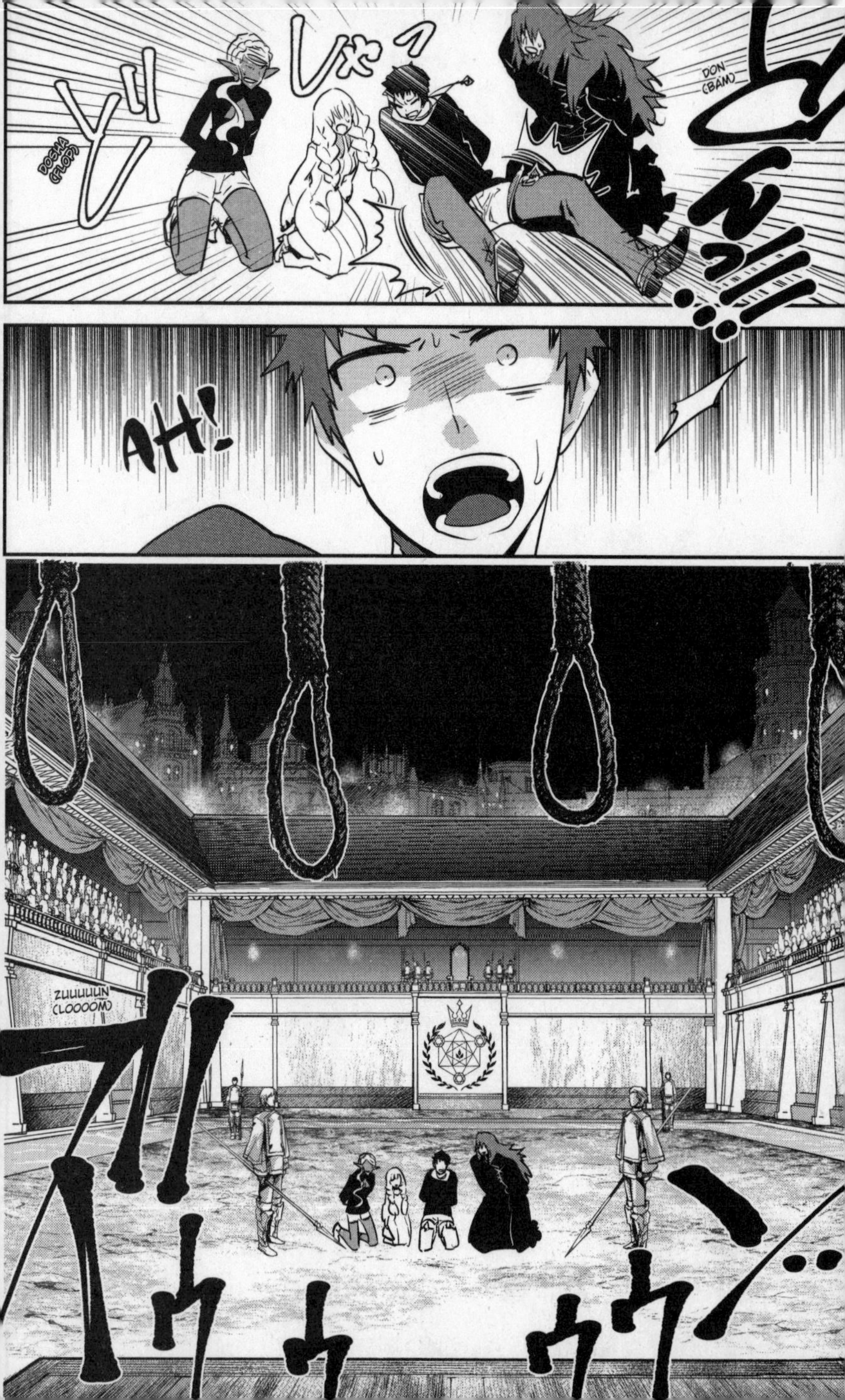
DON (BAM)
DOSHA (FLOP)
AH!
ZUUUUUN (LOOOOM)

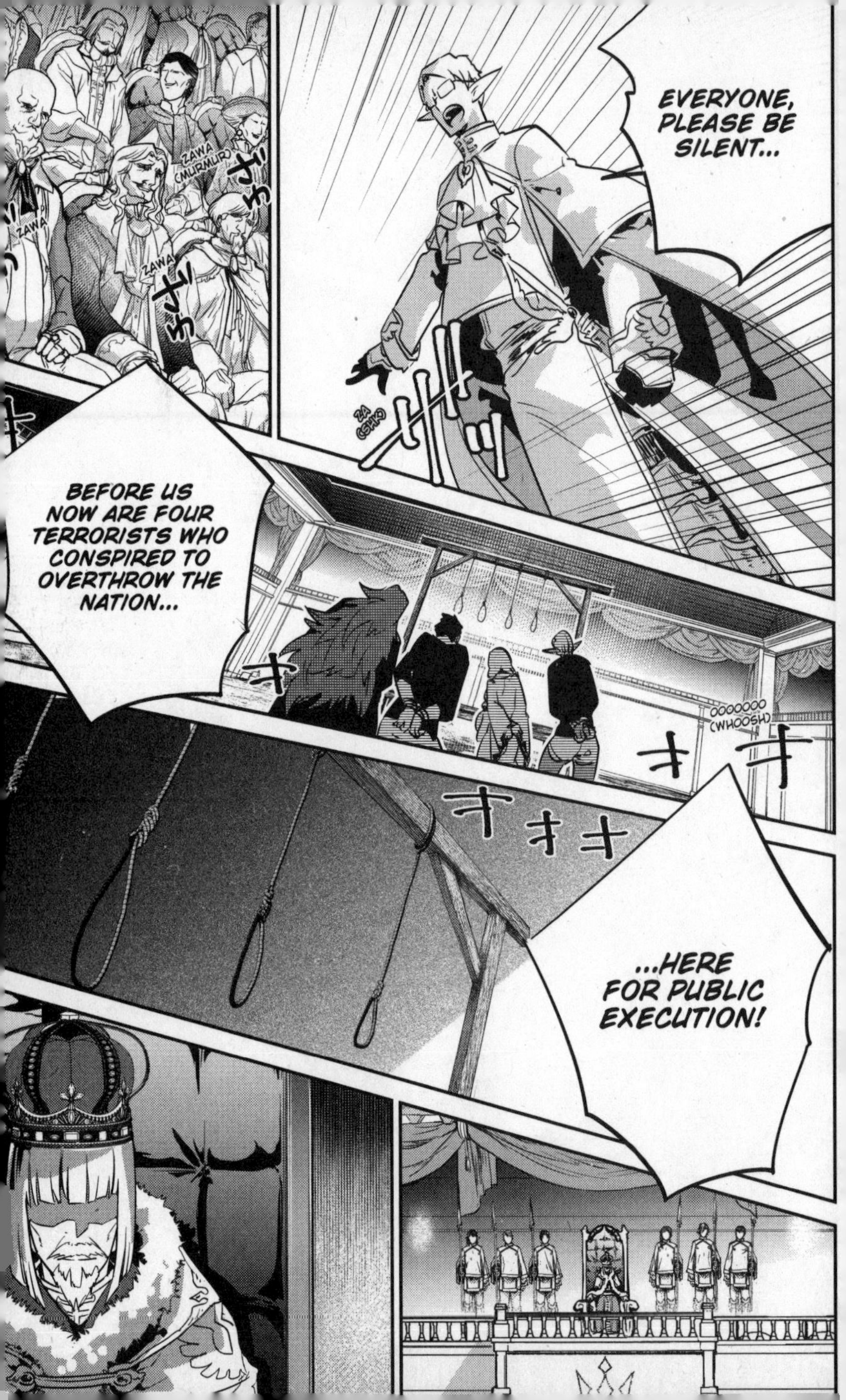
EVERYONE, PLEASE BE SILENT...
ZA (SHK)
ZAWA (MURMUR)
ZAWA
ZAWA
BEFORE US NOW ARE FOUR TERRORISTS WHO CONSPIRED TO OVERTHROW THE NATION...
OOOOOOO (WHOOSH)
...HERE FOR PUBLIC EXECUTION!

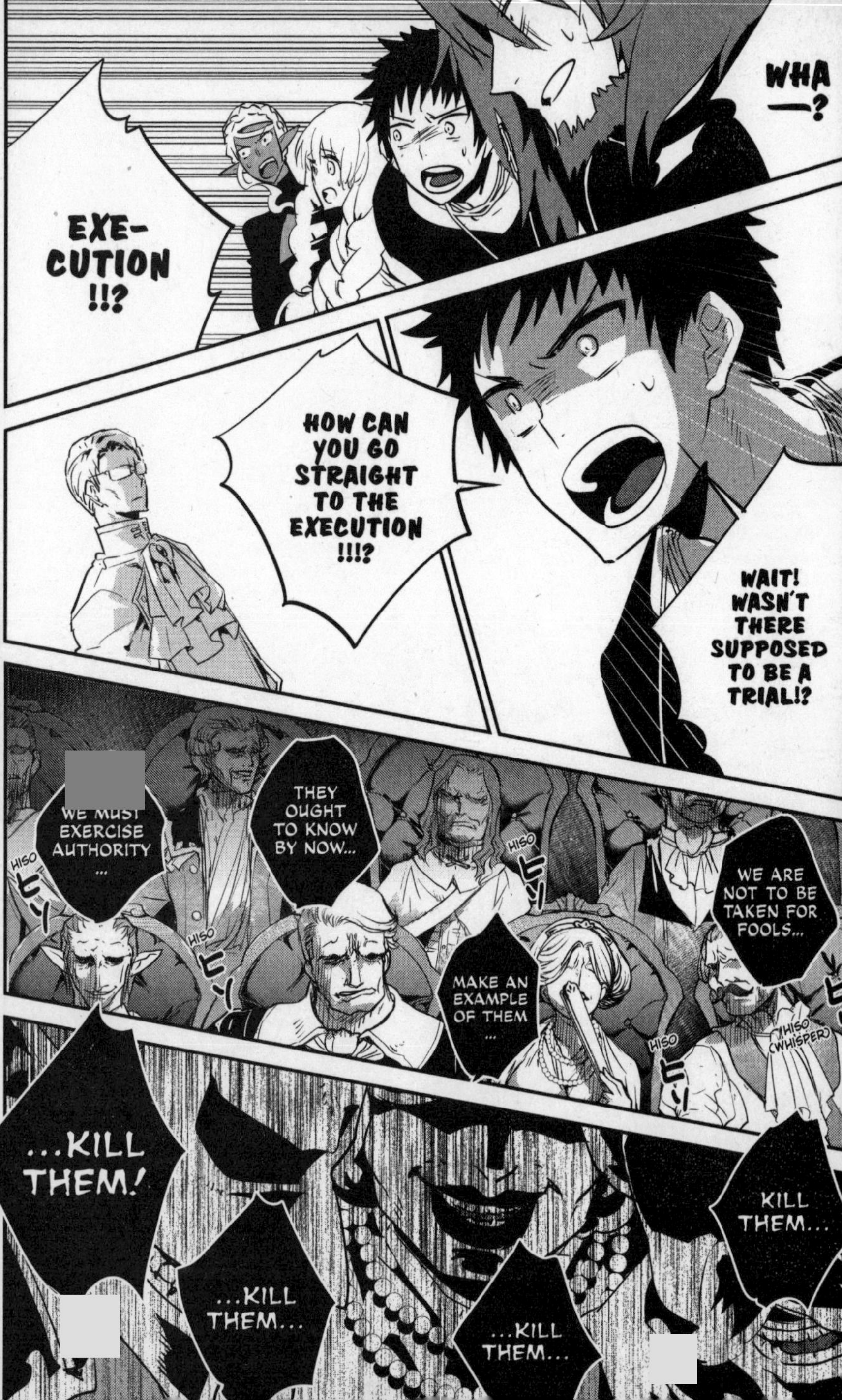
WHA—?
EXE-CUTION!!?
HOW CAN YOU GO STRAIGHT TO THE EXECUTION!!!?
WAIT! WASN'T THERE SUPPOSED TO BE A TRIAL!?
WE ARE NOT TO BE TAKEN FOR FOOLS...
HISO (WHISPER)
HISO
MAKE AN EXAMPLE OF THEM...
HISO
HISO
THEY OUGHT TO KNOW BY NOW...
HISO
WE MUST EXERCISE AUTHORITY...
KILL THEM...
...KILL THEM...
...KILL THEM...
...KILL THEM!

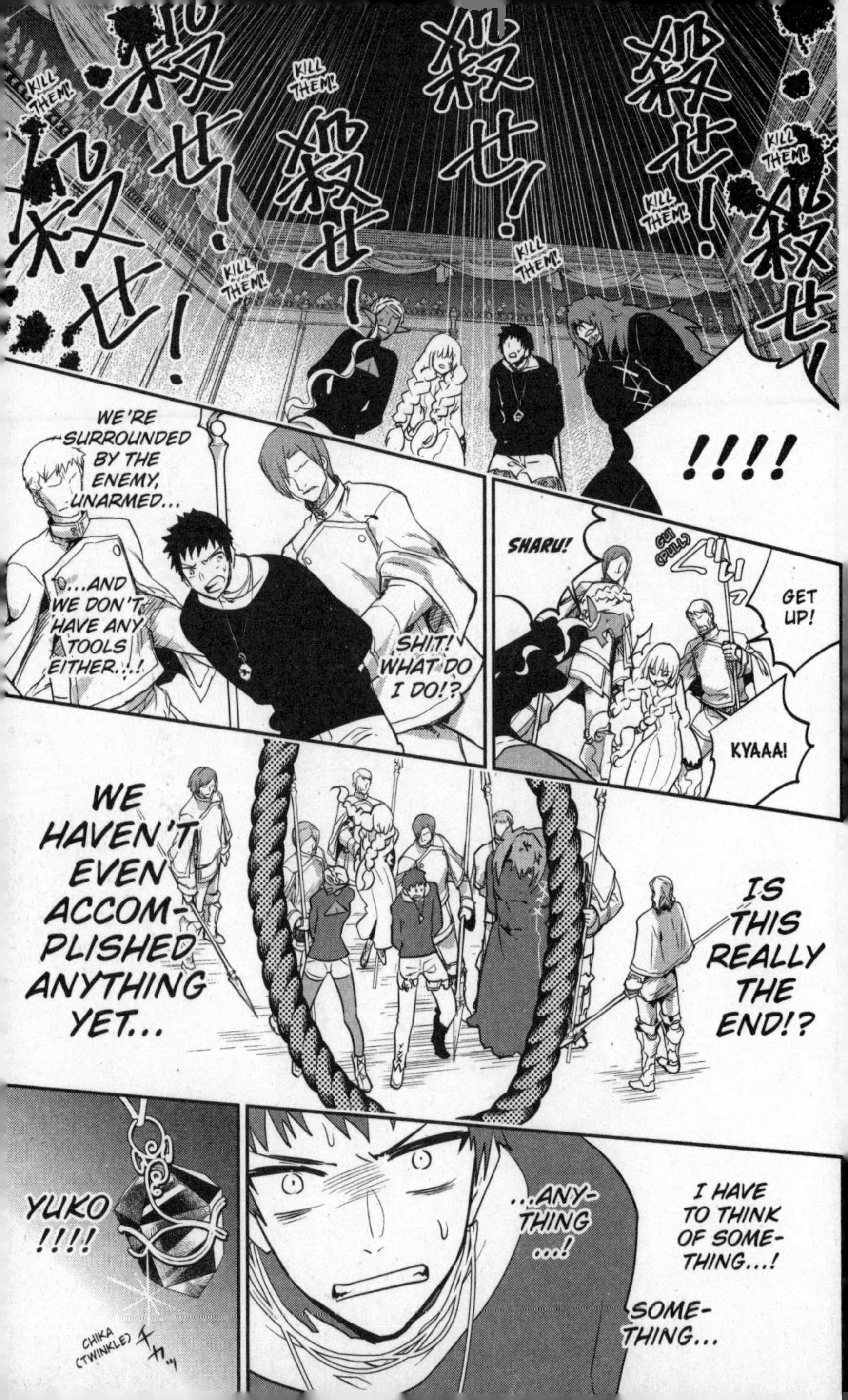
殺せ!
KILL THEM!
殺せ!
KILL THEM!
殺せ!
KILL THEM!
殺せ!
KILL THEM!
殺せ!
KILL THEM!
殺せ!
KILL THEM!
!!!!
WE'RE SURROUNDED BY THE ENEMY, UNARMED...
...AND WE DON'T HAVE ANY TOOLS EITHER...!
SHIT! WHAT DO I DO!?
SHARU!
GUI (PULL)
GET UP!
KYAAA!
WE HAVEN'T EVEN ACCOMPLISHED ANYTHING YET...
IS THIS REALLY THE END!?
I HAVE TO THINK OF SOMETHING...!
...ANYTHING...!
SOMETHING...
YUKO!!!!
CHIKA (TWINKLE)

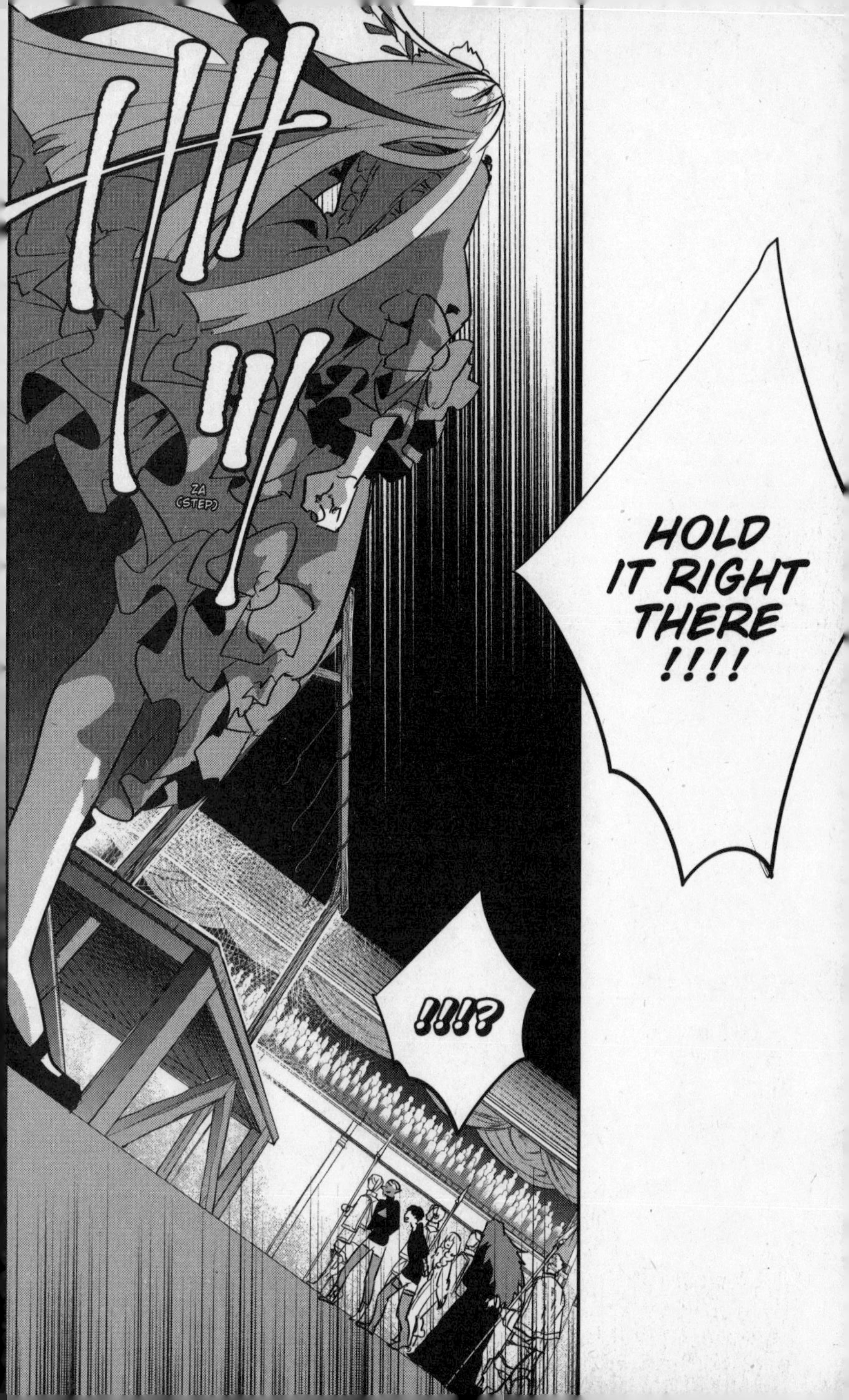
HOLD IT RIGHT THERE !!!!
ZA (STEP)
!!!?

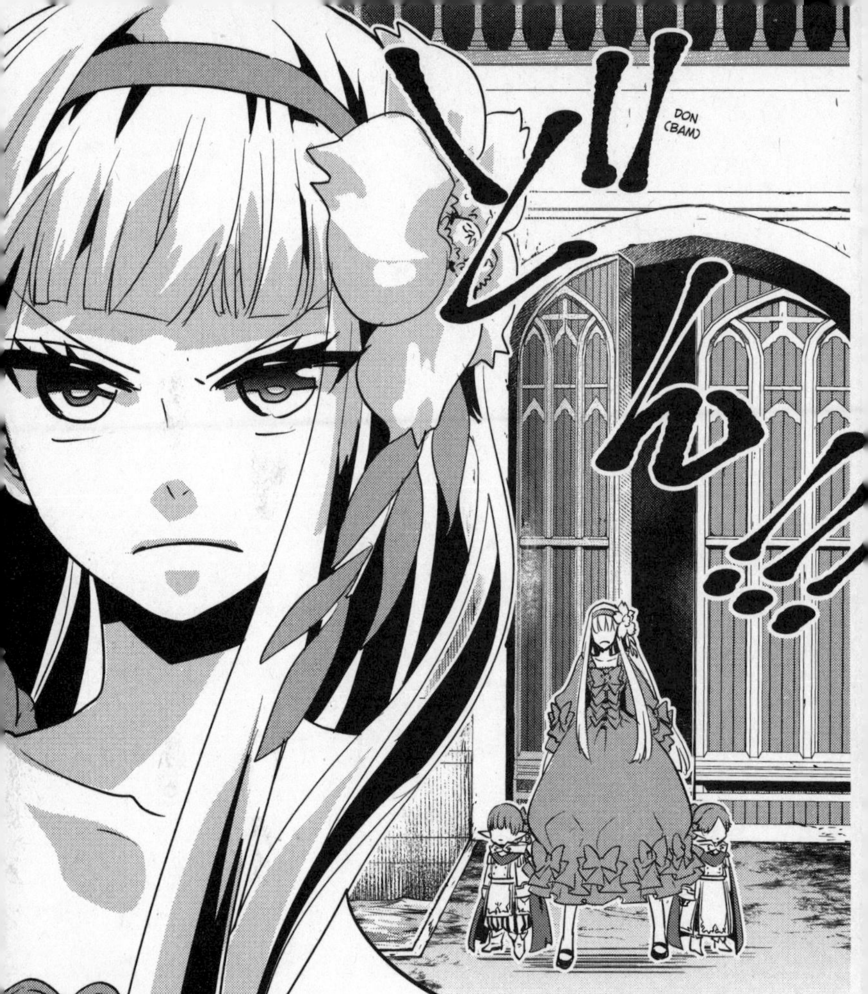
DON
(BAM)

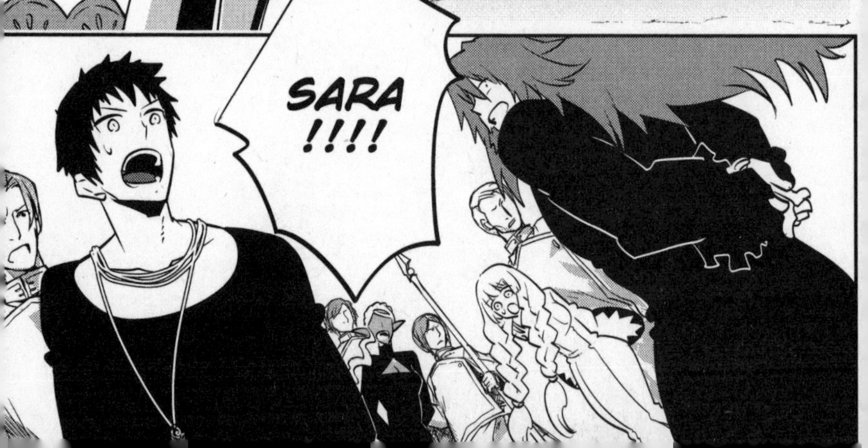
SARA
!!!!

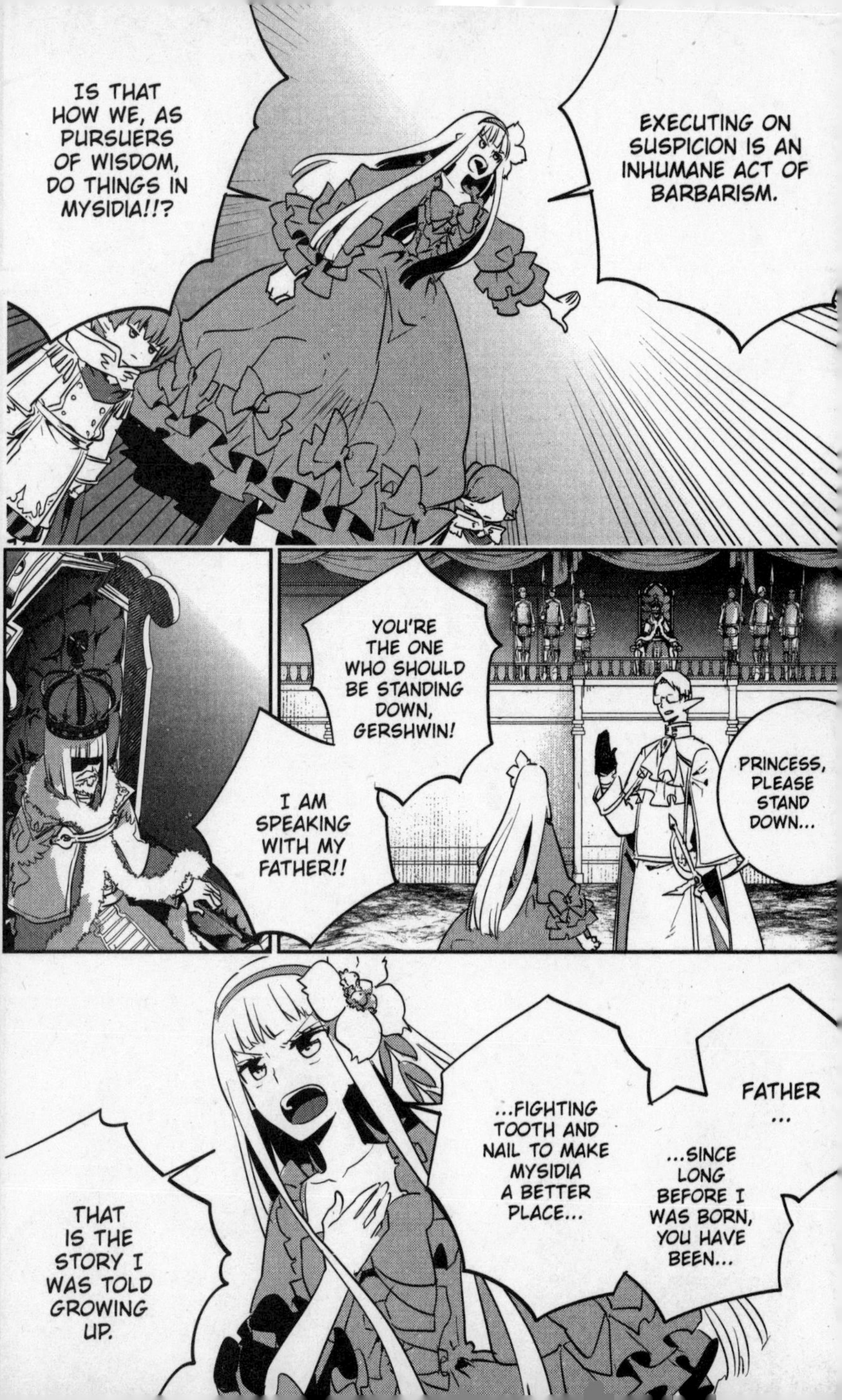
EXECUTING ON SUSPICION IS AN INHUMANE ACT OF BARBARISM.
IS THAT HOW WE, AS PURSUERS OF WISDOM, DO THINGS IN MYSIDIA!!?
PRINCESS, PLEASE STAND DOWN...
YOU'RE THE ONE WHO SHOULD BE STANDING DOWN, GERSHWIN!
I AM SPEAKING WITH MY FATHER!!
FATHER...
...SINCE LONG BEFORE I WAS BORN, YOU HAVE BEEN...
...FIGHTING TOOTH AND NAIL TO MAKE MYSIDIA A BETTER PLACE...
THAT IS THE STORY I WAS TOLD GROWING UP.

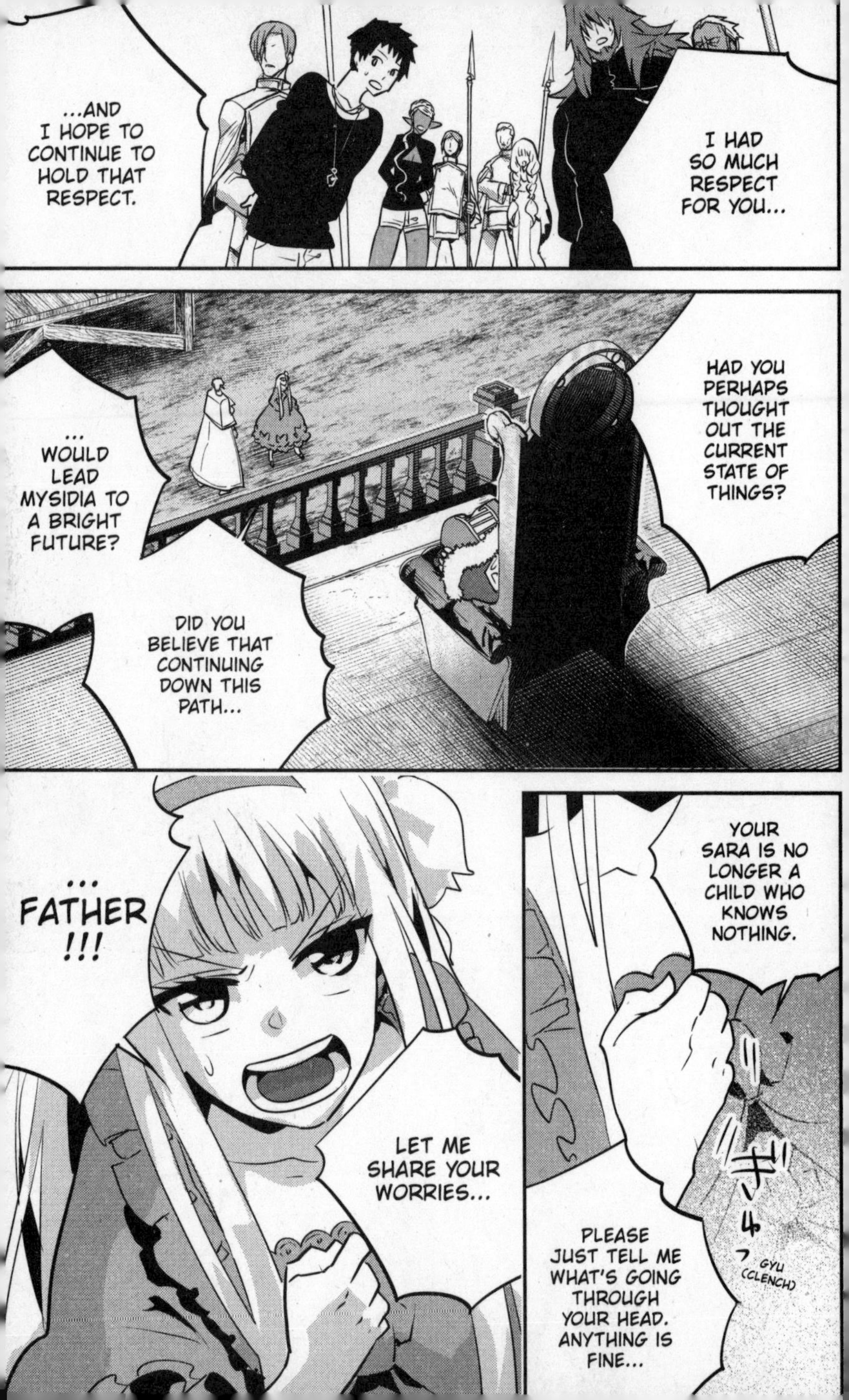
I HAD SO MUCH RESPECT FOR YOU...
...AND I HOPE TO CONTINUE TO HOLD THAT RESPECT.
HAD YOU PERHAPS THOUGHT OUT THE CURRENT STATE OF THINGS?
DID YOU BELIEVE THAT CONTINUING DOWN THIS PATH...
...WOULD LEAD MYSIDIA TO A BRIGHT FUTURE?
YOUR SARA IS NO LONGER A CHILD WHO KNOWS NOTHING.
GYU (CLENCH)
PLEASE JUST TELL ME WHAT'S GOING THROUGH YOUR HEAD. ANYTHING IS FINE...
LET ME SHARE YOUR WORRIES...
...FATHER!!!

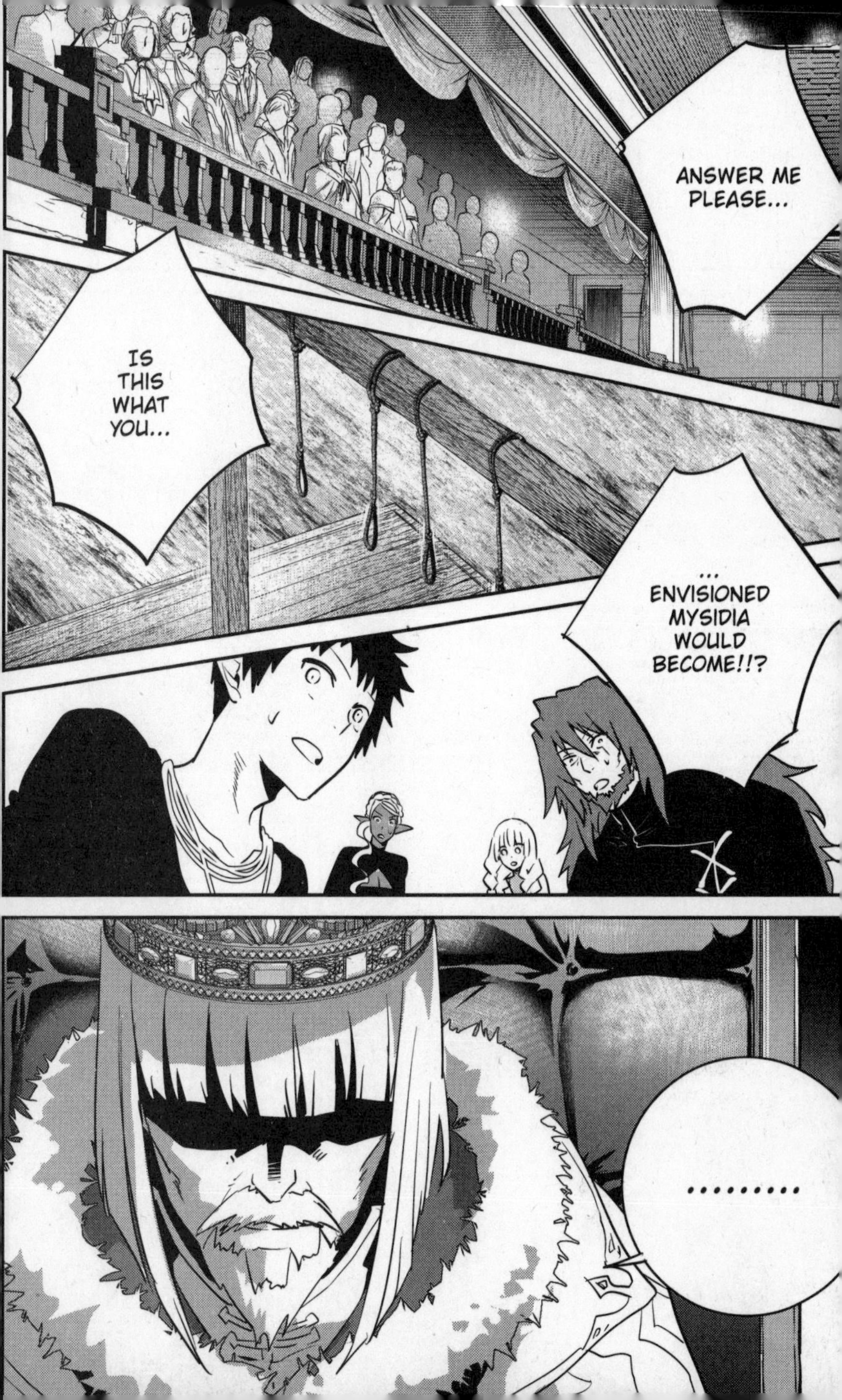
ANSWER ME PLEASE...
IS THIS WHAT YOU...
... ENVISIONED MYSIDIA WOULD BECOME!!?
....

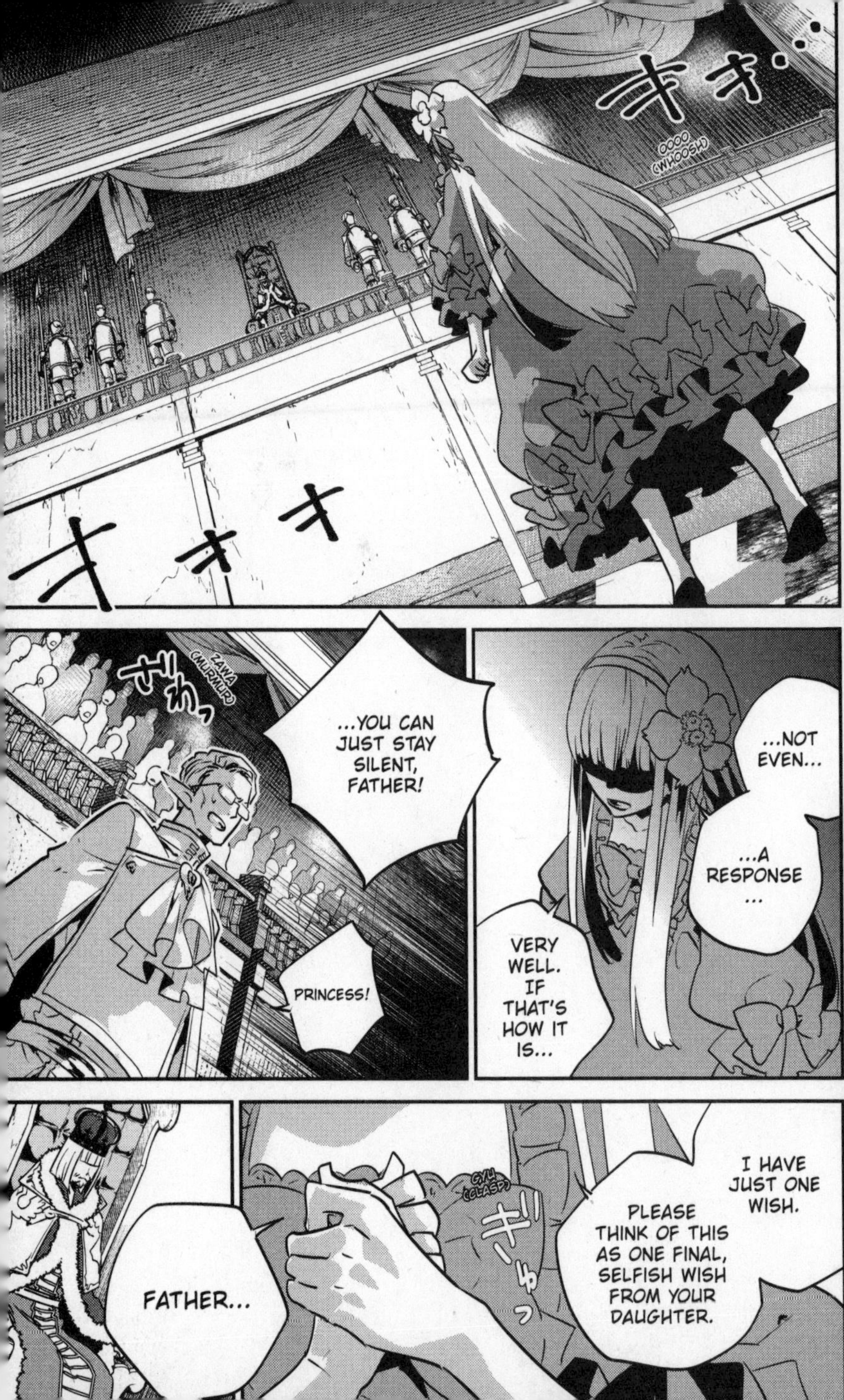
OOOO (WHOOSH)
...NOT EVEN...
...A RESPONSE ...
VERY WELL. IF THAT'S HOW IT IS...
ZAWA (MURMUR)
...YOU CAN JUST STAY SILENT, FATHER!
PRINCESS!
I HAVE JUST ONE WISH.
PLEASE THINK OF THIS AS ONE FINAL, SELFISH WISH FROM YOUR DAUGHTER.
GYU (CLASP)
FATHER...

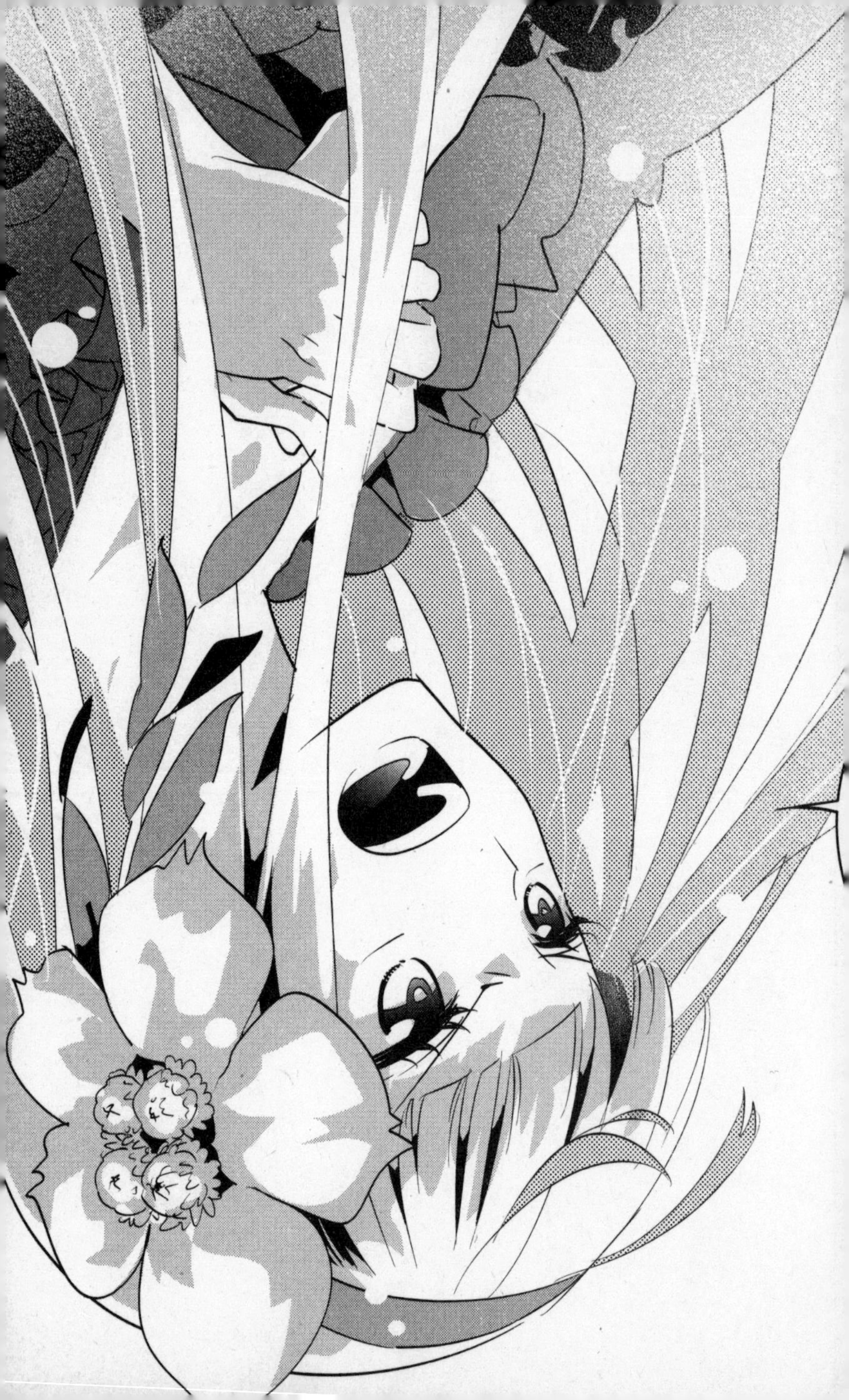

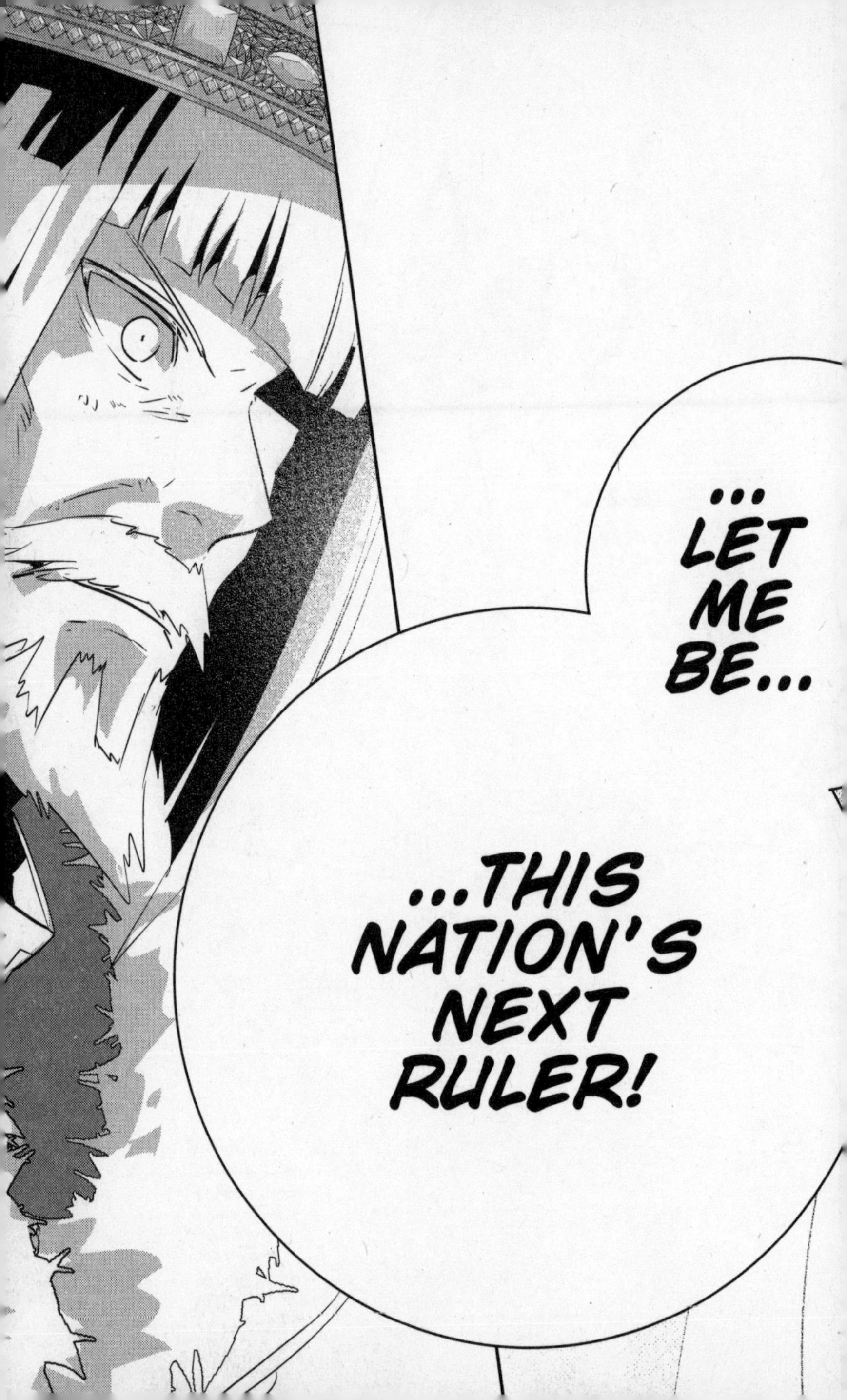
...LET ME BE...
...THIS NATION'S NEXT RULER!

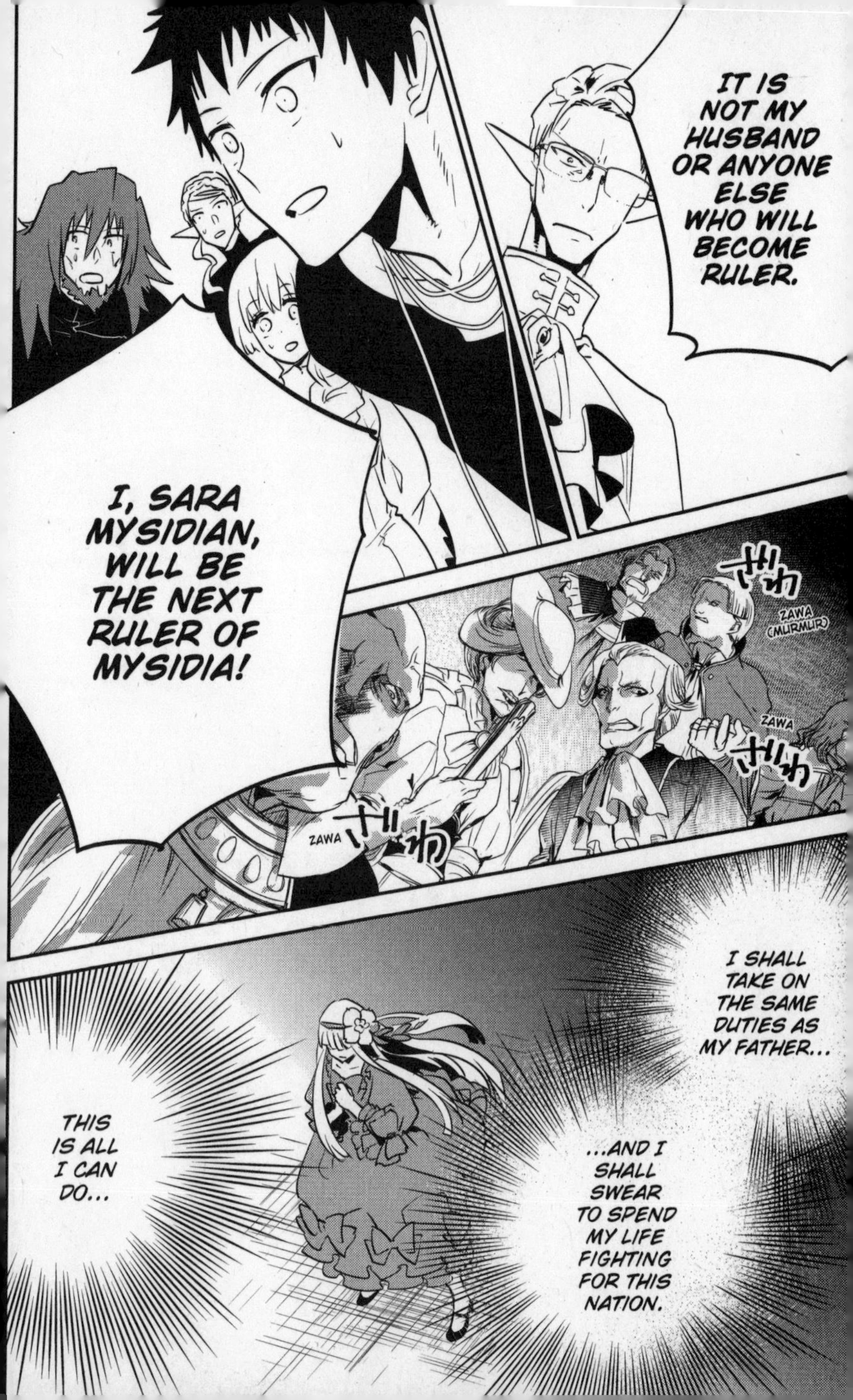
IT IS NOT MY HUSBAND OR ANYONE ELSE WHO WILL BECOME RULER.
I, SARA MYSIDIAN, WILL BE THE NEXT RULER OF MYSIDIA!
ざわ
ZAWA (MURMUR)
ZAWA
ざわ
ZAWA
ざわ
I SHALL TAKE ON THE SAME DUTIES AS MY FATHER...
...AND I SHALL SWEAR TO SPEND MY LIFE FIGHTING FOR THIS NATION.
THIS IS ALL I CAN DO...

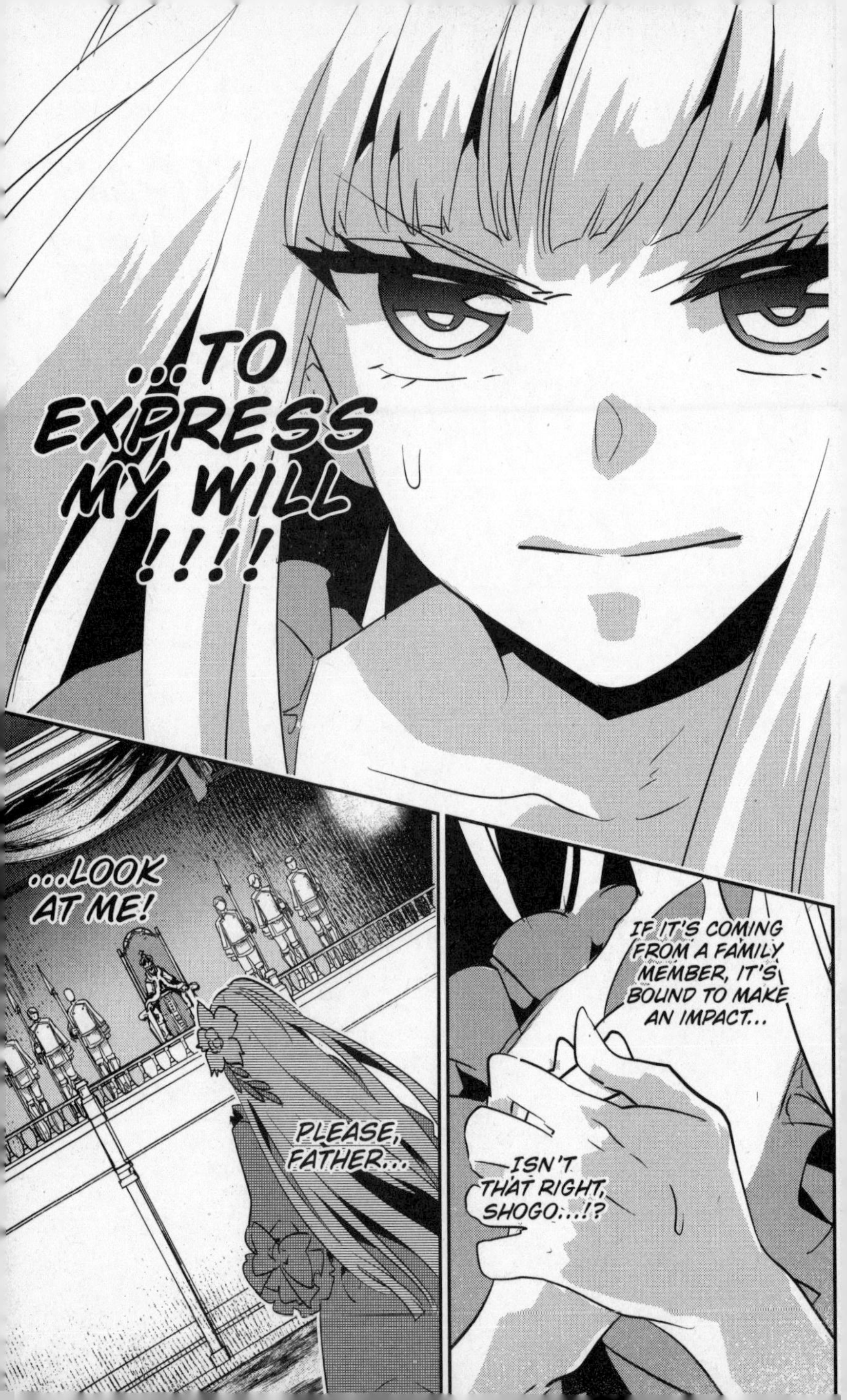
...TO EXPRESS MY WILL !!!!
IF IT'S COMING FROM A FAMILY MEMBER, IT'S BOUND TO MAKE AN IMPACT...
ISN'T THAT RIGHT, SHOGO...!?
PLEASE, FATHER...
...LOOK AT ME!

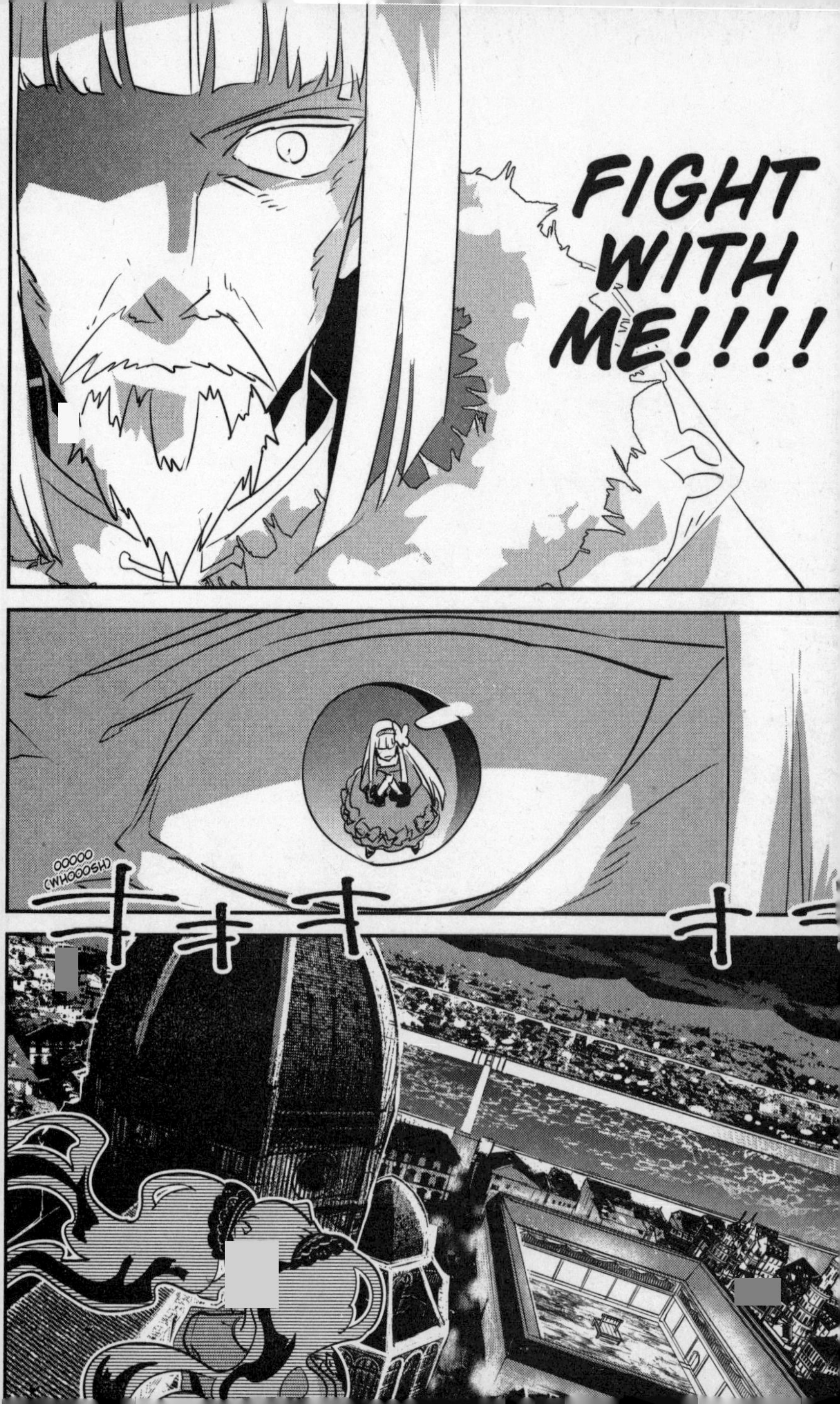
FIGHT WITH ME!!!!
OOOOO (WHOOOSH)

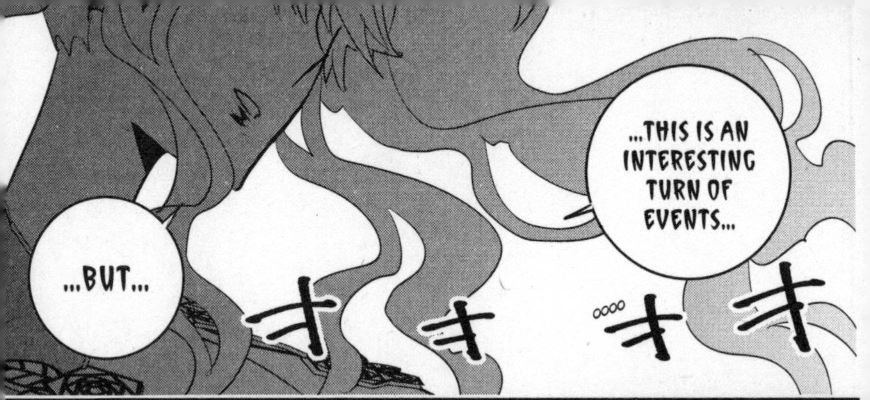
...THIS IS AN INTERESTING TURN OF EVENTS...
...BUT...
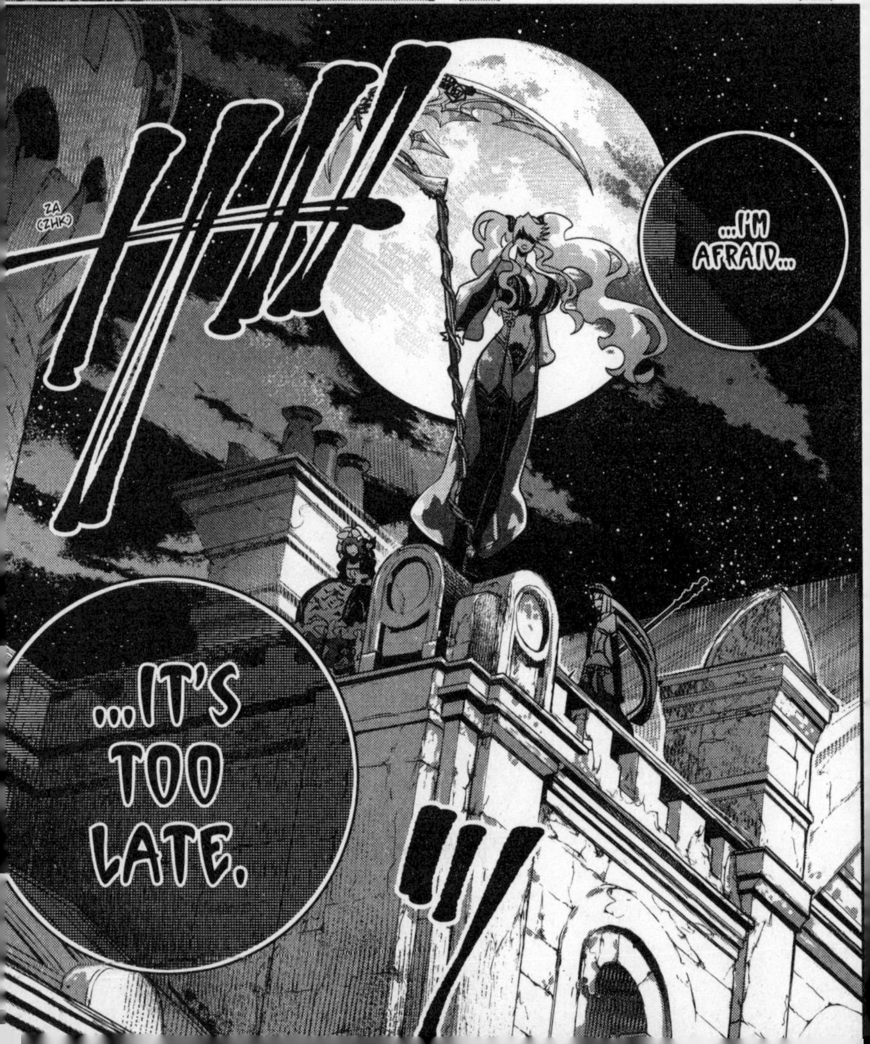
...I'M AFRAID...
ZA (ZHK)
...IT'S TOO LATE.

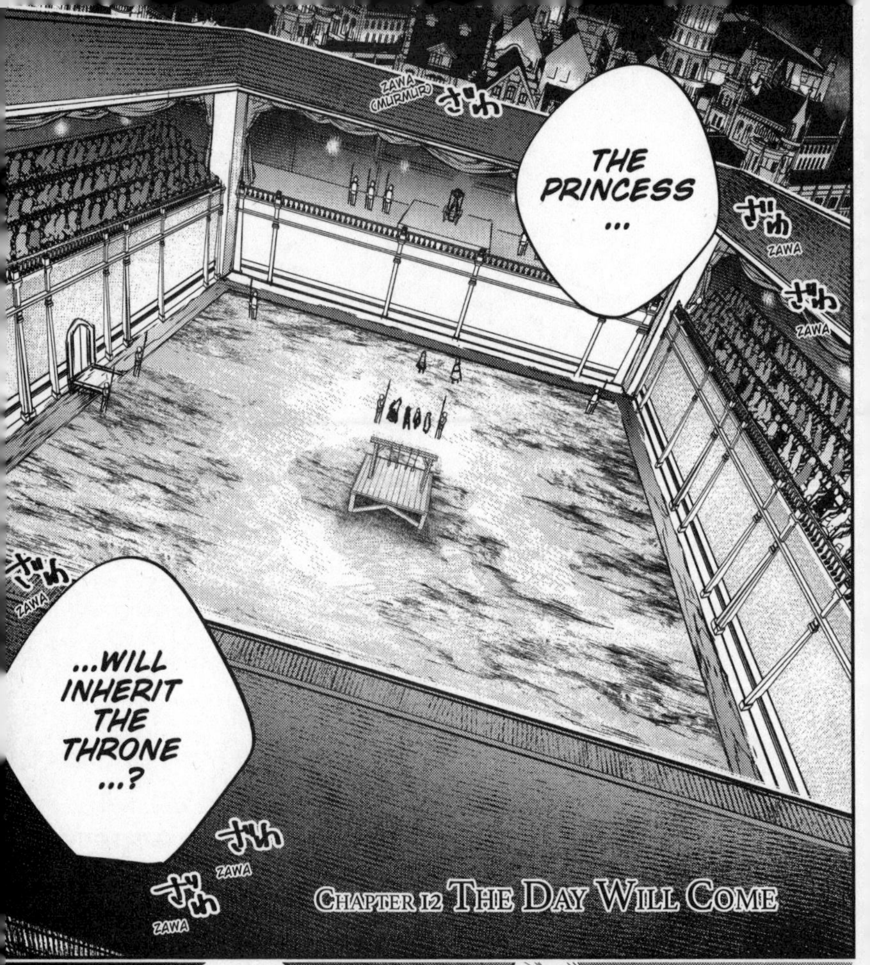
ZAWA (MURMUR)
THE PRINCESS ...
ZAWA
ZAWA
ZAWA
...WILL INHERIT THE THRONE ...?
ZAWA
ZAWA
CHAPTER 12 THE DAY WILL COME
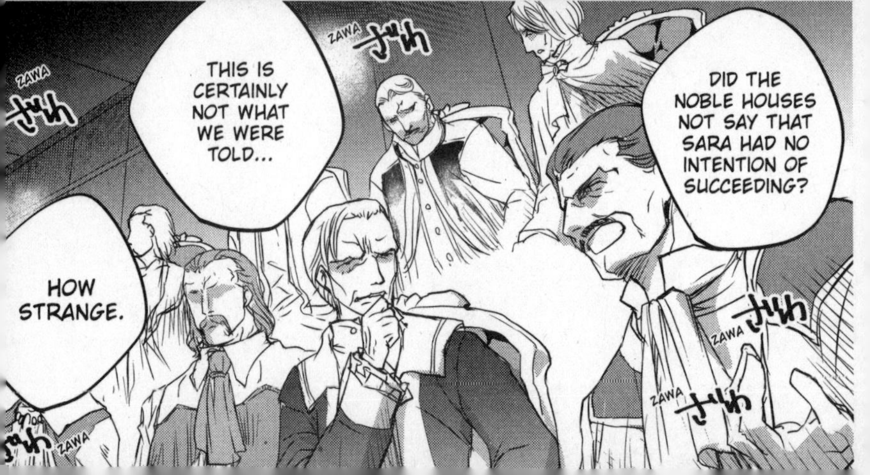
DID THE NOBLE HOUSES NOT SAY THAT SARA HAD NO INTENTION OF SUCCEEDING?
ZAWA
THIS IS CERTAINLY NOT WHAT WE WERE TOLD...
ZAWA
ZAWA
ZAWA
HOW STRANGE.
ZAWA

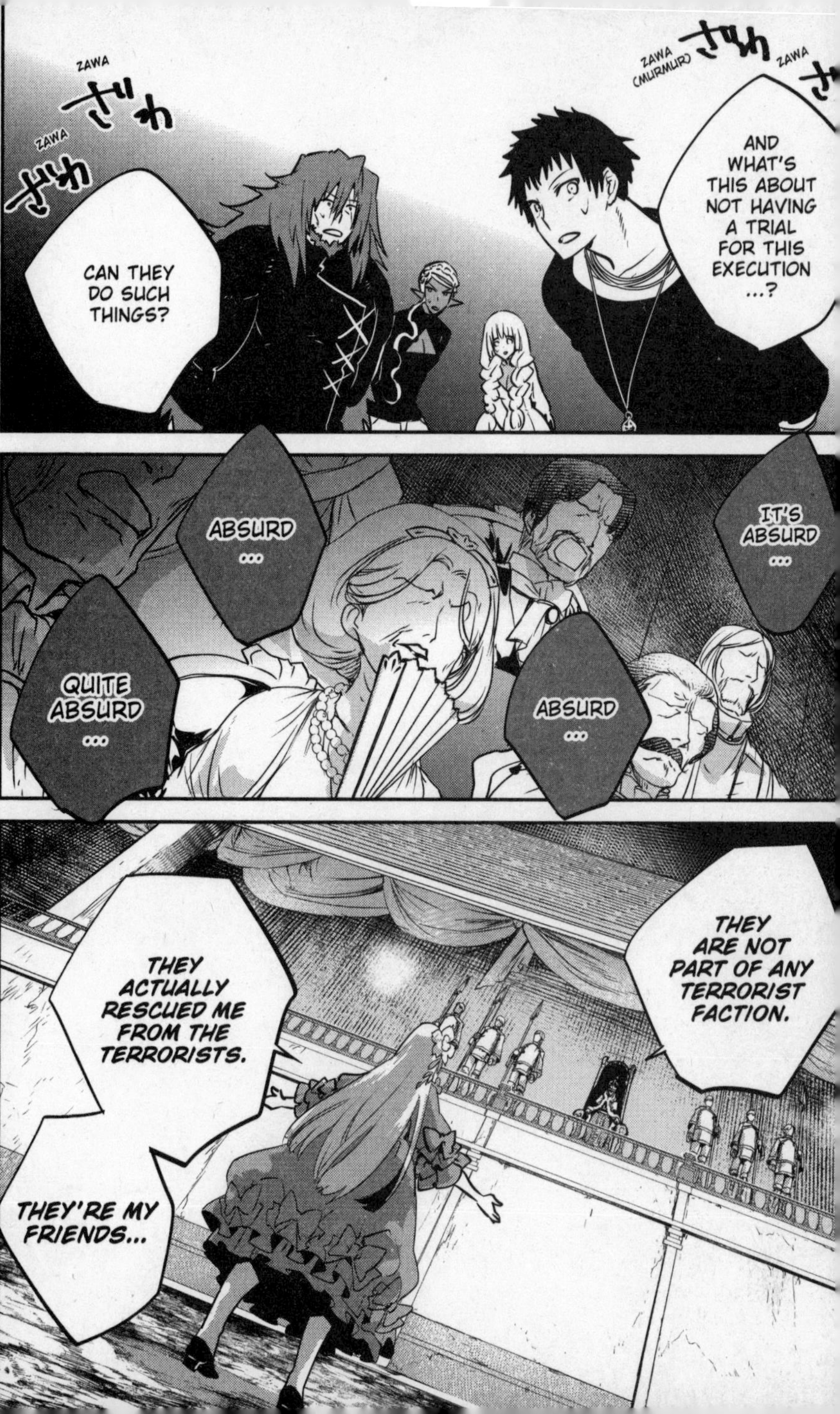
ZAWA
ざわ
ZAWA (MURMUR)
ざわ
AND WHAT'S THIS ABOUT NOT HAVING A TRIAL FOR THIS EXECUTION ...?
ZAWA
ざわ
ZAWA
ざわ
CAN THEY DO SUCH THINGS?
IT'S ABSURD ...
ABSURD ...
ABSURD ...
QUITE ABSURD ...
THEY ARE NOT PART OF ANY TERRORIST FACTION.
THEY ACTUALLY RESCUED ME FROM THE TERRORISTS.
THEY'RE MY FRIENDS...

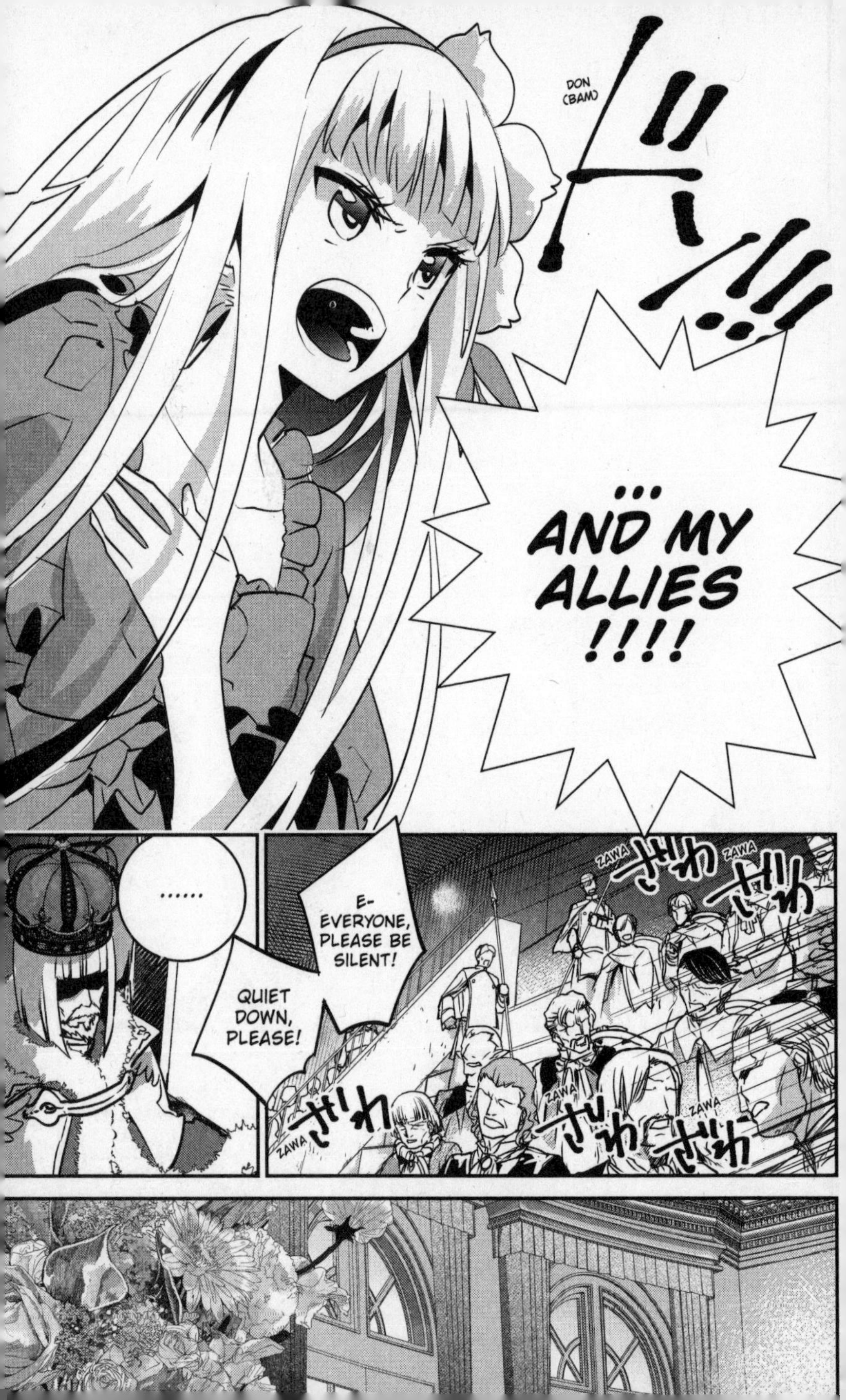
DON (BAM)
...AND MY ALLIES !!!!
ZAWA ZAWA ZAWA ZAWA ZAWA ZAWA ZAWA ZAWA
E-EVERYONE, PLEASE BE SILENT!
QUIET DOWN, PLEASE!
......

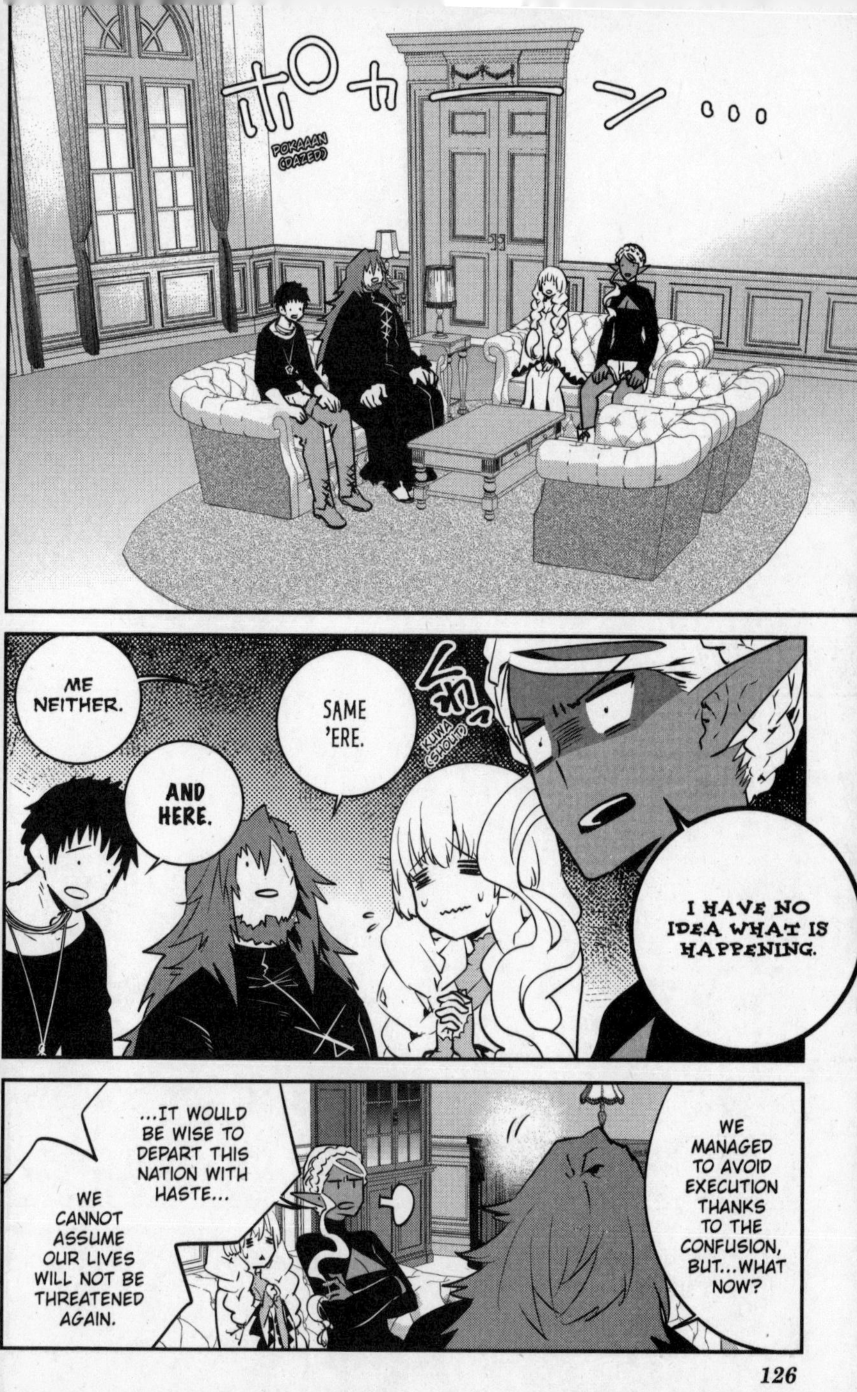
POKAAAN (DAZED)
I HAVE NO IDEA WHAT IS HAPPENING.
KUWA (SHOUT)
SAME 'ERE.
AND HERE.
ME NEITHER.
WE MANAGED TO AVOID EXECUTION THANKS TO THE CONFUSION, BUT...WHAT NOW?
...IT WOULD BE WISE TO DEPART THIS NATION WITH HASTE...
WE CANNOT ASSUME OUR LIVES WILL NOT BE THREATENED AGAIN.

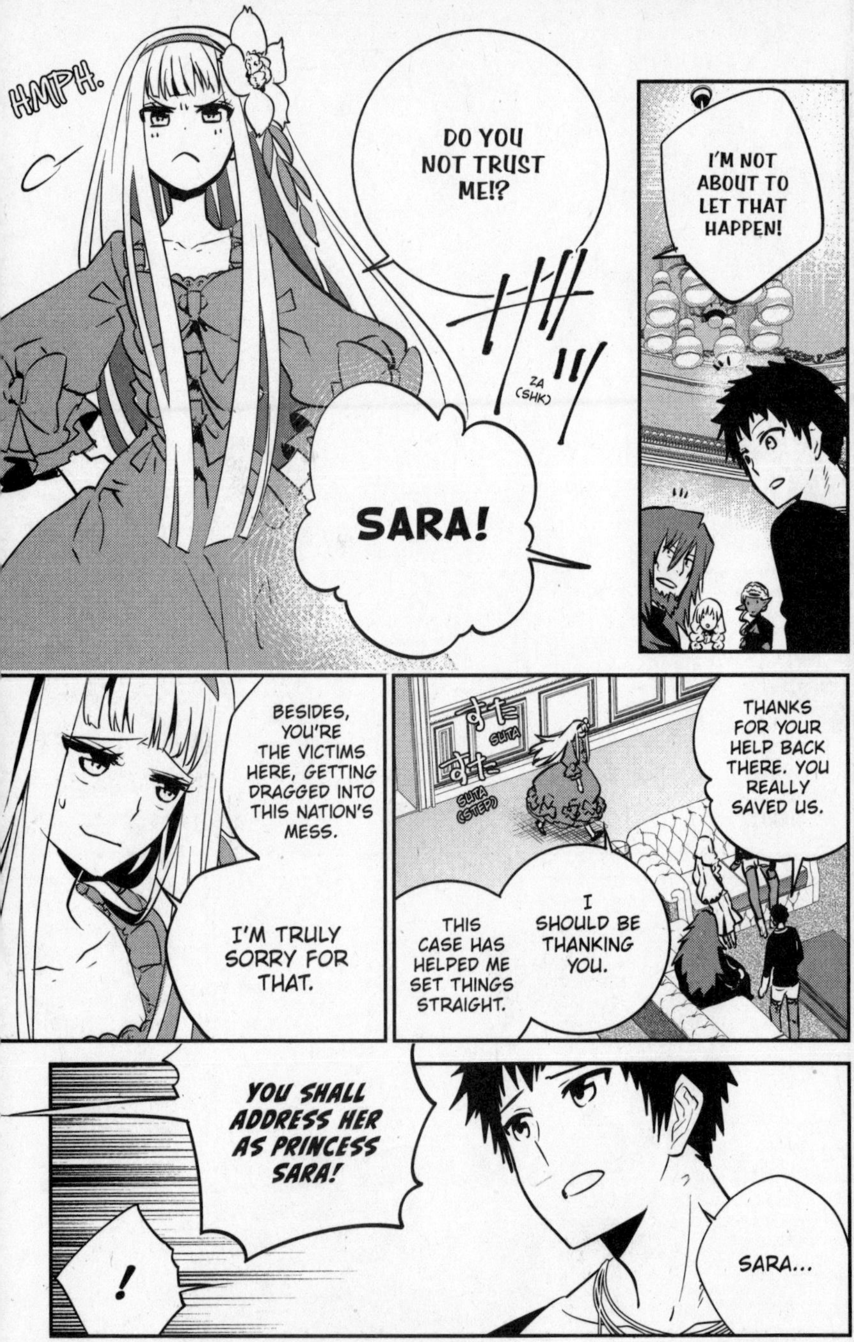
I'M NOT ABOUT TO LET THAT HAPPEN!
DO YOU NOT TRUST ME!?
ZA (SHK)
SARA!
HMPH.
THANKS FOR YOUR HELP BACK THERE. YOU REALLY SAVED US.
すた SUTA
すた SUTA (STEP)
I SHOULD BE THANKING YOU.
THIS CASE HAS HELPED ME SET THINGS STRAIGHT.
BESIDES, YOU'RE THE VICTIMS HERE, GETTING DRAGGED INTO THIS NATION'S MESS.
I'M TRULY SORRY FOR THAT.
SARA...
YOU SHALL ADDRESS HER AS PRINCESS SARA!
!

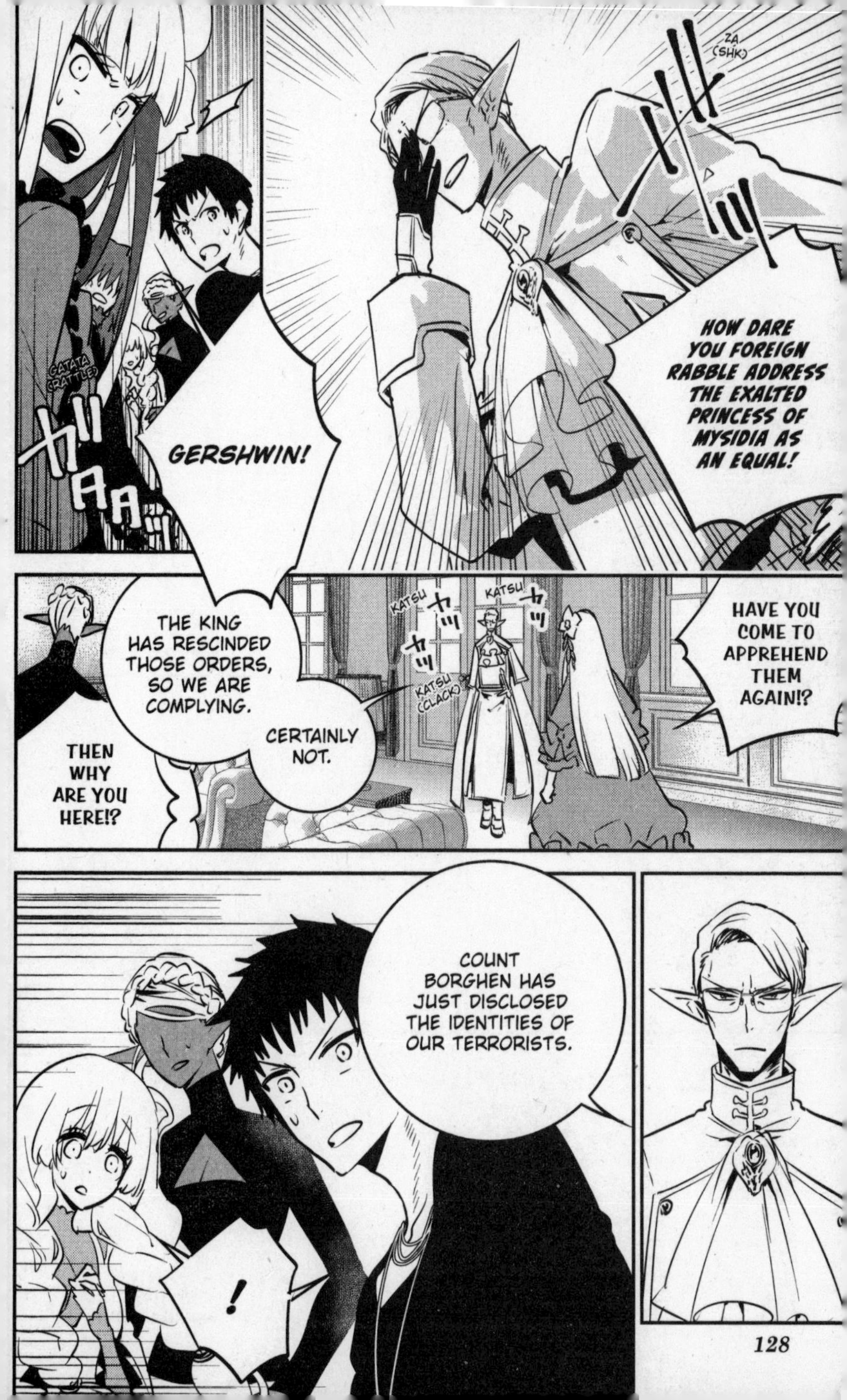
ZA (SHK)
HOW DARE YOU FOREIGN RABBLE ADDRESS THE EXALTED PRINCESS OF MYSIDIA AS AN EQUAL!
GERSHWIN!
GATATA (RATTLE)
HAVE YOU COME TO APPREHEND THEM AGAIN!?
KATSU
KATSU
KATSU (CLACK)
CERTAINLY NOT.
THE KING HAS RESCINDED THOSE ORDERS, SO WE ARE COMPLYING.
THEN WHY ARE YOU HERE!?
COUNT BORGHEN HAS JUST DISCLOSED THE IDENTITIES OF OUR TERRORISTS.
!

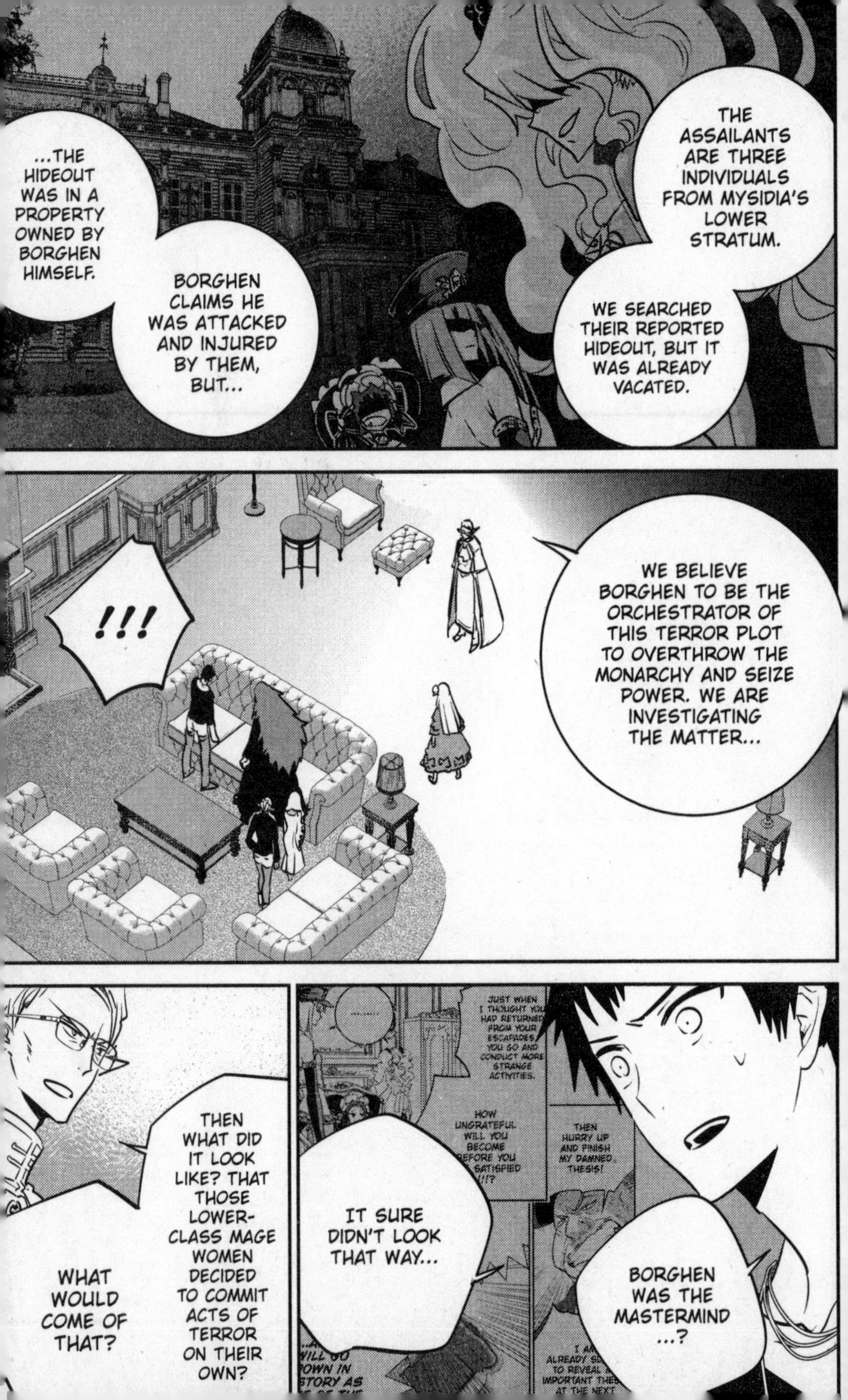
THE ASSAILANTS ARE THREE INDIVIDUALS FROM MYSIDIA'S LOWER STRATUM.
WE SEARCHED THEIR REPORTED HIDEOUT, BUT IT WAS ALREADY VACATED.
BORGHEN CLAIMS HE WAS ATTACKED AND INJURED BY THEM, BUT...
...THE HIDEOUT WAS IN A PROPERTY OWNED BY BORGHEN HIMSELF.
WE BELIEVE BORGHEN TO BE THE ORCHESTRATOR OF THIS TERROR PLOT TO OVERTHROW THE MONARCHY AND SEIZE POWER. WE ARE INVESTIGATING THE MATTER...
!!!
JUST WHEN I THOUGHT YOU HAD RETURNED FROM YOUR ESCAPADES, YOU GO AND CONDUCT MORE STRANGE ACTIVITIES.
THEN HURRY UP AND FINISH MY DAMNED THESIS!
BORGHEN WAS THE MASTERMIND ...?
IT SURE DIDN'T LOOK THAT WAY...
THEN WHAT DID IT LOOK LIKE? THAT THOSE LOWER-CLASS MAGE WOMEN DECIDED TO COMMIT ACTS OF TERROR ON THEIR OWN?
WHAT WOULD COME OF THAT?

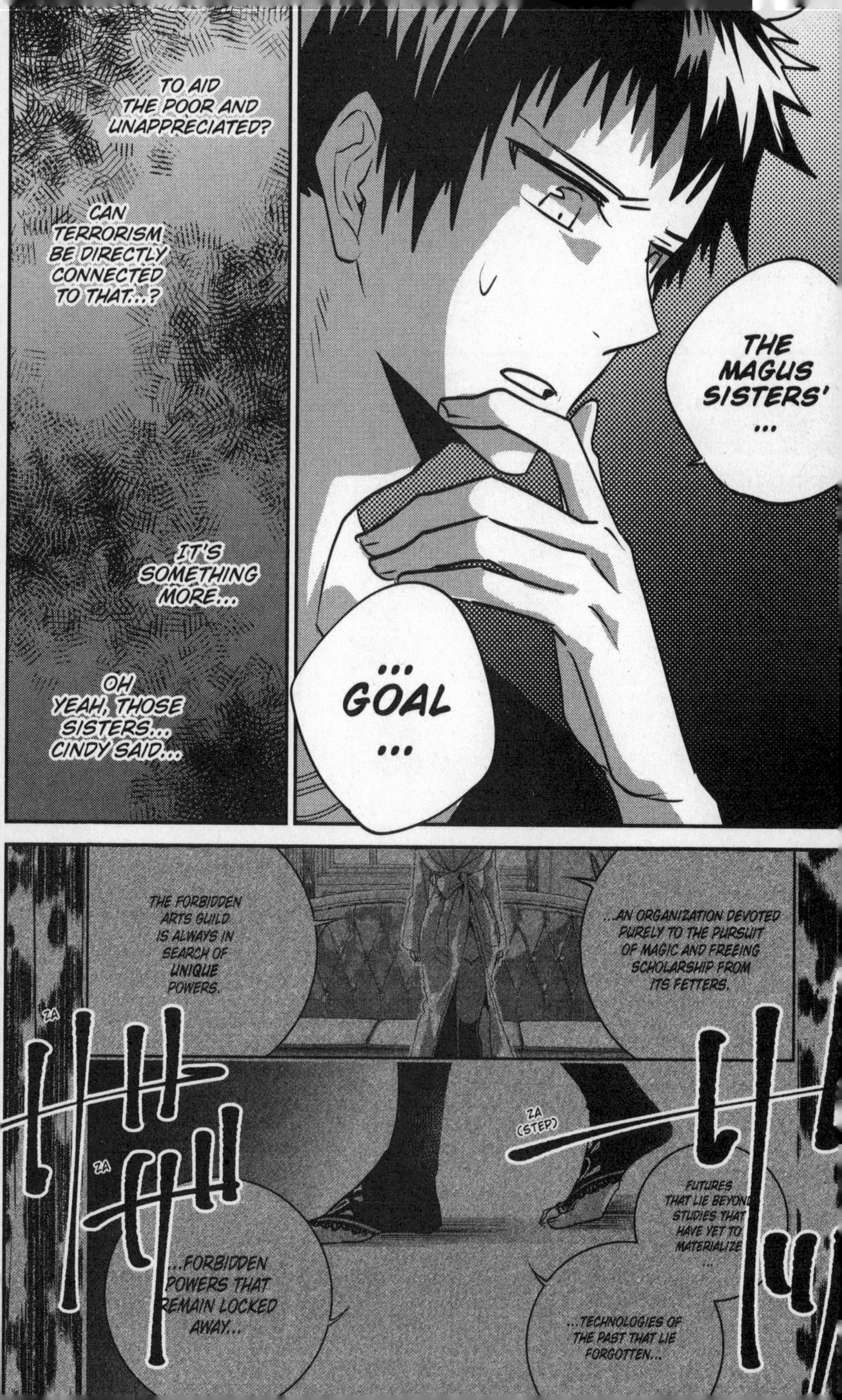
THE MAGUS SISTERS' ...
...GÖAL...
TO AID THE POOR AND UNAPPRECIATED?
CAN TERRORISM BE DIRECTLY CONNECTED TO THAT...?
IT'S SOMETHING MORE...
OH YEAH, THOSE SISTERS... CINDY SAID...
...AN ORGANIZATION DEVOTED PURELY TO THE PURSUIT OF MAGIC AND FREEING SCHOLARSHIP FROM ITS FETTERS.
THE FORBIDDEN ARTS GUILD IS ALWAYS IN SEARCH OF UNIQUE POWERS.
ZA
ZA (STEP)
FUTURES THAT LIE BEYOND STUDIES THAT HAVE YET TO MATERIALIZE...
...TECHNOLOGIES OF THE PAST THAT LIE FORGOTTEN...
ZA
...FORBIDDEN POWERS THAT REMAIN LOCKED AWAY...

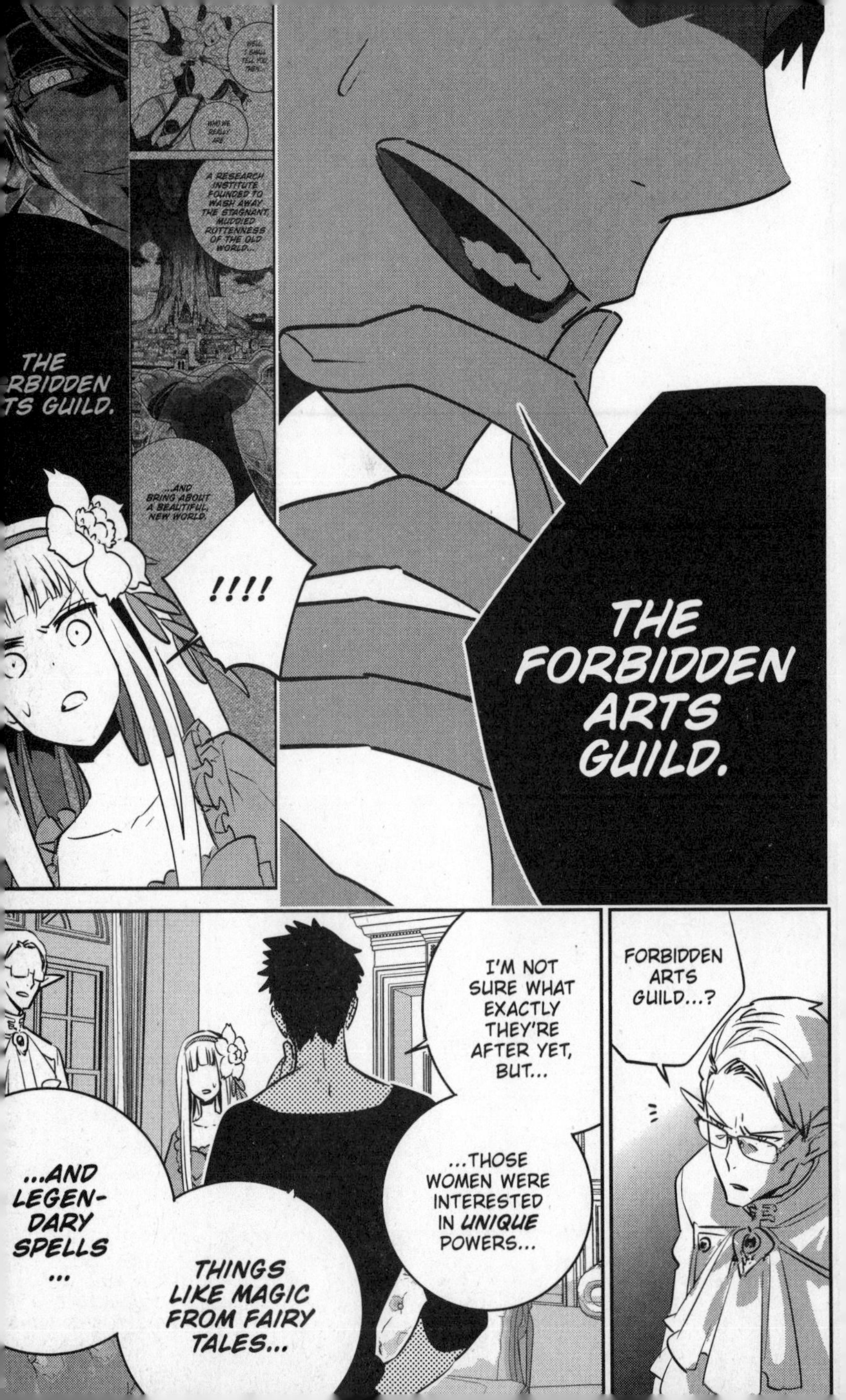
THE FORBIDDEN ARTS GUILD.
WELL, I SHALL TELL YOU, THEN...
WHO WE REALLY ARE
A RESEARCH INSTITUTE FOUNDED TO WASH AWAY THE STAGNANT, MUDDIED ROTTENNESS OF THE OLD WORLD...
...AND BRING ABOUT A BEAUTIFUL NEW WORLD.
THE FORBIDDEN ARTS GUILD.
!!!!
FORBIDDEN ARTS GUILD...?
I'M NOT SURE WHAT EXACTLY THEY'RE AFTER YET, BUT...
...THOSE WOMEN WERE INTERESTED IN *UNIQUE* POWERS...
THINGS LIKE MAGIC FROM FAIRY TALES...
...AND LEGEN-DARY SPELLS ...

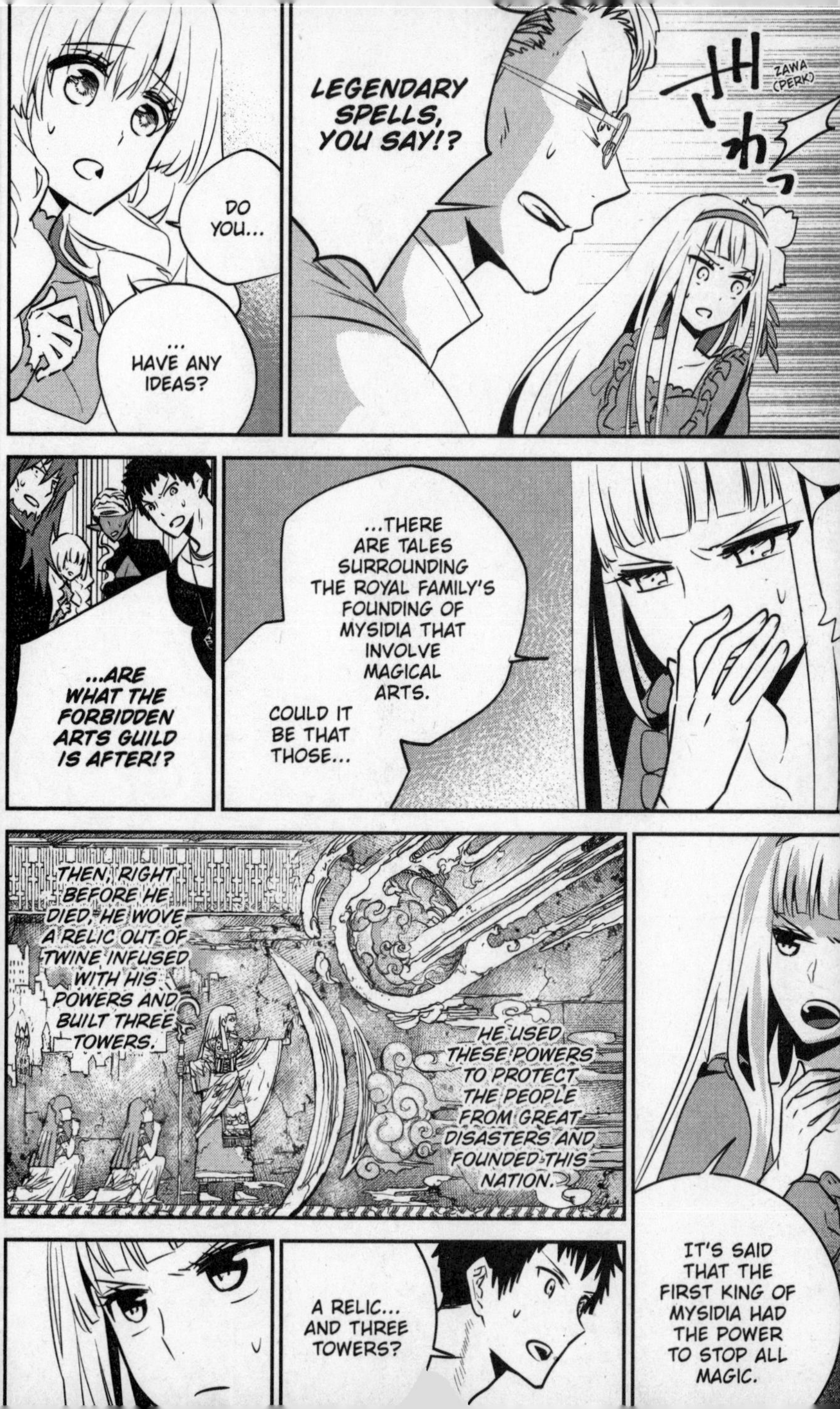
LEGENDARY SPELLS, YOU SAY!?
ZAWA (PERK)
DO YOU...
...HAVE ANY IDEAS?
...THERE ARE TALES SURROUNDING THE ROYAL FAMILY'S FOUNDING OF MYSIDIA THAT INVOLVE MAGICAL ARTS.
COULD IT BE THAT THOSE...
...ARE WHAT THE FORBIDDEN ARTS GUILD IS AFTER!?
IT'S SAID THAT THE FIRST KING OF MYSIDIA HAD THE POWER TO STOP ALL MAGIC.
HE USED THESE POWERS TO PROTECT THE PEOPLE FROM GREAT DISASTERS AND FOUNDED THIS NATION.
THEN, RIGHT BEFORE HE DIED, HE WOVE A RELIC OUT OF TWINE INFUSED WITH HIS POWERS AND BUILT THREE TOWERS.
A RELIC... AND THREE TOWERS?

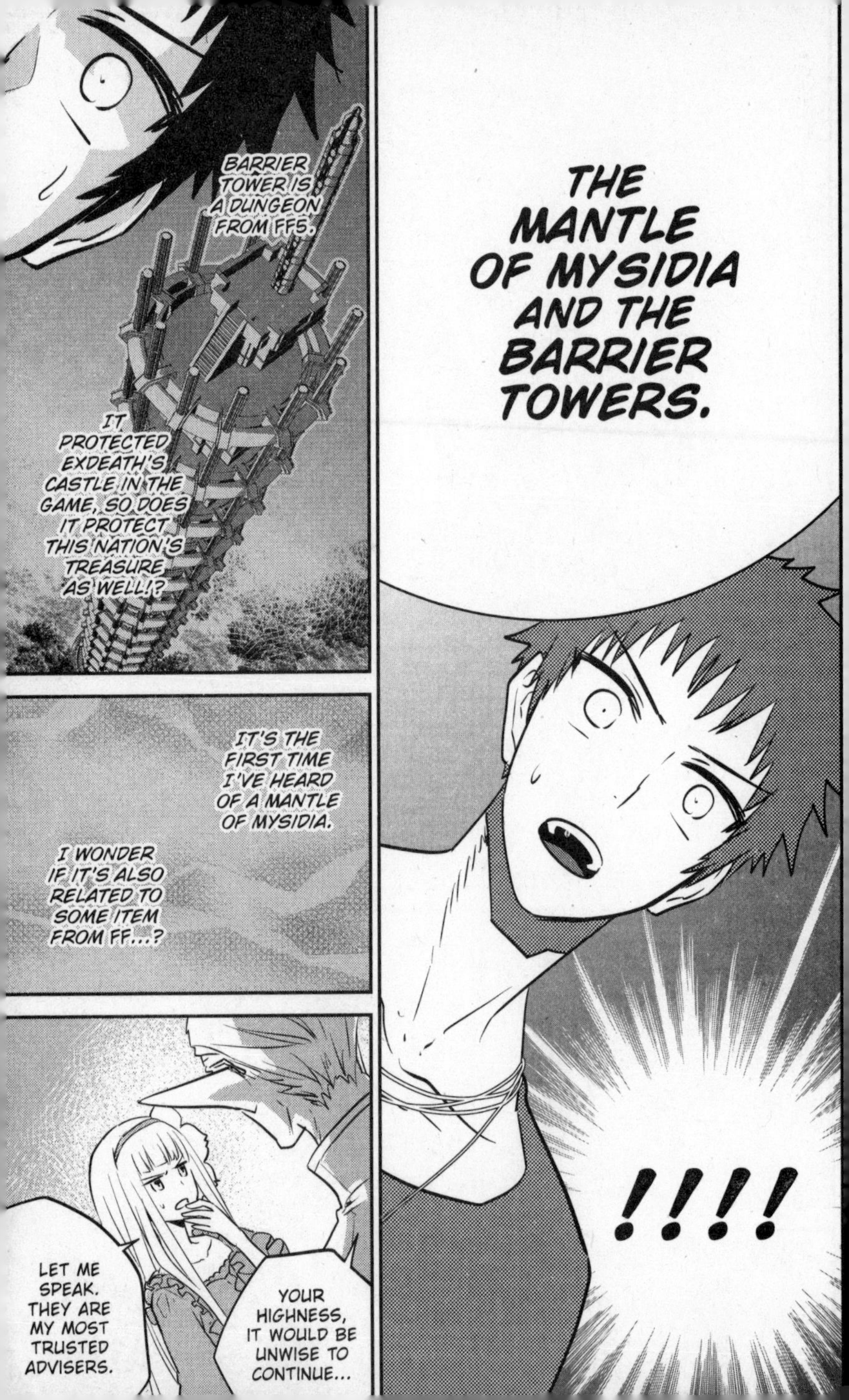
THE MANTLE OF MYSIDIA AND THE BARRIER TOWERS.
!!!!
BARRIER TOWER IS A DUNGEON FROM FF5.
IT PROTECTED EXDEATH'S CASTLE IN THE GAME, SO DOES IT PROTECT THIS NATION'S TREASURE AS WELL!?
IT'S THE FIRST TIME I'VE HEARD OF A MANTLE OF MYSIDIA.
I WONDER IF IT'S ALSO RELATED TO SOME ITEM FROM FF...?
YOUR HIGHNESS, IT WOULD BE UNWISE TO CONTINUE...
LET ME SPEAK. THEY ARE MY MOST TRUSTED ADVISERS.

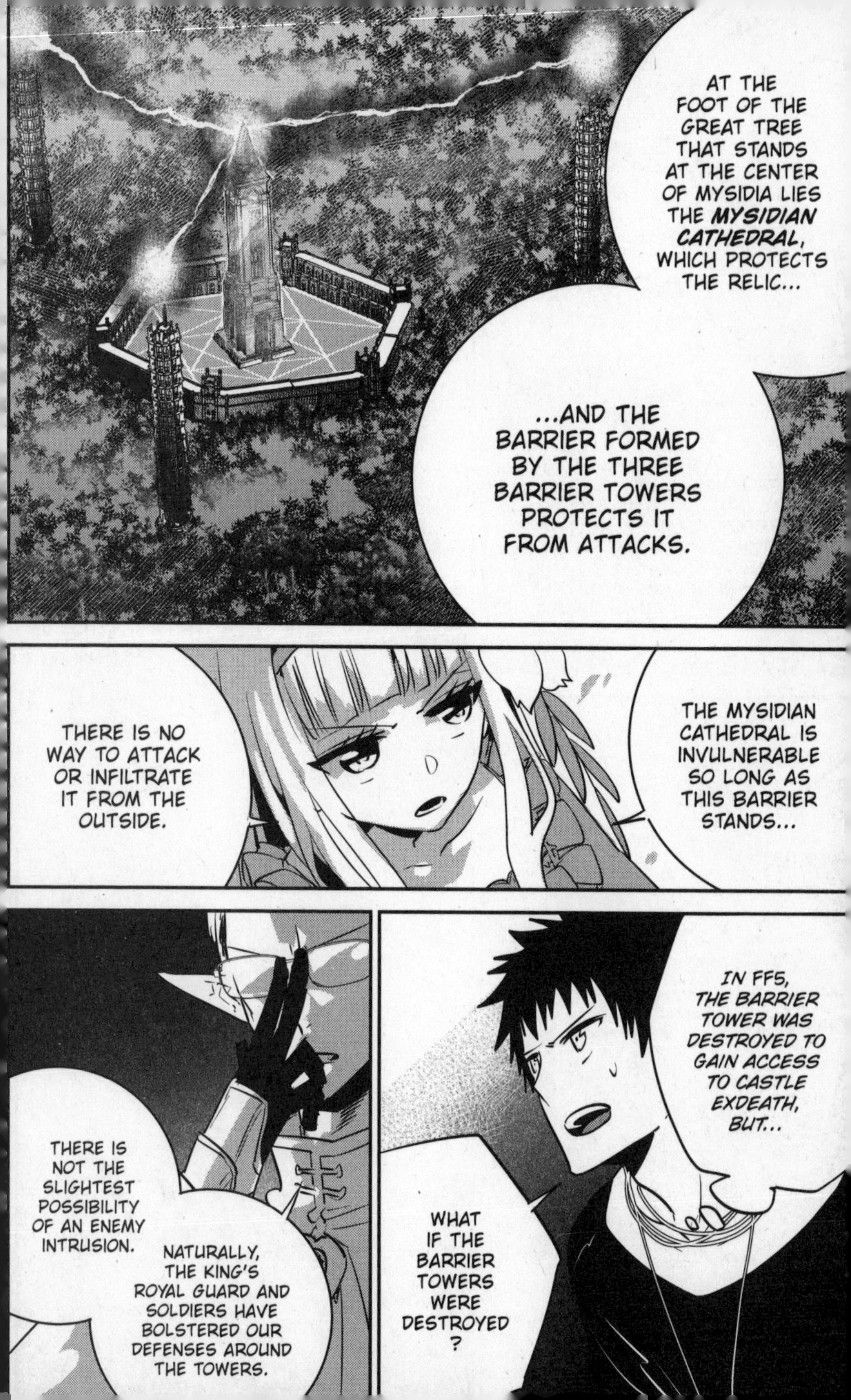
AT THE FOOT OF THE GREAT TREE THAT STANDS AT THE CENTER OF MYSIDIA LIES THE ***MYSIDIAN CATHEDRAL***, WHICH PROTECTS THE RELIC...
...AND THE BARRIER FORMED BY THE THREE BARRIER TOWERS PROTECTS IT FROM ATTACKS.
THE MYSIDIAN CATHEDRAL IS INVULNERABLE SO LONG AS THIS BARRIER STANDS...
THERE IS NO WAY TO ATTACK OR INFILTRATE IT FROM THE OUTSIDE.
IN FF5, THE BARRIER TOWER WAS DESTROYED TO GAIN ACCESS TO CASTLE EXDEATH, BUT...
WHAT IF THE BARRIER TOWERS WERE DESTROYED ?
THERE IS NOT THE SLIGHTEST POSSIBILITY OF AN ENEMY INTRUSION.
NATURALLY, THE KING'S ROYAL GUARD AND SOLDIERS HAVE BOLSTERED OUR DEFENSES AROUND THE TOWERS.

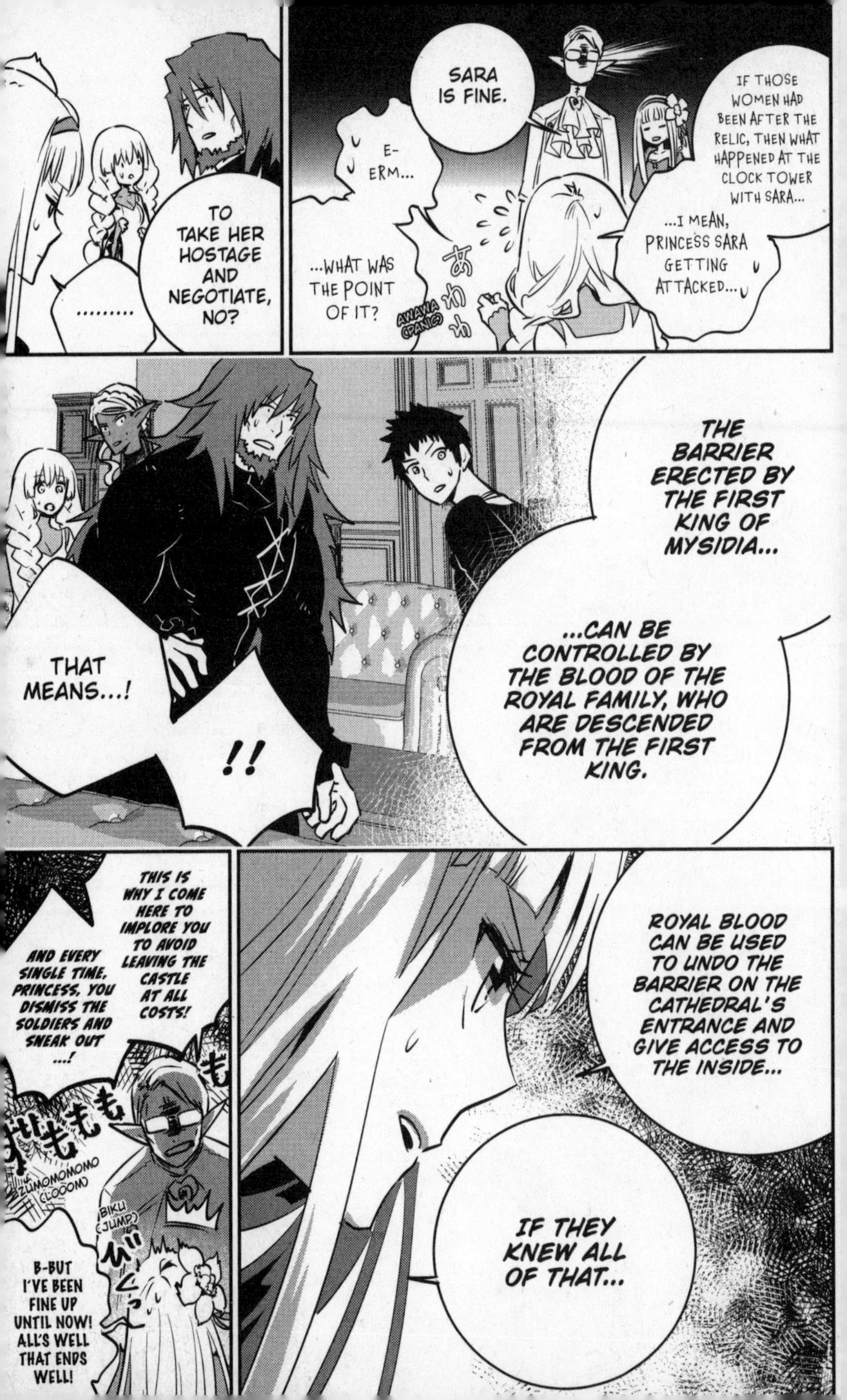

IF THOSE WOMEN HAD BEEN AFTER THE RELIC, THEN WHAT HAPPENED AT THE CLOCK TOWER WITH SARA...
SARA IS FINE.
E-ERM...
...I MEAN, PRINCESS SARA GETTING ATTACKED...
あわわ
AWAWA (PANIC)
...WHAT WAS THE POINT OF IT?
TO TAKE HER HOSTAGE AND NEGOTIATE, NO?
....
THE BARRIER ERECTED BY THE FIRST KING OF MYSIDIA...
...CAN BE CONTROLLED BY THE BLOOD OF THE ROYAL FAMILY, WHO ARE DESCENDED FROM THE FIRST KING.
!!
THAT MEANS...!
ROYAL BLOOD CAN BE USED TO UNDO THE BARRIER ON THE CATHEDRAL'S ENTRANCE AND GIVE ACCESS TO THE INSIDE...
IF THEY KNEW ALL OF THAT...
THIS IS WHY I COME HERE TO IMPLORE YOU TO AVOID LEAVING THE CASTLE AT ALL COSTS!
AND EVERY SINGLE TIME, PRINCESS, YOU DISMISS THE SOLDIERS AND SNEAK OUT ...!
ZUMOMOMOMO (LOOOM)
BIKU (JUMP)
B-BUT I'VE BEEN FINE UP UNTIL NOW! ALL'S WELL THAT ENDS WELL!

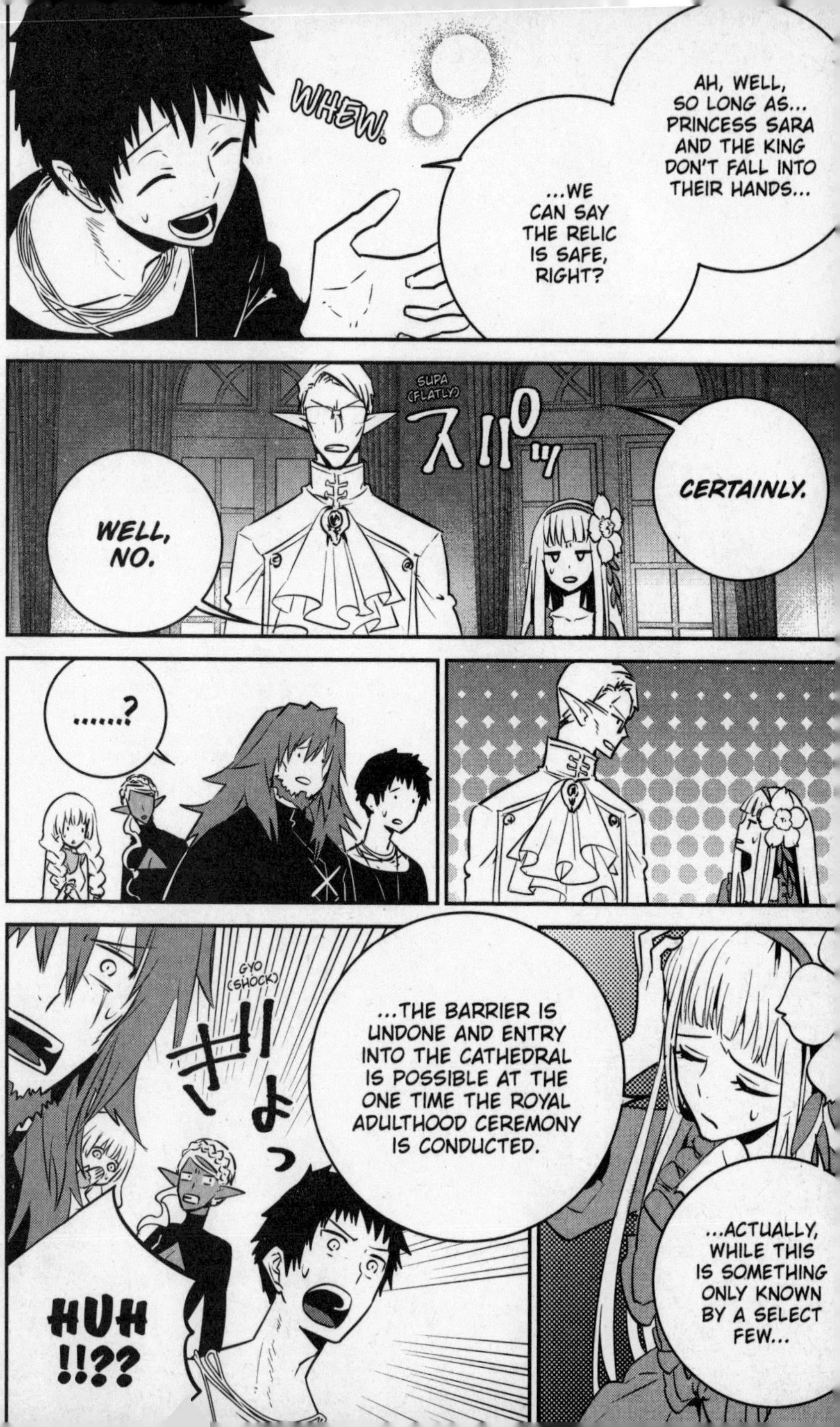
AH, WELL, SO LONG AS... PRINCESS SARA AND THE KING DON'T FALL INTO THEIR HANDS...
...WE CAN SAY THE RELIC IS SAFE, RIGHT?
WHEW.
CERTAINLY.
SUPA (FLATLY)
WELL, NO.
......?
...ACTUALLY, WHILE THIS IS SOMETHING ONLY KNOWN BY A SELECT FEW...
...THE BARRIER IS UNDONE AND ENTRY INTO THE CATHEDRAL IS POSSIBLE AT THE ONE TIME THE ROYAL ADULTHOOD CEREMONY IS CONDUCTED.
GYO (SHOCK)
HUH !!??

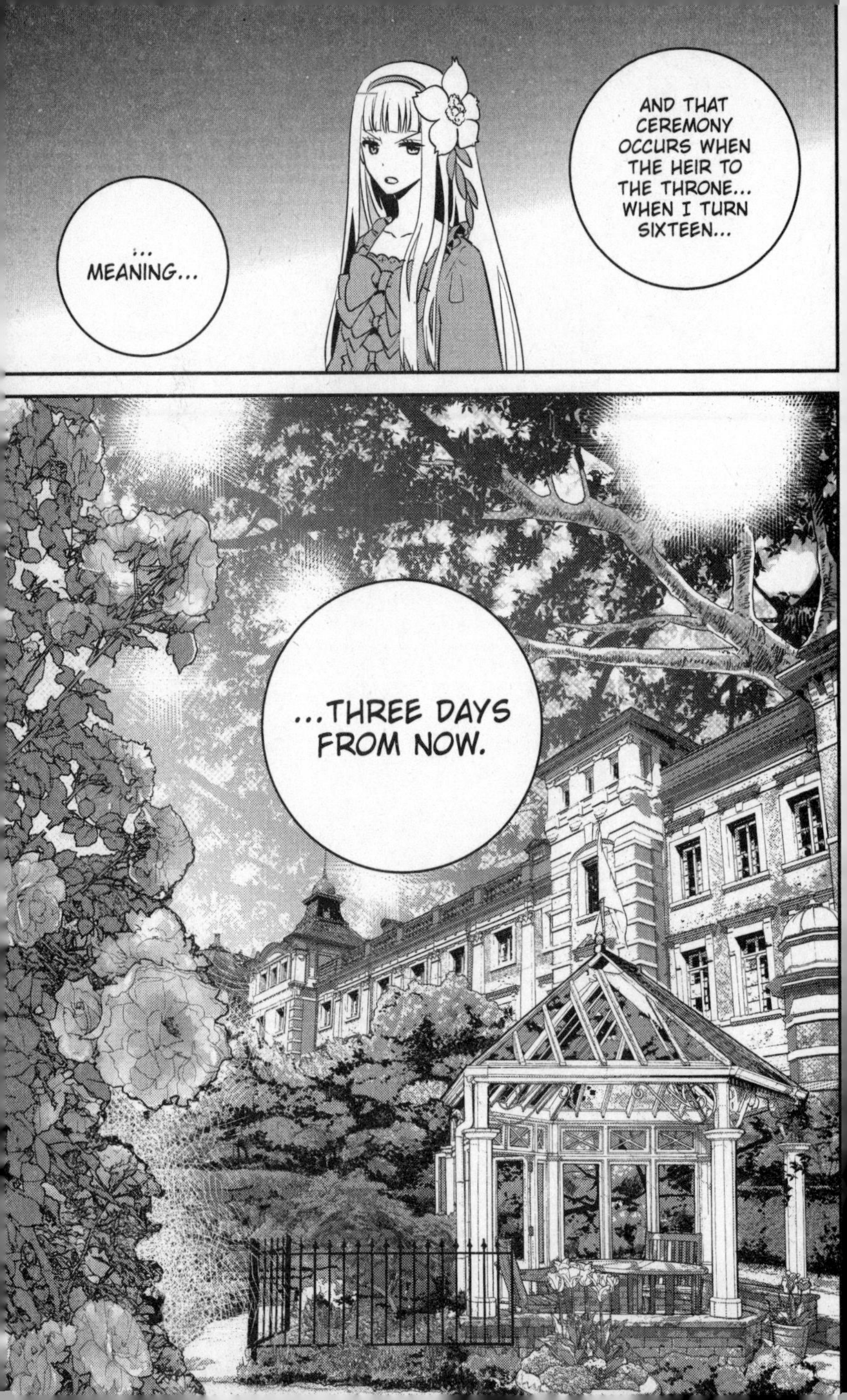
AND THAT CEREMONY OCCURS WHEN THE HEIR TO THE THRONE... WHEN I TURN SIXTEEN...
...
MEANING...
...THREE DAYS FROM NOW.

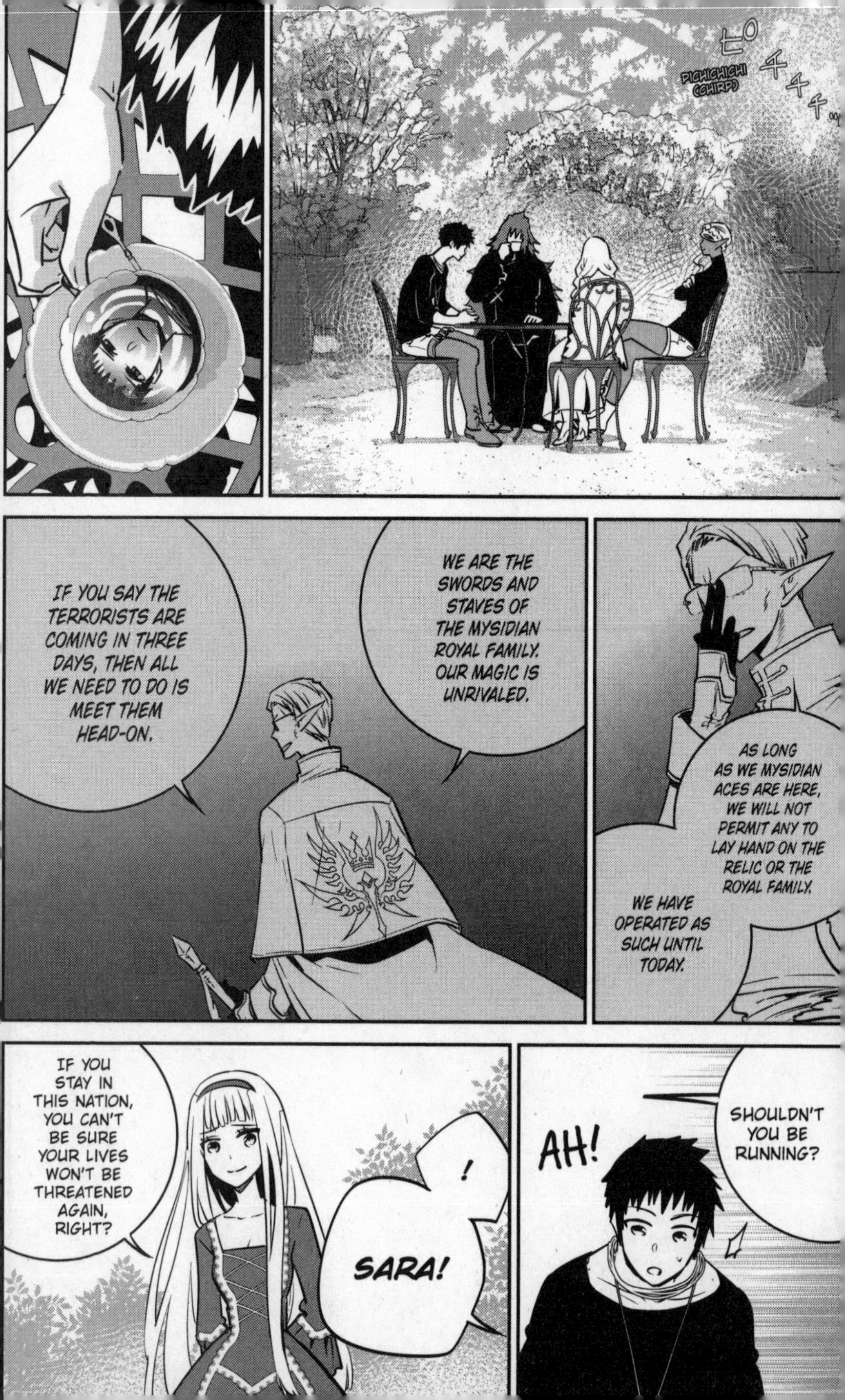

PICHICHICHI (CHIRP)
AS LONG AS WE MYSIDIAN ACES ARE HERE, WE WILL NOT PERMIT ANY TO LAY HAND ON THE RELIC OR THE ROYAL FAMILY.
WE HAVE OPERATED AS SUCH UNTIL TODAY.
WE ARE THE SWORDS AND STAVES OF THE MYSIDIAN ROYAL FAMILY. OUR MAGIC IS UNRIVALED.
IF YOU SAY THE TERRORISTS ARE COMING IN THREE DAYS, THEN ALL WE NEED TO DO IS MEET THEM HEAD-ON.
SHOULDN'T YOU BE RUNNING?
AH!
!
SARA!
IF YOU STAY IN THIS NATION, YOU CAN'T BE SURE YOUR LIVES WON'T BE THREATENED AGAIN, RIGHT?

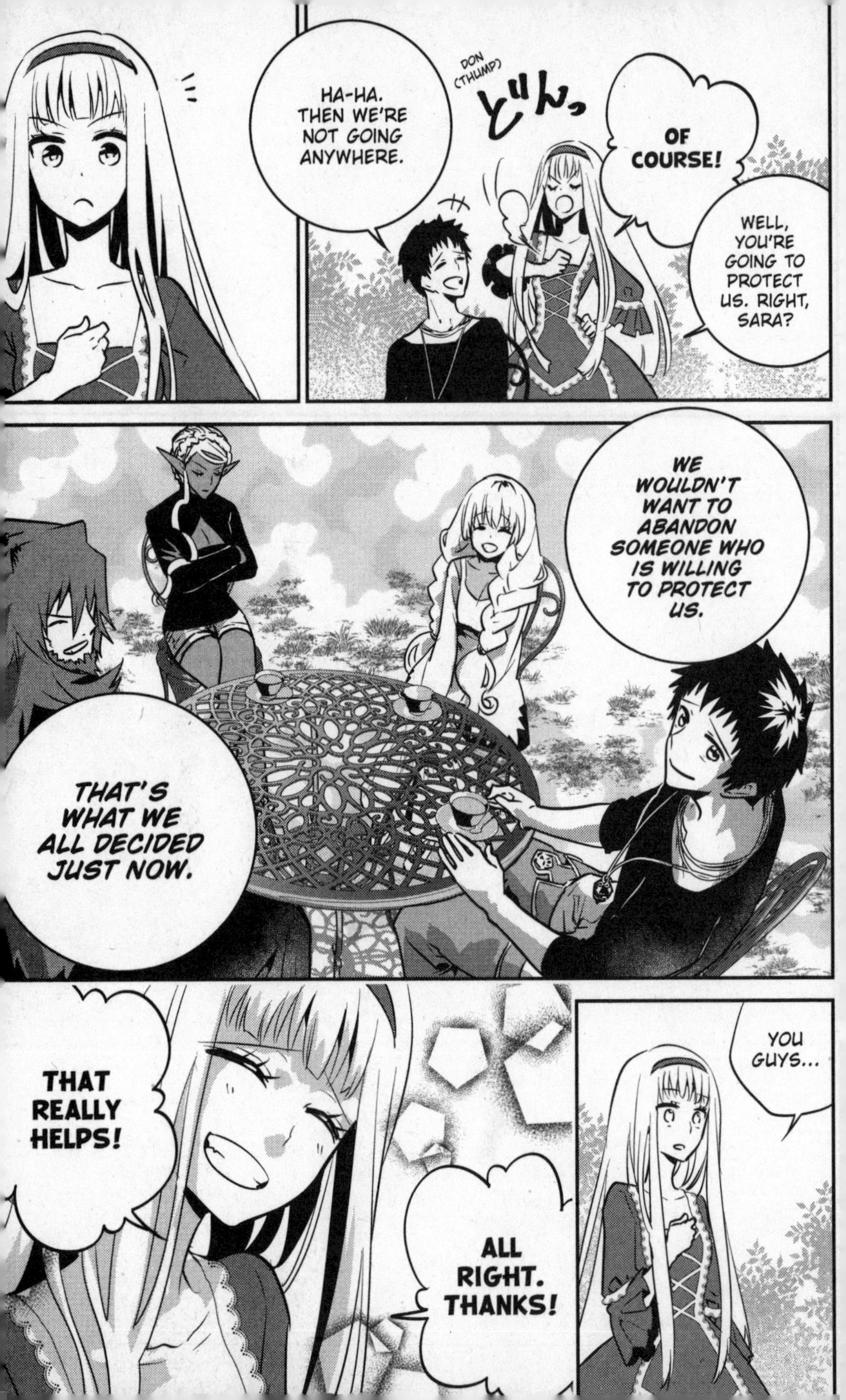
WELL, YOU'RE GOING TO PROTECT US. RIGHT, SARA?
OF COURSE!
DON (THUMP)
どりんっ
HA-HA. THEN WE'RE NOT GOING ANYWHERE.
WE WOULDN'T WANT TO ABANDON SOMEONE WHO IS WILLING TO PROTECT US.
THAT'S WHAT WE ALL DECIDED JUST NOW.
YOU GUYS...
ALL RIGHT. THANKS!
THAT REALLY HELPS!

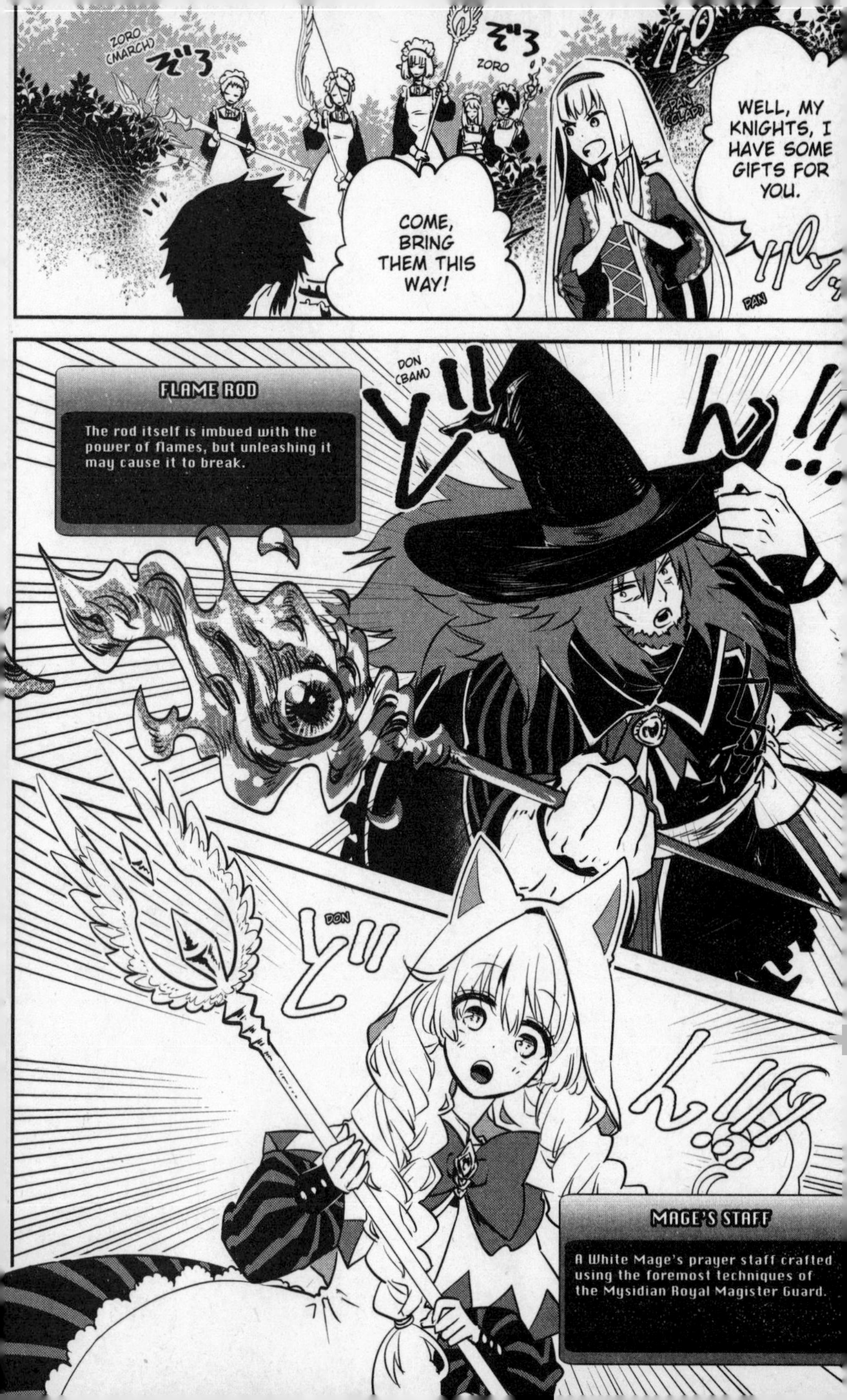
PAN (CLAP)
WELL, MY KNIGHTS, I HAVE SOME GIFTS FOR YOU.
PAN
ZORO
COME, BRING THEM THIS WAY!
ZORO (MARCH)
DON (BAM)
FLAME ROD
The rod itself is imbued with the power of flames, but unleashing it may cause it to break.
DON
MAGE'S STAFF
A White Mage's prayer staff crafted using the foremost techniques of the Mysidian Royal Magister Guard.

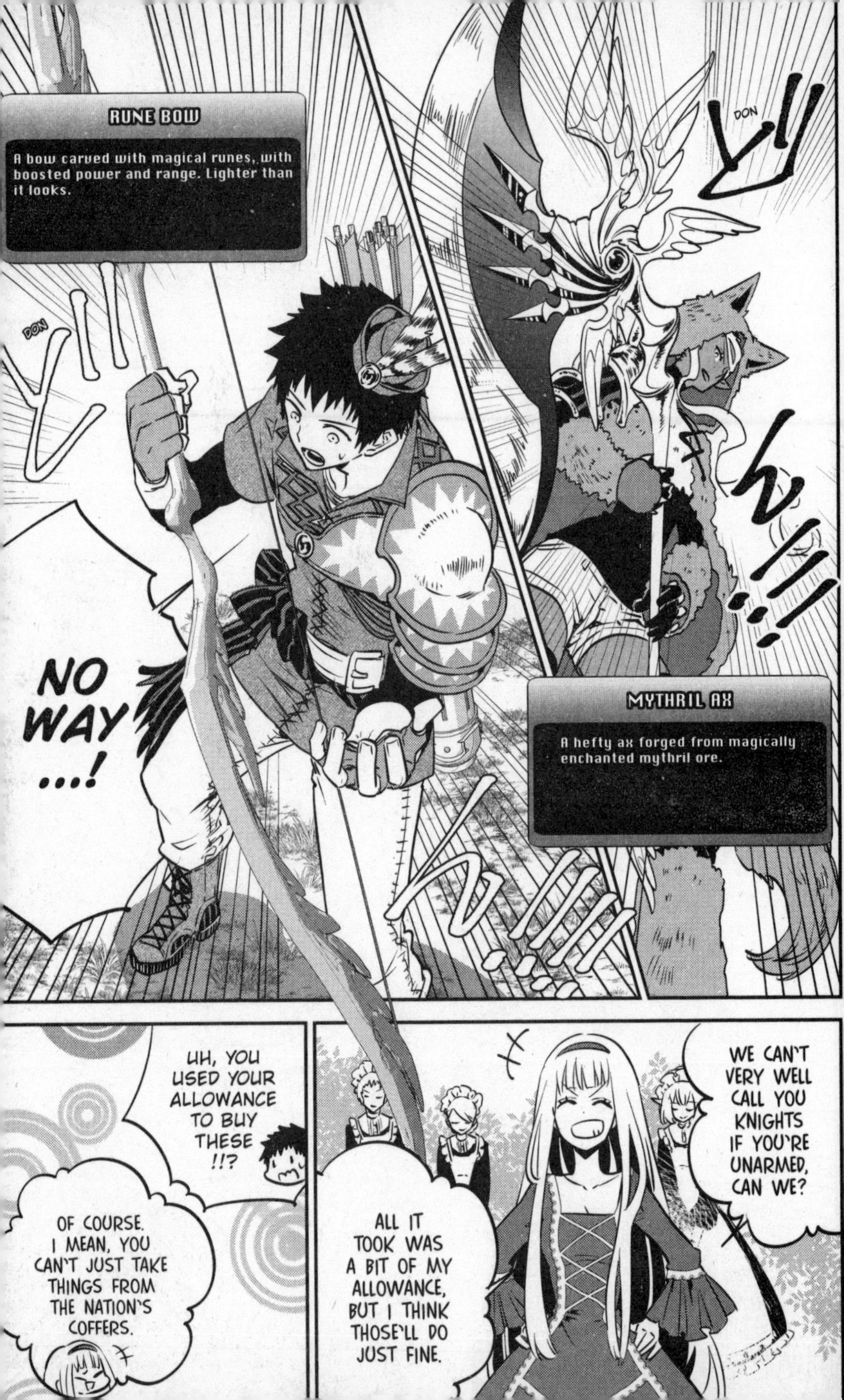
DON
ZU!
MYTHRIL AX
A hefty ax forged from magically enchanted mythril ore.
DON
ZU!!
RUNE BOW
A bow carved with magical runes, with boosted power and range. Lighter than it looks.
NO WAY ...!
WE CAN'T VERY WELL CALL YOU KNIGHTS IF YOU'RE UNARMED, CAN WE?
ALL IT TOOK WAS A BIT OF MY ALLOWANCE, BUT I THINK THOSE'LL DO JUST FINE.
UH, YOU USED YOUR ALLOWANCE TO BUY THESE !!?
OF COURSE. I MEAN, YOU CAN'T JUST TAKE THINGS FROM THE NATION'S COFFERS.

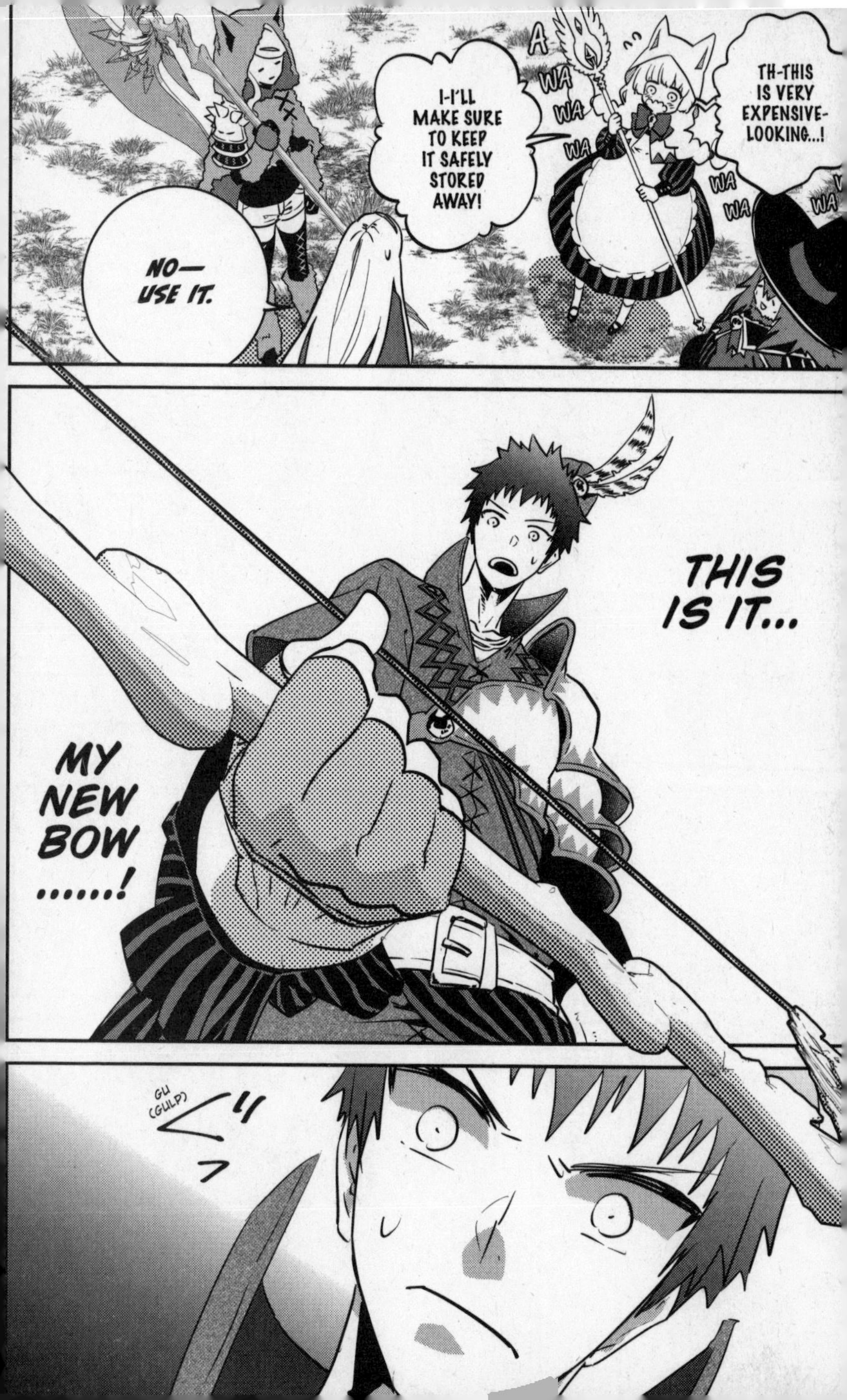
TH-THIS IS VERY EXPENSIVE-LOOKING...!
A WA WA WA WA WA WA
I-I'LL MAKE SURE TO KEEP IT SAFELY STORED AWAY!
NO— USE IT.
THIS IS IT...
MY NEW BOW ......!
GU (GULP)

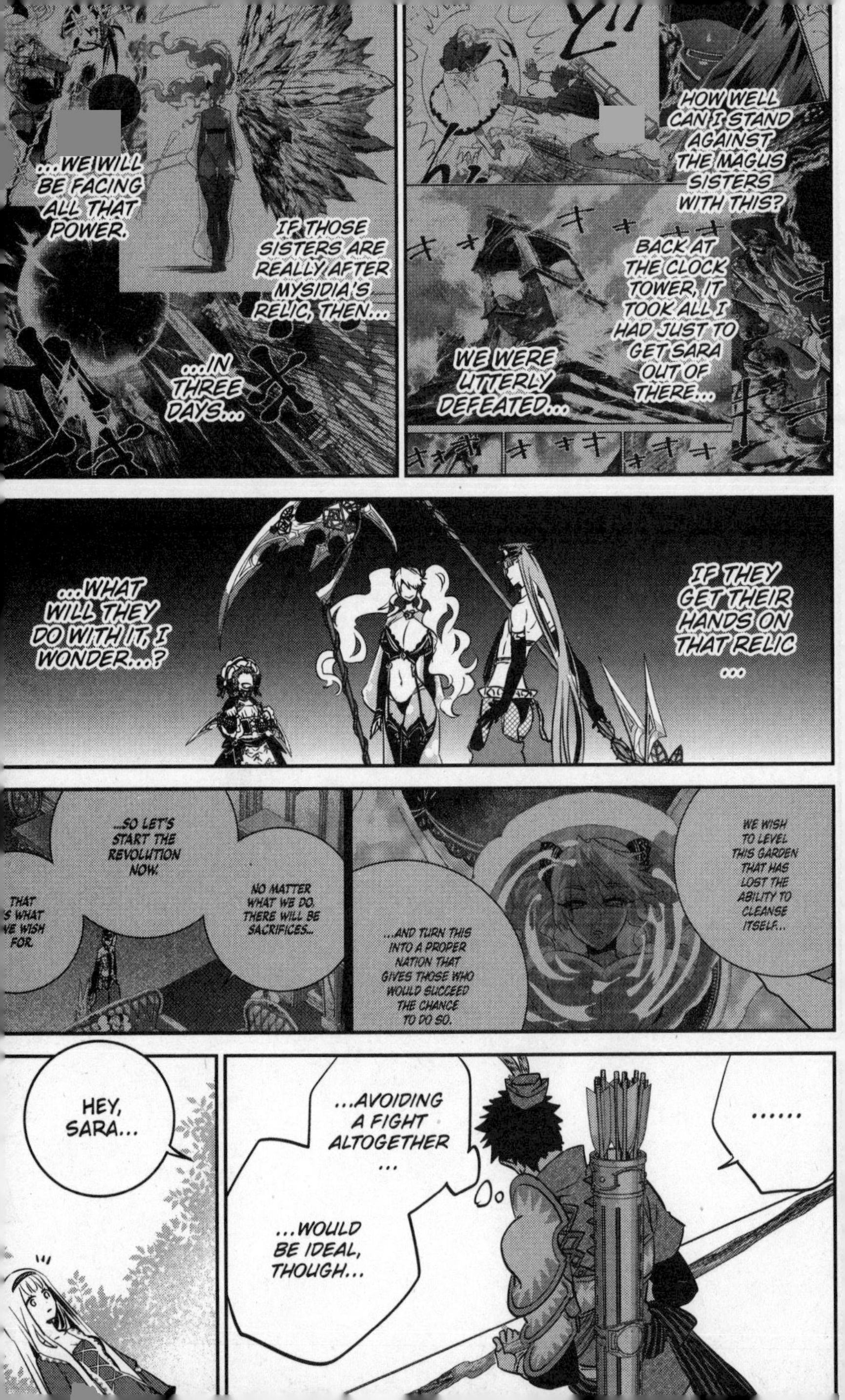
HOW WELL CAN I STAND AGAINST THE MAGUS SISTERS WITH THIS?
BACK AT THE CLOCK TOWER, IT TOOK ALL I HAD JUST TO GET SARA OUT OF THERE...
WE WERE UTTERLY DEFEATED...
IF THOSE SISTERS ARE REALLY AFTER MYSIDIA'S RELIC, THEN...
...IN THREE DAYS...
...WE WILL BE FACING ALL THAT POWER.
IF THEY GET THEIR HANDS ON THAT RELIC ...
...WHAT WILL THEY DO WITH IT, I WONDER...?
WE WISH TO LEVEL THIS GARDEN THAT HAS LOST THE ABILITY TO CLEANSE ITSELF...
...AND TURN THIS INTO A PROPER NATION THAT GIVES THOSE WHO WOULD SUCCEED THE CHANCE TO DO SO.
NO MATTER WHAT WE DO, THERE WILL BE SACRIFICES...
...SO LET'S START THE REVOLUTION NOW.
......
...AVOIDING A FIGHT ALTOGETHER ...
...WOULD BE IDEAL, THOUGH...
HEY, SARA...

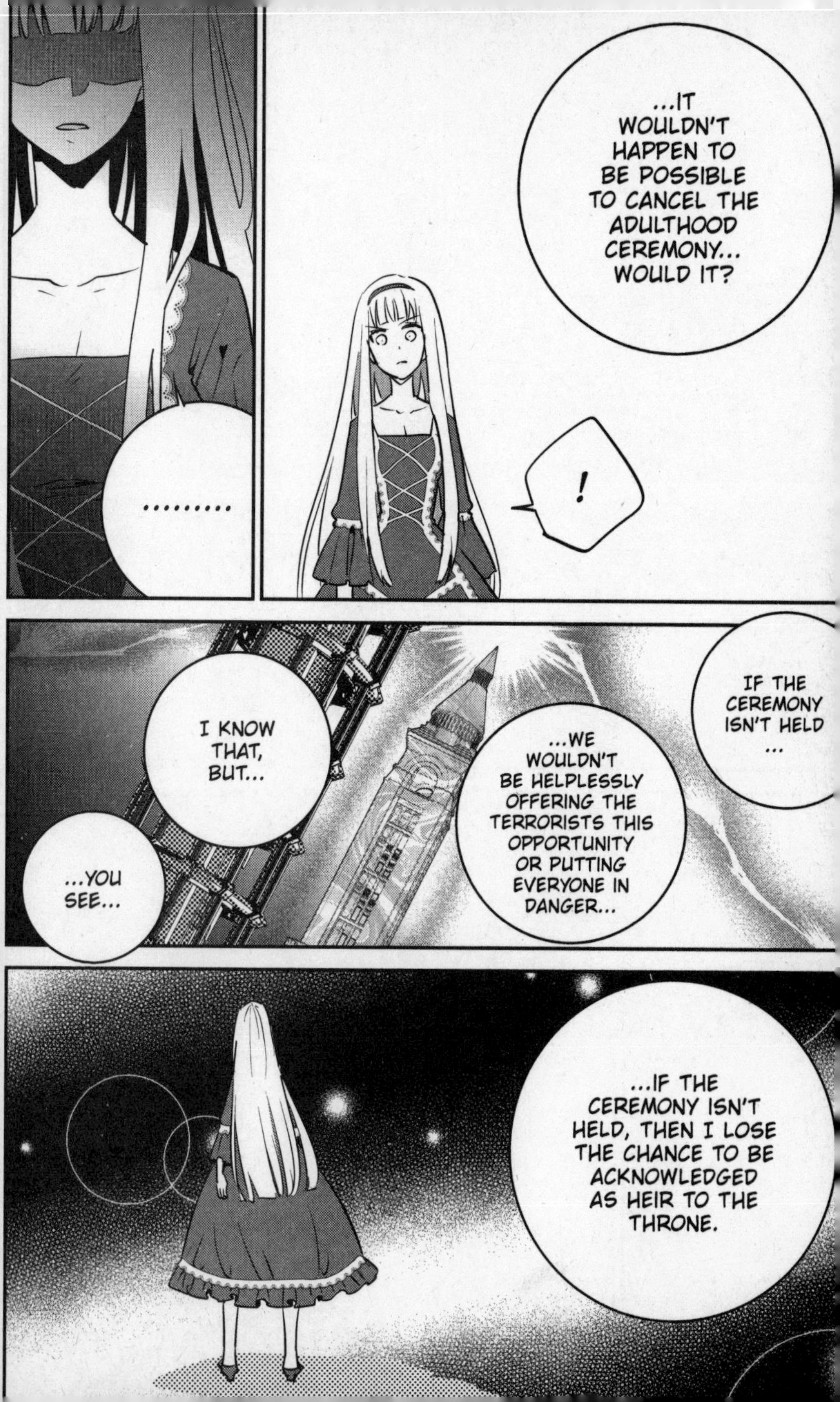
...IT WOULDN'T HAPPEN TO BE POSSIBLE TO CANCEL THE ADULTHOOD CEREMONY... WOULD IT?
!
....
IF THE CEREMONY ISN'T HELD ...
...WE WOULDN'T BE HELPLESSLY OFFERING THE TERRORISTS THIS OPPORTUNITY OR PUTTING EVERYONE IN DANGER...
I KNOW THAT, BUT...
...YOU SEE...
...IF THE CEREMONY ISN'T HELD, THEN I LOSE THE CHANCE TO BE ACKNOWLEDGED AS HEIR TO THE THRONE.

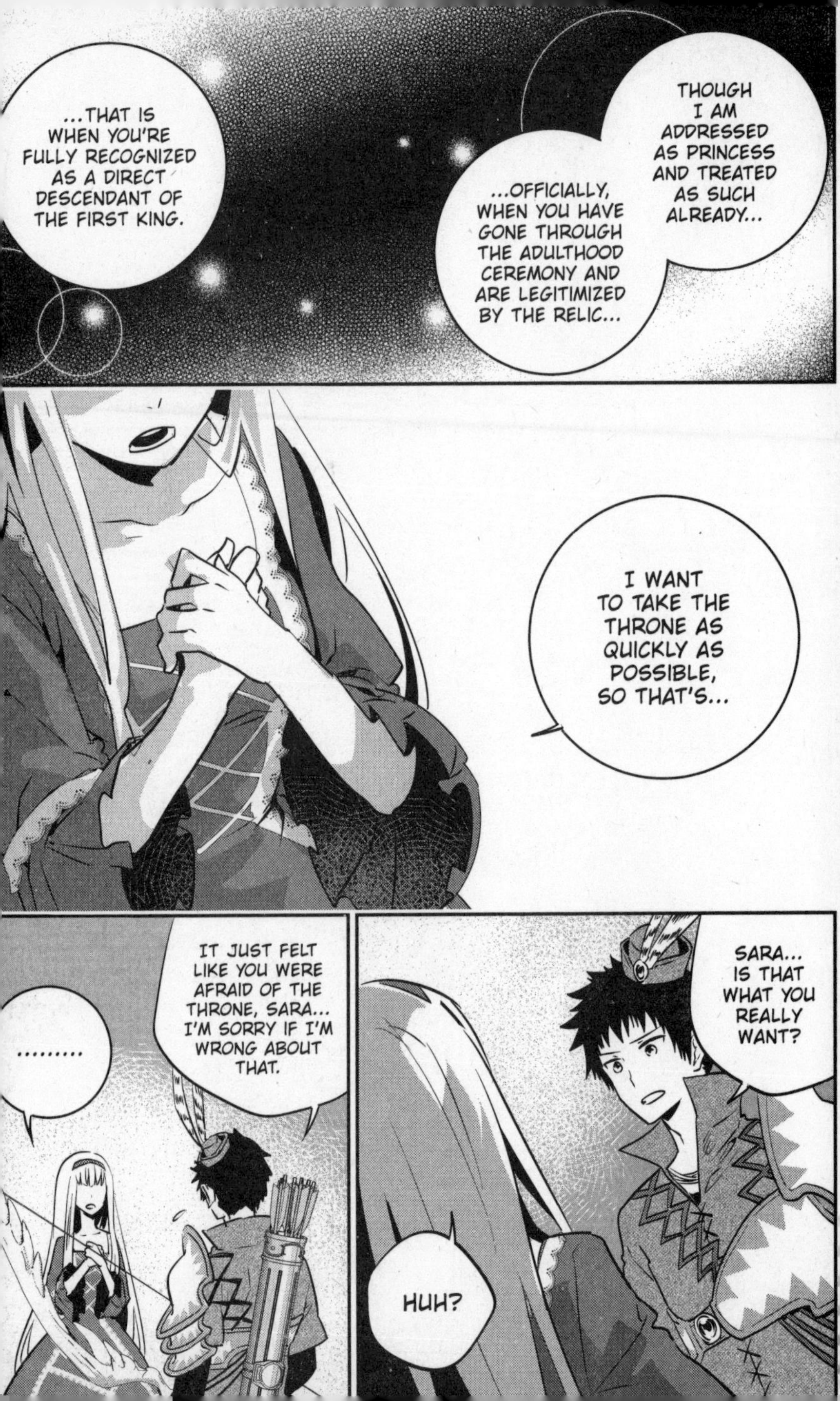
THOUGH I AM ADDRESSED AS PRINCESS AND TREATED AS SUCH ALREADY...
...OFFICIALLY, WHEN YOU HAVE GONE THROUGH THE ADULTHOOD CEREMONY AND ARE LEGITIMIZED BY THE RELIC...
...THAT IS WHEN YOU'RE FULLY RECOGNIZED AS A DIRECT DESCENDANT OF THE FIRST KING.
I WANT TO TAKE THE THRONE AS QUICKLY AS POSSIBLE, SO THAT'S...
SARA... IS THAT WHAT YOU REALLY WANT?
HUH?
IT JUST FELT LIKE YOU WERE AFRAID OF THE THRONE, SARA... I'M SORRY IF I'M WRONG ABOUT THAT.
....

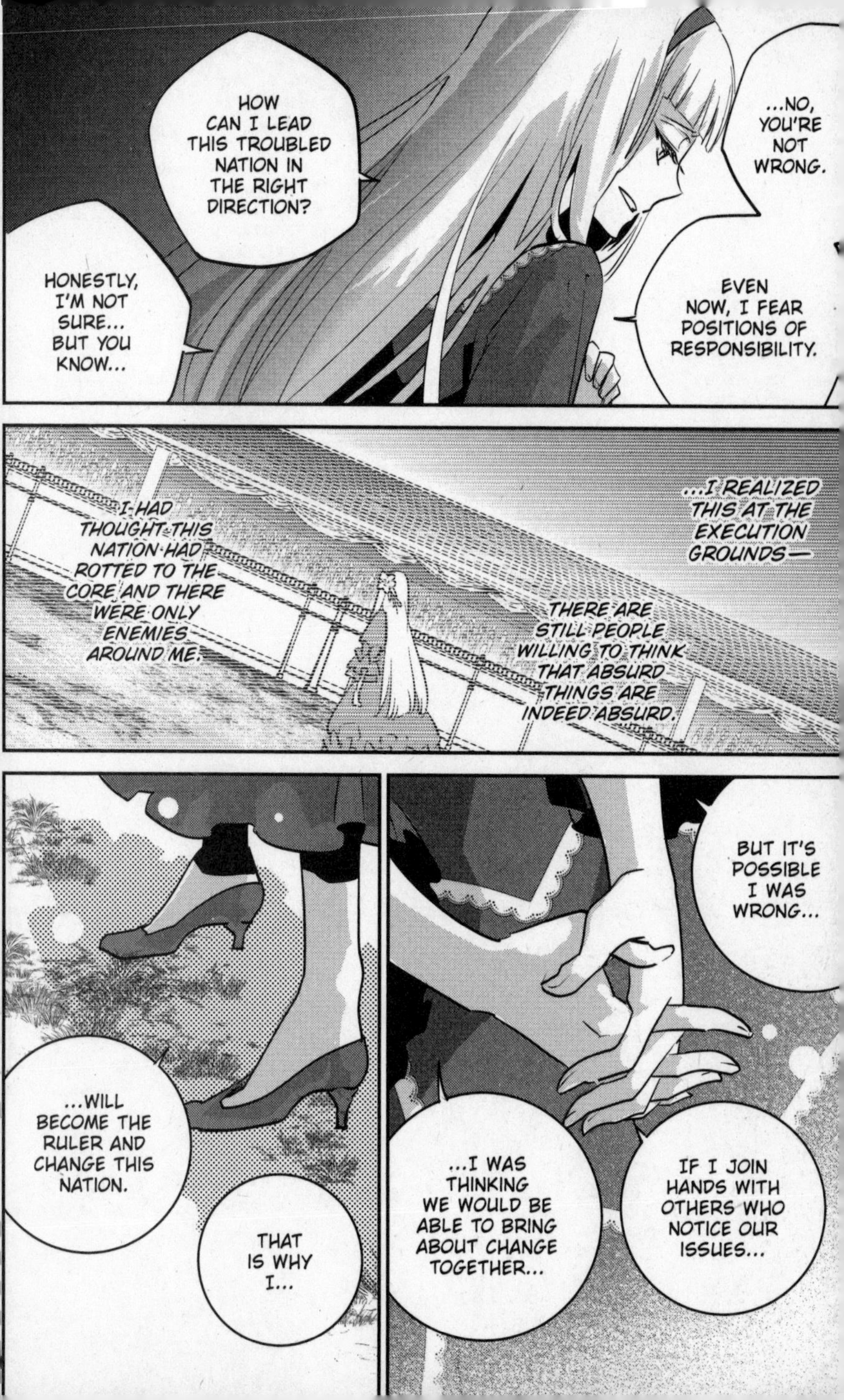
...NO, YOU'RE NOT WRONG.
EVEN NOW, I FEAR POSITIONS OF RESPONSIBILITY.
HOW CAN I LEAD THIS TROUBLED NATION IN THE RIGHT DIRECTION?
HONESTLY, I'M NOT SURE... BUT YOU KNOW...
...I REALIZED THIS AT THE EXECUTION GROUNDS—
THERE ARE STILL PEOPLE WILLING TO THINK THAT ABSURD THINGS ARE INDEED ABSURD.
I HAD THOUGHT THIS NATION HAD ROTTED TO THE CORE AND THERE WERE ONLY ENEMIES AROUND ME.
BUT IT'S POSSIBLE I WAS WRONG...
IF I JOIN HANDS WITH OTHERS WHO NOTICE OUR ISSUES...
...I WAS THINKING WE WOULD BE ABLE TO BRING ABOUT CHANGE TOGETHER...
...WILL BECOME THE RULER AND CHANGE THIS NATION.
THAT IS WHY I...

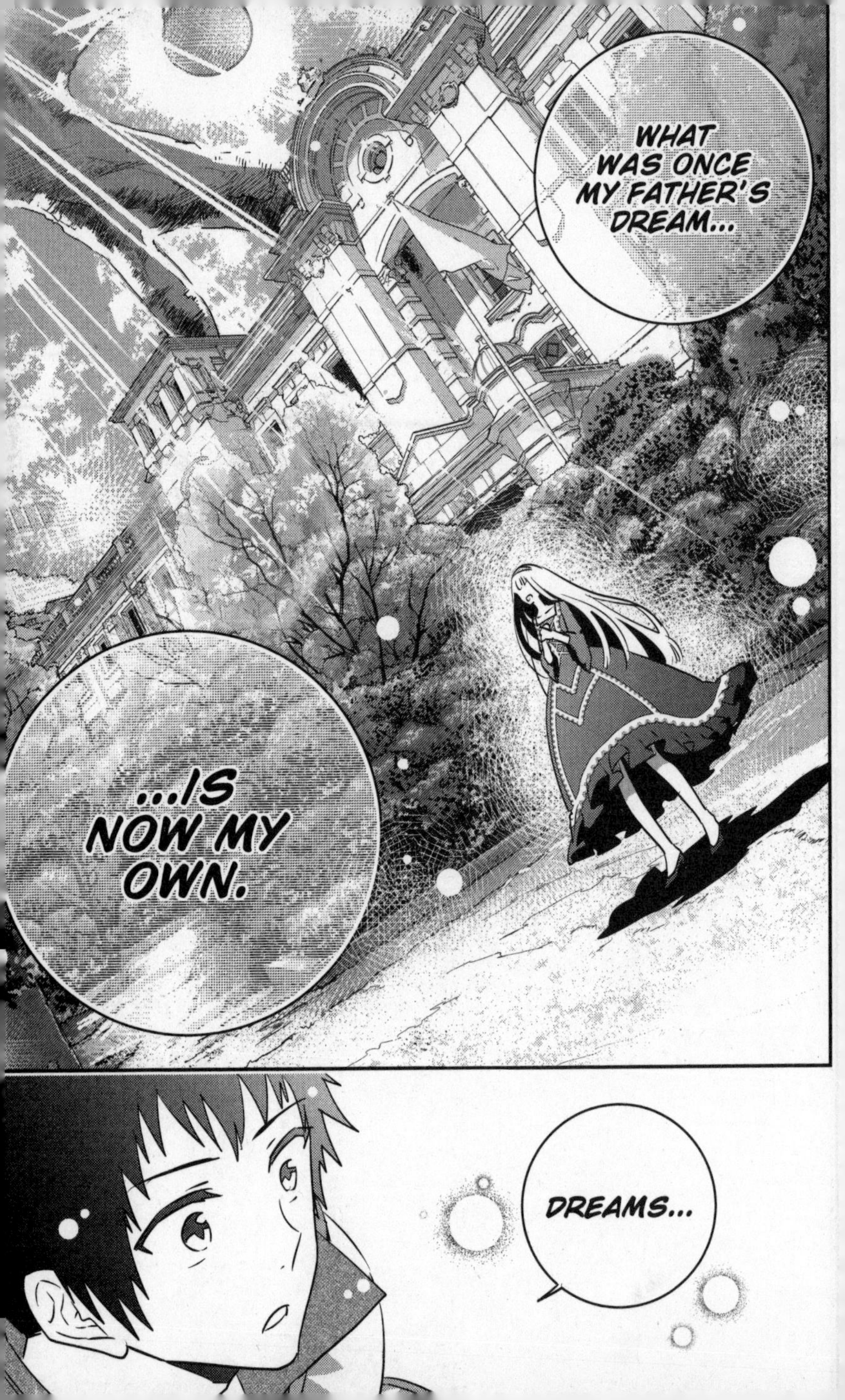
WHAT WAS ONCE MY FATHER'S DREAM...
...IS NOW MY OWN.
DREAMS...

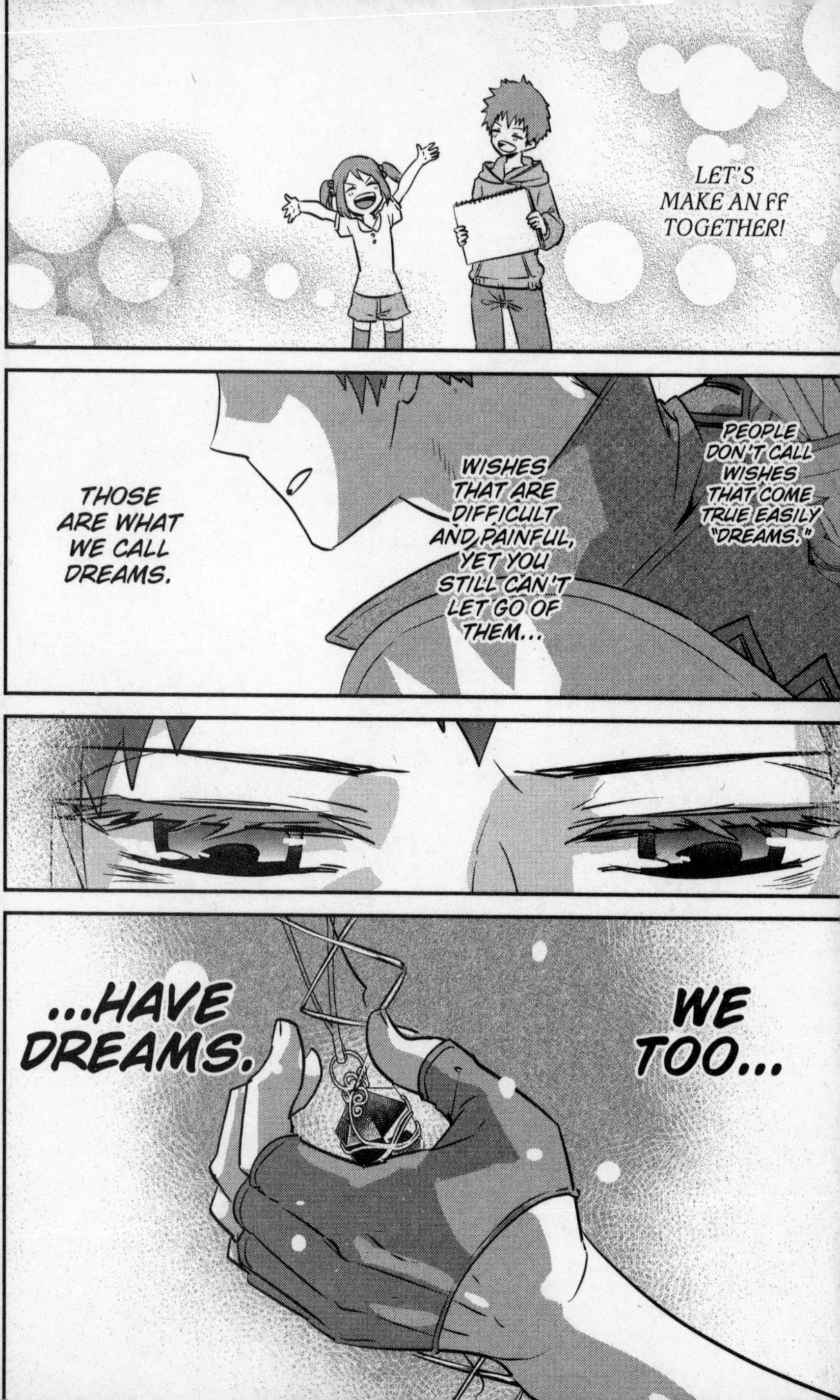
LET'S MAKE AN FF TOGETHER!
PEOPLE DON'T CALL WISHES THAT COME TRUE EASILY "DREAMS."
WISHES THAT ARE DIFFICULT AND PAINFUL, YET YOU STILL CAN'T LET GO OF THEM...
THOSE ARE WHAT WE CALL DREAMS.
WE TOO...
...HAVE DREAMS.

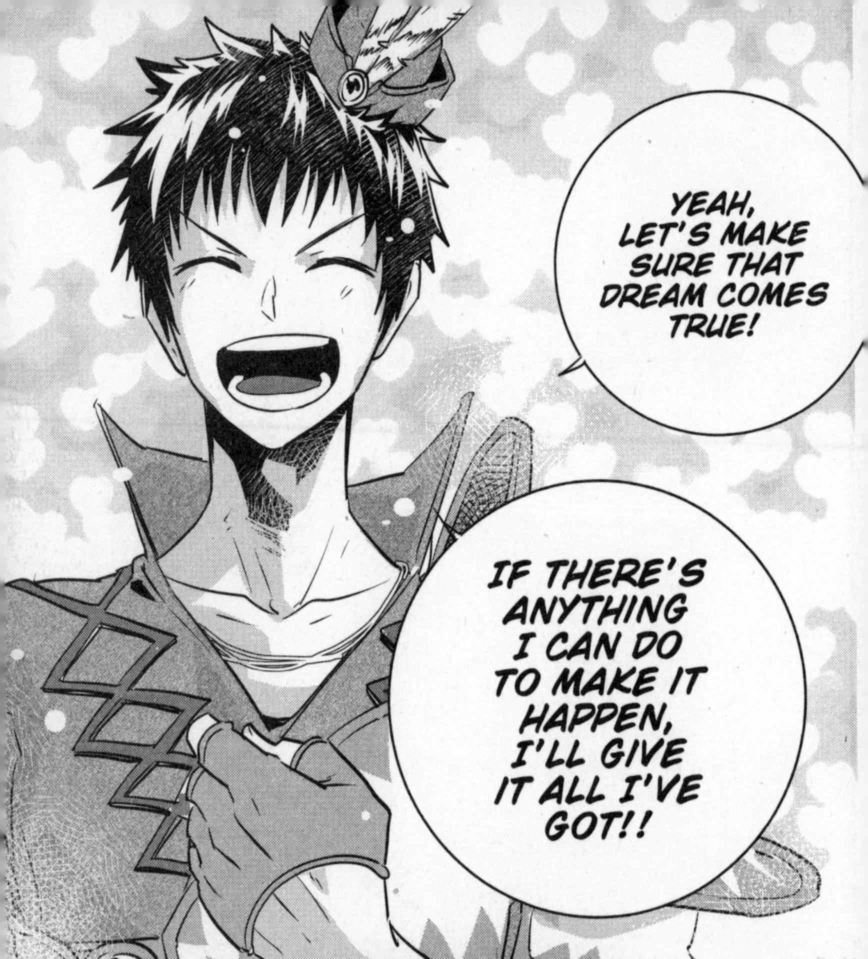
YEAH, LET'S MAKE SURE THAT DREAM COMES TRUE!
IF THERE'S ANYTHING I CAN DO TO MAKE IT HAPPEN, I'LL GIVE IT ALL I'VE GOT!!
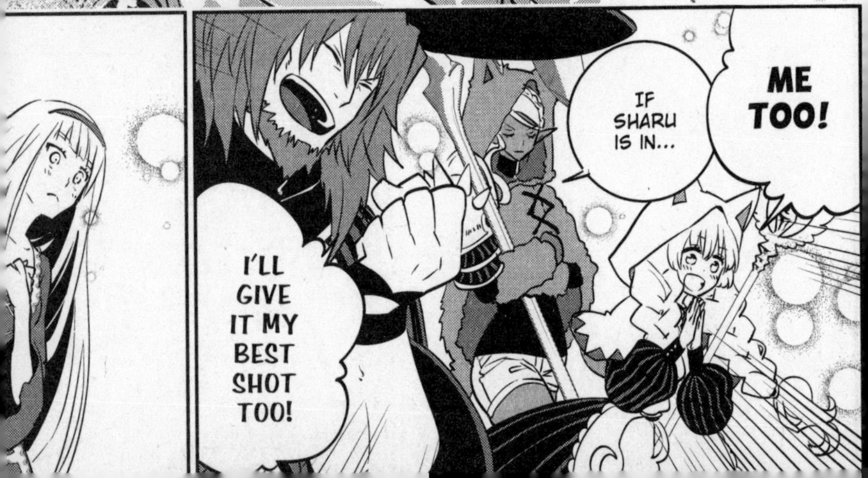
ME TOO!
IF SHARU IS IN...
I'LL GIVE IT MY BEST SHOT TOO!

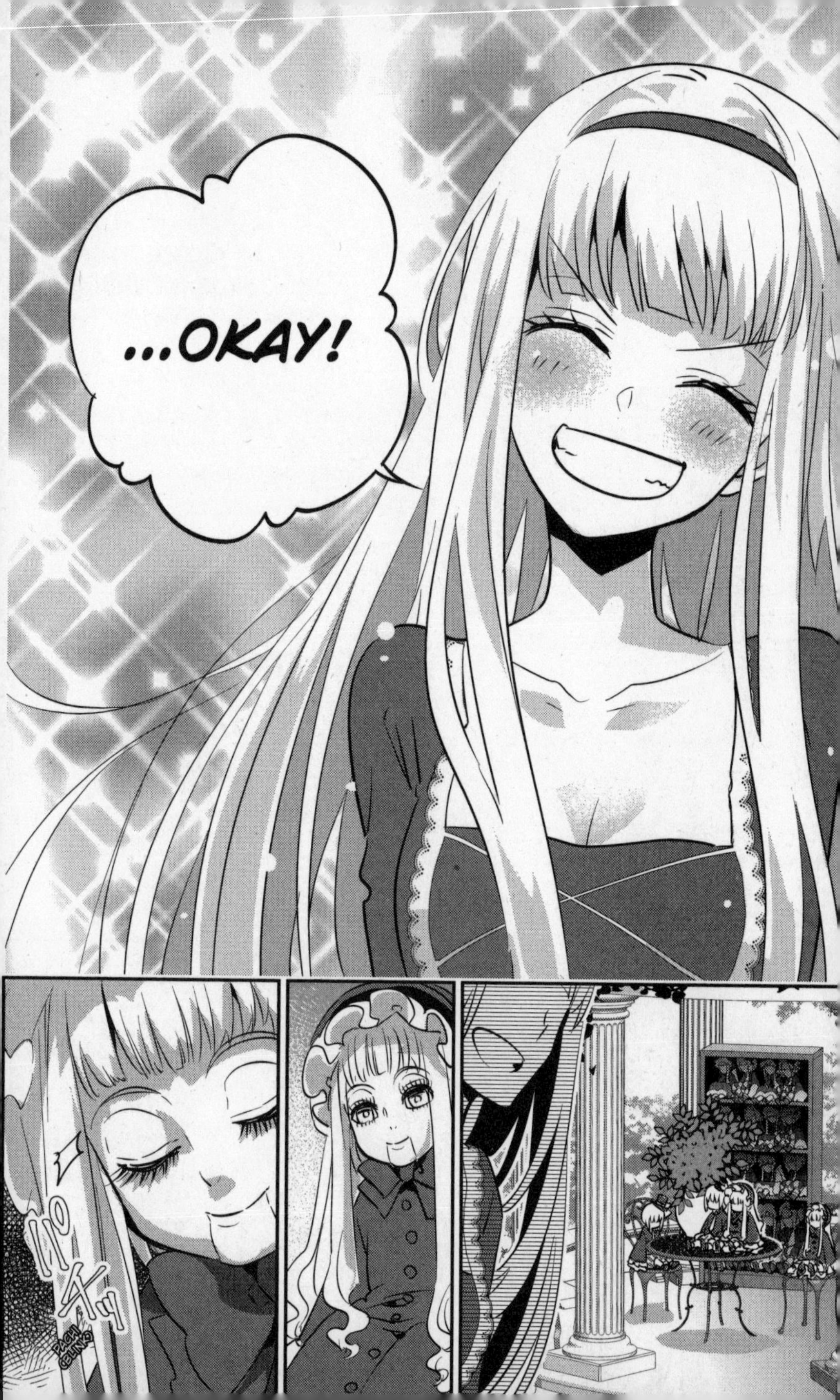
...OKAY!
PACHI (BLINK)

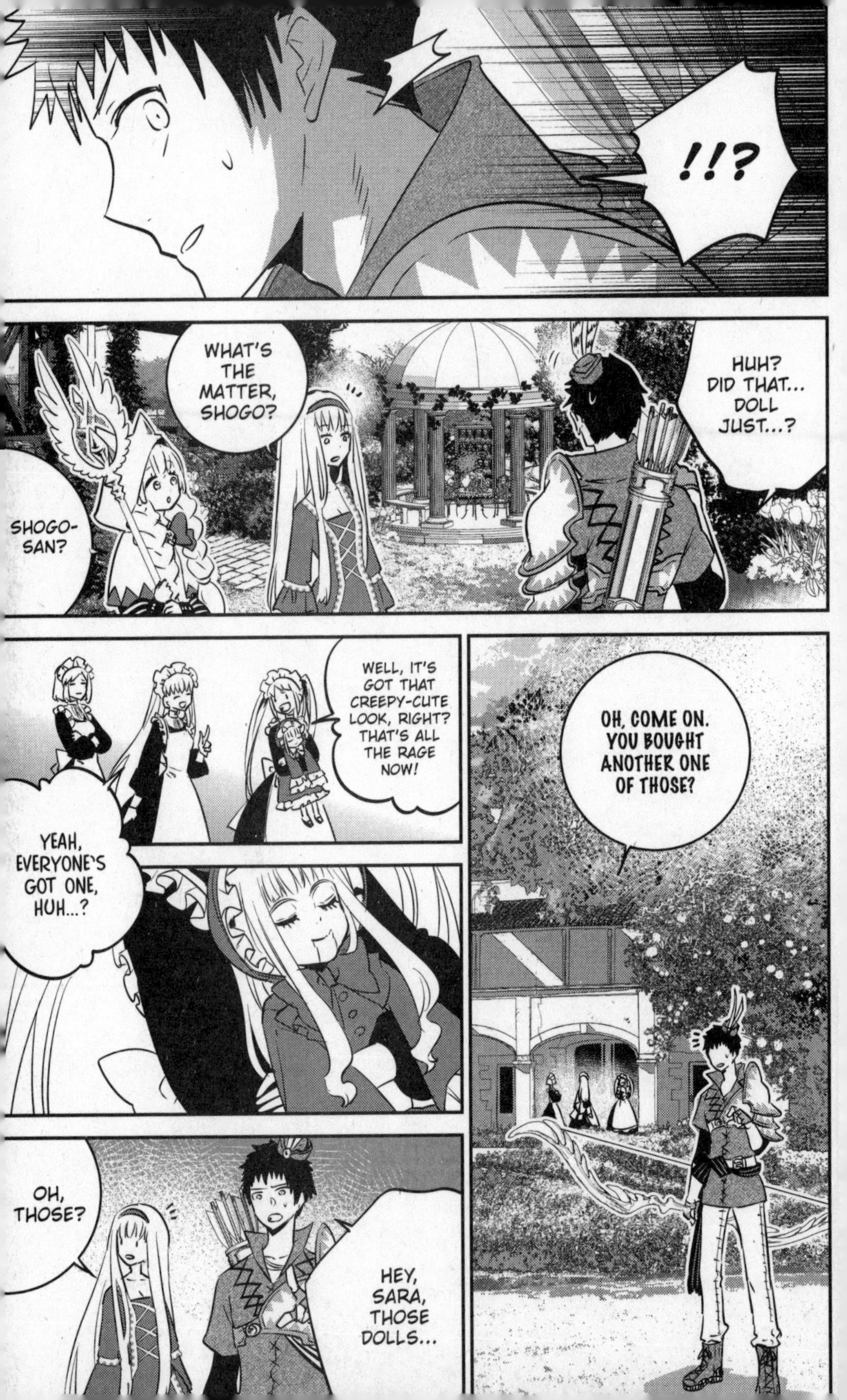
!!?
HUH? DID THAT... DOLL JUST...?
WHAT'S THE MATTER, SHOGO?
SHOGO-SAN?
OH, COME ON. YOU BOUGHT ANOTHER ONE OF THOSE?
WELL, IT'S GOT THAT CREEPY-CUTE LOOK, RIGHT? THAT'S ALL THE RAGE NOW!
YEAH, EVERYONE'S GOT ONE, HUH...?
HEY, SARA, THOSE DOLLS...
OH, THOSE?

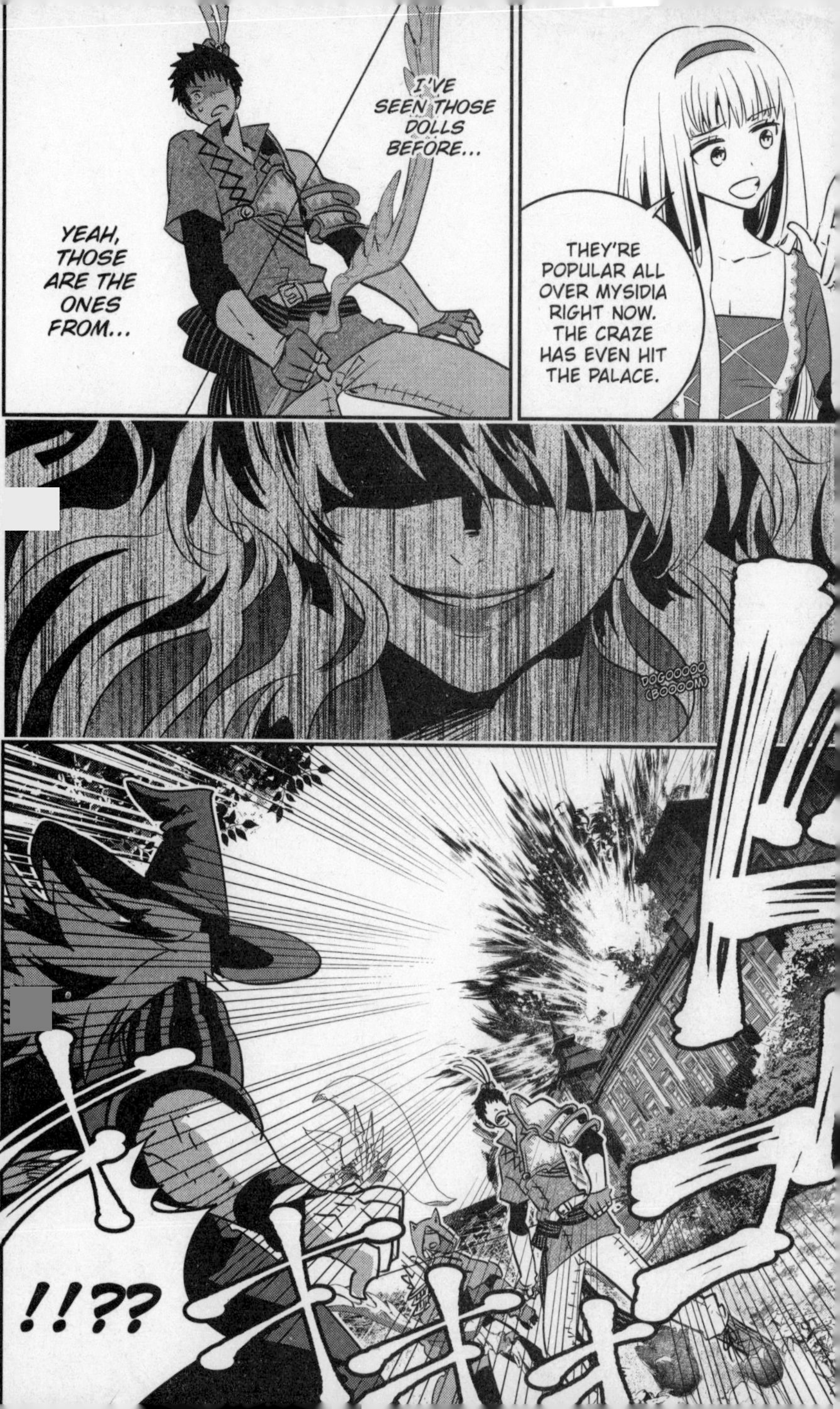
THEY'RE POPULAR ALL OVER MYSIDIA RIGHT NOW. THE CRAZE HAS EVEN HIT THE PALACE.
I'VE SEEN THOSE DOLLS BEFORE...
YEAH, THOSE ARE THE ONES FROM...
DOGOOOOO (BOOOOM)
!!??

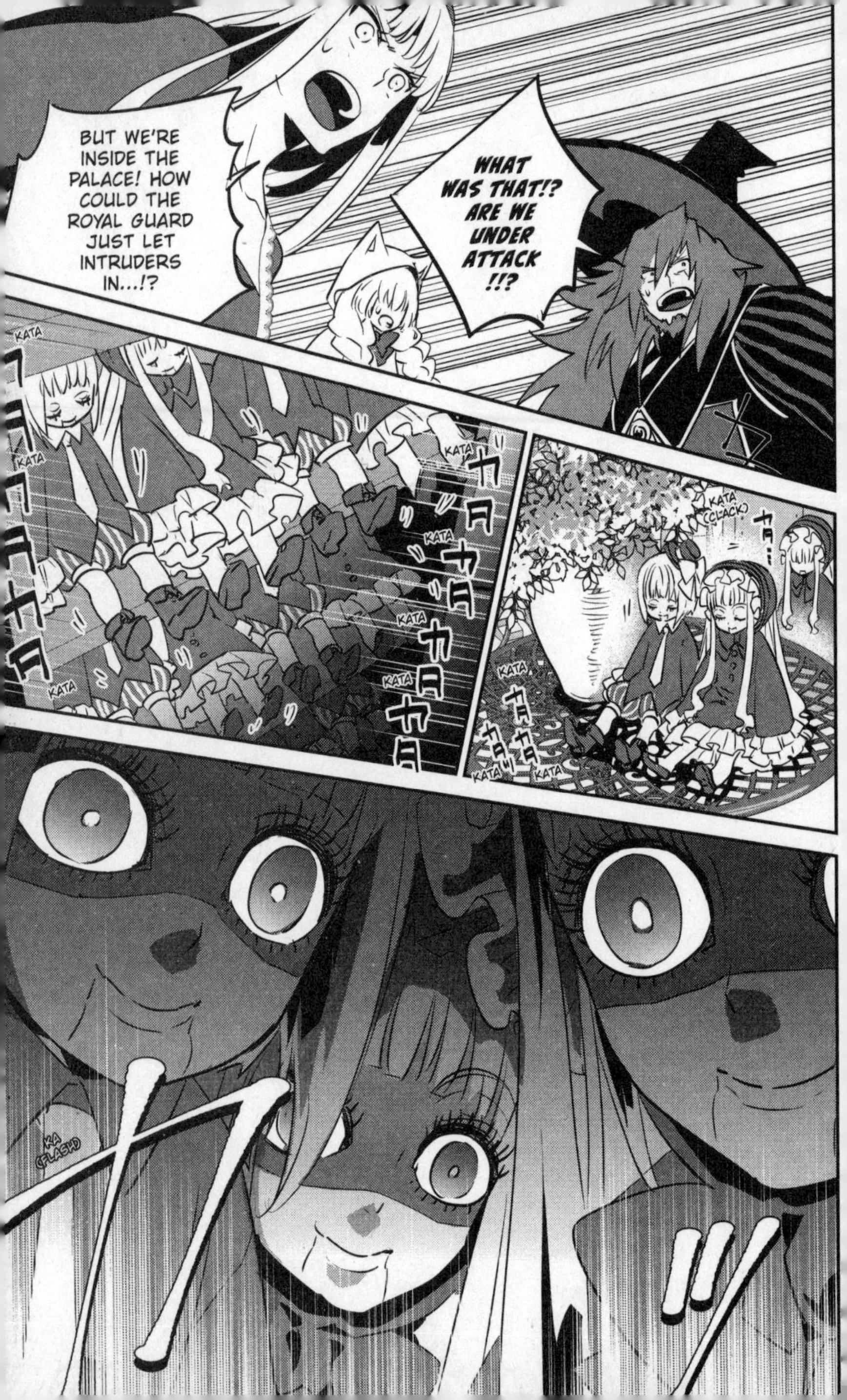
WHAT WAS THAT!? ARE WE UNDER ATTACK !!?
BUT WE'RE INSIDE THE PALACE! HOW COULD THE ROYAL GUARD JUST LET INTRUDERS IN...!?
KATA (CLACK)
KATA
KATA
KATA
KATA
KATA
KATA
KATA
KATA
KATA
KA (FLASH)

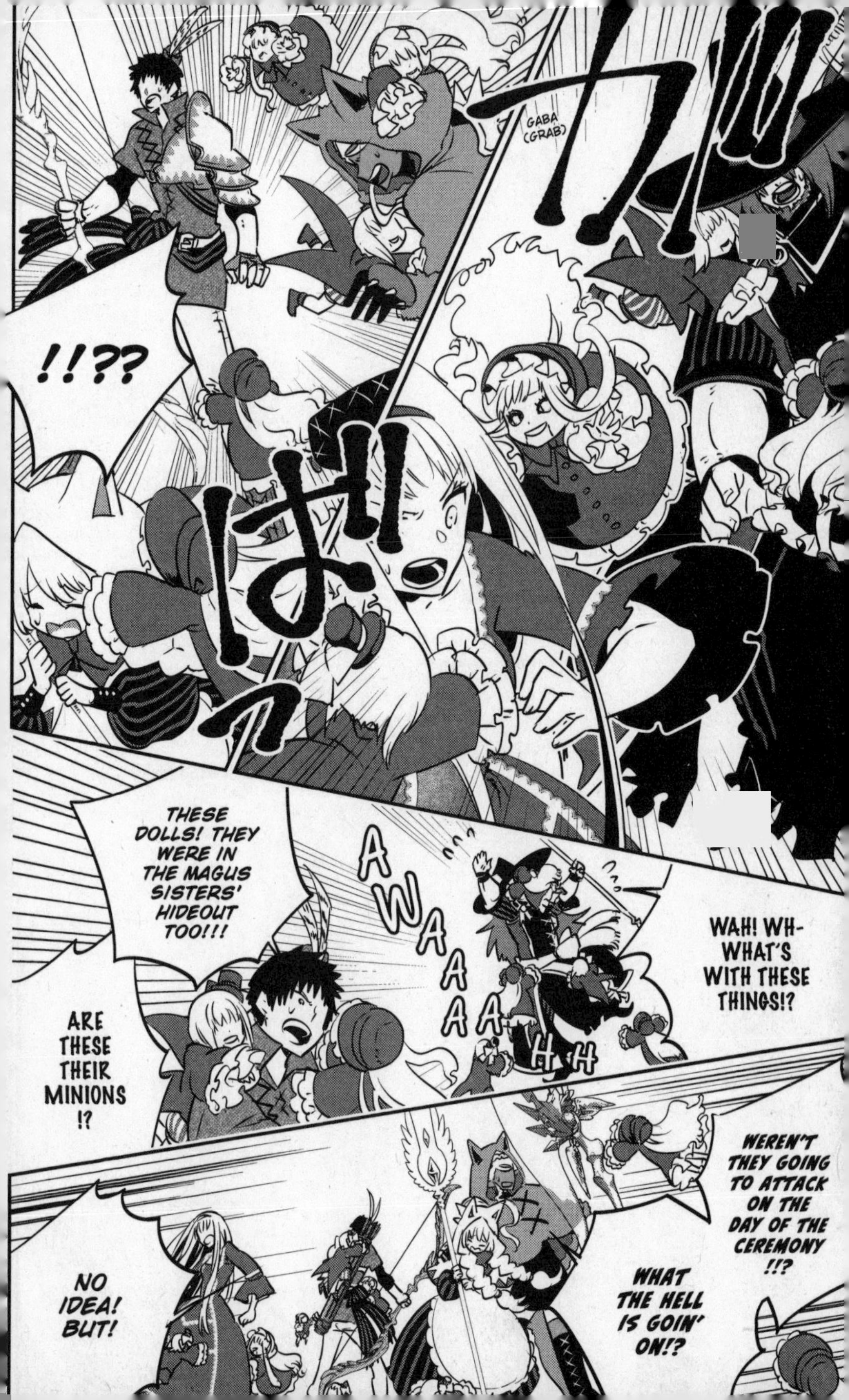
GABA (GRAB)
はっ!!
!!??
WAH! WH-WHAT'S WITH THESE THINGS!?
AWAAAAAHH
THESE DOLLS! THEY WERE IN THE MAGUS SISTERS' HIDEOUT TOO!!!
ARE THESE THEIR MINIONS!?
WEREN'T THEY GOING TO ATTACK ON THE DAY OF THE CEREMONY!!?
WHAT THE HELL IS GOIN' ON!?
NO IDEA! BUT!

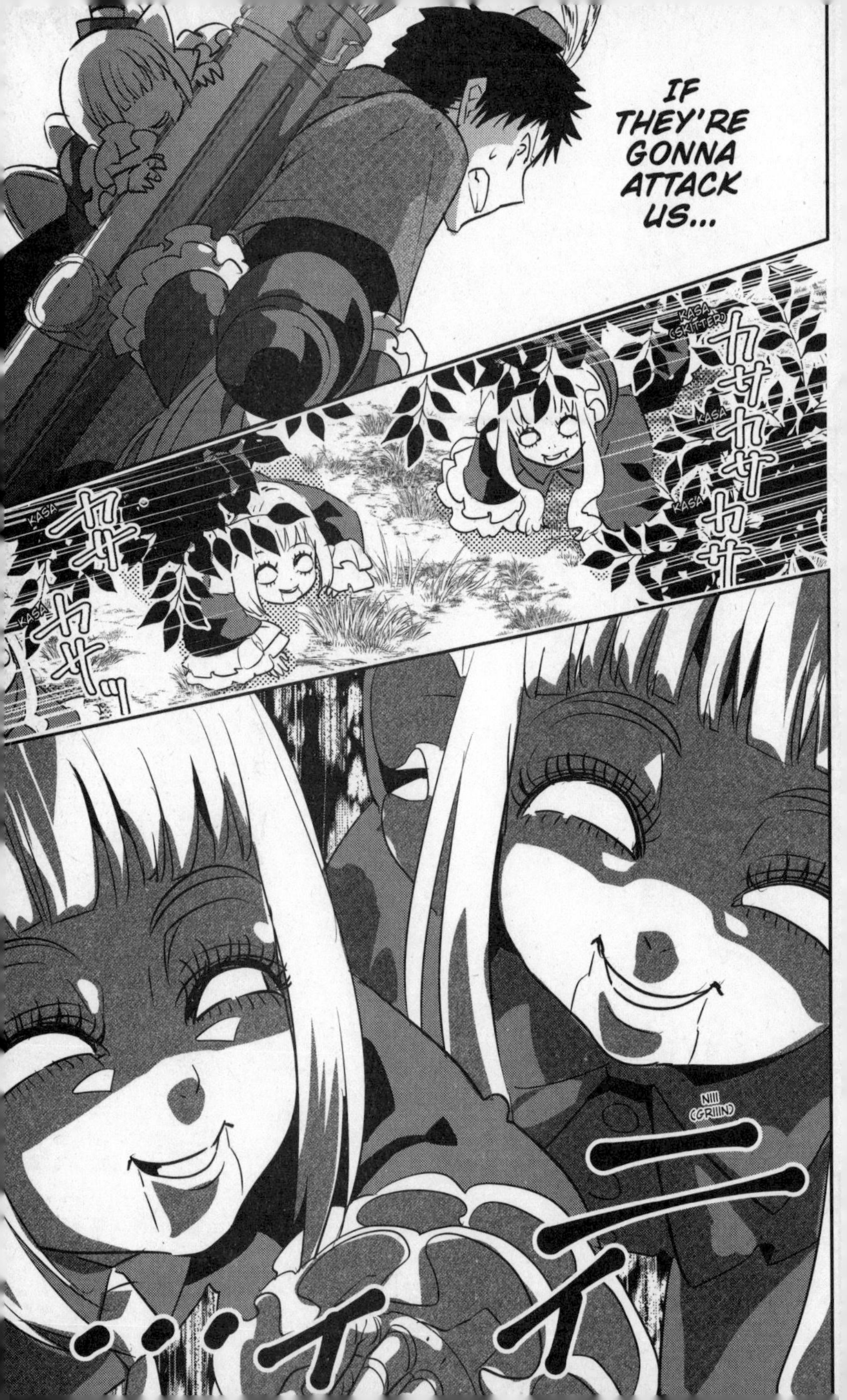
IF THEY'RE GONNA ATTACK US...
KASA (SKITTER)
KASA
KASA
KASA
KASA
NIII (GRIIIN)

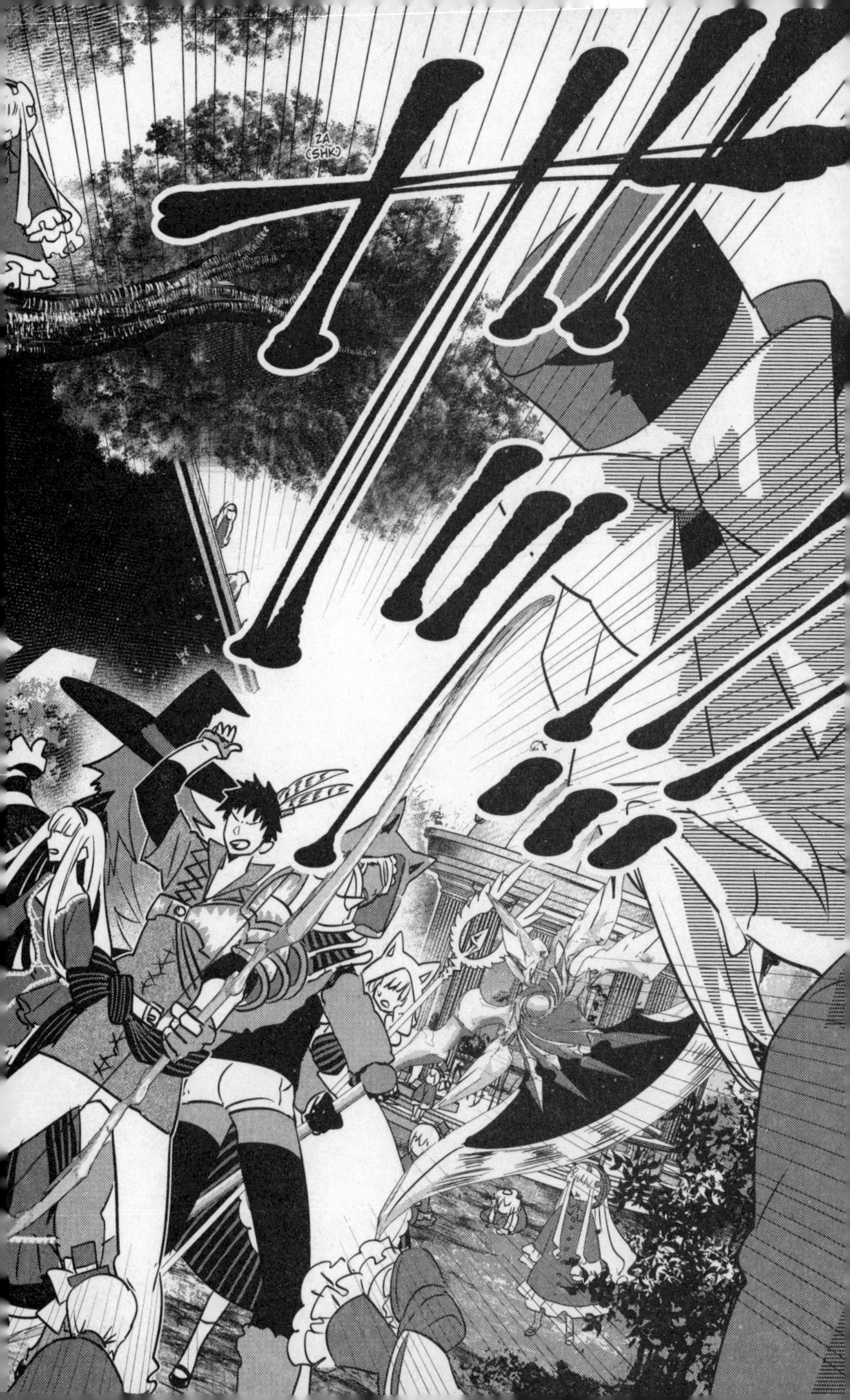
ZA
(SHK)

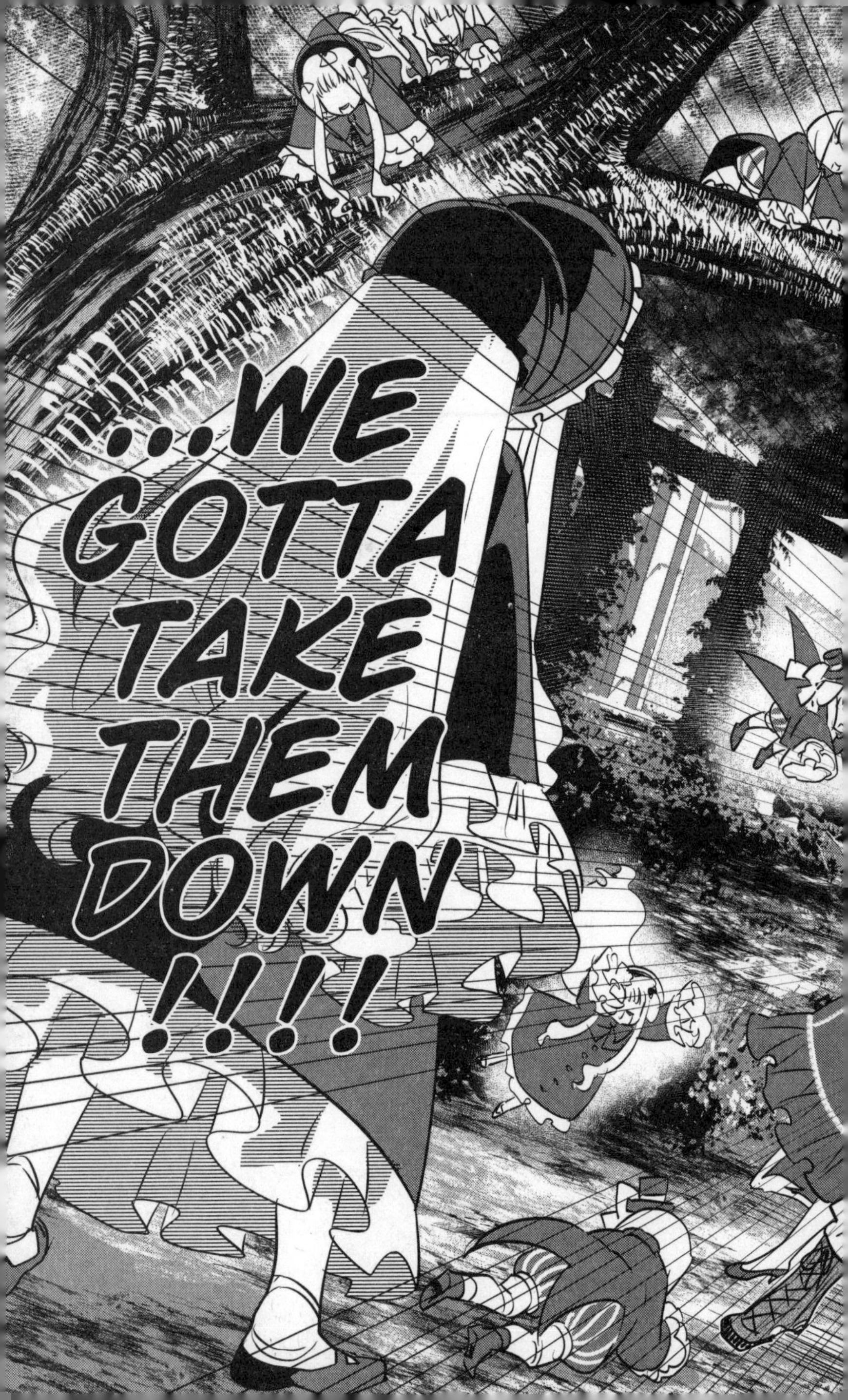
...WE GOTTA TAKE THEM DOWN!!!!

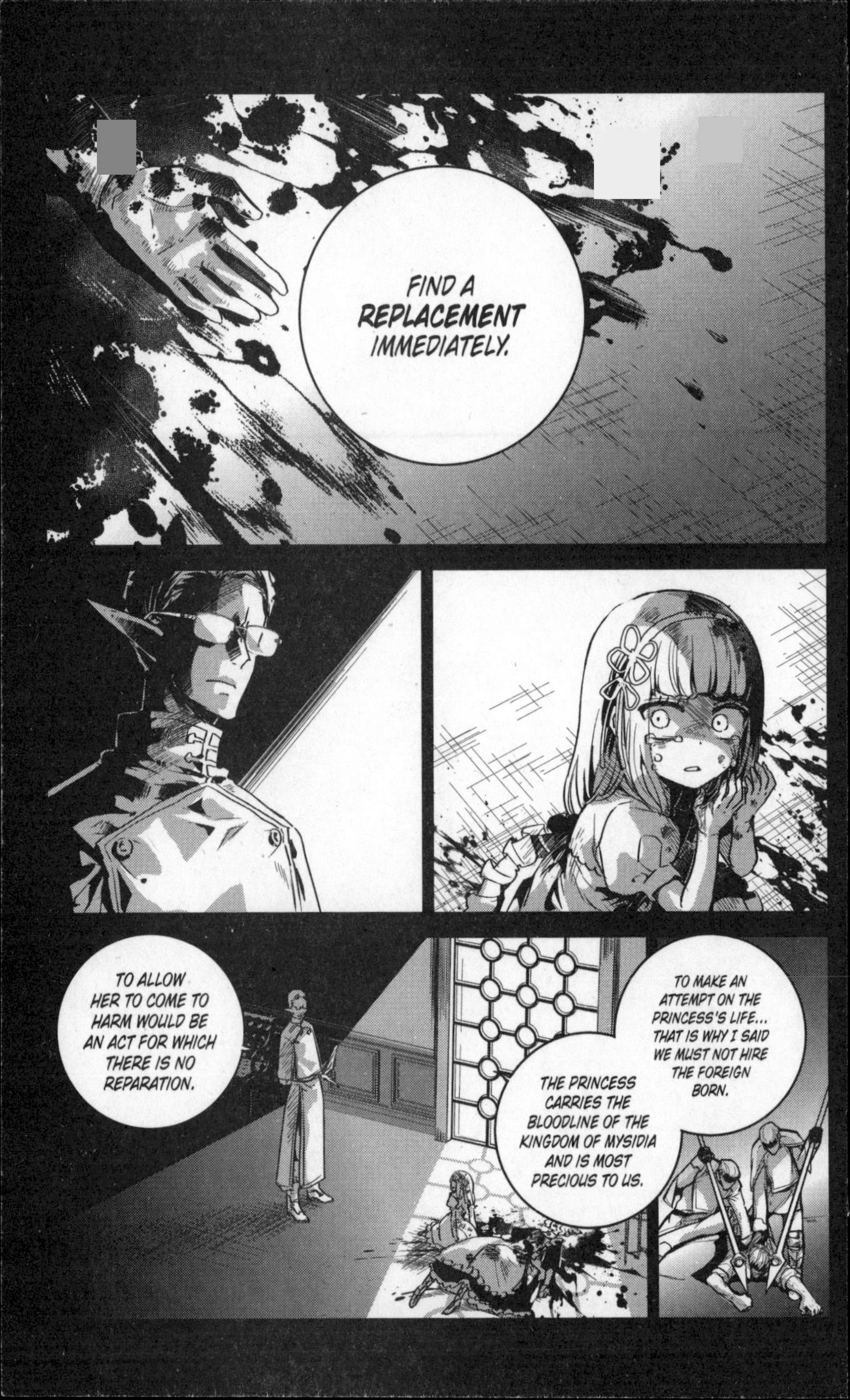
FIND A REPLACEMENT IMMEDIATELY.
TO MAKE AN ATTEMPT ON THE PRINCESS'S LIFE... THAT IS WHY I SAID WE MUST NOT HIRE THE FOREIGN BORN.
THE PRINCESS CARRIES THE BLOODLINE OF THE KINGDOM OF MYSIDIA AND IS MOST PRECIOUS TO US.
TO ALLOW HER TO COME TO HARM WOULD BE AN ACT FOR WHICH THERE IS NO REPARATION.

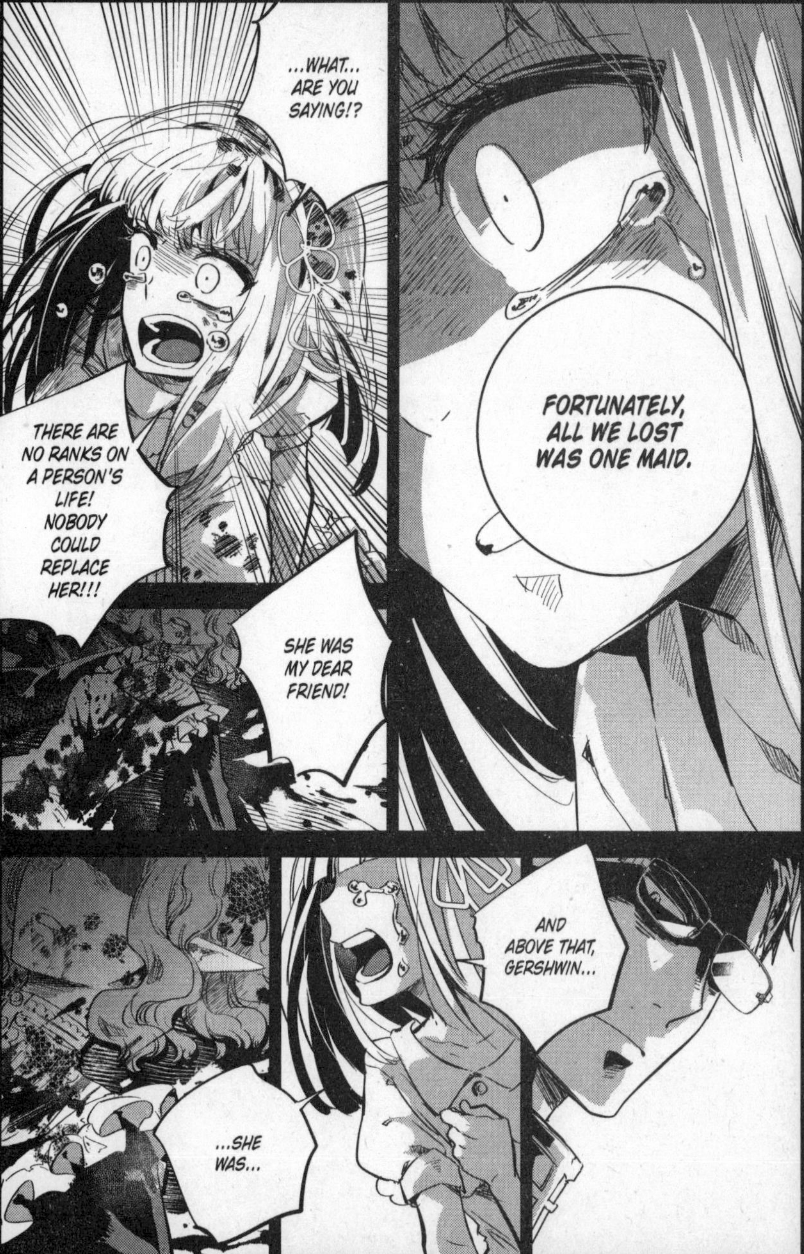
FORTUNATELY, ALL WE LOST WAS ONE MAID.
...WHAT... ARE YOU SAYING!?
THERE ARE NO RANKS ON A PERSON'S LIFE! NOBODY COULD REPLACE HER!!!
SHE WAS MY DEAR FRIEND!
AND ABOVE THAT, GERSHWIN...
...SHE WAS...

Chapter 13 Dancing Calcabrina

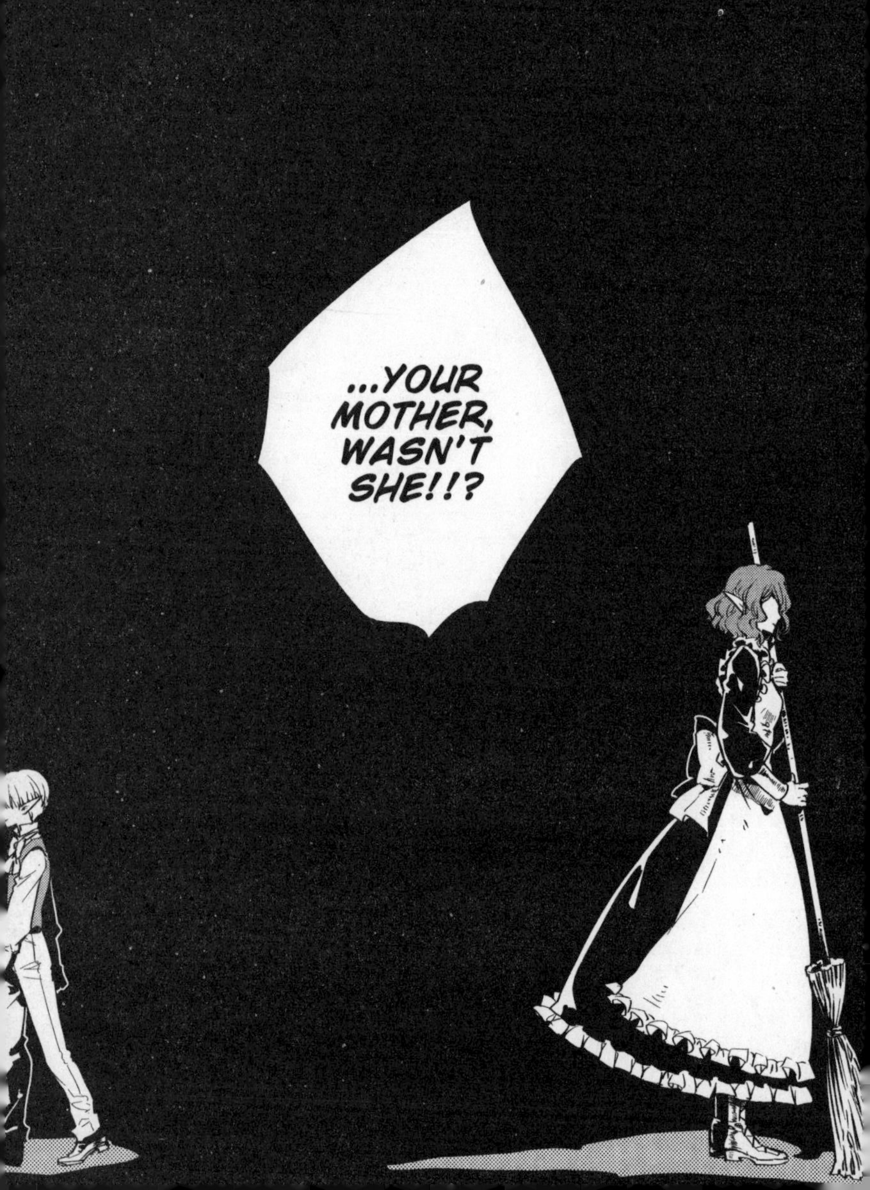
...YOUR MOTHER, WASN'T SHE!!?

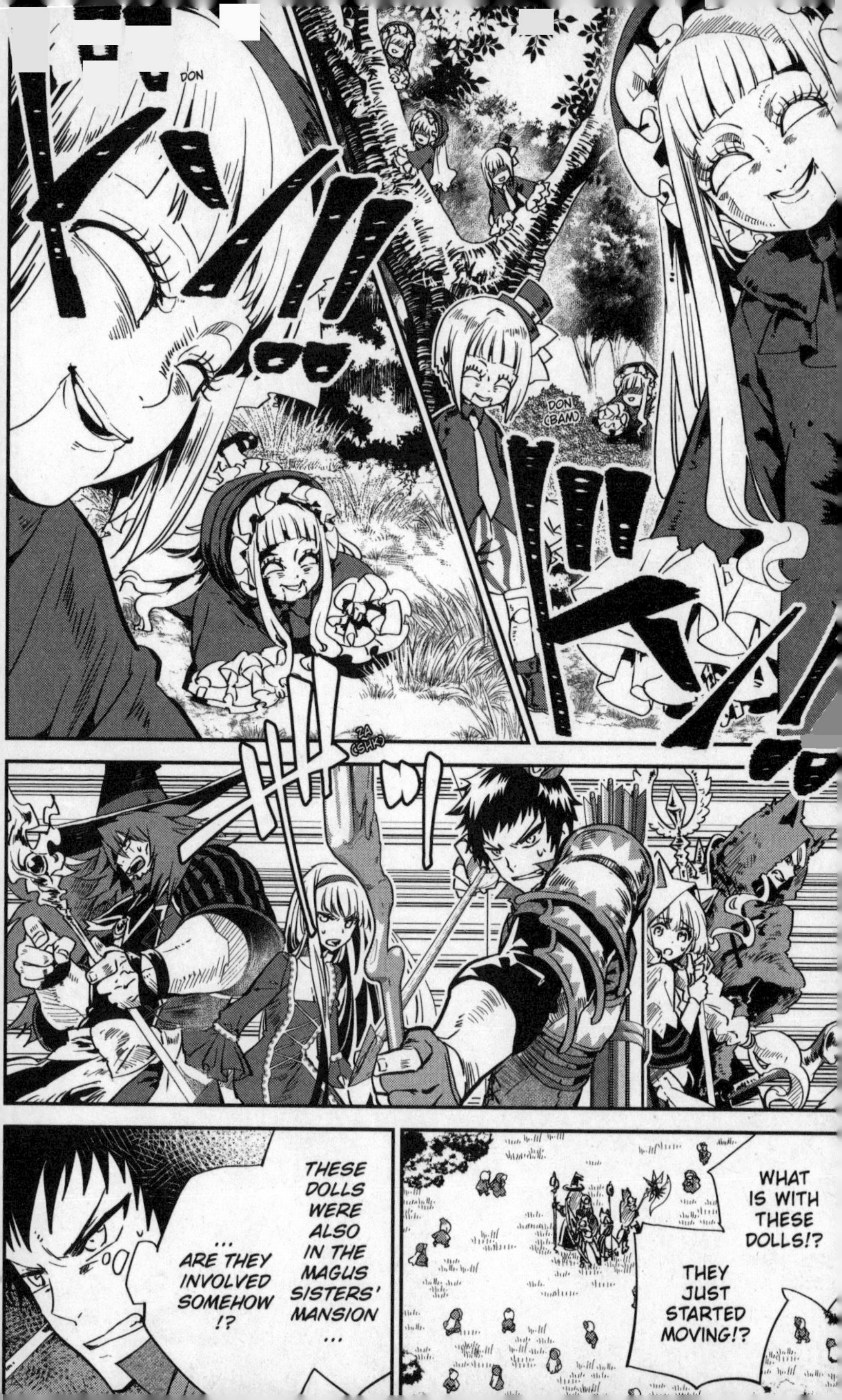
DON
DON (BAM)
ZA (SHK)
WHAT IS WITH THESE DOLLS!?
THEY JUST STARTED MOVING!?
THESE DOLLS WERE ALSO IN THE MAGUS SISTERS' MANSION...
...ARE THEY INVOLVED SOMEHOW!?

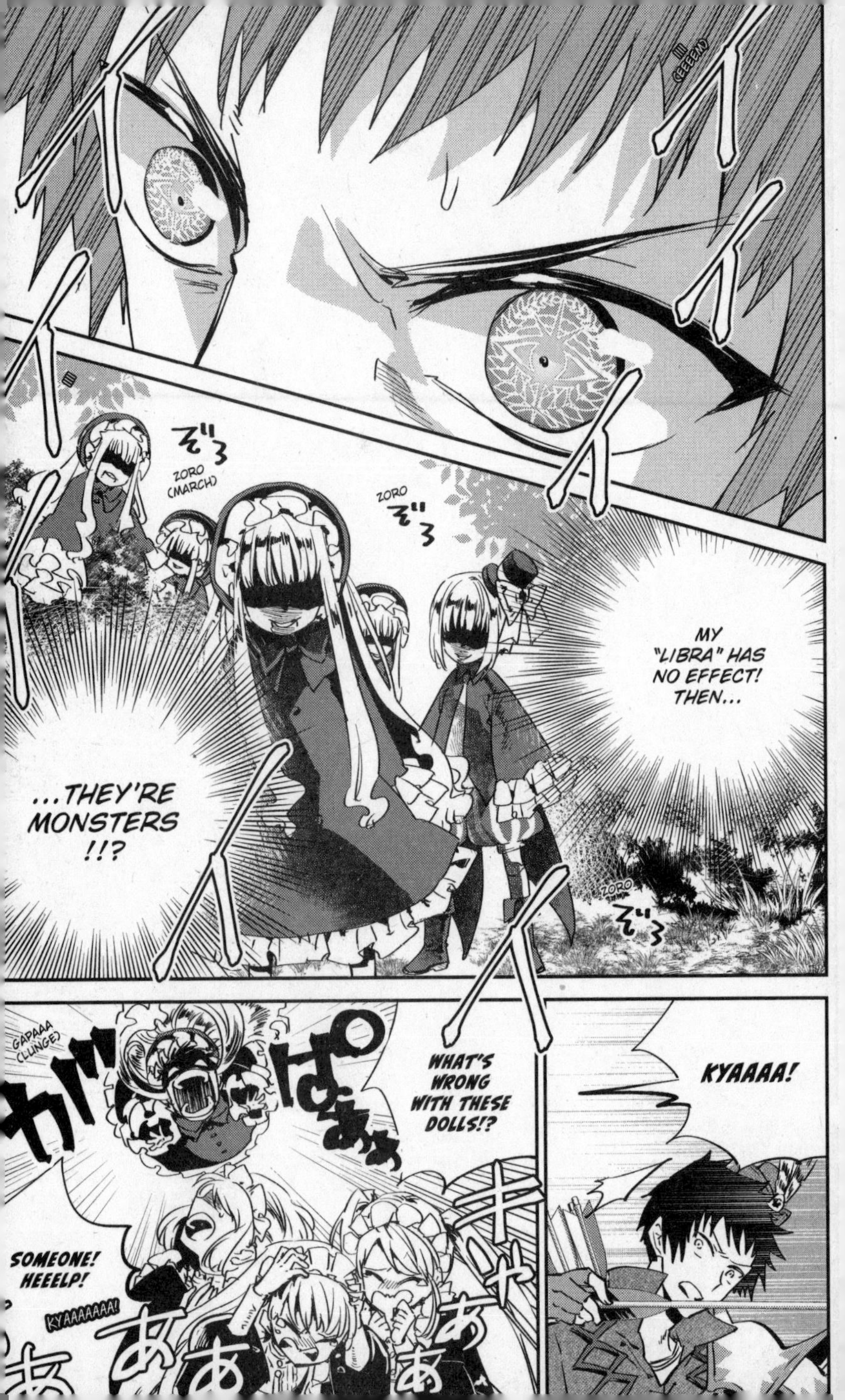
GEEEND
ZORO (MARCH)
ZORO
MY "LIBRA" HAS NO EFFECT! THEN...
...THEY'RE MONSTERS !!?
ZORO
KYAAAA!
WHAT'S WRONG WITH THESE DOLLS!?
GAPAAA (LUNGE)
SOMEONE! HEEELP!
KYAAAAAAA!

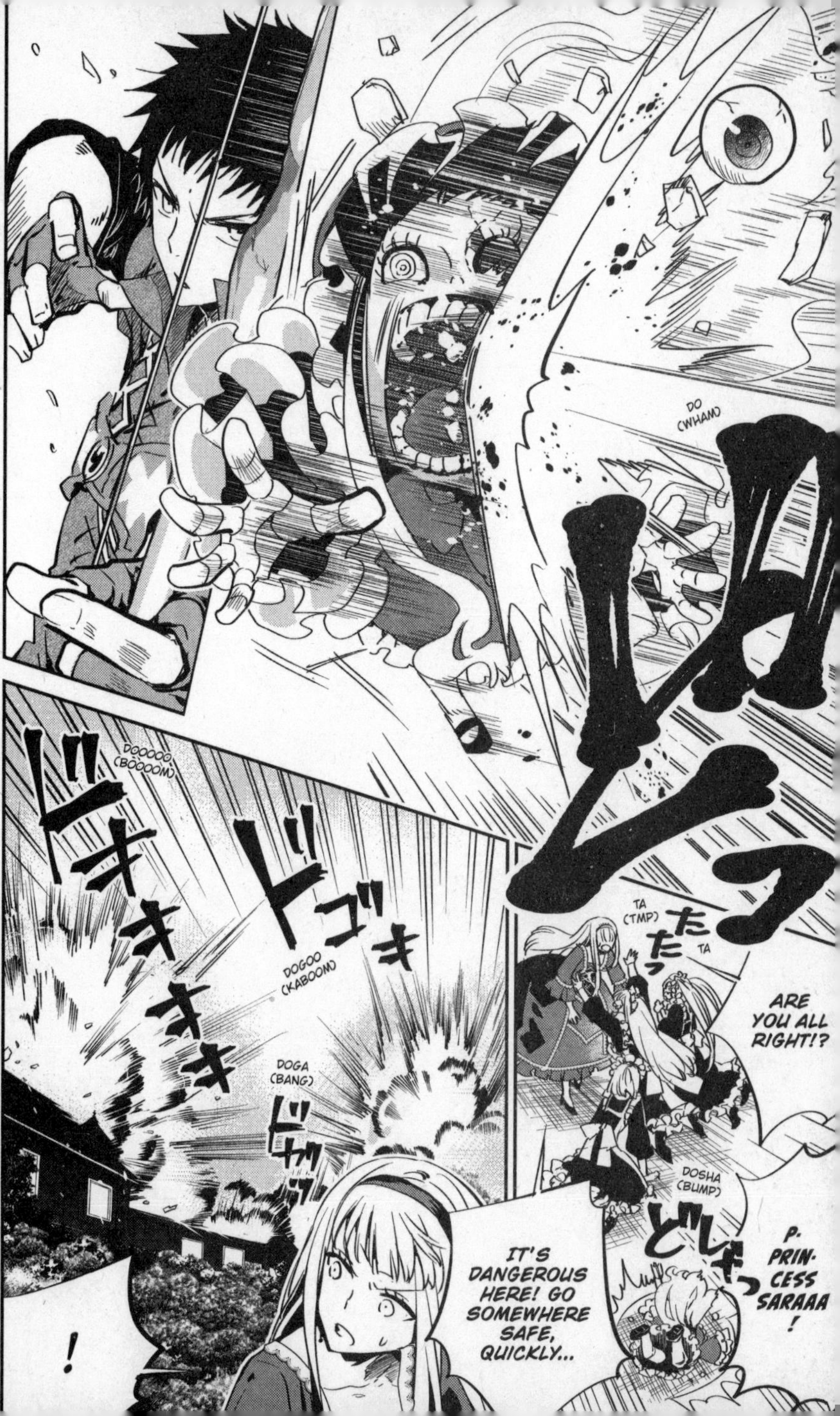
DO
(WHAM)
TA
(TMP)
TA
ARE YOU ALL RIGHT!?
DOSHA
(BUMP)
P. PRINCESS SARAAA!
DOOOOO
(BOOOOM)
DOGOO
(KABOOM)
DOGA
(BANG)
IT'S DANGEROUS HERE! GO SOMEWHERE SAFE, QUICKLY...
!

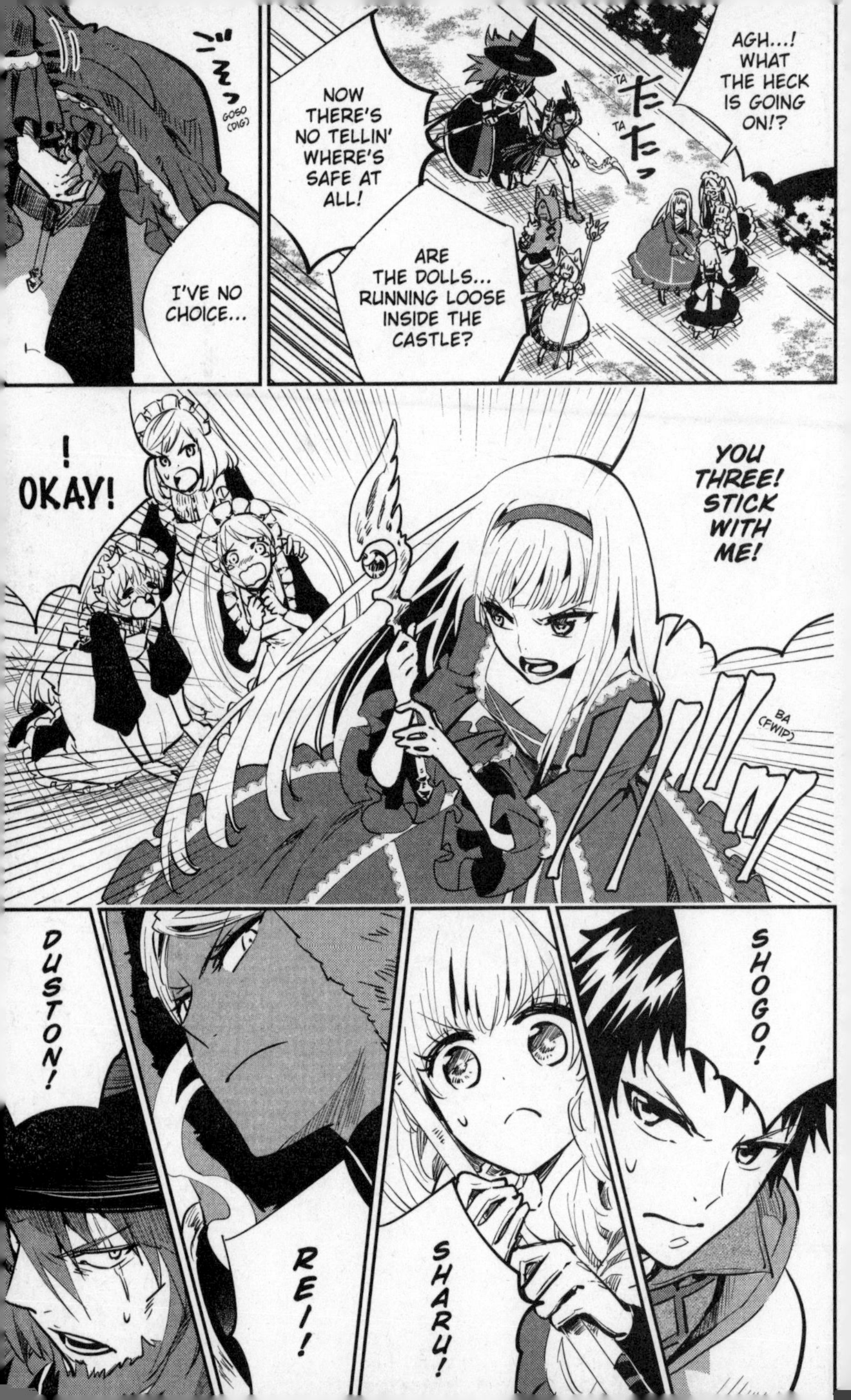
AGH...! WHAT THE HECK IS GOING ON!?
TA TA
NOW THERE'S NO TELLIN' WHERE'S SAFE AT ALL!
ARE THE DOLLS... RUNNING LOOSE INSIDE THE CASTLE?
GOSO (DIG)
I'VE NO CHOICE...
YOU THREE! STICK WITH ME!
BA (FWIP)
! OKAY!
SHOGO!
SHARU!
REI!
DUSTON!

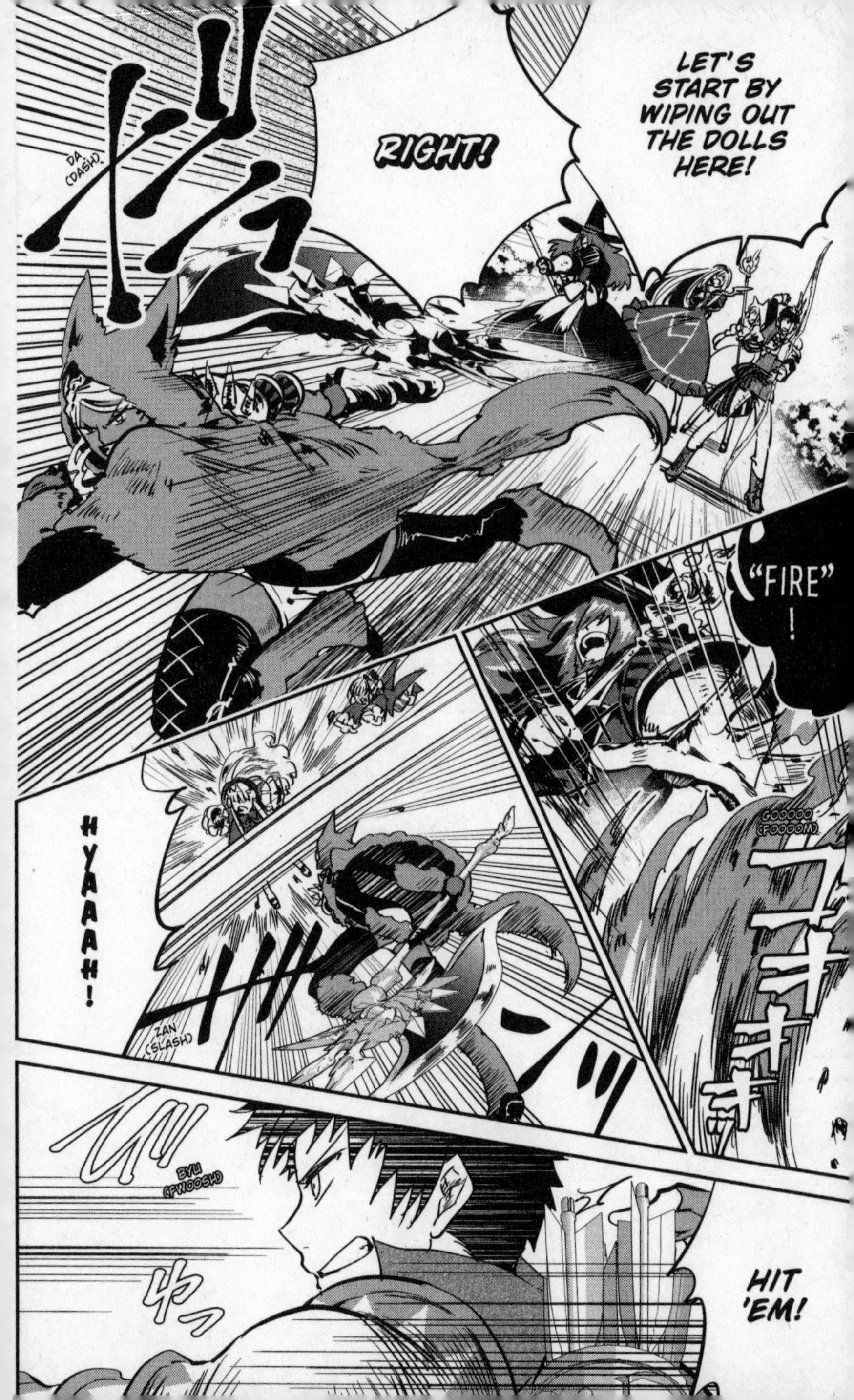
LET'S START BY WIPING OUT THE DOLLS HERE!
RIGHT!
DA (DASH)
"FIRE"!
GOOOOO (FOOOOM)
HYAAAAH!
ZAN (SLASH)
BYU (FWOOSH)
HIT 'EM!

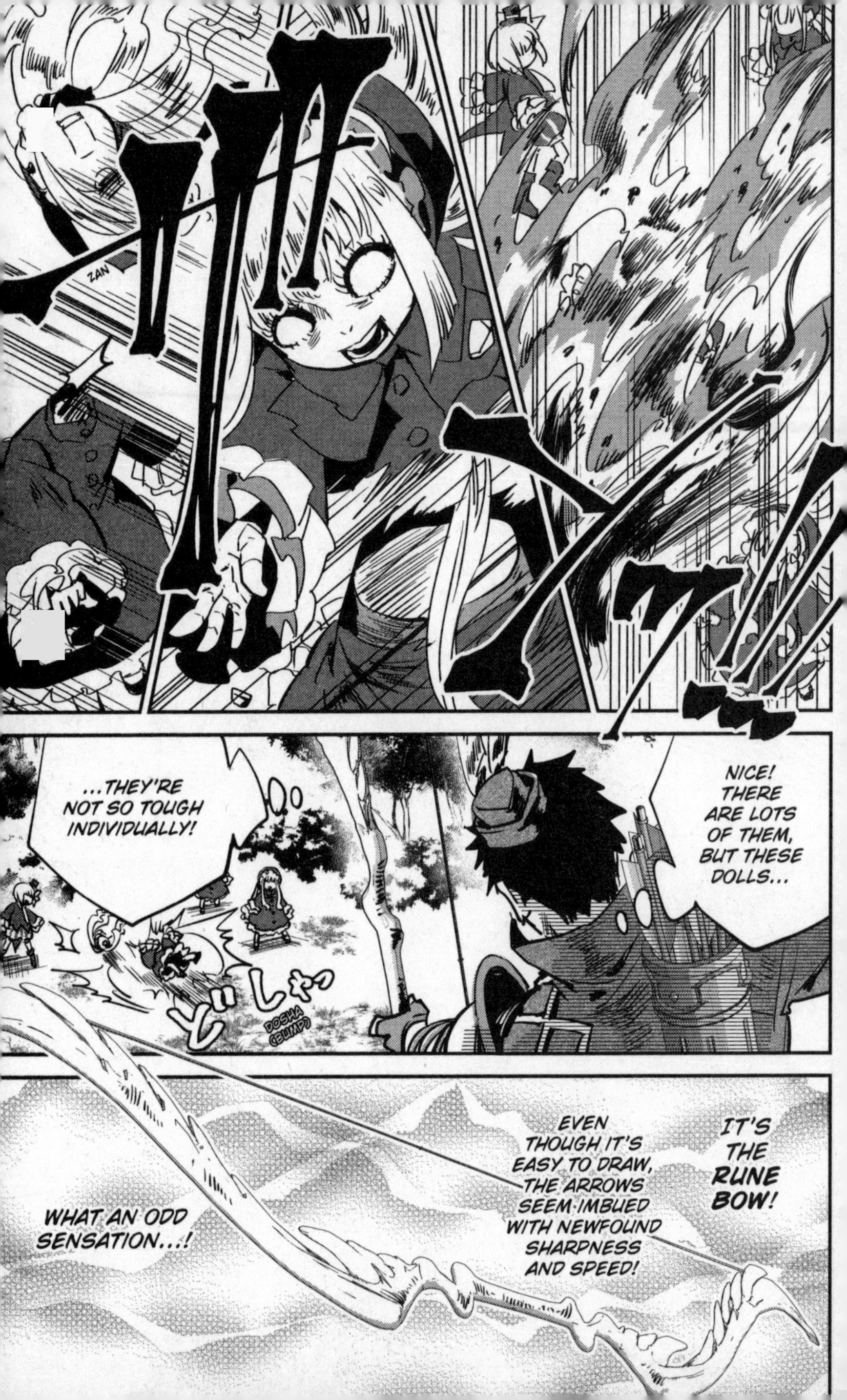
ZAN
NICE! THERE ARE LOTS OF THEM, BUT THESE DOLLS...
...THEY'RE NOT SO TOUGH INDIVIDUALLY!
DOSHA (BUMP)
IT'S THE RUNE BOW!
EVEN THOUGH IT'S EASY TO DRAW, THE ARROWS SEEM IMBUED WITH NEWFOUND SHARPNESS AND SPEED!
WHAT AN ODD SENSATION...!

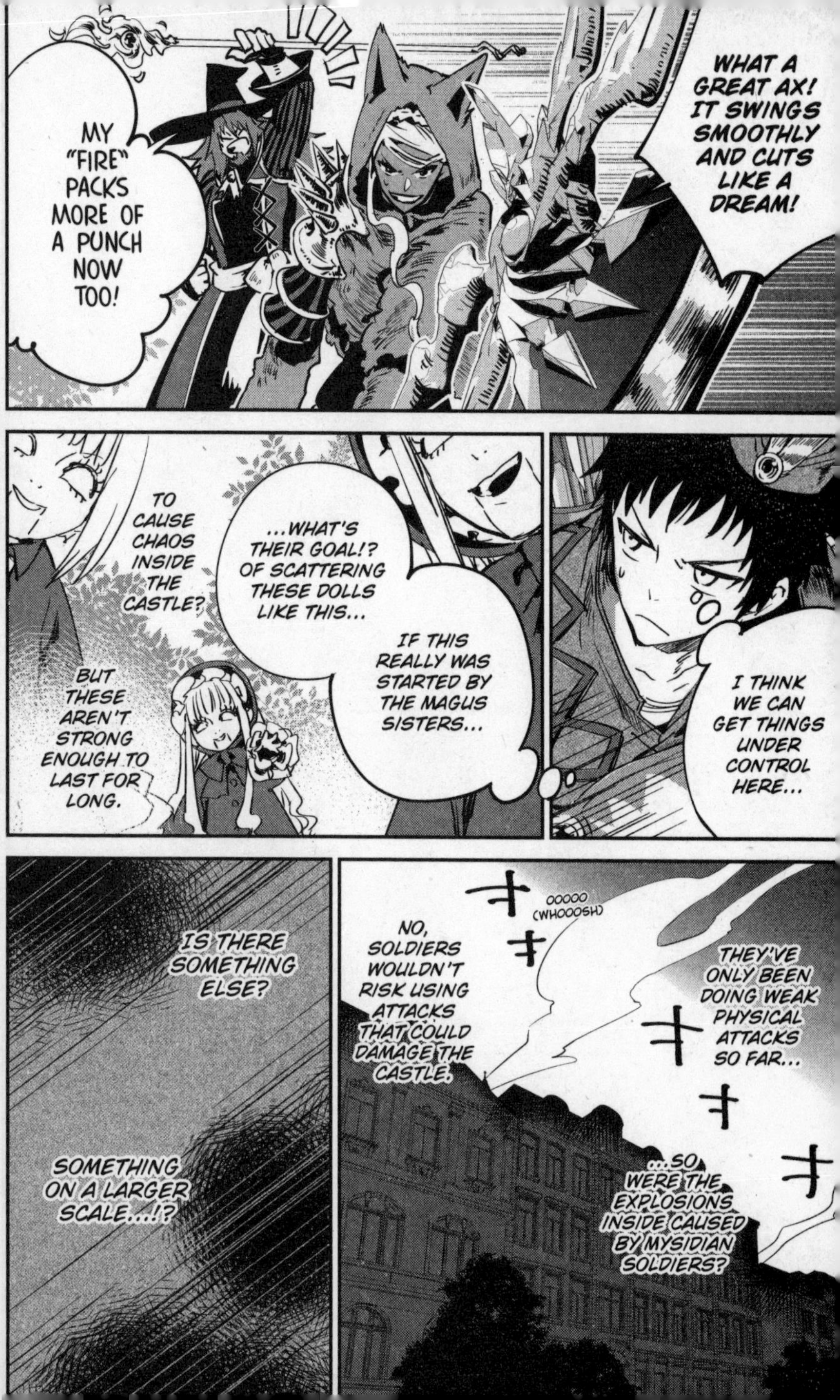
WHAT A GREAT AX! IT SWINGS SMOOTHLY AND CUTS LIKE A DREAM!
MY "FIRE" PACKS MORE OF A PUNCH NOW TOO!
I THINK WE CAN GET THINGS UNDER CONTROL HERE...
IF THIS REALLY WAS STARTED BY THE MAGUS SISTERS...
...WHAT'S THEIR GOAL!? OF SCATTERING THESE DOLLS LIKE THIS...
TO CAUSE CHAOS INSIDE THE CASTLE?
BUT THESE AREN'T STRONG ENOUGH TO LAST FOR LONG.
OOOOO (WHOOOSH)
THEY'VE ONLY BEEN DOING WEAK PHYSICAL ATTACKS SO FAR...
...SO WERE THE EXPLOSIONS INSIDE CAUSED BY MYSIDIAN SOLDIERS?
NO, SOLDIERS WOULDN'T RISK USING ATTACKS THAT COULD DAMAGE THE CASTLE.
IS THERE SOMETHING ELSE?
SOMETHING ON A LARGER SCALE...!?

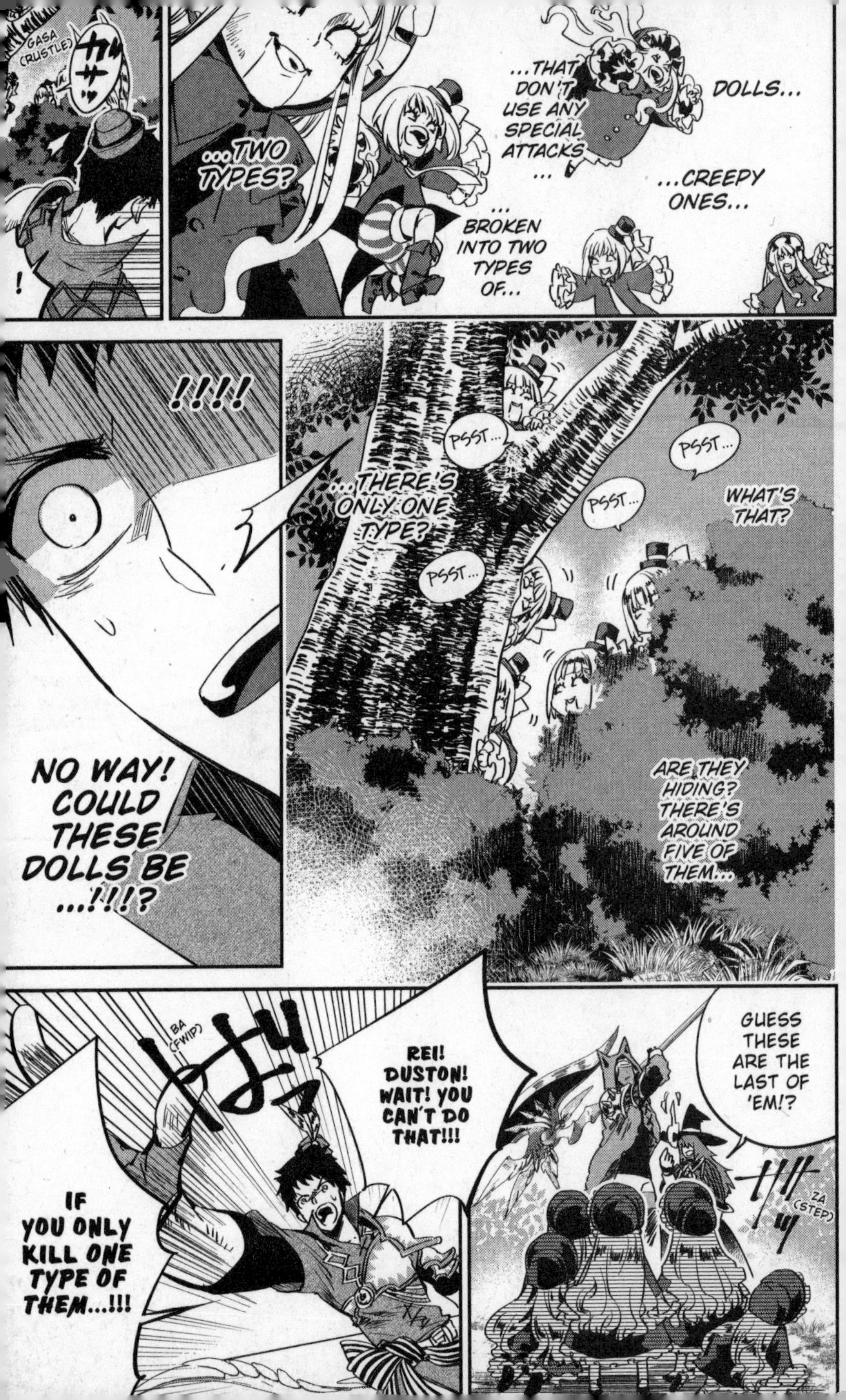
DOLLS...
...THAT DON'T USE ANY SPECIAL ATTACKS...
...CREEPY ONES...
...BROKEN INTO TWO TYPES OF...
...TWO TYPES?
GASA (RUSTLE)
!
WHAT'S THAT?
PSST...
PSST...
PSST...
PSST...
...THERE'S ONLY ONE TYPE?
ARE THEY HIDING? THERE'S AROUND FIVE OF THEM...
!!!!
NO WAY! COULD THESE DOLLS BE ...!!!?
GUESS THESE ARE THE LAST OF 'EM!?
ZA (STEP)
REI! DUSTON! WAIT! YOU CAN'T DO THAT!!!
BA (FWIP)
IF YOU ONLY KILL ONE TYPE OF THEM...!!!

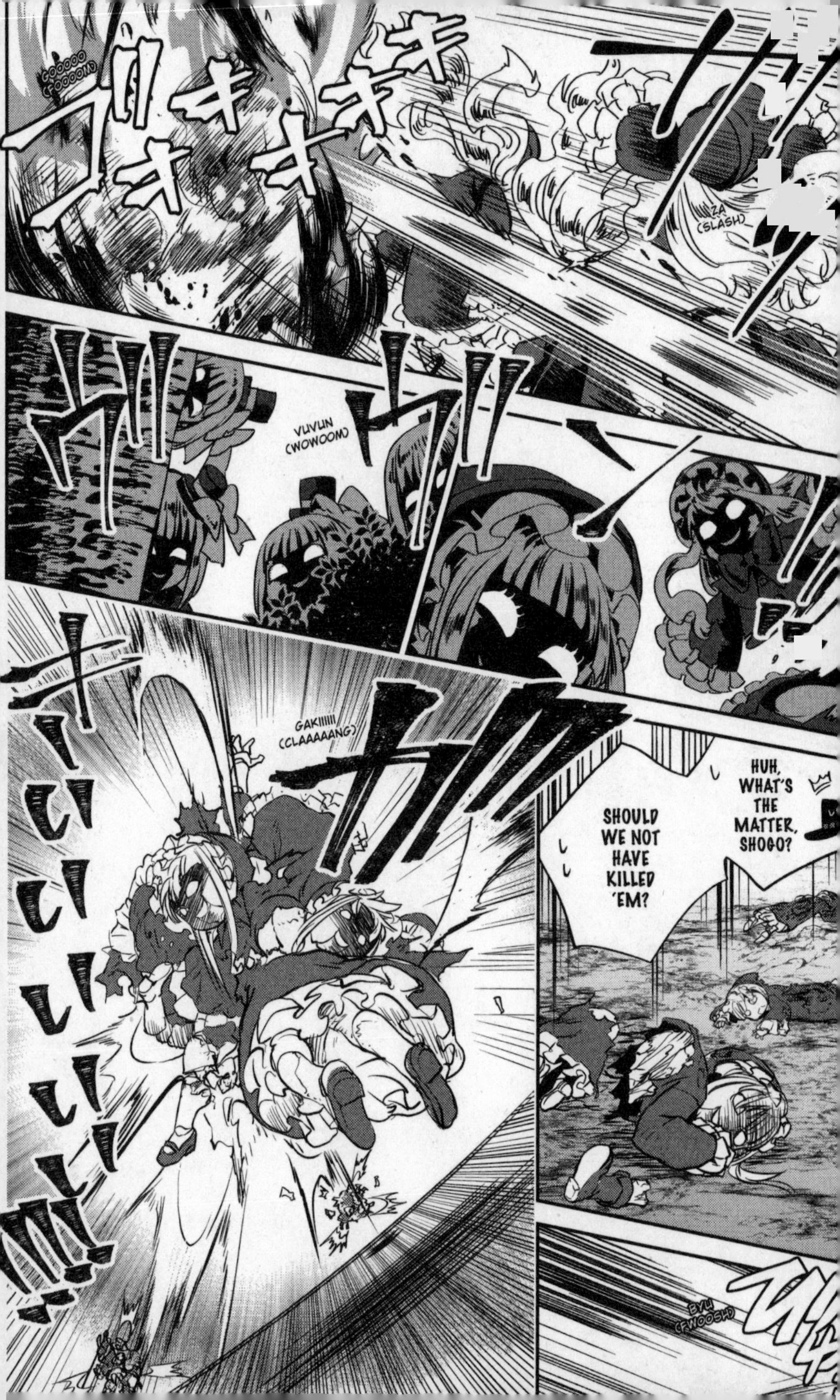
ZA
(SLASH)
GOOOOO
(FOOOOM)
VUVUN
(WOWOOM)
GAKIIIIII
(CLAAAAANG)
HUH, WHAT'S THE MATTER, SHOGO?
SHOULD WE NOT HAVE KILLED 'EM?
BYU
(FWOOSH)

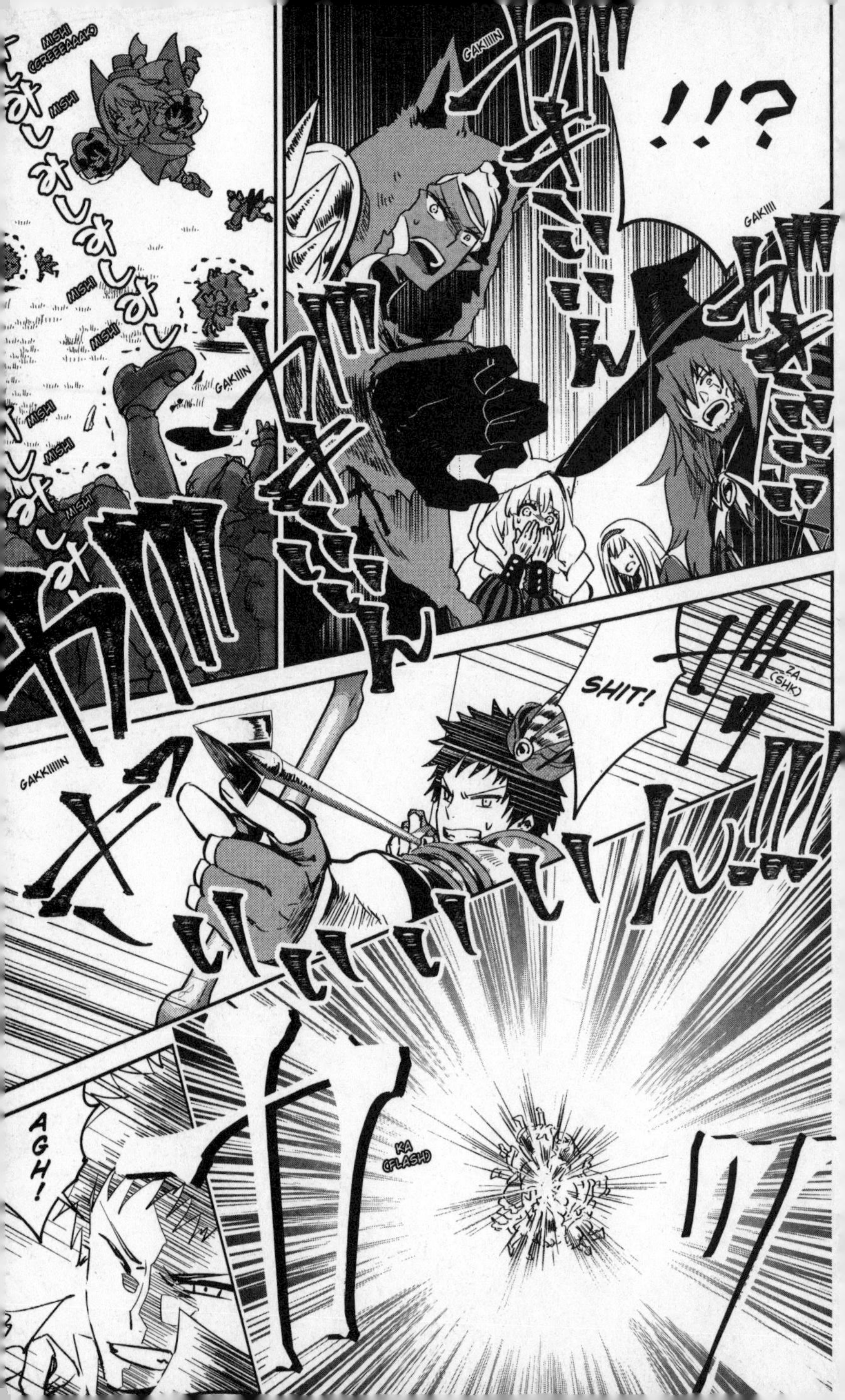
!!?
GAKIIII
GAKIIIN
MISHI (CREEEAAAK)
MISHI
MISHI
MISHI
GAKIIIN
MISHI
MISHI
MISHI
SHIT!
ZA (SHK)
GAKKIIIIIN
KA (FLASH)
AGH!

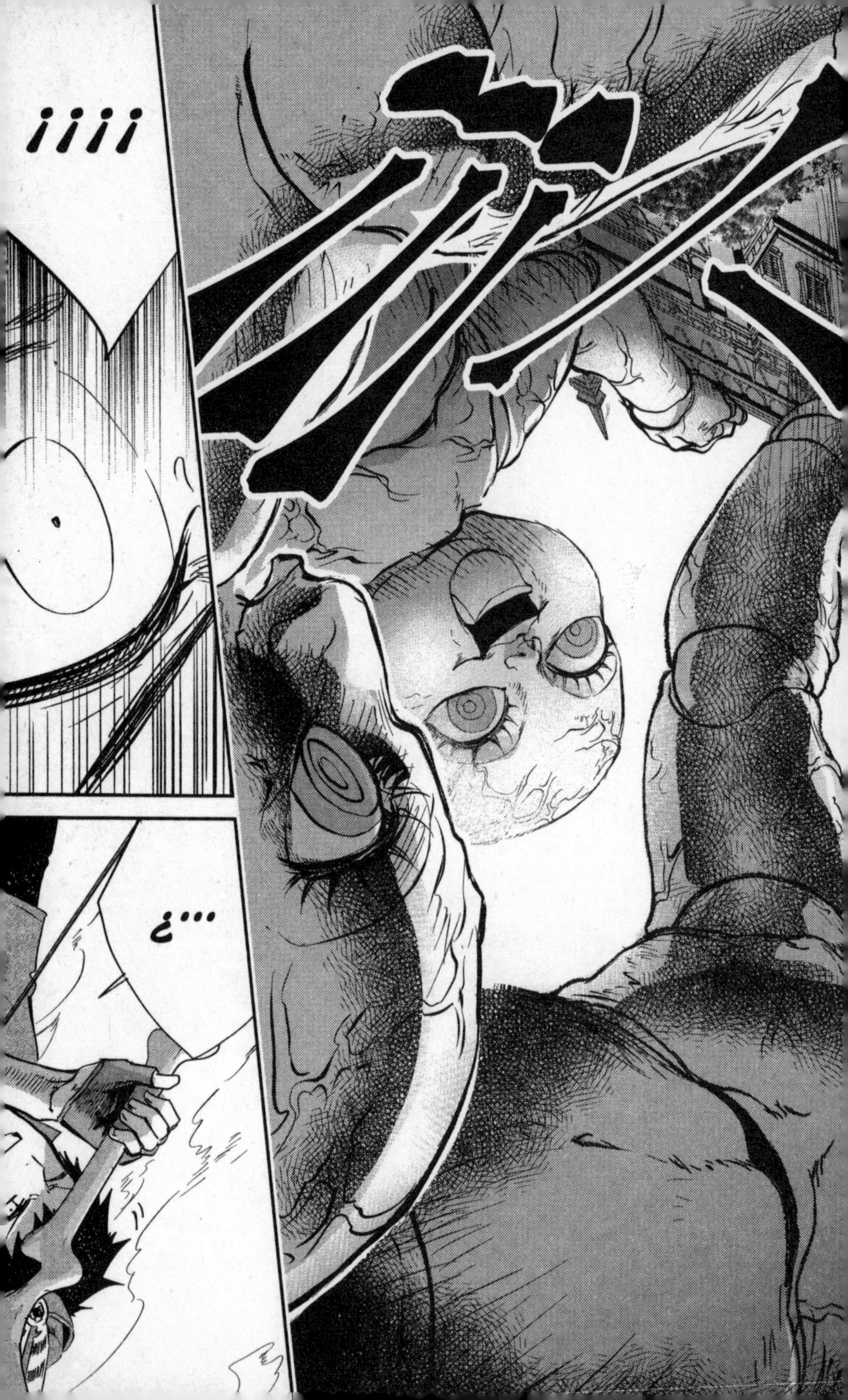
¡¡¡¡
¿...

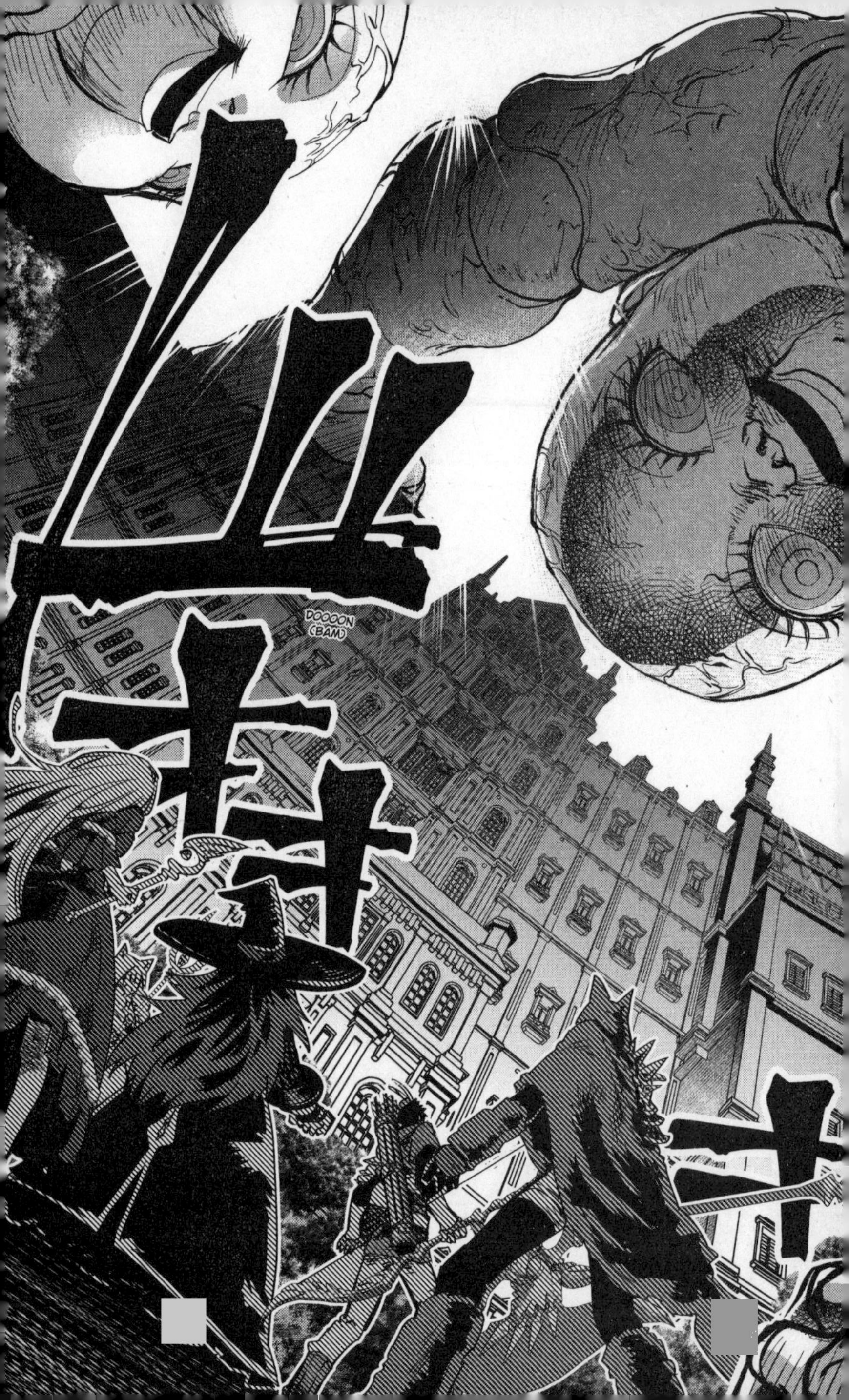
DOOOON
(BAM)

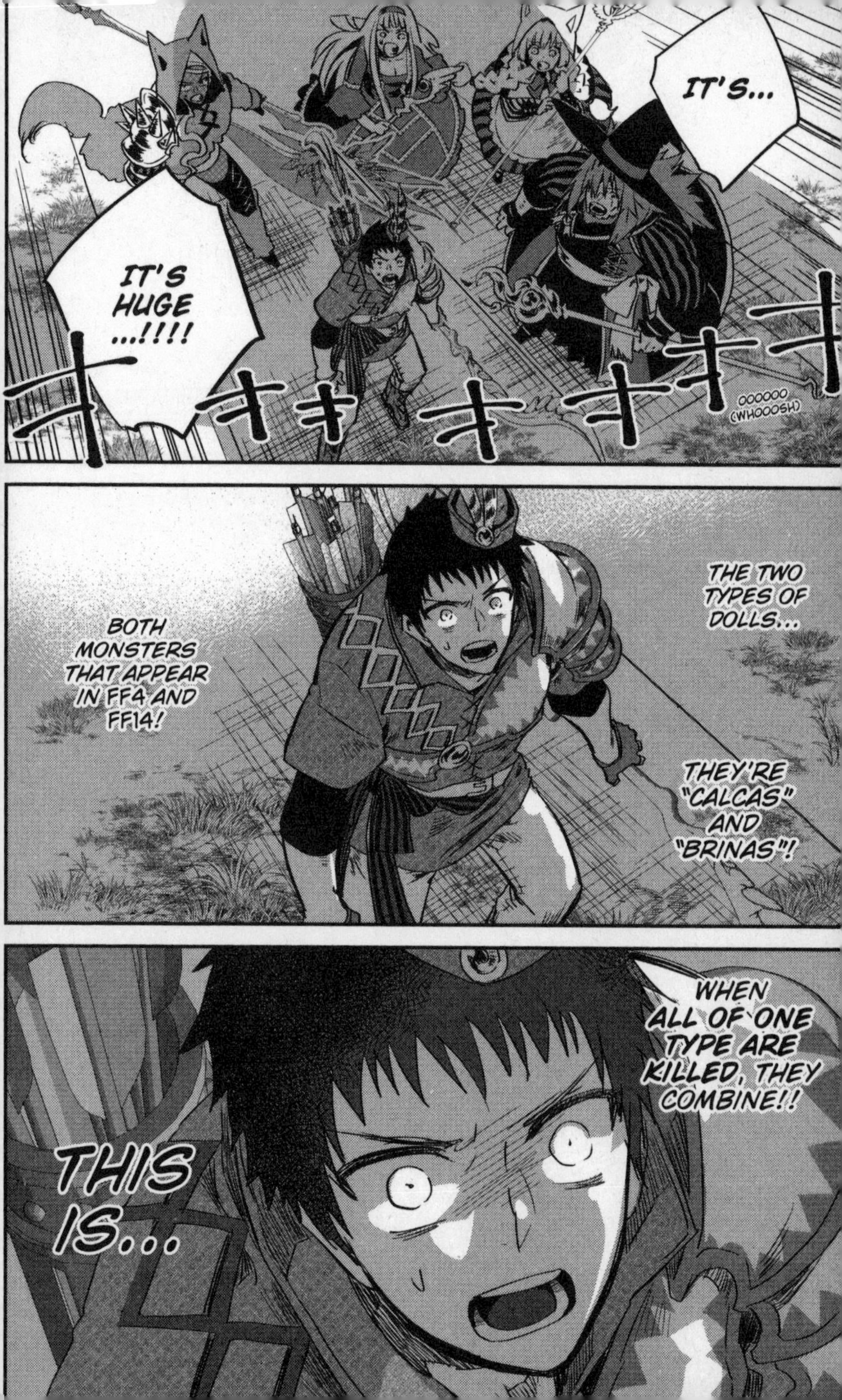
IT'S...
OOOOOO (WHOOOSH)
IT'S HUGE ...!!!!
THE TWO TYPES OF DOLLS...
THEY'RE "CALCAS" AND "BRINAS"!
BOTH MONSTERS THAT APPEAR IN FF4 AND FF14!
WHEN ALL OF ONE TYPE ARE KILLED, THEY COMBINE!!
THIS IS...

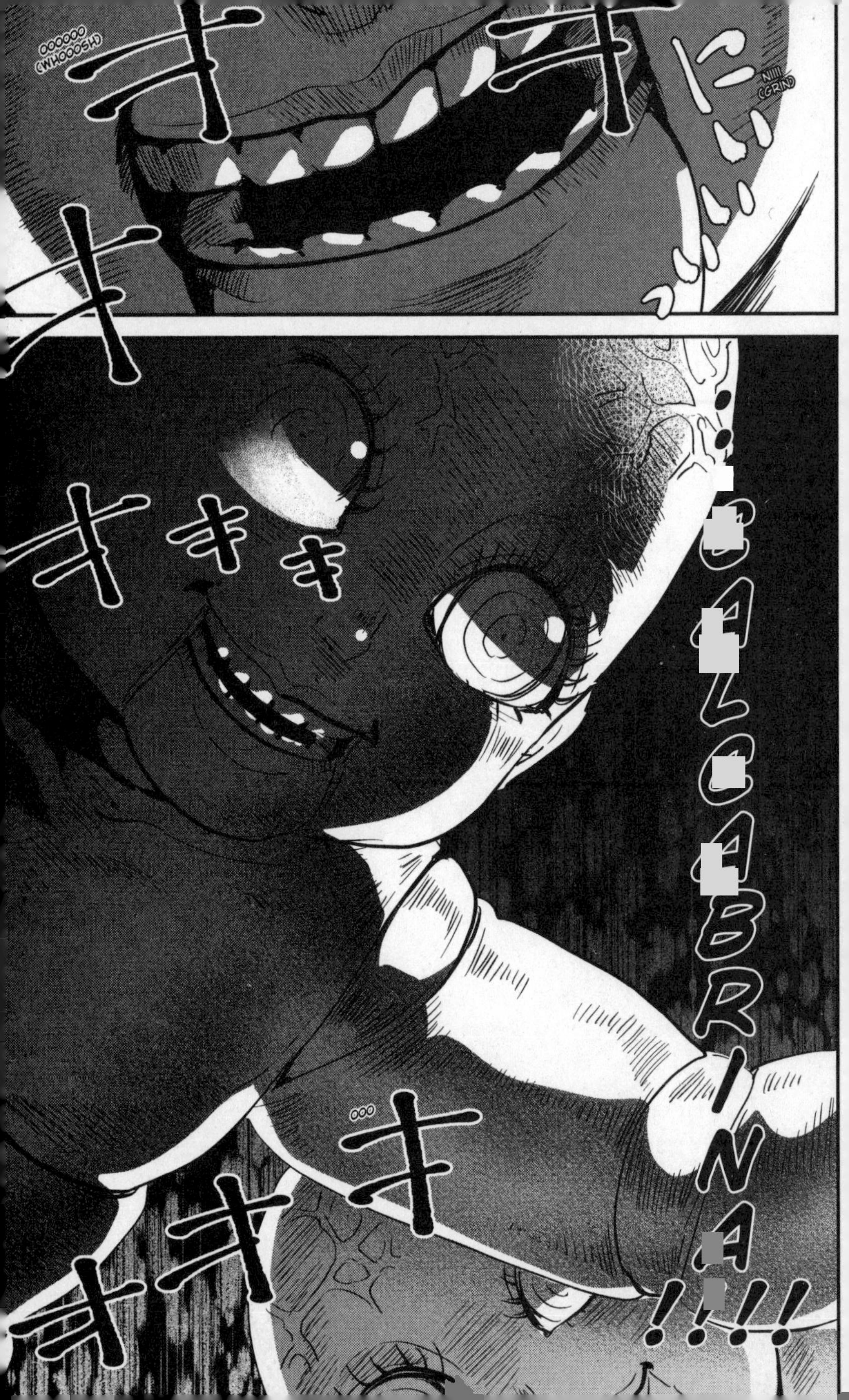
にぃぃ
NIII (GRIN)
オオ
OOOOOO (WHOOOSH)
...CALCABRINA!!!!
キキキ
キキキ...

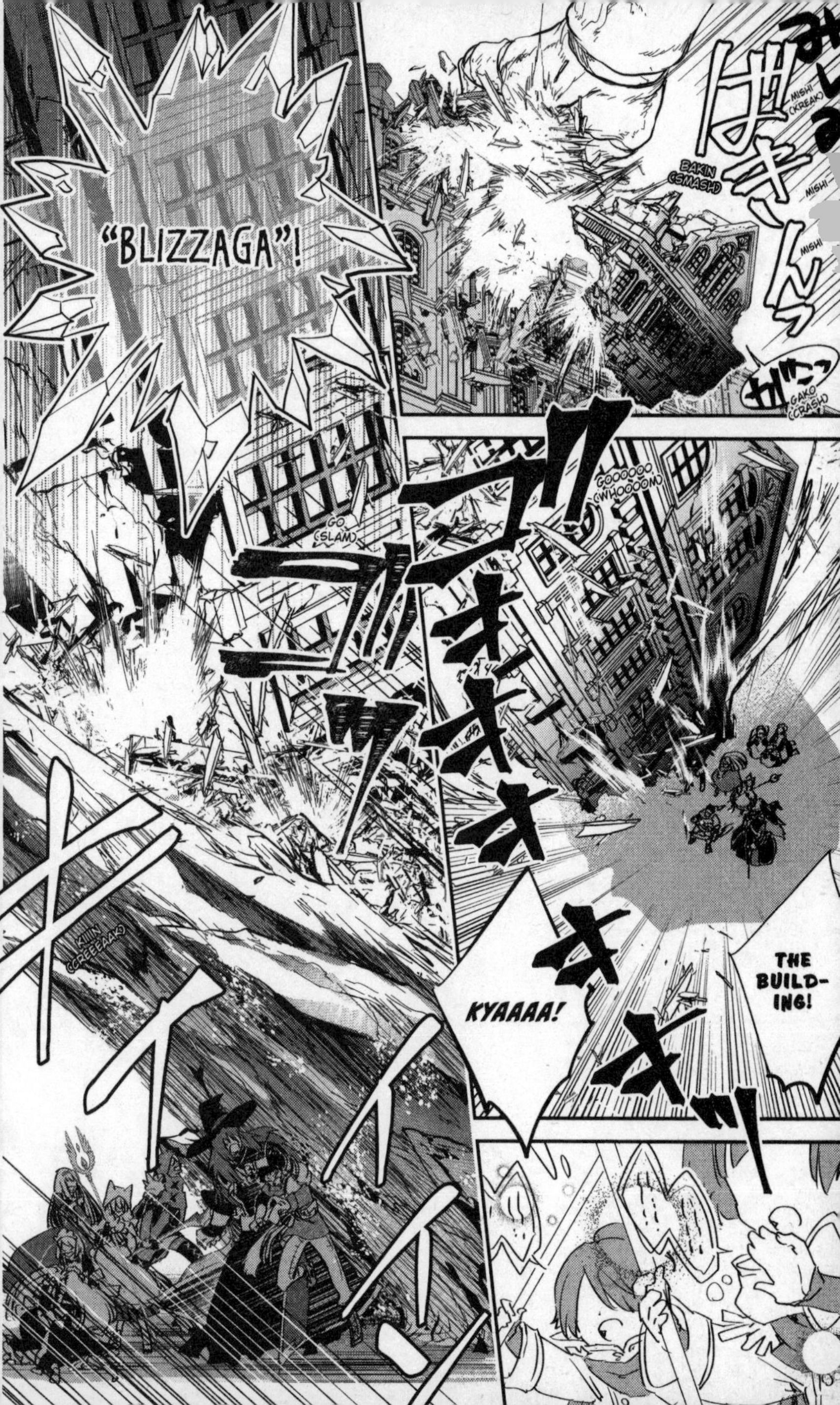

MISHI (KREAK)
MISHI
MISHI
BAKIN (SMASH)
GAKO (CRASH)
"BLIZZAGA"!
GOOOOOO (WHOOOOM)
GO (SLAM)
THE BUILD-ING!
KYAAAA!
KIIIN (CREEEAAK)

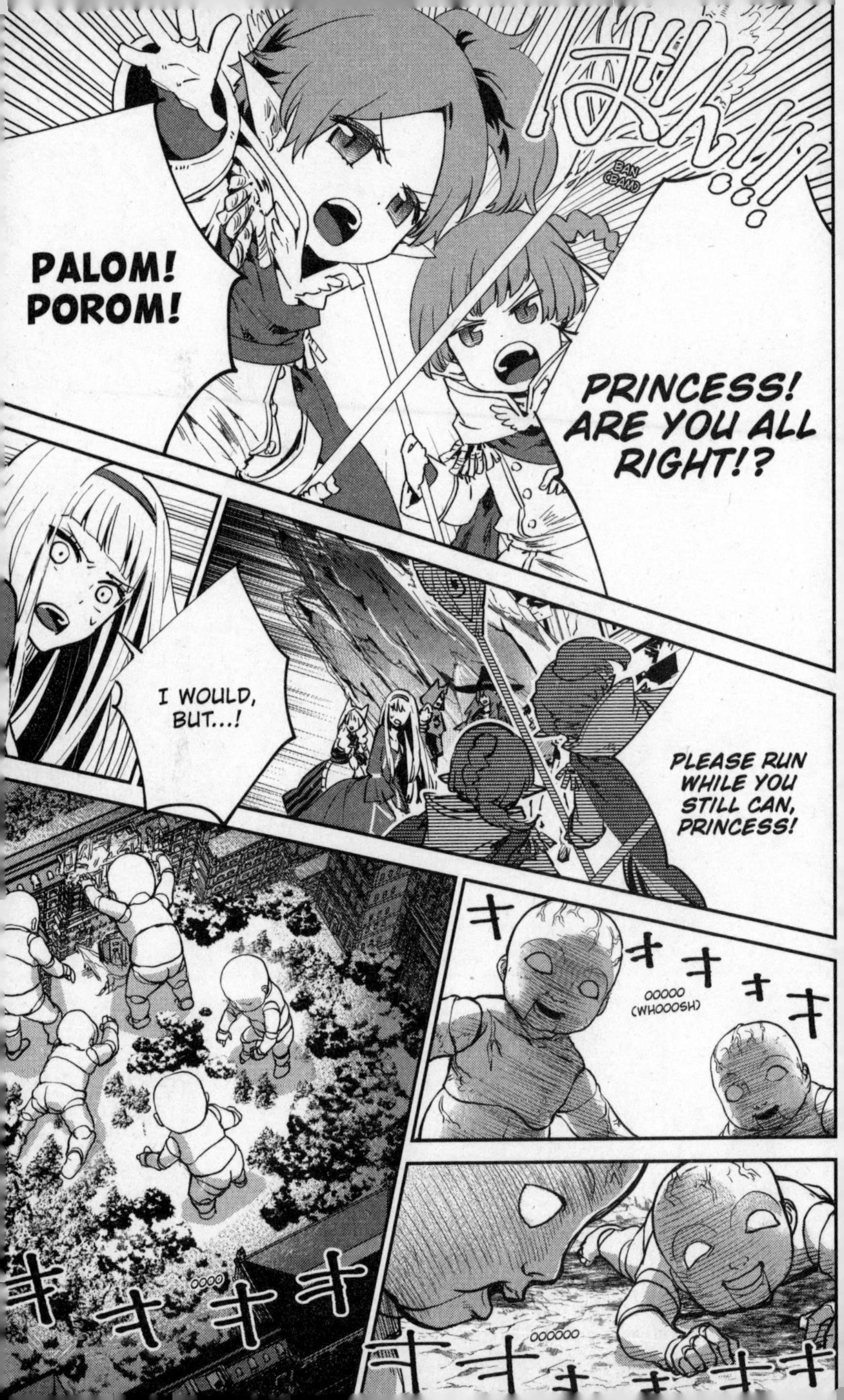
BAN (BAM)
PRINCESS! ARE YOU ALL RIGHT!?
PALOM! POROM!
PLEASE RUN WHILE YOU STILL CAN, PRINCESS!
I WOULD, BUT...!
OOOOO (WHOOOSH)
OOOO
OOOOOO

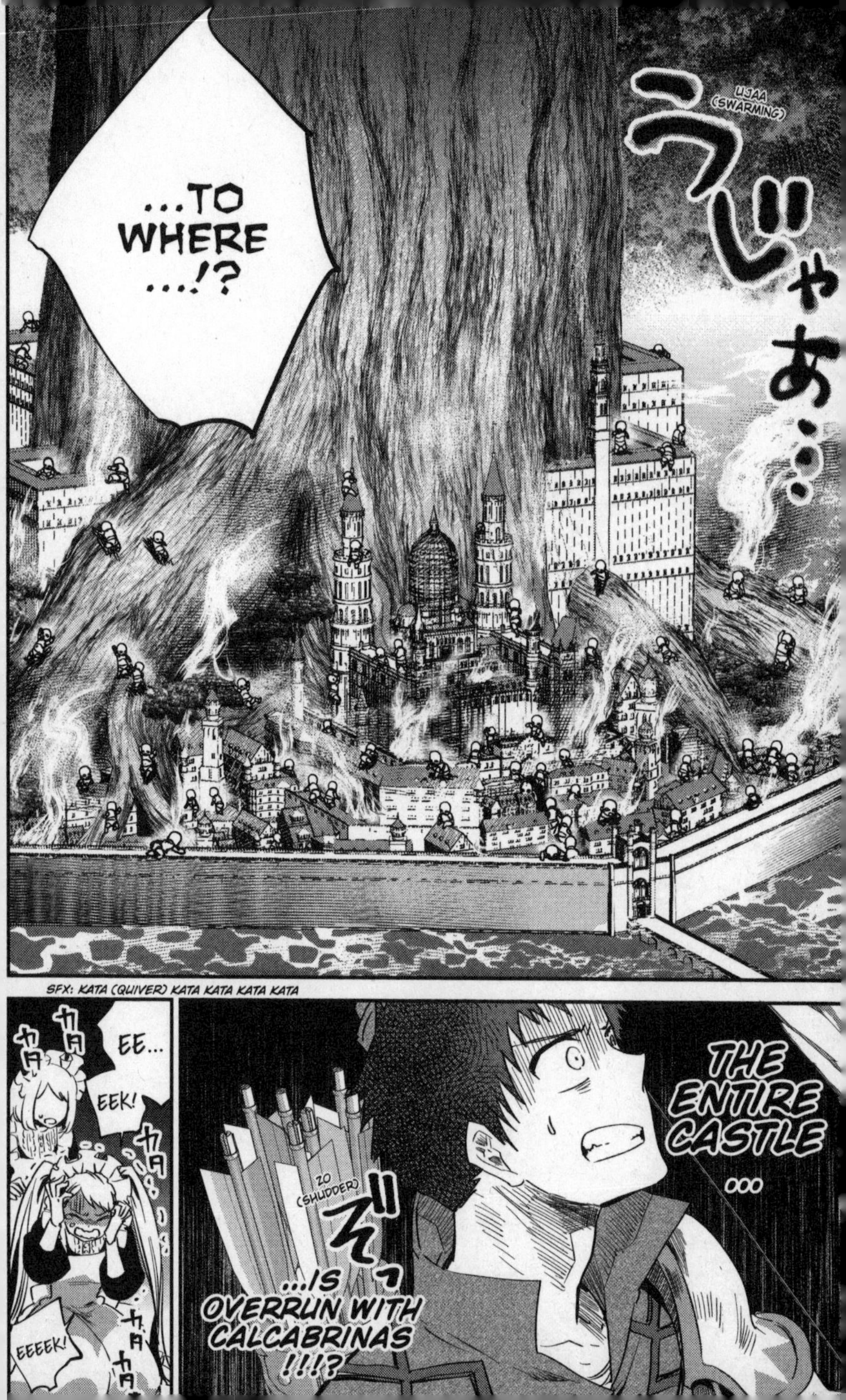
うじゃあ…
UJAA (SWARMING)
...TO WHERE ...!?
SFX: KATA (QUIVER) KATA KATA KATA KATA
THE ENTIRE CASTLE ...
ZO (SHUDDER)
ぞっ
...IS OVERRUN WITH CALCABRINAS !!!?
カタ
カタ
EE...
EEK!
カタ
EEEEK!
カタ
カタ

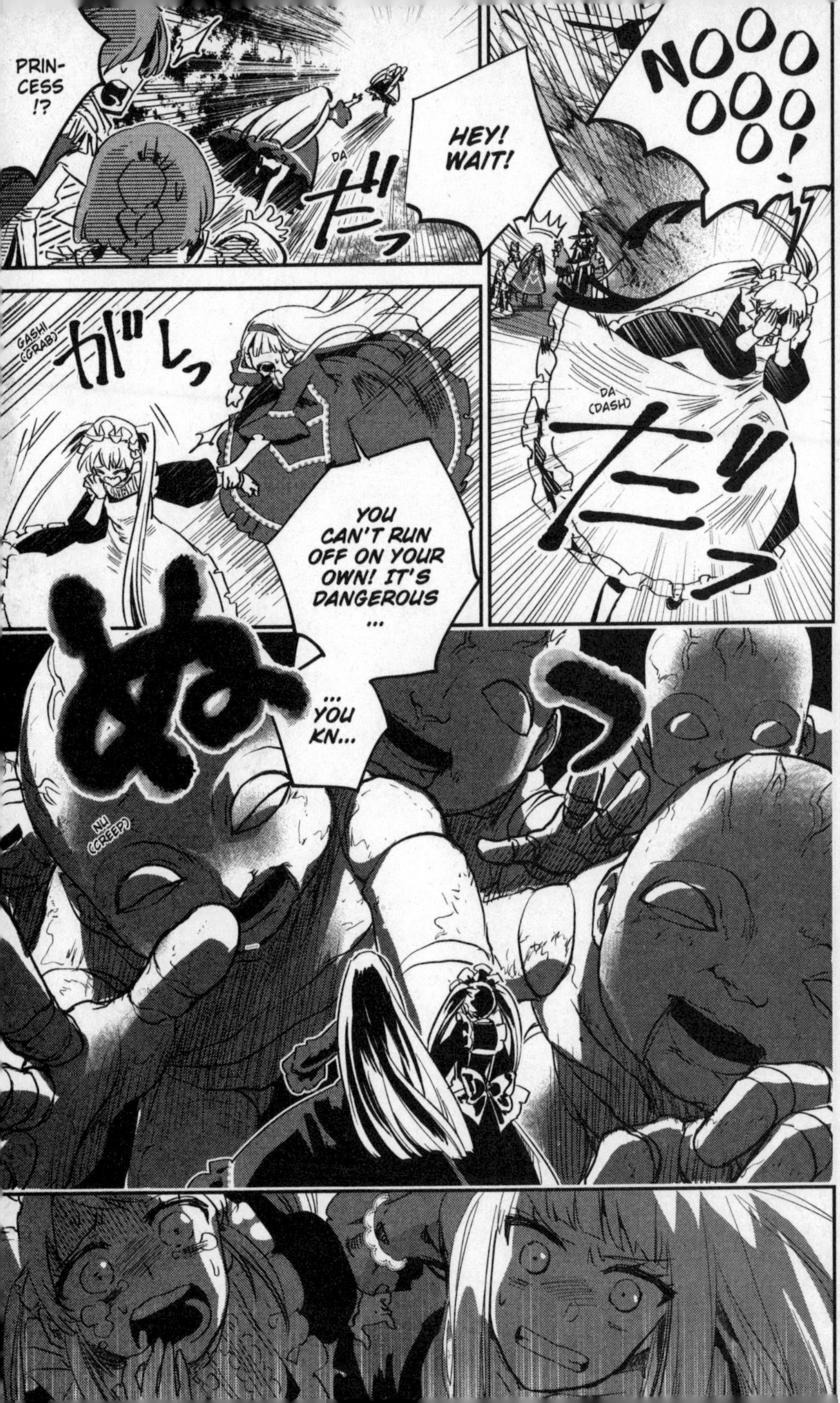
NOOOOOOOO!
DA (DASH)
HEY! WAIT!
DA
PRIN-CESS!?
GASHI (GRAB)
YOU CAN'T RUN OFF ON YOUR OWN! IT'S DANGEROUS...
...YOU KN...
NU (CREEP)

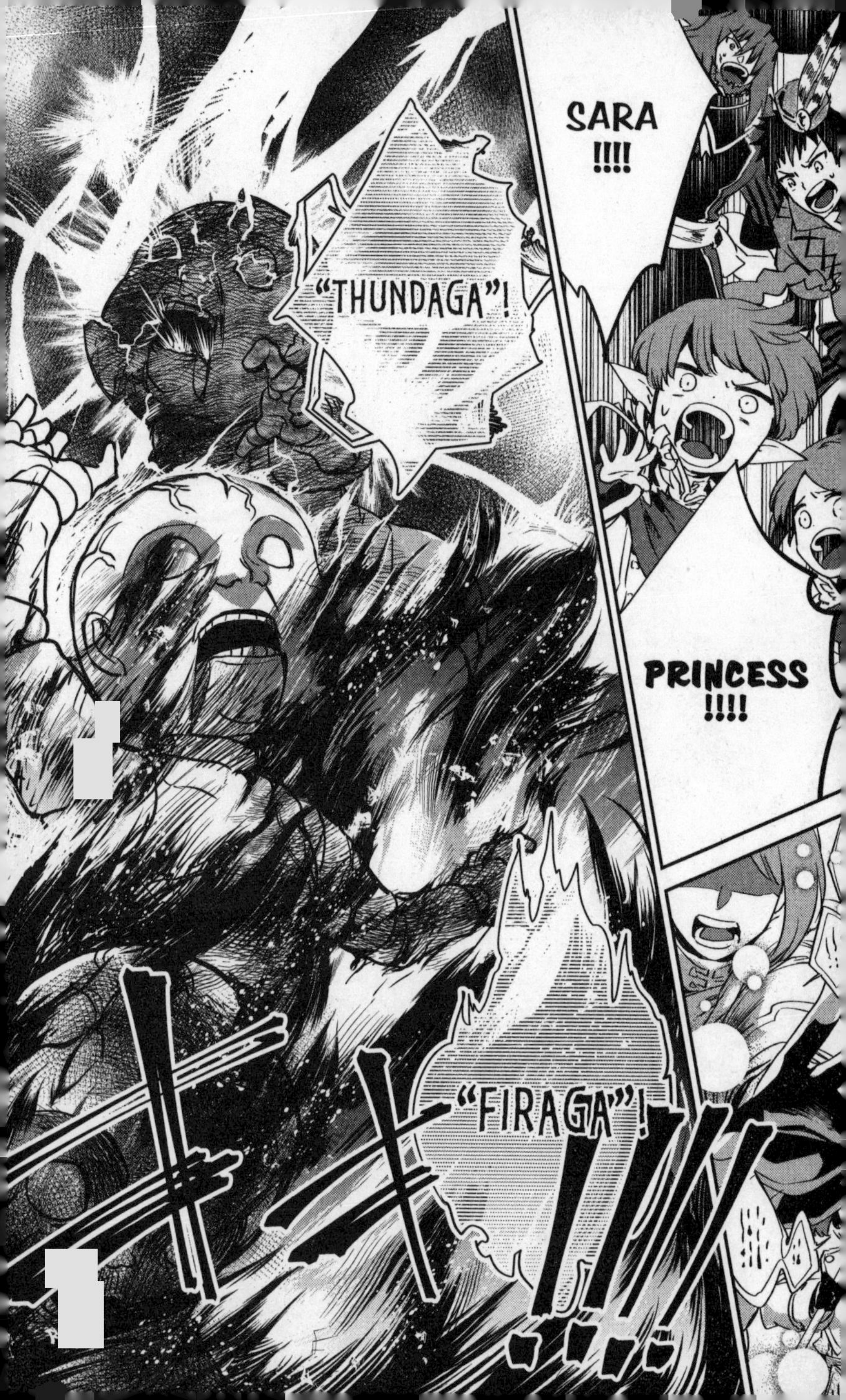
SARA !!!!
PRINCESS !!!!
"THUNDAGA"!
"FIRAGA"!

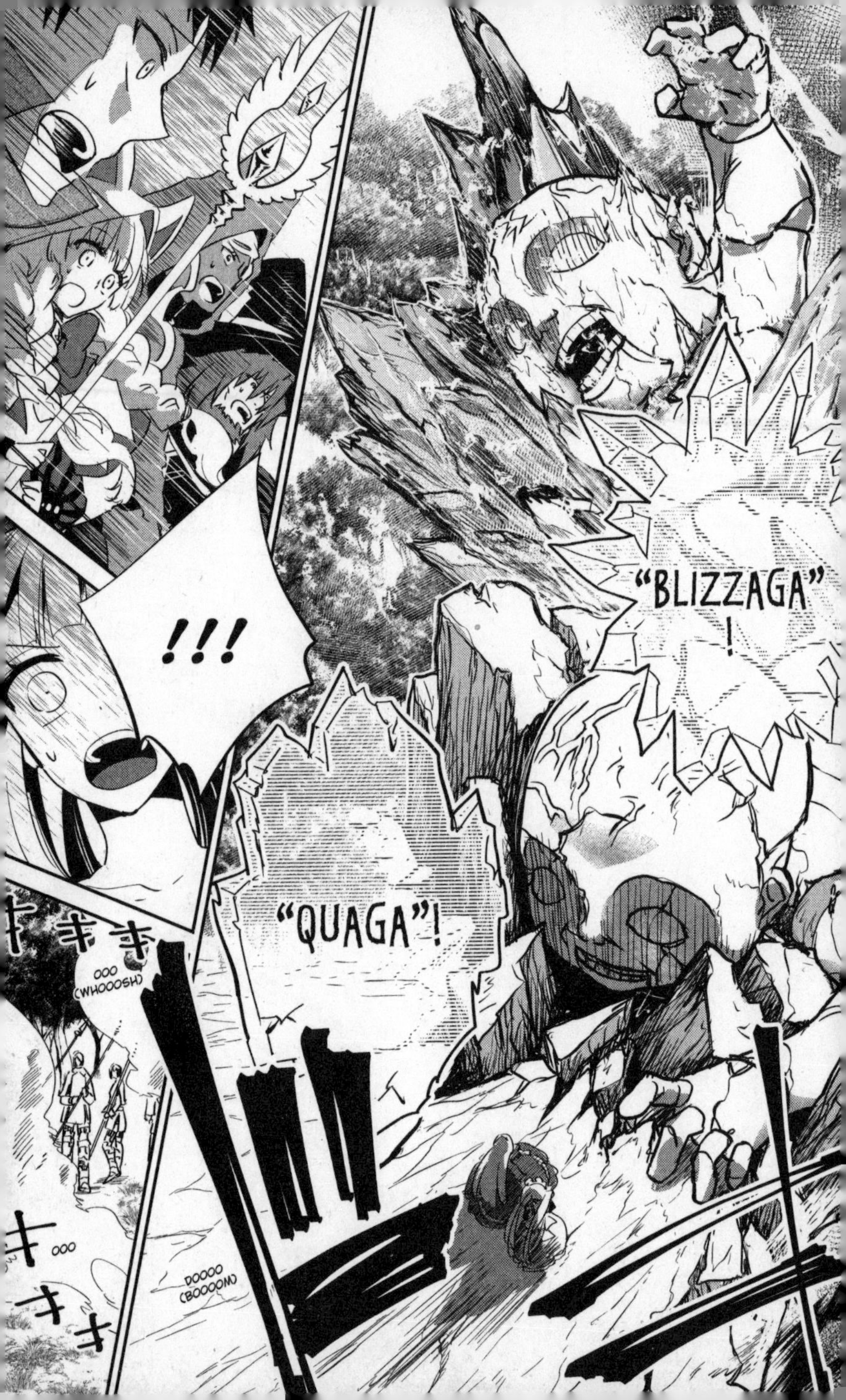
"BLIZZAGA"!
"QUAGA"!
!!!
OOO (WHOOOSH)
DOOOO (BOOOOM)

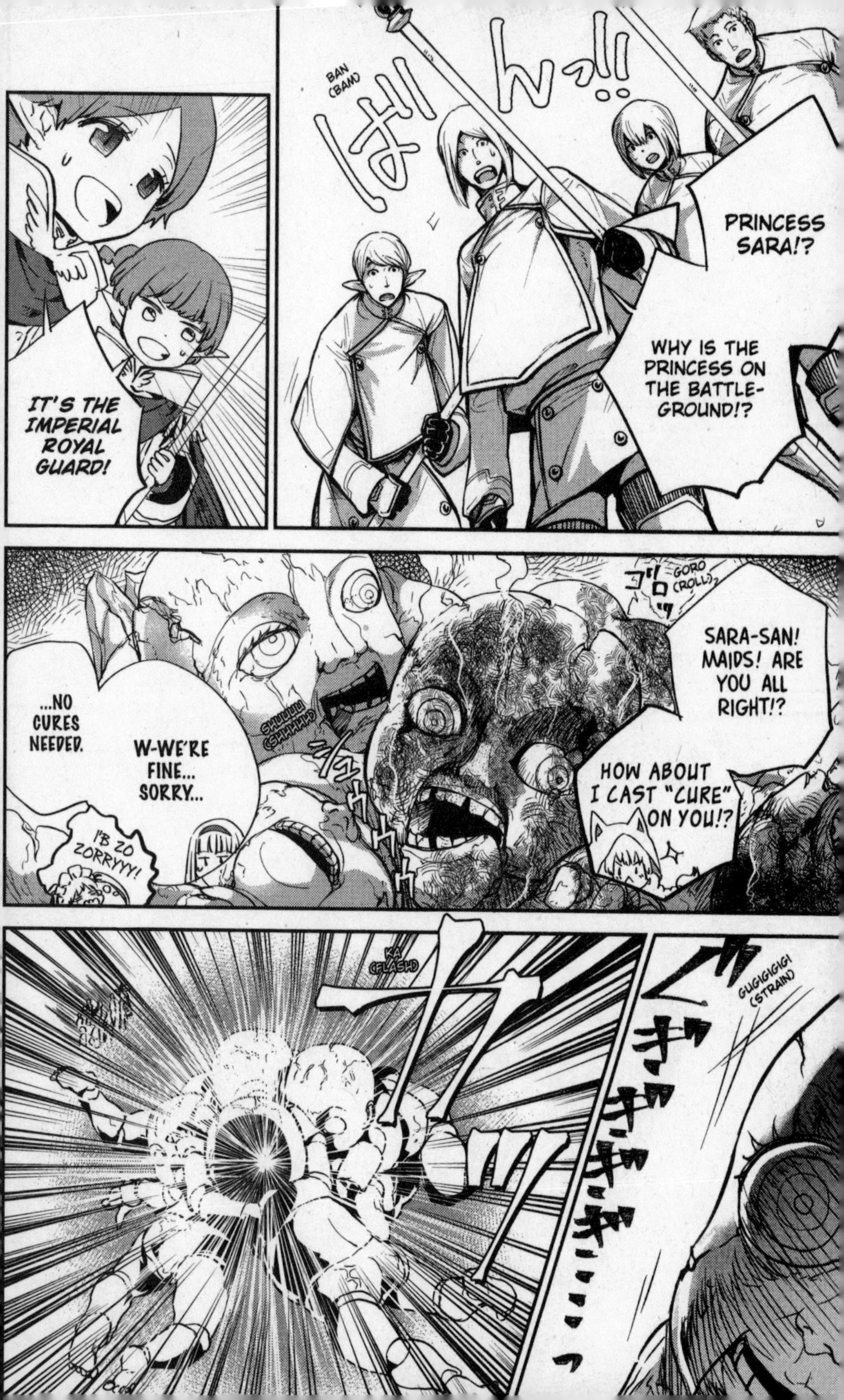
BAN (BAM)
PRINCESS SARA!?
WHY IS THE PRINCESS ON THE BATTLE-GROUND!?
IT'S THE IMPERIAL ROYAL GUARD!
GORO (ROLL)
SARA-SAN! MAIDS! ARE YOU ALL RIGHT!?
HOW ABOUT I CAST "CURE" ON YOU!?
SHUUUU (SHHHHH)
W-WE'RE FINE... SORRY...
...NO CURES NEEDED.
I'B ZO ZORRYYY!
GUGIGIGIGI (STRAIN)
KA (FLASH)

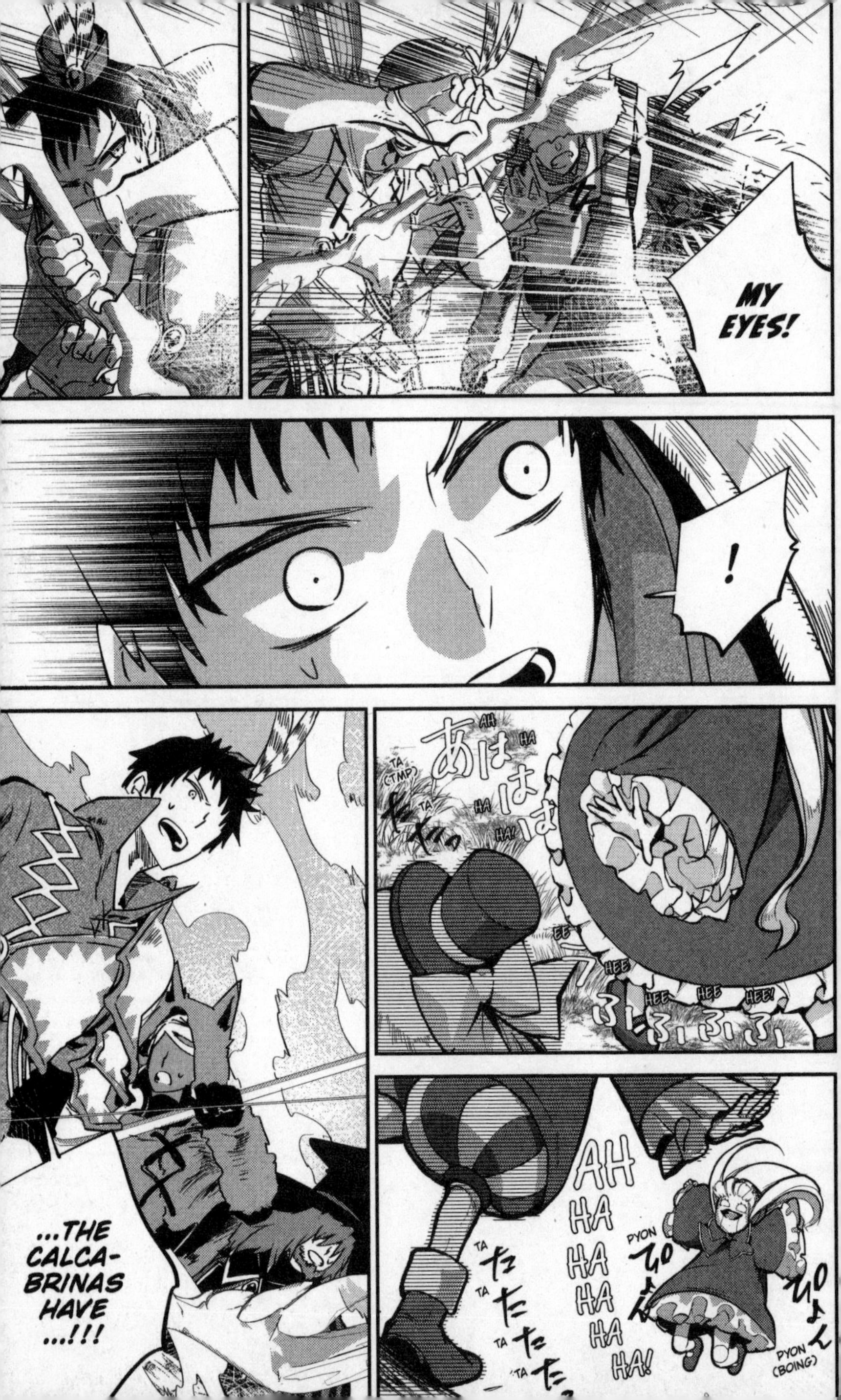
MY EYES!
!
あはは AH HA HA HA!
たたたっ TA TA TA (TMP)
ふふふふ EE HEE HEE HEE HEE!
AH HA HA HA HA HA HA!
たたたた TA TA TA TA
ぴょん PYON
ぴょん PYON (BOING)
...THE CALCA-BRINAS HAVE ...!!!

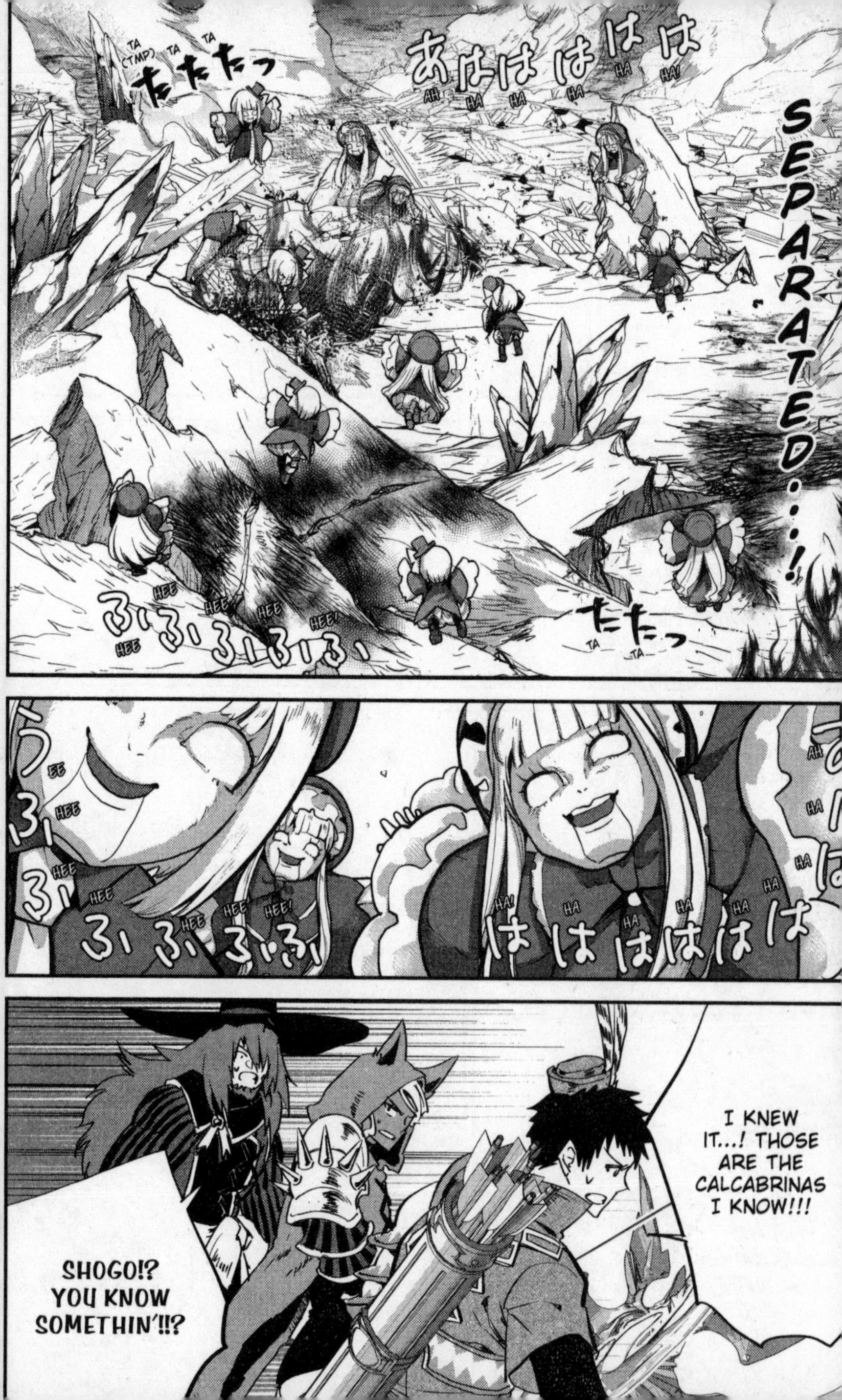
SEPARATED...!!
あははははは
AH HA HA HA HA!
たたたっ
TA (TMP) TA TA
ふぃふぃふぃふぃ
HEE HEE HEE HEE!
たたっ
TA TA
はははははは
AH HA HA HA HA HA!
ふふふふふ
HEE HEE HEE HEE!
うふふ
EE HEE HEE
I KNEW IT...! THOSE ARE THE CALCABRINAS I KNOW!!!
SHOGO!? YOU KNOW SOMETHIN'!!?

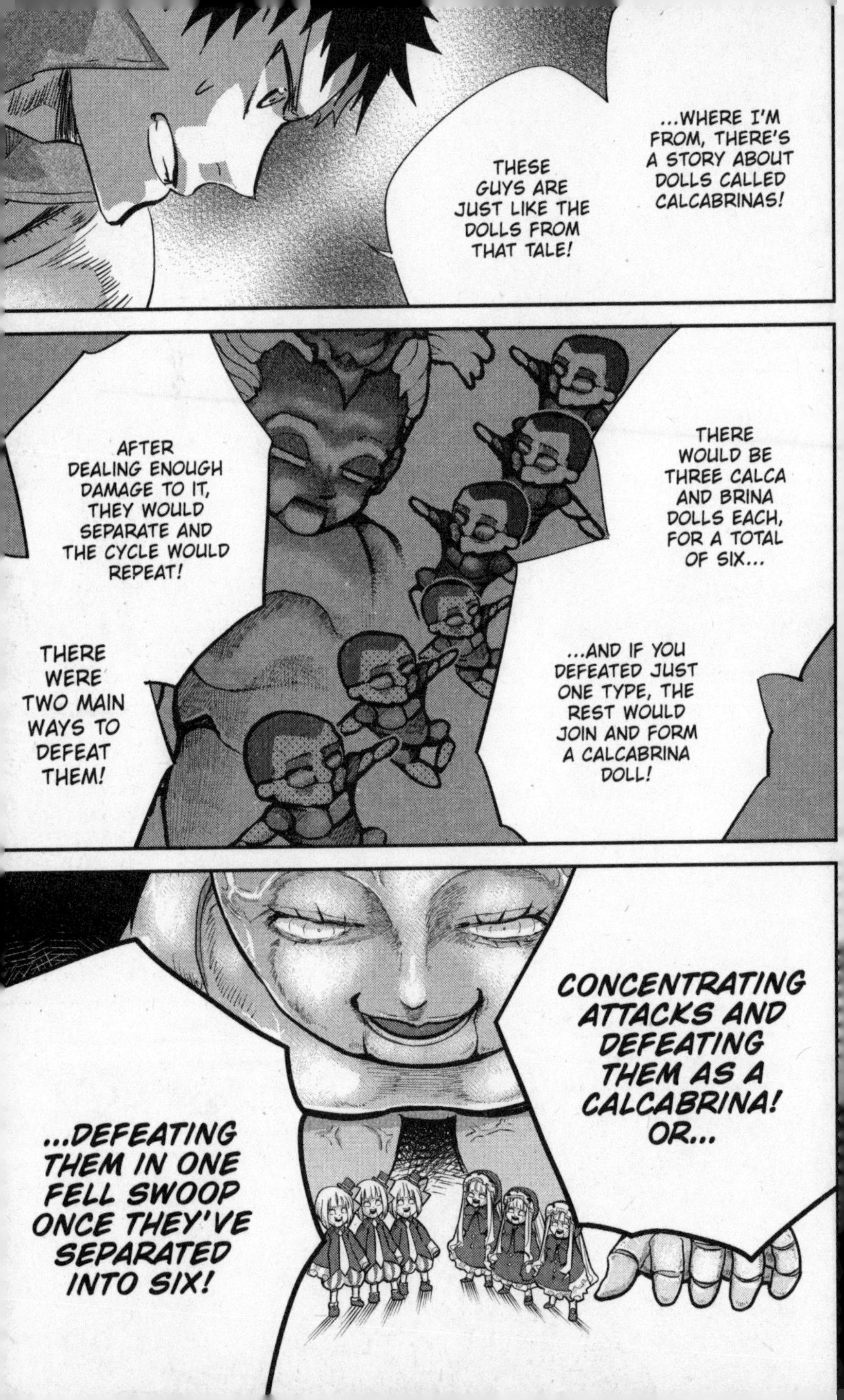
...WHERE I'M FROM, THERE'S A STORY ABOUT DOLLS CALLED CALCABRINAS!
THESE GUYS ARE JUST LIKE THE DOLLS FROM THAT TALE!
THERE WOULD BE THREE CALCA AND BRINA DOLLS EACH, FOR A TOTAL OF SIX...
AFTER DEALING ENOUGH DAMAGE TO IT, THEY WOULD SEPARATE AND THE CYCLE WOULD REPEAT!
...AND IF YOU DEFEATED JUST ONE TYPE, THE REST WOULD JOIN AND FORM A CALCABRINA DOLL!
THERE WERE TWO MAIN WAYS TO DEFEAT THEM!
CONCENTRATING ATTACKS AND DEFEATING THEM AS A CALCABRINA! OR...
...DEFEATING THEM IN ONE FELL SWOOP ONCE THEY'VE SEPARATED INTO SIX!

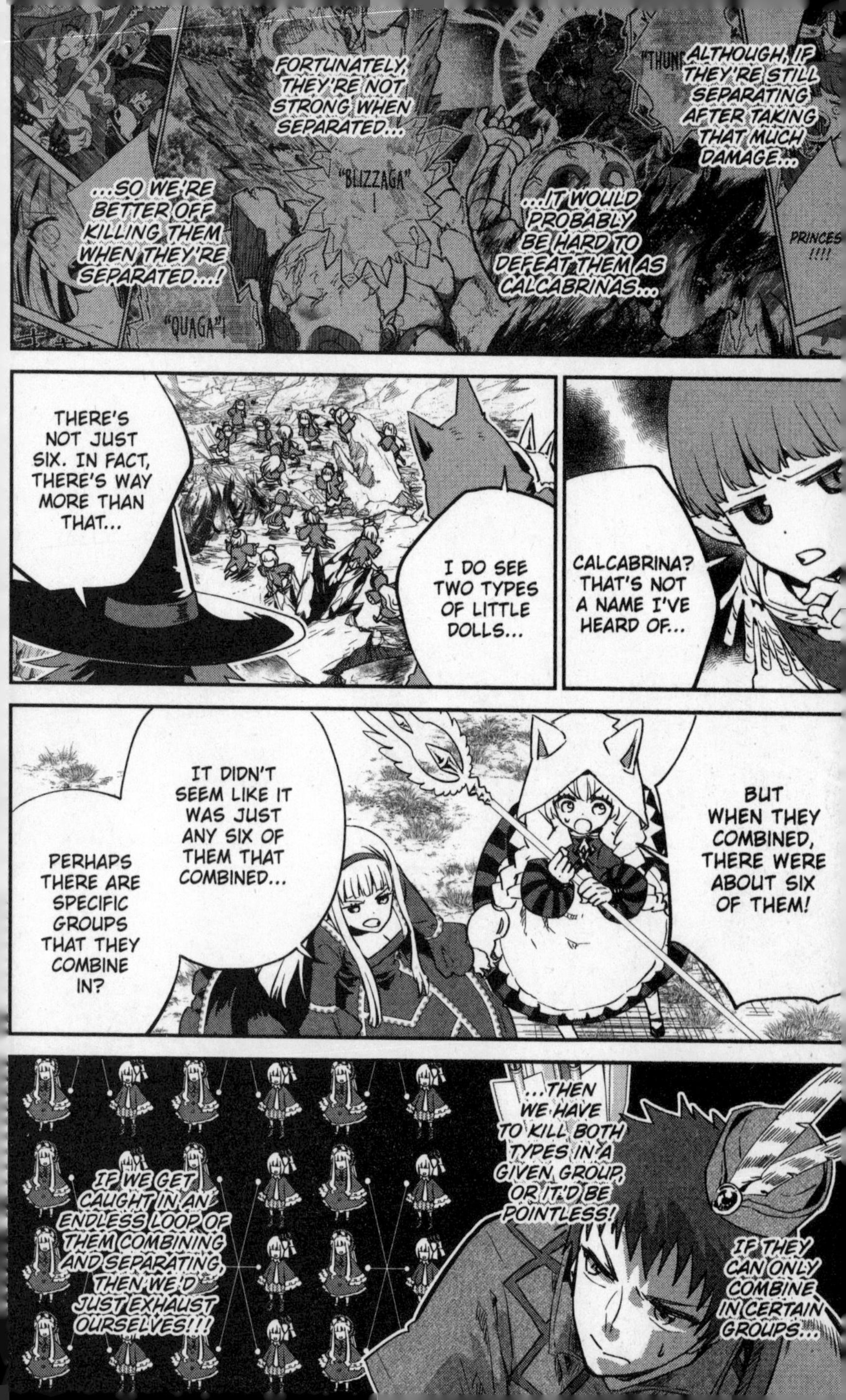
PRINCES !!!!
"THUN
ALTHOUGH, IF THEY'RE STILL SEPARATING AFTER TAKING THAT MUCH DAMAGE...
...IT WOULD PROBABLY BE HARD TO DEFEAT THEM AS CALCABRINAS...
FORTUNATELY, THEY'RE NOT STRONG WHEN SEPARATED...
"BLIZZAGA"!
...SO WE'RE BETTER OFF KILLING THEM WHEN THEY'RE SEPARATED...!
"QUAGA"!
CALCABRINA? THAT'S NOT A NAME I'VE HEARD OF...
I DO SEE TWO TYPES OF LITTLE DOLLS...
THERE'S NOT JUST SIX. IN FACT, THERE'S WAY MORE THAN THAT...
BUT WHEN THEY COMBINED, THERE WERE ABOUT SIX OF THEM!
IT DIDN'T SEEM LIKE IT WAS JUST ANY SIX OF THEM THAT COMBINED...
PERHAPS THERE ARE SPECIFIC GROUPS THAT THEY COMBINE IN?
IF THEY CAN ONLY COMBINE IN CERTAIN GROUPS...
...THEN WE HAVE TO KILL BOTH TYPES IN A GIVEN GROUP, OR IT'D BE POINTLESS!
IF WE GET CAUGHT IN AN ENDLESS LOOP OF THEM COMBINING AND SEPARATING, THEN WE'D JUST EXHAUST OURSELVES!!!

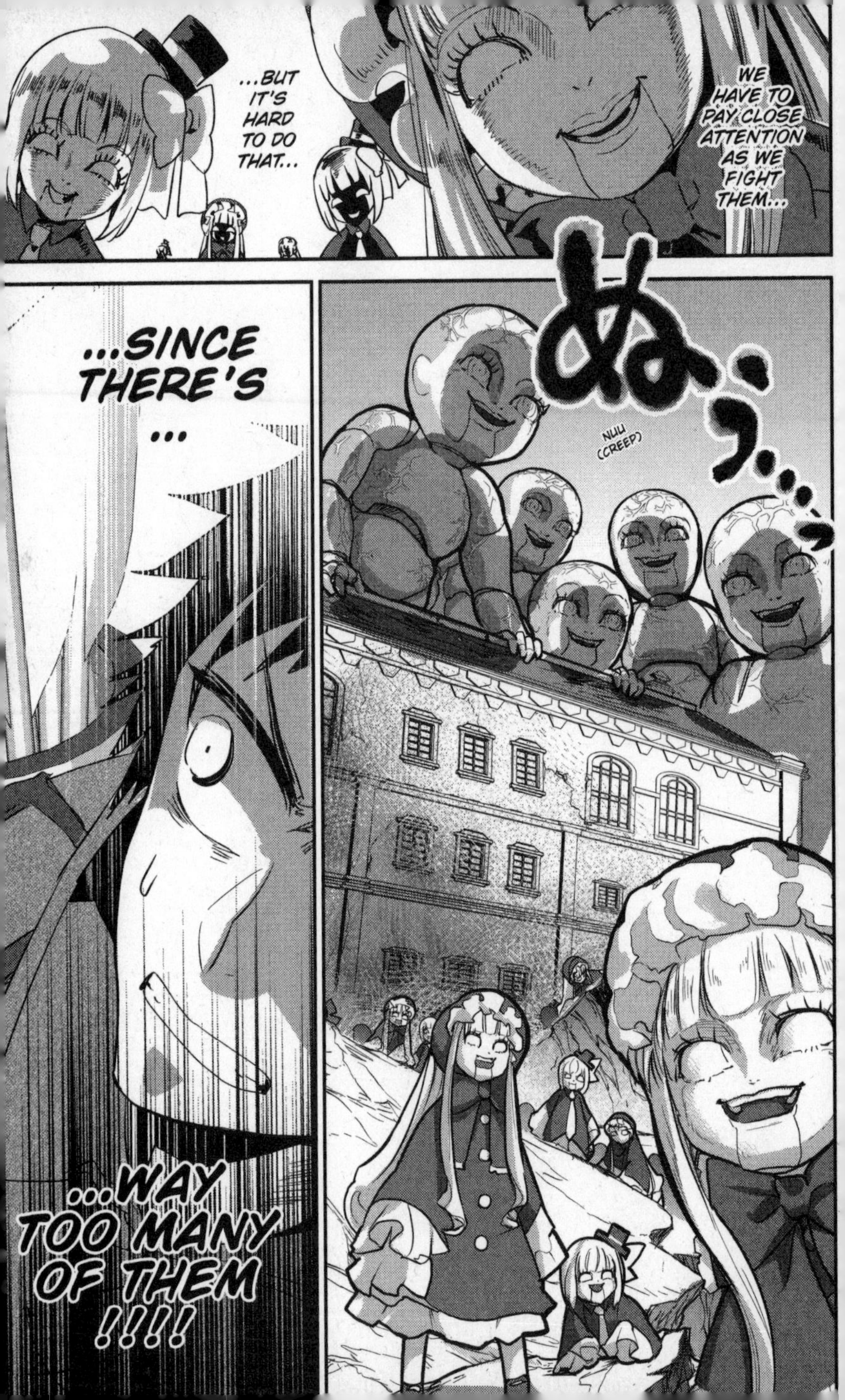
WE HAVE TO PAY CLOSE ATTENTION AS WE FIGHT THEM...
...BUT IT'S HARD TO DO THAT...
ぬっ...
NUU (CREEP)
...SINCE THERE'S ...
...WAY TOO MANY OF THEM !!!!

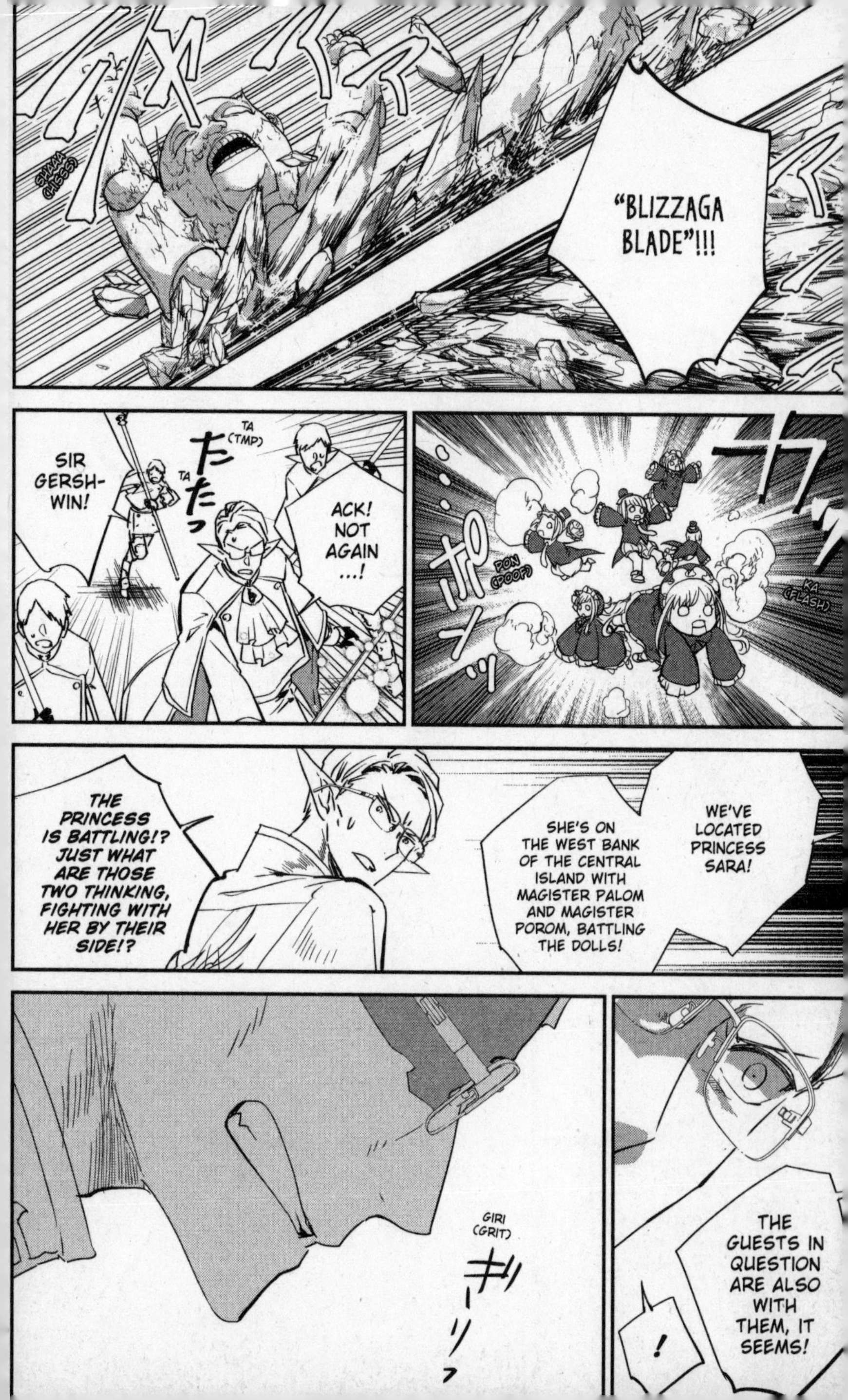
"BLIZZAGA BLADE"!!!
SHAA (HISSS)
KA (FLASH)
PON (POOF)
TA TA (TMP)
SIR GERSH-WIN!
ACK! NOT AGAIN...!
WE'VE LOCATED PRINCESS SARA!
SHE'S ON THE WEST BANK OF THE CENTRAL ISLAND WITH MAGISTER PALOM AND MAGISTER POROM, BATTLING THE DOLLS!
THE PRINCESS IS BATTLING!? JUST WHAT ARE THOSE TWO THINKING, FIGHTING WITH HER BY THEIR SIDE!?
THE GUESTS IN QUESTION ARE ALSO WITH THEM, IT SEEMS!
!
GIRI (GRIT)

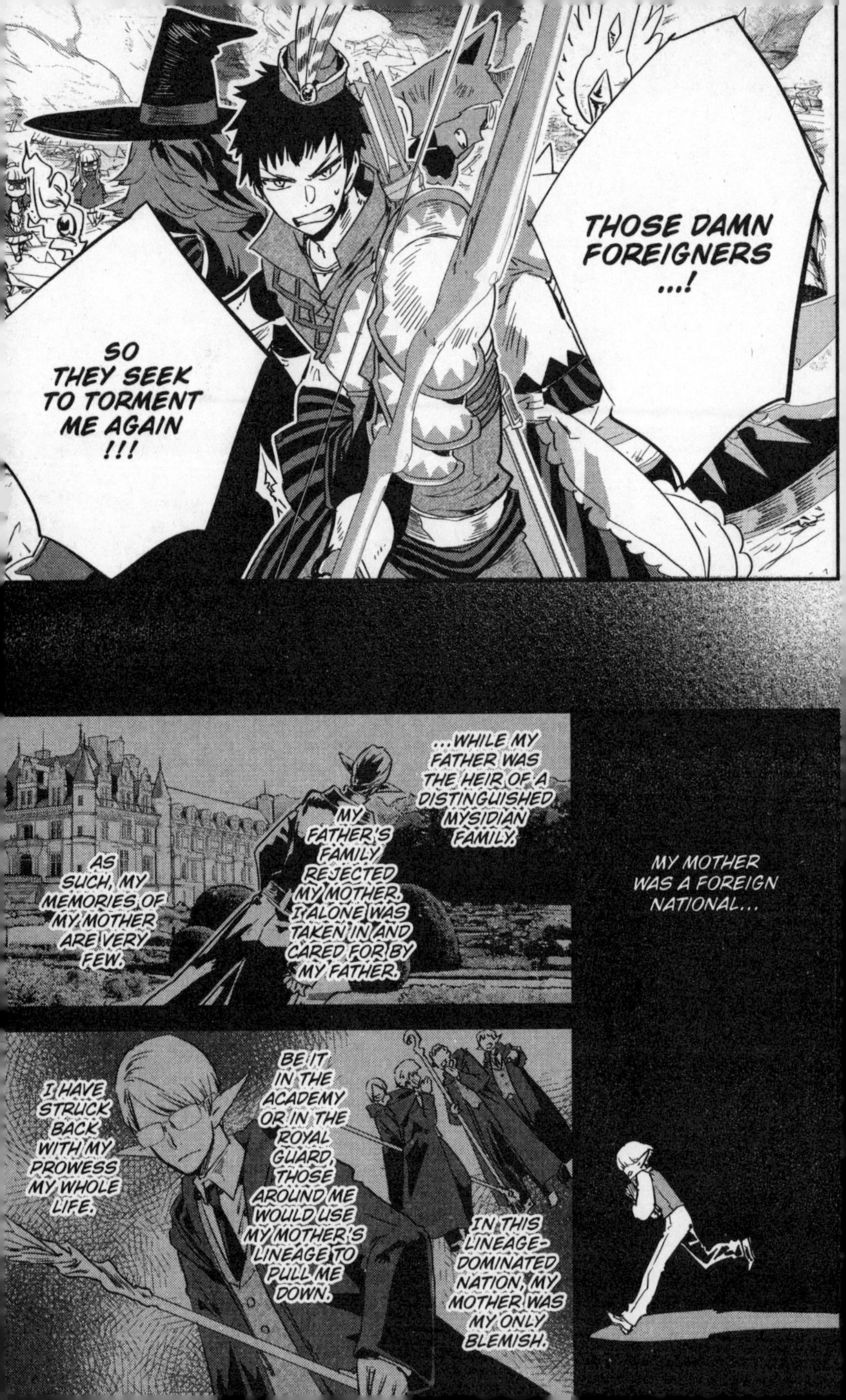
THOSE DAMN FOREIGNERS ...!
SO THEY SEEK TO TORMENT ME AGAIN !!!
MY MOTHER WAS A FOREIGN NATIONAL...
...WHILE MY FATHER WAS THE HEIR OF A DISTINGUISHED MYSIDIAN FAMILY.
MY FATHER'S FAMILY REJECTED MY MOTHER. I ALONE WAS TAKEN IN AND CARED FOR BY MY FATHER.
AS SUCH, MY MEMORIES OF MY MOTHER ARE VERY FEW.
IN THIS LINEAGE-DOMINATED NATION, MY MOTHER WAS MY ONLY BLEMISH.
BE IT IN THE ACADEMY OR IN THE ROYAL GUARD, THOSE AROUND ME WOULD USE MY MOTHER'S LINEAGE TO PULL ME DOWN.
I HAVE STRUCK BACK WITH MY PROWESS MY WHOLE LIFE.

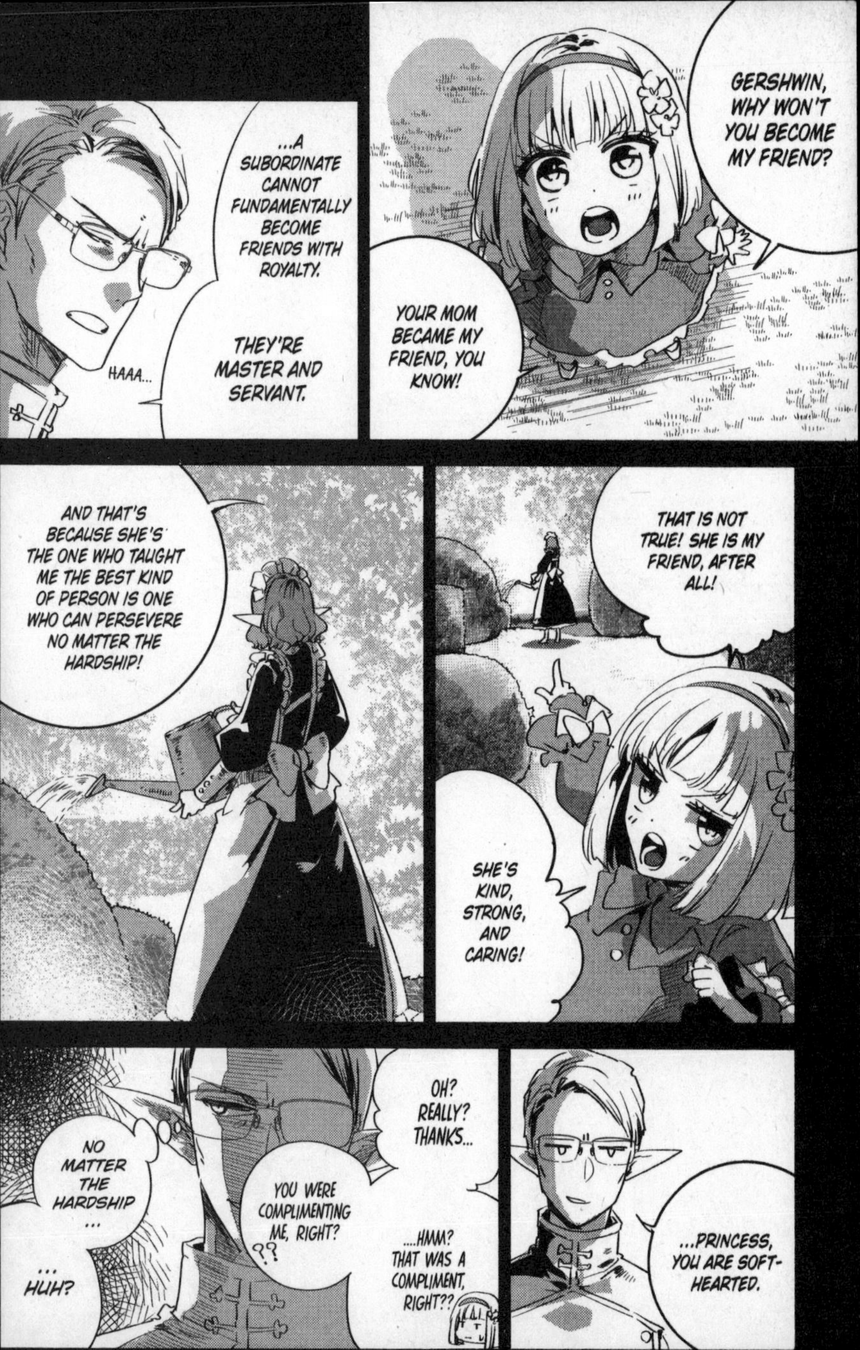
GERSHWIN, WHY WON'T YOU BECOME MY FRIEND?
YOUR MOM BECAME MY FRIEND, YOU KNOW!
...A SUBORDINATE CANNOT FUNDAMENTALLY BECOME FRIENDS WITH ROYALTY.
THEY'RE MASTER AND SERVANT.
HAAA...
THAT IS NOT TRUE! SHE IS MY FRIEND, AFTER ALL!
SHE'S KIND, STRONG, AND CARING!
AND THAT'S BECAUSE SHE'S THE ONE WHO TAUGHT ME THE BEST KIND OF PERSON IS ONE WHO CAN PERSEVERE NO MATTER THE HARDSHIP!
...PRINCESS, YOU ARE SOFT-HEARTED.
OH? REALLY? THANKS...
YOU WERE COMPLIMENTING ME, RIGHT?
??
...HMM? THAT WAS A COMPLIMENT, RIGHT??
NO MATTER THE HARDSHIP ...
... HUH?

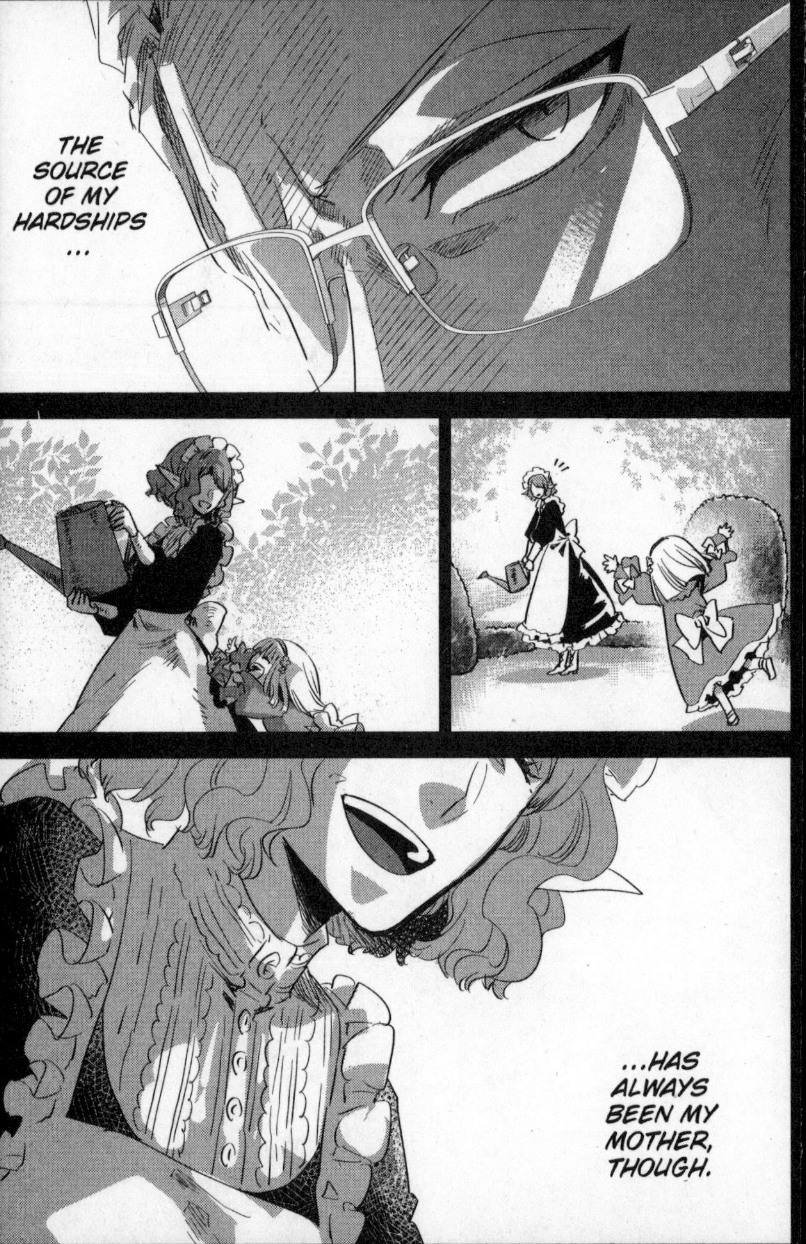
THE SOURCE OF MY HARDSHIPS ...
...HAS ALWAYS BEEN MY MOTHER, THOUGH.

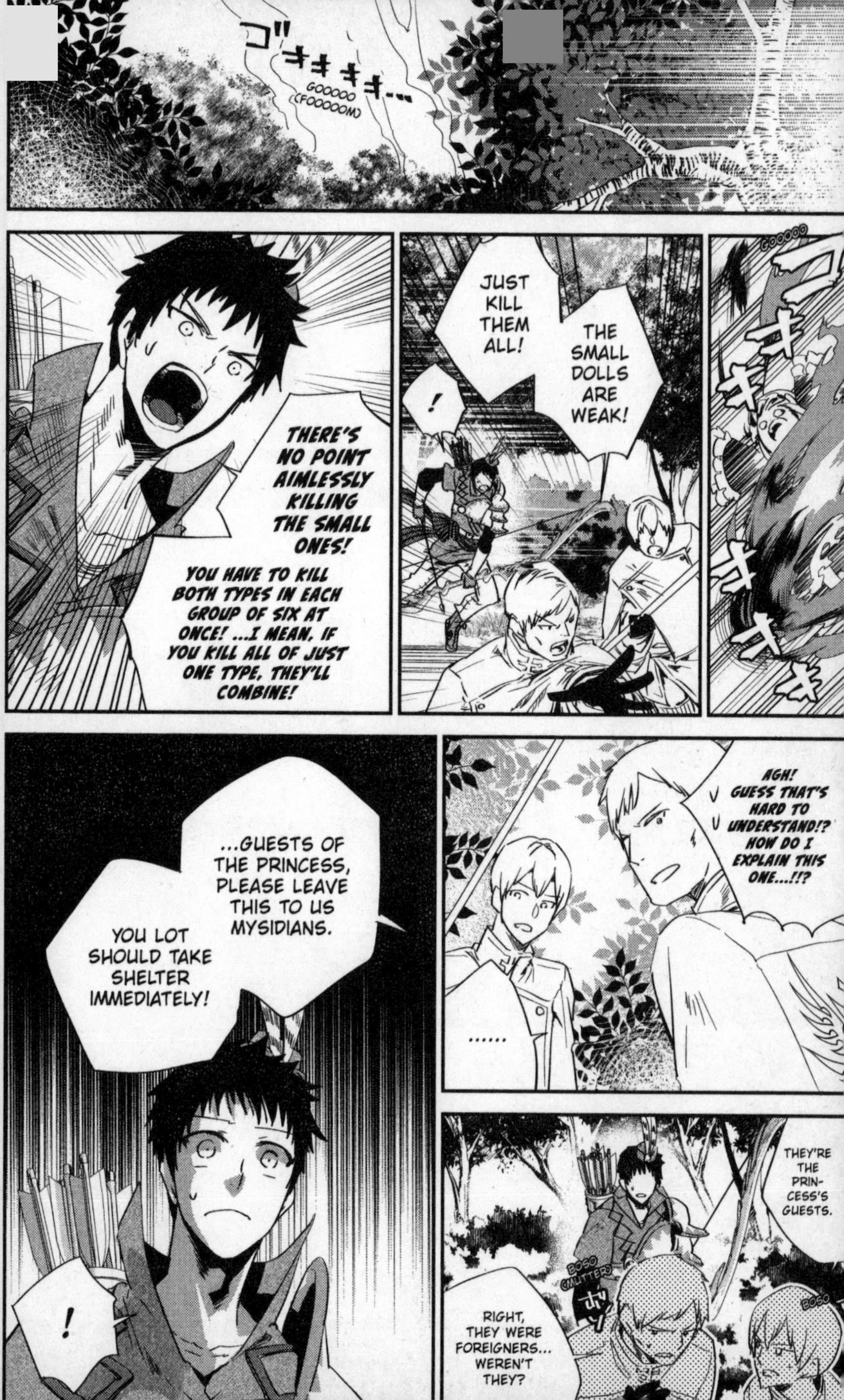
GOOOOO (FOOOOOM)
GOOOOO
JUST KILL THEM ALL!
THE SMALL DOLLS ARE WEAK!
!
THERE'S NO POINT AIMLESSLY KILLING THE SMALL ONES!
YOU HAVE TO KILL BOTH TYPES IN EACH GROUP OF SIX AT ONCE! ...I MEAN, IF YOU KILL ALL OF JUST ONE TYPE, THEY'LL COMBINE!
AGH! GUESS THAT'S HARD TO UNDERSTAND!? HOW DO I EXPLAIN THIS ONE...!!?
......
THEY'RE THE PRIN-CESS'S GUESTS.
BOSO
BOSO (MUTTER)
RIGHT, THEY WERE FOREIGNERS... WEREN'T THEY?
...GUESTS OF THE PRINCESS, PLEASE LEAVE THIS TO US MYSIDIANS.
YOU LOT SHOULD TAKE SHELTER IMMEDIATELY!
!

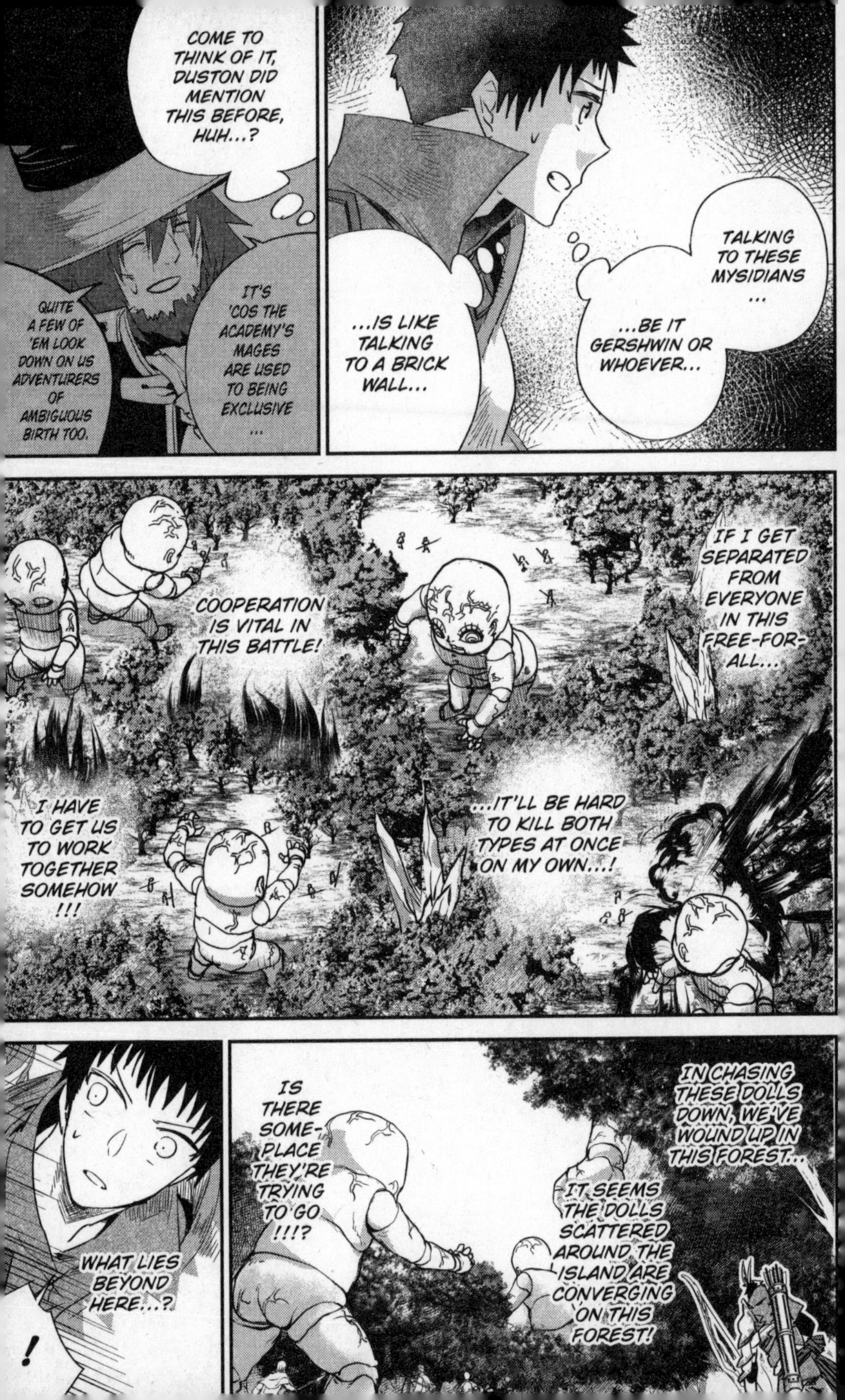
TALKING TO THESE MYSIDIANS ...
...BE IT GERSHWIN OR WHOEVER...
...IS LIKE TALKING TO A BRICK WALL...
COME TO THINK OF IT, DUSTON DID MENTION THIS BEFORE, HUH...?
IT'S 'COS THE ACADEMY'S MAGES ARE USED TO BEING EXCLUSIVE ...
QUITE A FEW OF 'EM LOOK DOWN ON US ADVENTURERS OF AMBIGUOUS BIRTH TOO.
IF I GET SEPARATED FROM EVERYONE IN THIS FREE-FOR-ALL...
...IT'LL BE HARD TO KILL BOTH TYPES AT ONCE ON MY OWN...!
COOPERATION IS VITAL IN THIS BATTLE!
I HAVE TO GET US TO WORK TOGETHER SOMEHOW !!!
IN CHASING THESE DOLLS DOWN, WE'VE WOUND UP IN THIS FOREST...
IT SEEMS THE DOLLS SCATTERED AROUND THE ISLAND ARE CONVERGING ON THIS FOREST!
IS THERE SOME-PLACE THEY'RE TRYING TO GO !!!?
WHAT LIES BEYOND HERE...?
!

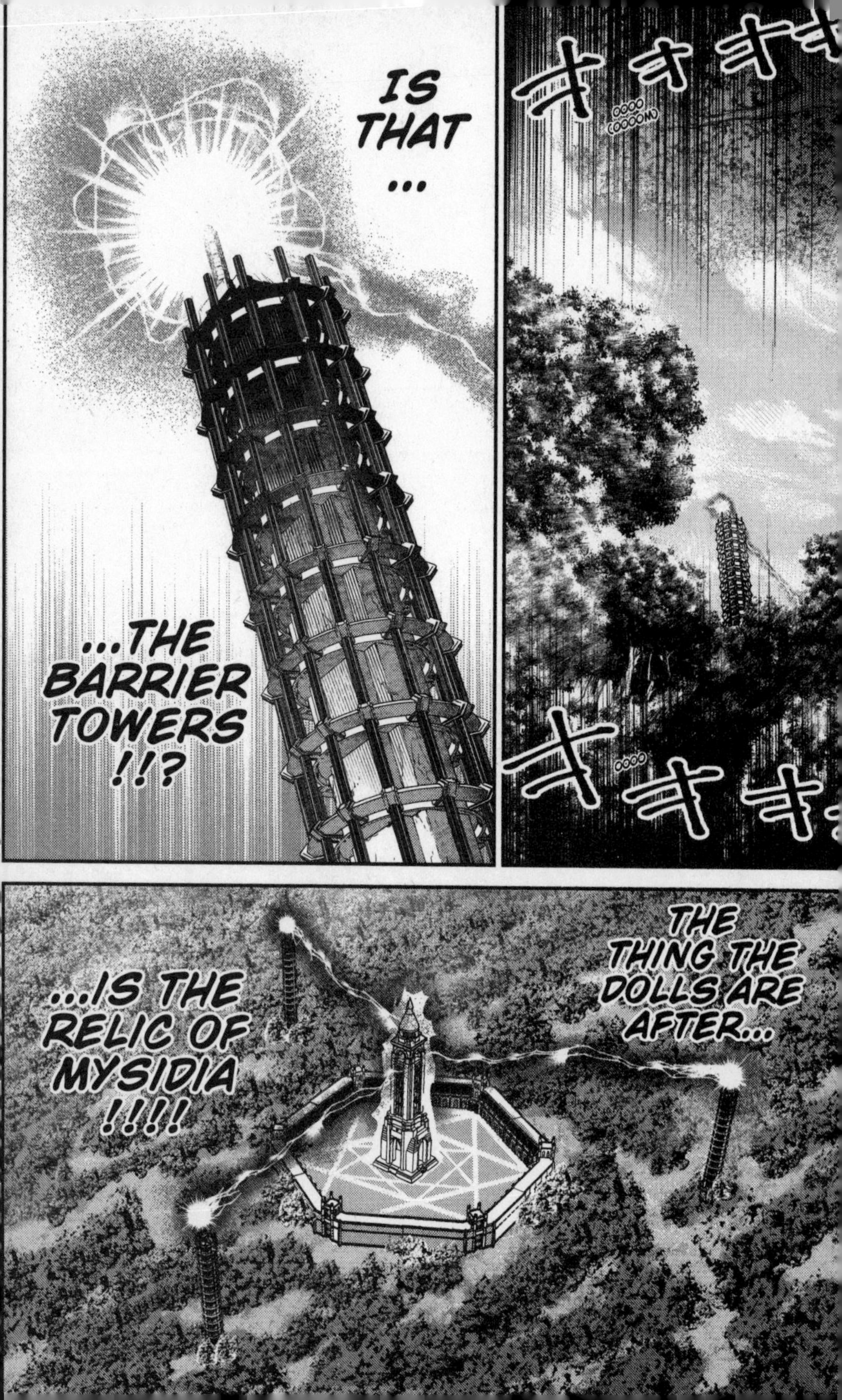
OOOO (OOOOM)
OOOO
IS THAT ...
...THE BARRIER TOWERS !!?
THE THING THE DOLLS ARE AFTER...
...IS THE RELIC OF MYSIDIA !!!!

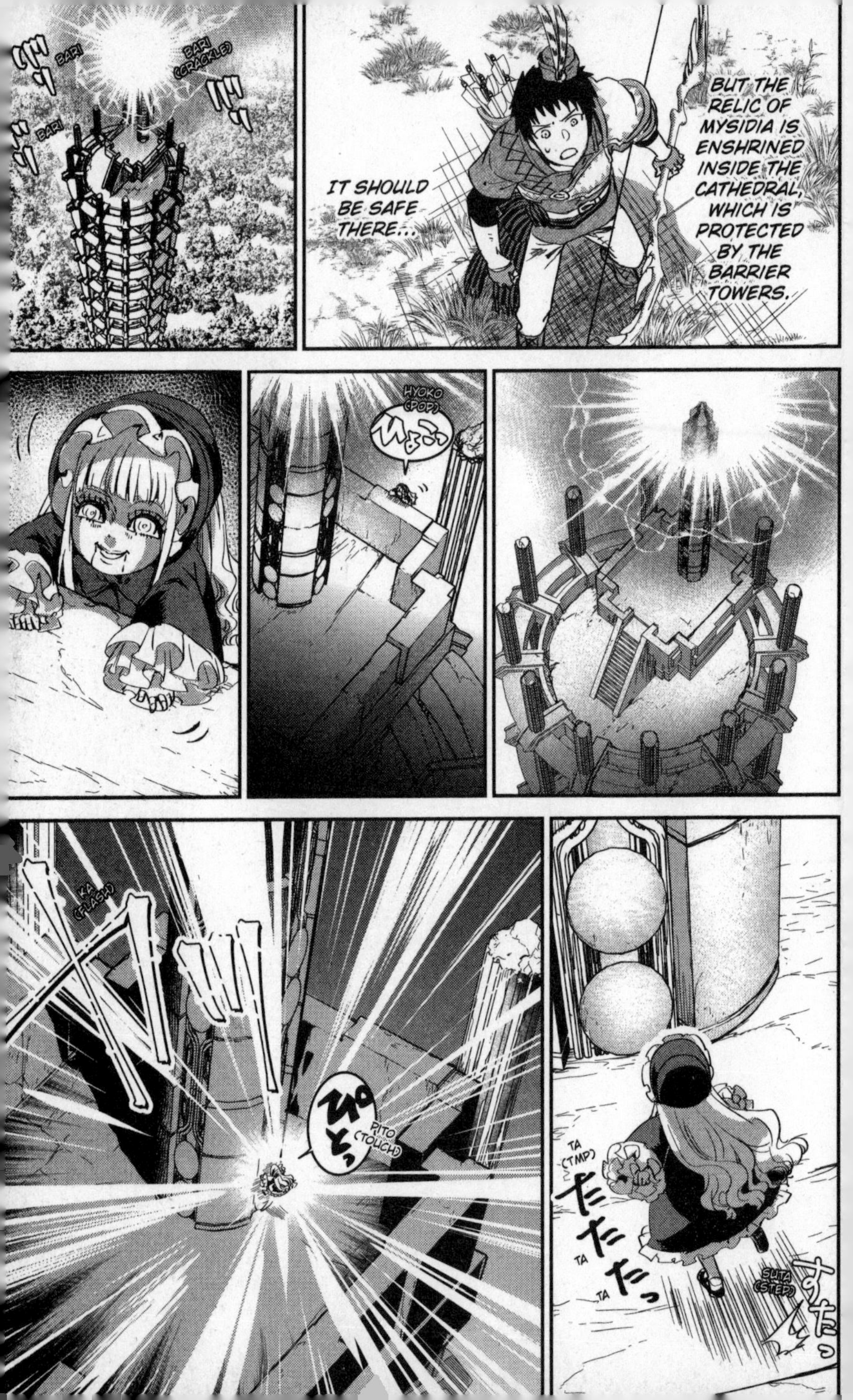
BUT THE RELIC OF MYSIDIA IS ENSHRINED INSIDE THE CATHEDRAL, WHICH IS PROTECTED BY THE BARRIER TOWERS.
IT SHOULD BE SAFE THERE...
BARI (CRACKLE)
BARI
BARI
HYOKO (POP)
SUTA (STEP)
TA (TMP)
TA
TA
PITO (TOUCH)
KA (FLASH)

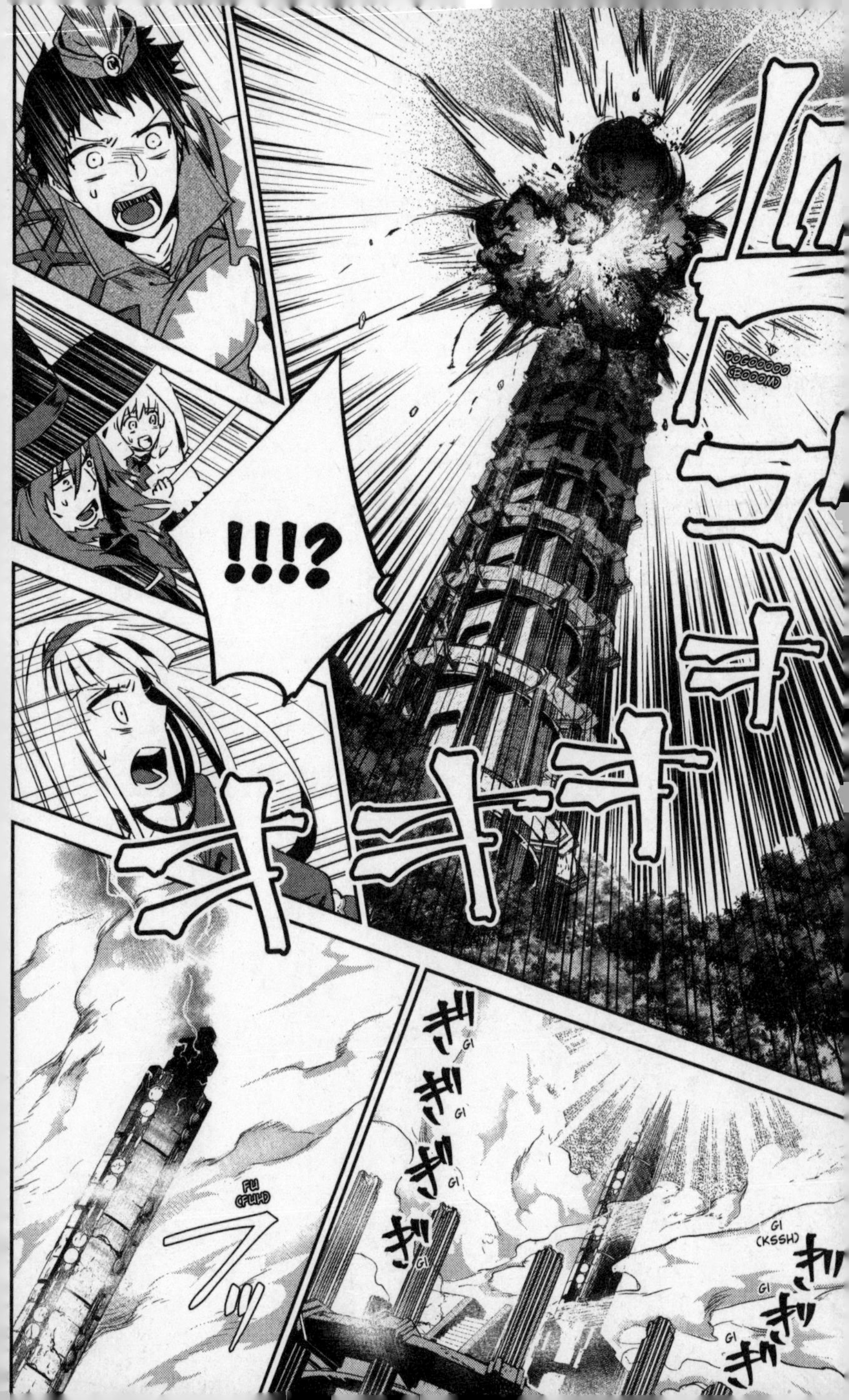
GI
GI
GI
GI
GI (KSSH)
GI
GI
FU (FLIHD)
DOGOOOOO (BOOOM)
!!!?

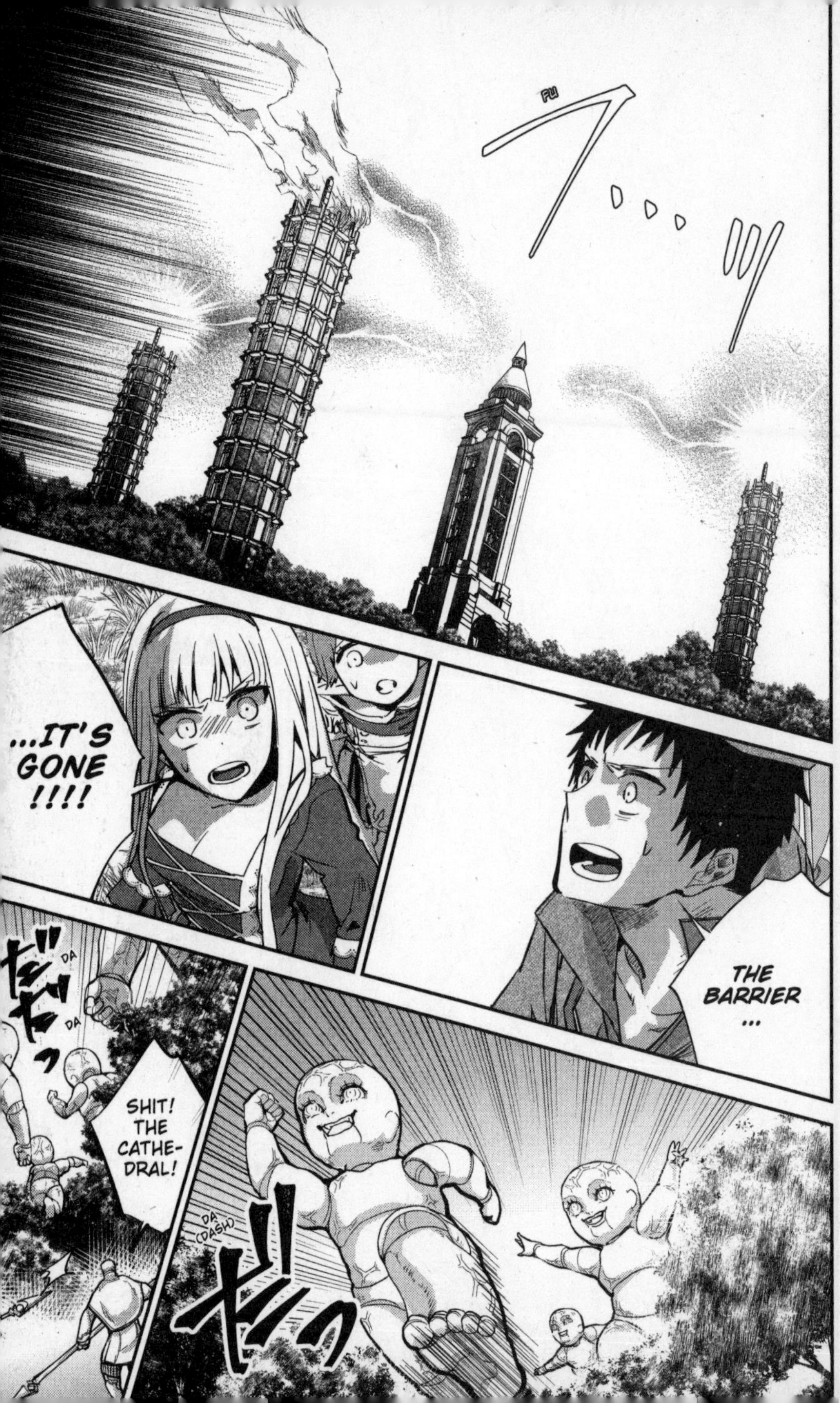
FU
THE BARRIER ...
...IT'S GONE !!!!
DA (DASH)
DA
DA
SHIT! THE CATHE-DRAL!

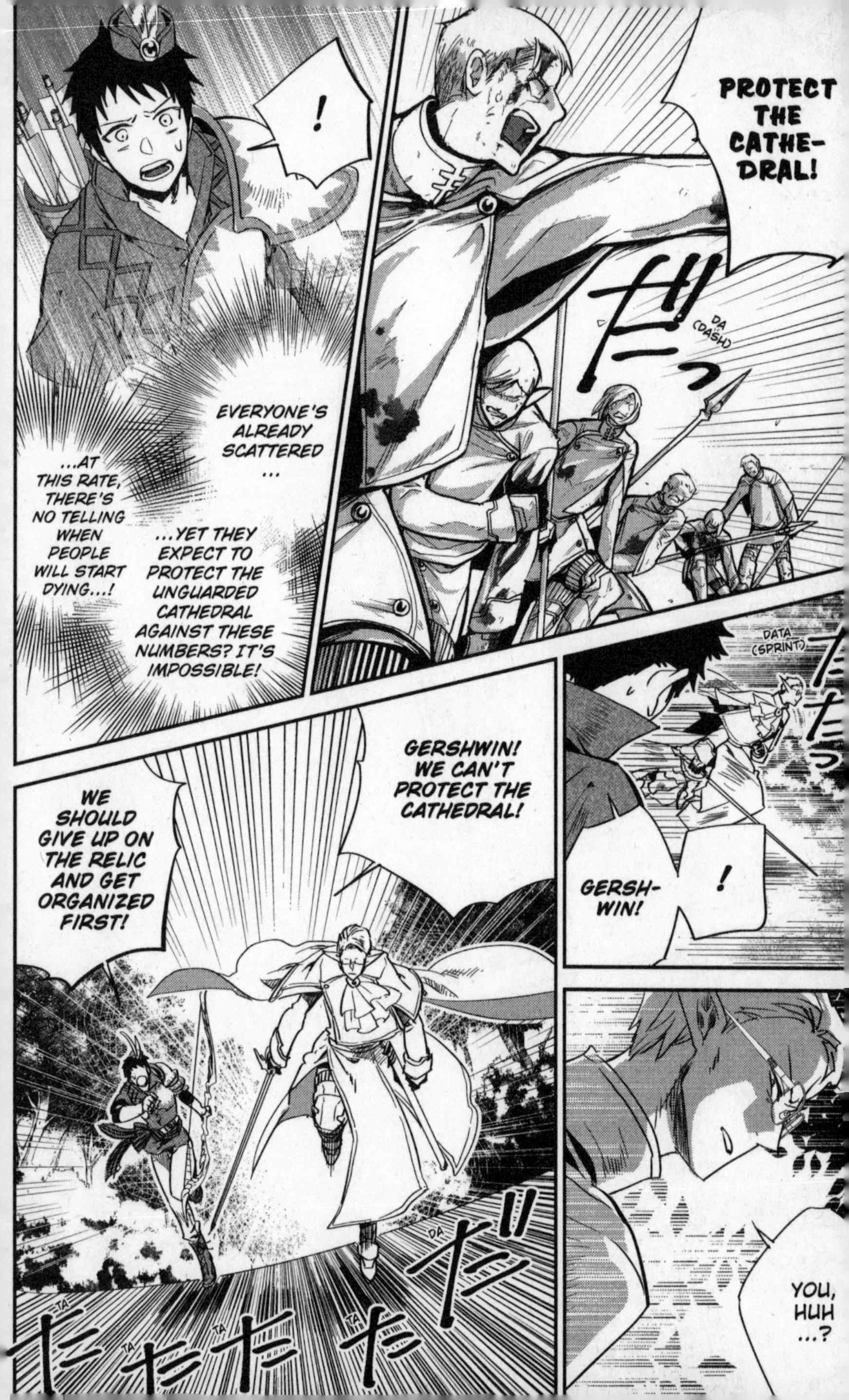
PROTECT THE CATHE-DRAL!
DA (DASH)
!
EVERYONE'S ALREADY SCATTERED ...
...AT THIS RATE, THERE'S NO TELLING WHEN PEOPLE WILL START DYING...!
...YET THEY EXPECT TO PROTECT THE UNGUARDED CATHEDRAL AGAINST THESE NUMBERS? IT'S IMPOSSIBLE!
DATA (SPRINT)
!
GERSH-WIN!
GERSHWIN! WE CAN'T PROTECT THE CATHEDRAL!
WE SHOULD GIVE UP ON THE RELIC AND GET ORGANIZED FIRST!
DA
TA
TA
TA
TA
YOU, HUH ...?

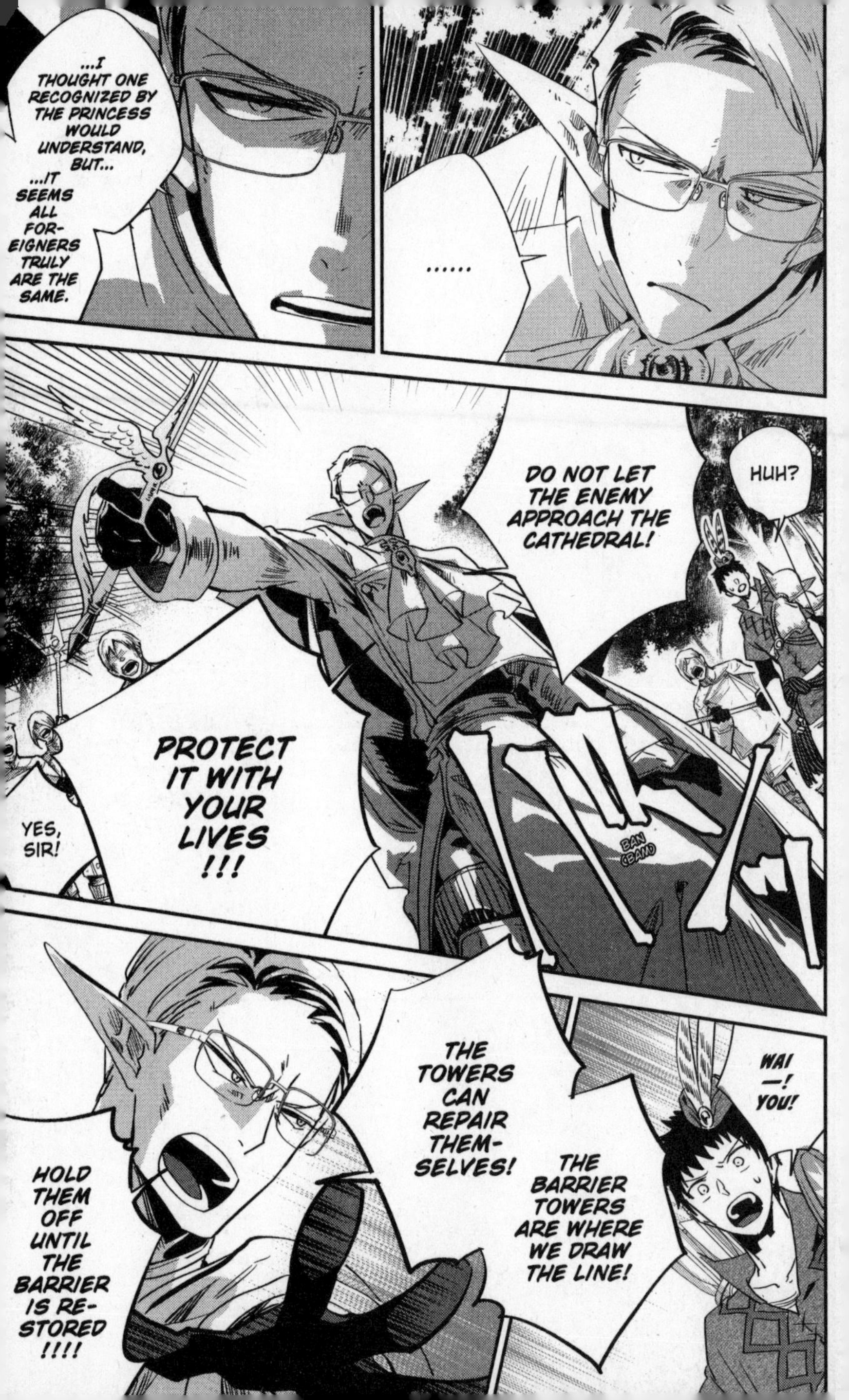
......
...I THOUGHT ONE RECOGNIZED BY THE PRINCESS WOULD UNDERSTAND, BUT...
...IT SEEMS ALL FOR-EIGNERS TRULY ARE THE SAME.
HUH?
DO NOT LET THE ENEMY APPROACH THE CATHEDRAL!
BAN (BAM)
PROTECT IT WITH YOUR LIVES!!!
YES, SIR!
WAI—! YOU!
THE BARRIER TOWERS ARE WHERE WE DRAW THE LINE!
THE TOWERS CAN REPAIR THEM-SELVES!
HOLD THEM OFF UNTIL THE BARRIER IS RE-STORED!!!!

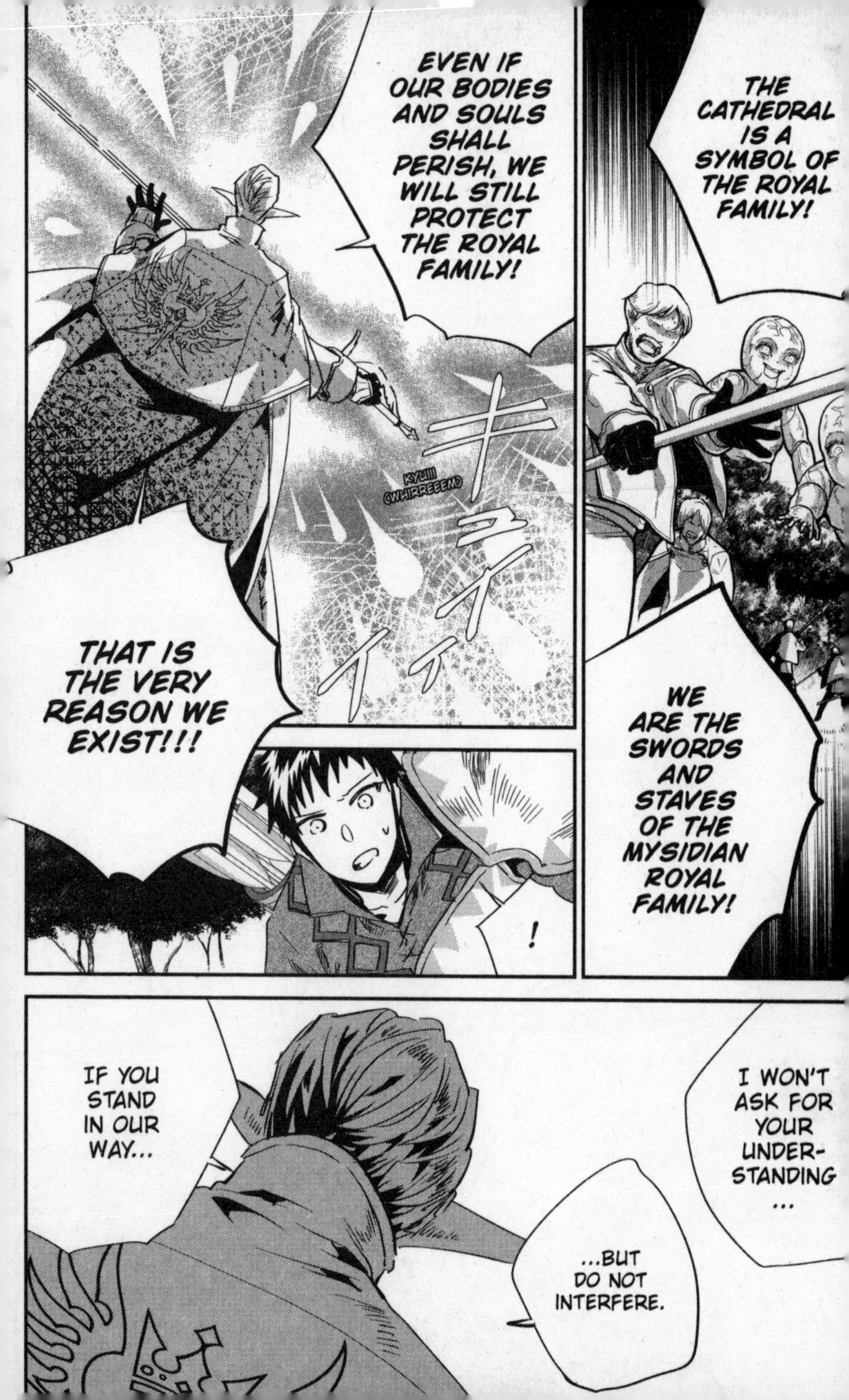
THE CATHEDRAL IS A SYMBOL OF THE ROYAL FAMILY!
EVEN IF OUR BODIES AND SOULS SHALL PERISH, WE WILL STILL PROTECT THE ROYAL FAMILY!
KYUIII (WHIRREEEM)
WE ARE THE SWORDS AND STAVES OF THE MYSIDIAN ROYAL FAMILY!
THAT IS THE VERY REASON WE EXIST!!!
!
I WON'T ASK FOR YOUR UNDER-STANDING ...
...BUT DO NOT INTERFERE.
IF YOU STAND IN OUR WAY...

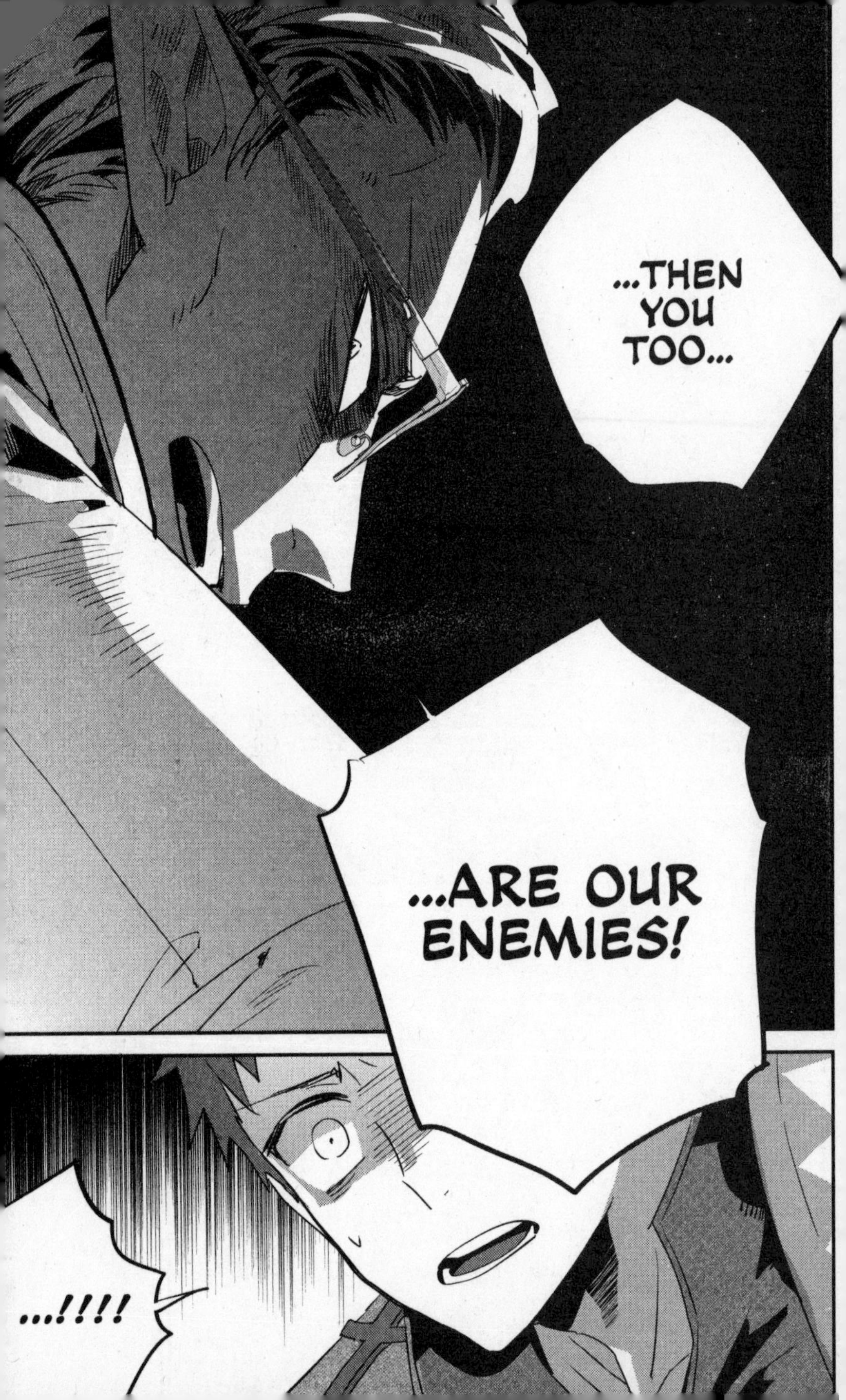
...THEN YOU TOO...
...ARE OUR ENEMIES!
...!!!!

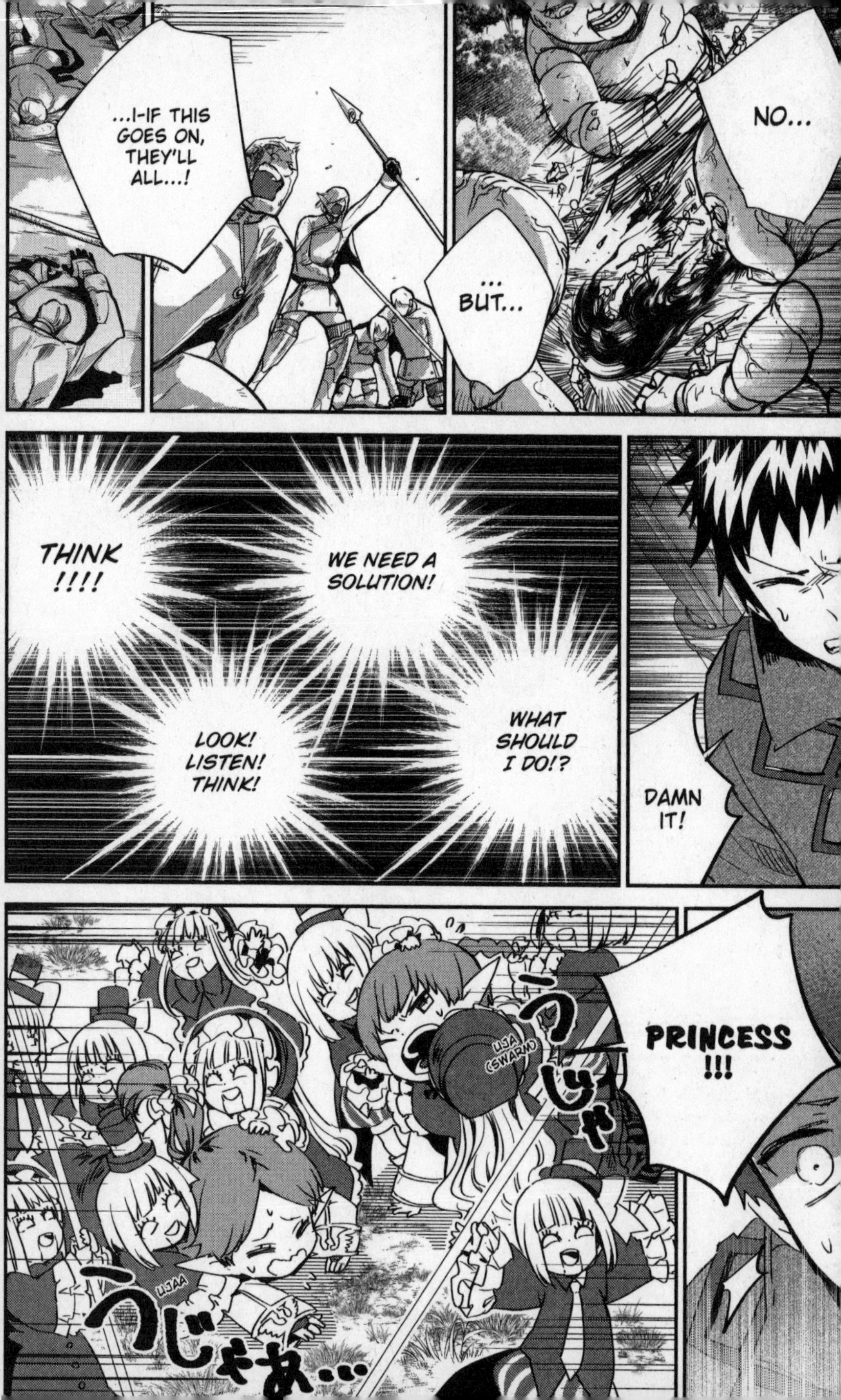
NO...
... BUT...
...I-IF THIS GOES ON, THEY'LL ALL...!
DAMN IT!
WHAT SHOULD I DO!?
WE NEED A SOLUTION!
LOOK! LISTEN! THINK!
THINK !!!!
PRINCESS !!!
うじゃ
UJA (SWARM)
うじゃあ…
UJAA

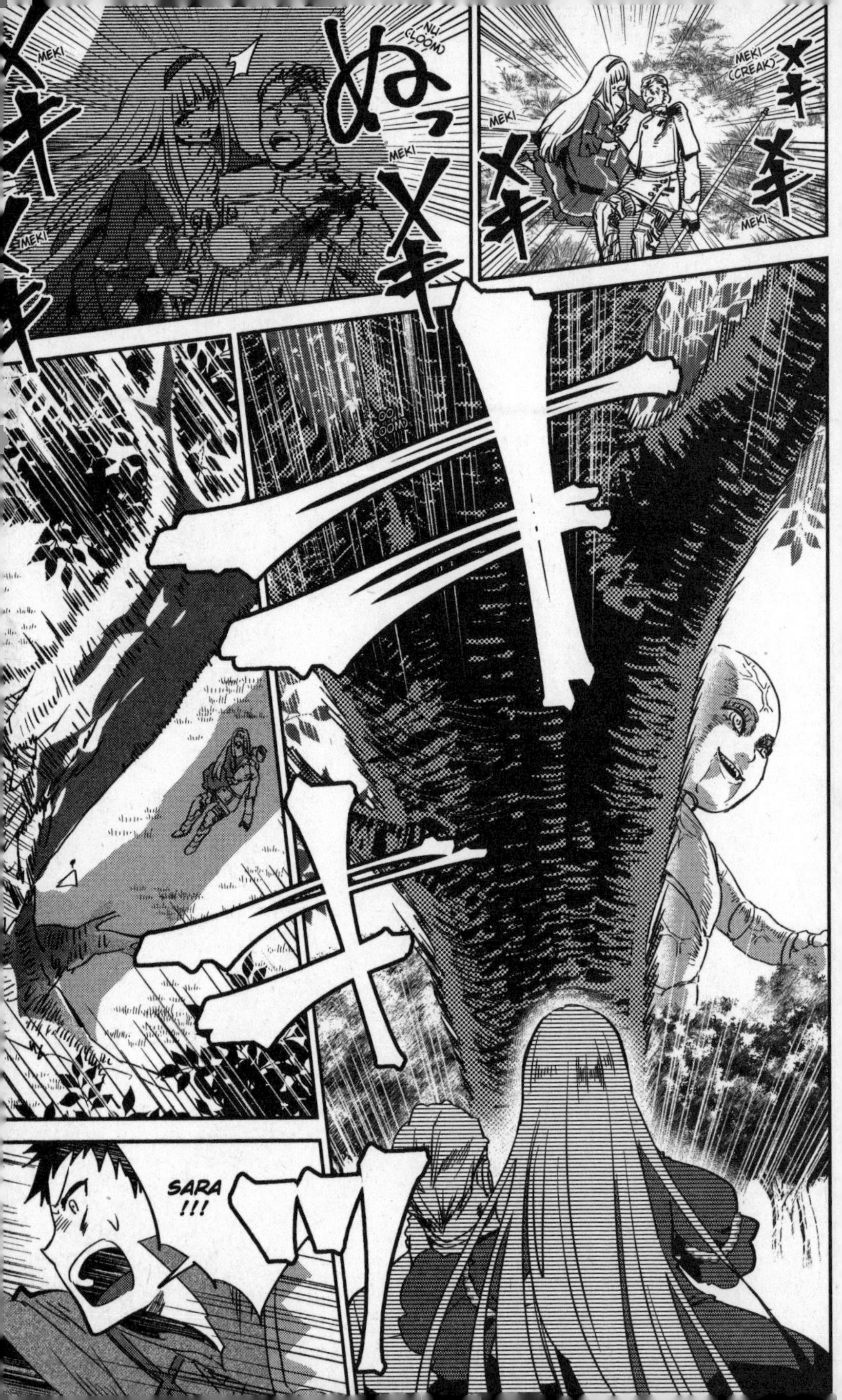
メキ
MEKI
(CREAK)
メキ
MEKI
メキ
MEKI
ぬっ
NU
(LOOM)
メキ
MEKI
メキ
MEKI
メキ
MEKI
DOO
SARA
!!!

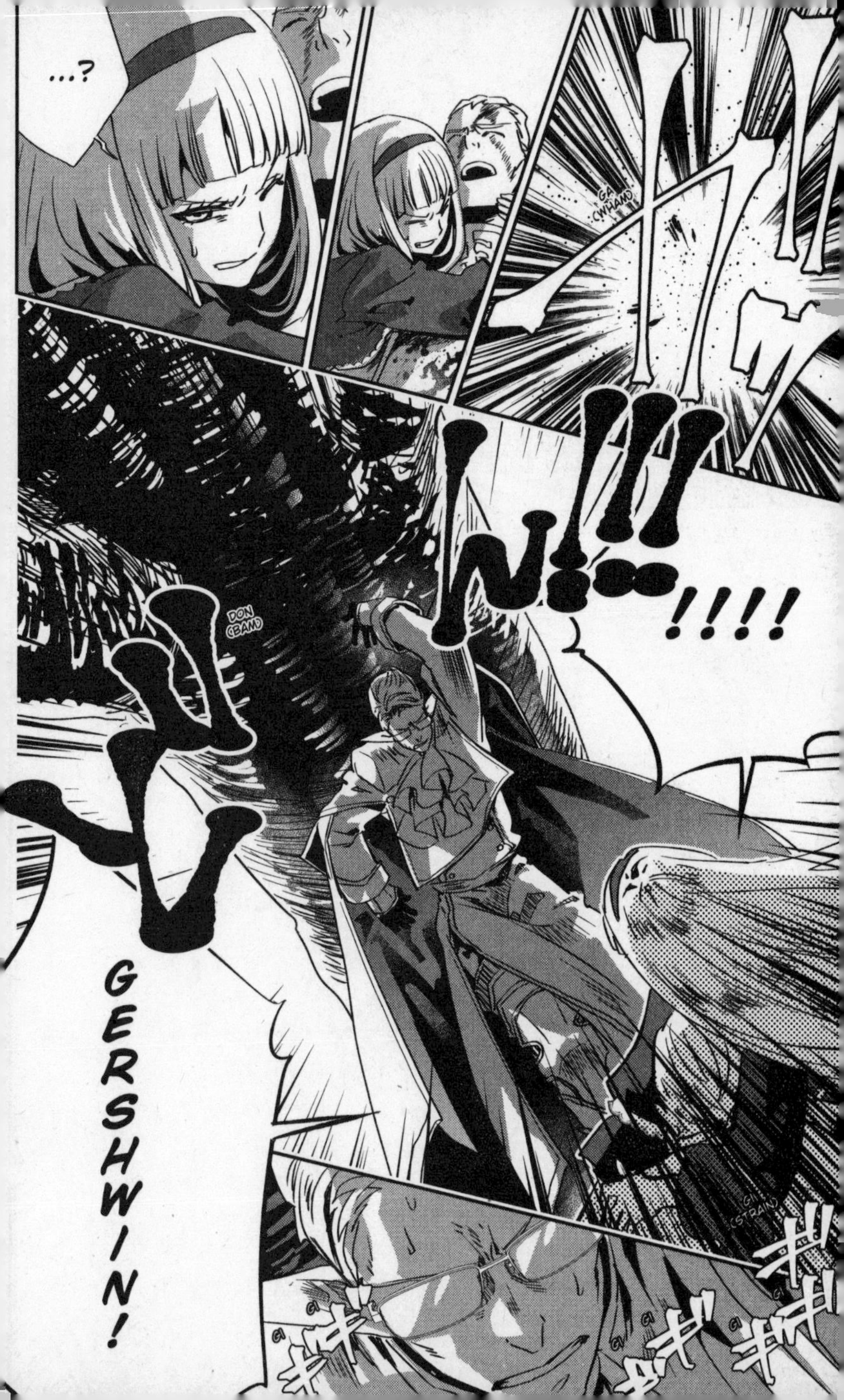
GA (WHAM)
...?
N!!!!!
DON (BAM)
GERSHWIN!
GI (STRAIN)

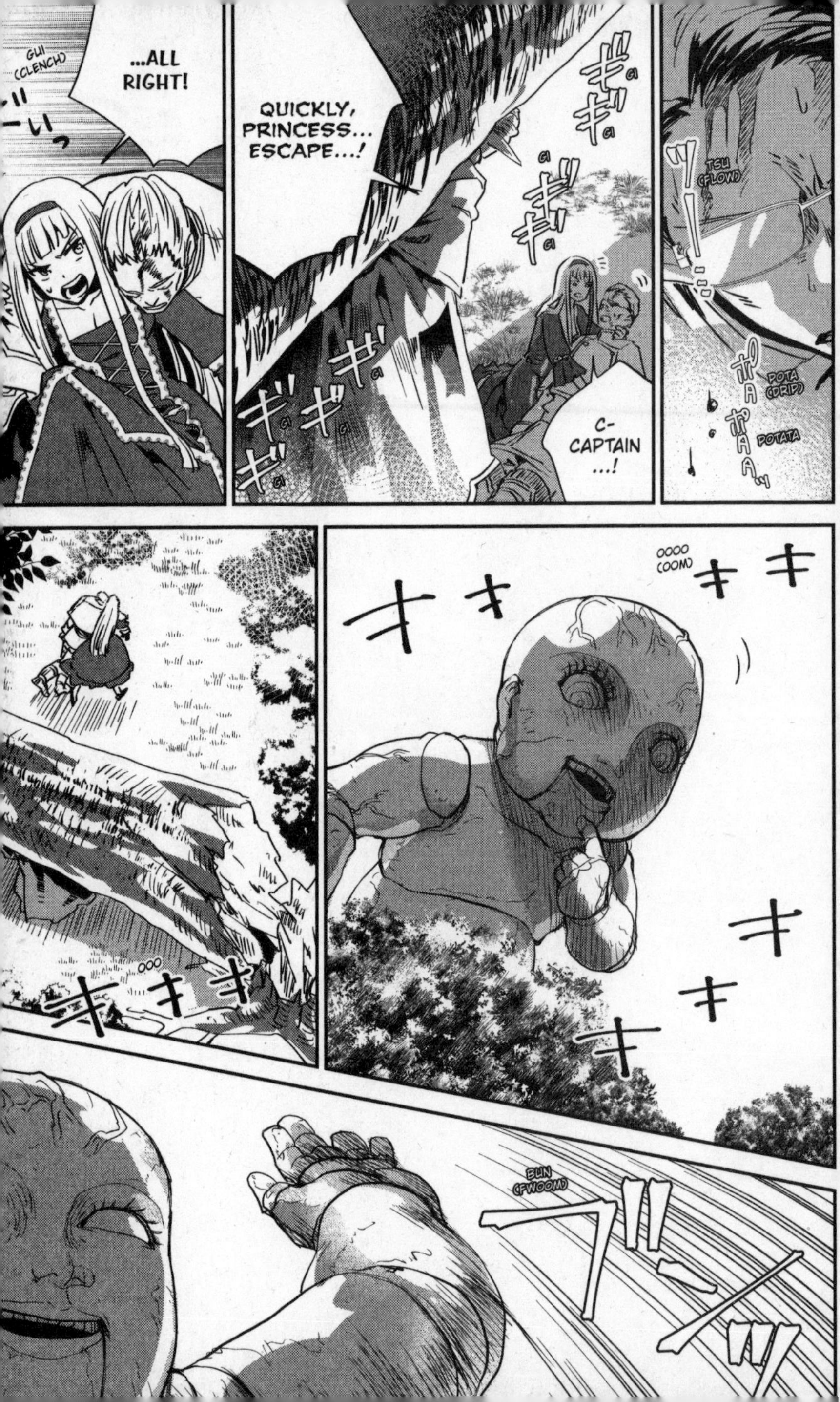
TSU (FLOW)
POTA (DRIP)
POTATA
C-CAPTAIN ...!
QUICKLY, PRINCESS... ESCAPE...!
...ALL RIGHT!
GUI (CLENCH)
OOOO (OOM)
BUN (FWOOM)

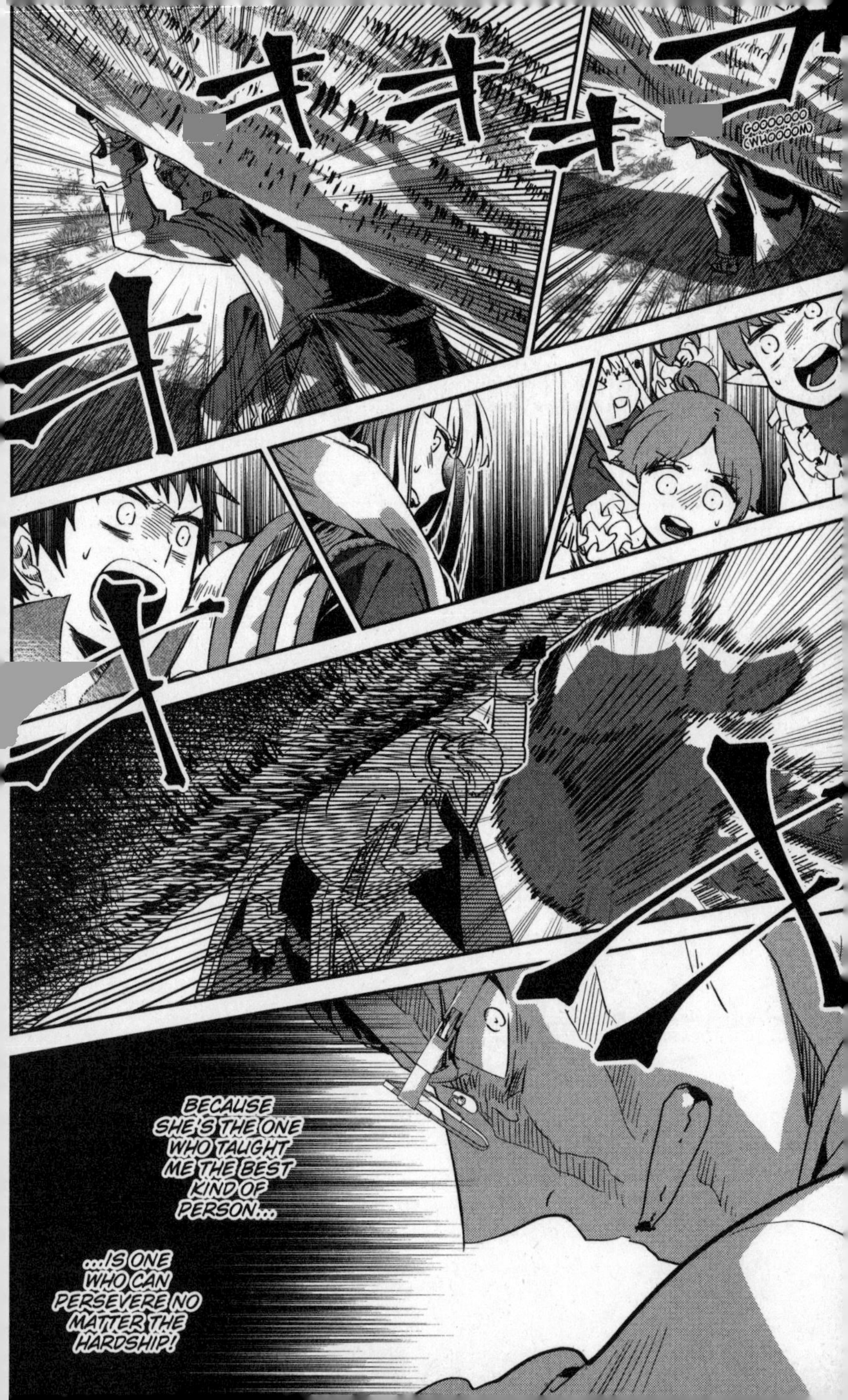
GOOOOOOO (WHOOOOM)
BECAUSE SHE'S THE ONE WHO TAUGHT ME THE BEST KIND OF PERSON...
...IS ONE WHO CAN PERSEVERE NO MATTER THE HARDSHIP!

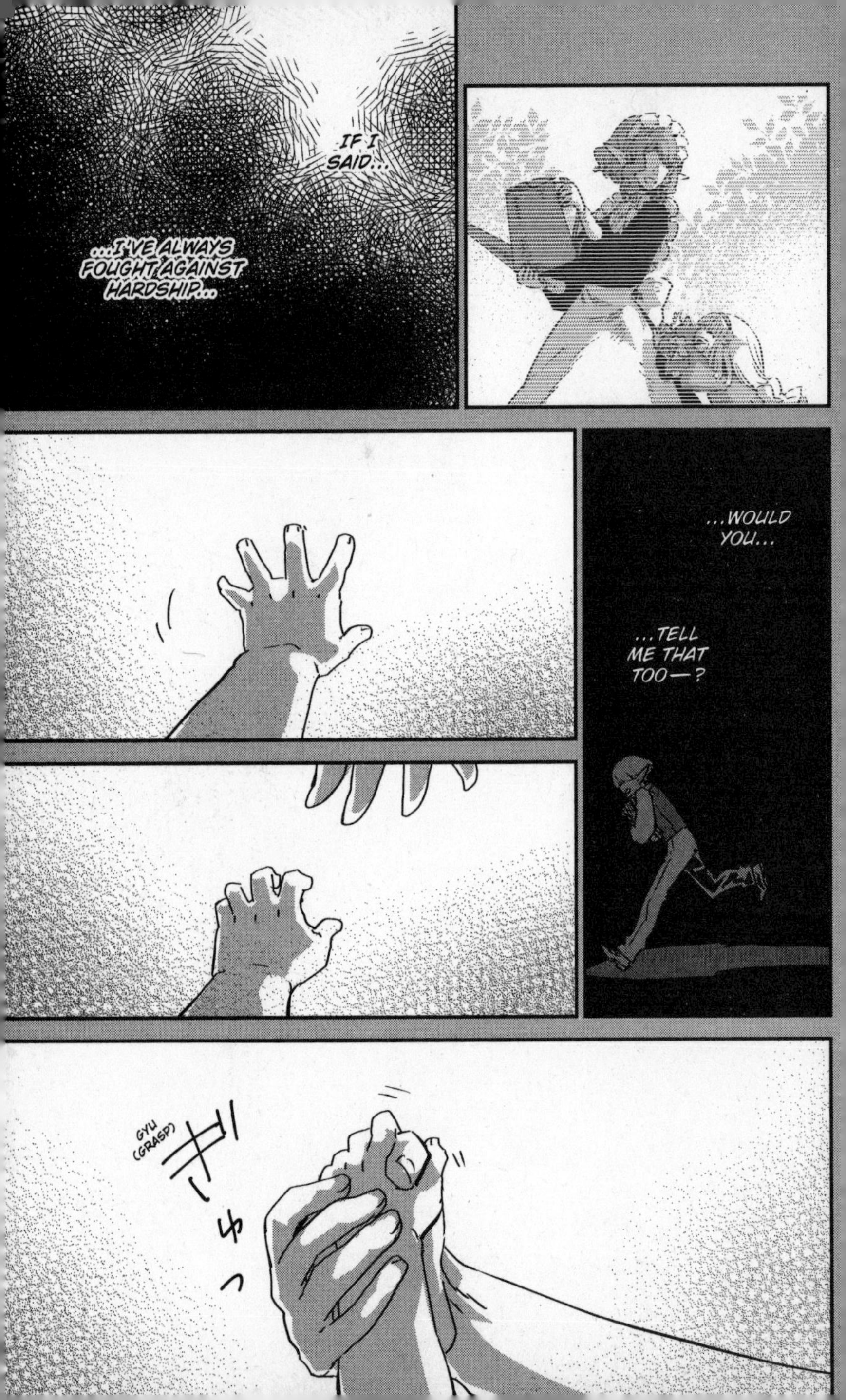
IF I SAID...
...I'VE ALWAYS FOUGHT AGAINST HARDSHIP...
...WOULD YOU...
...TELL ME THAT TOO—?
ぎゅっ
GYU (GRASP)

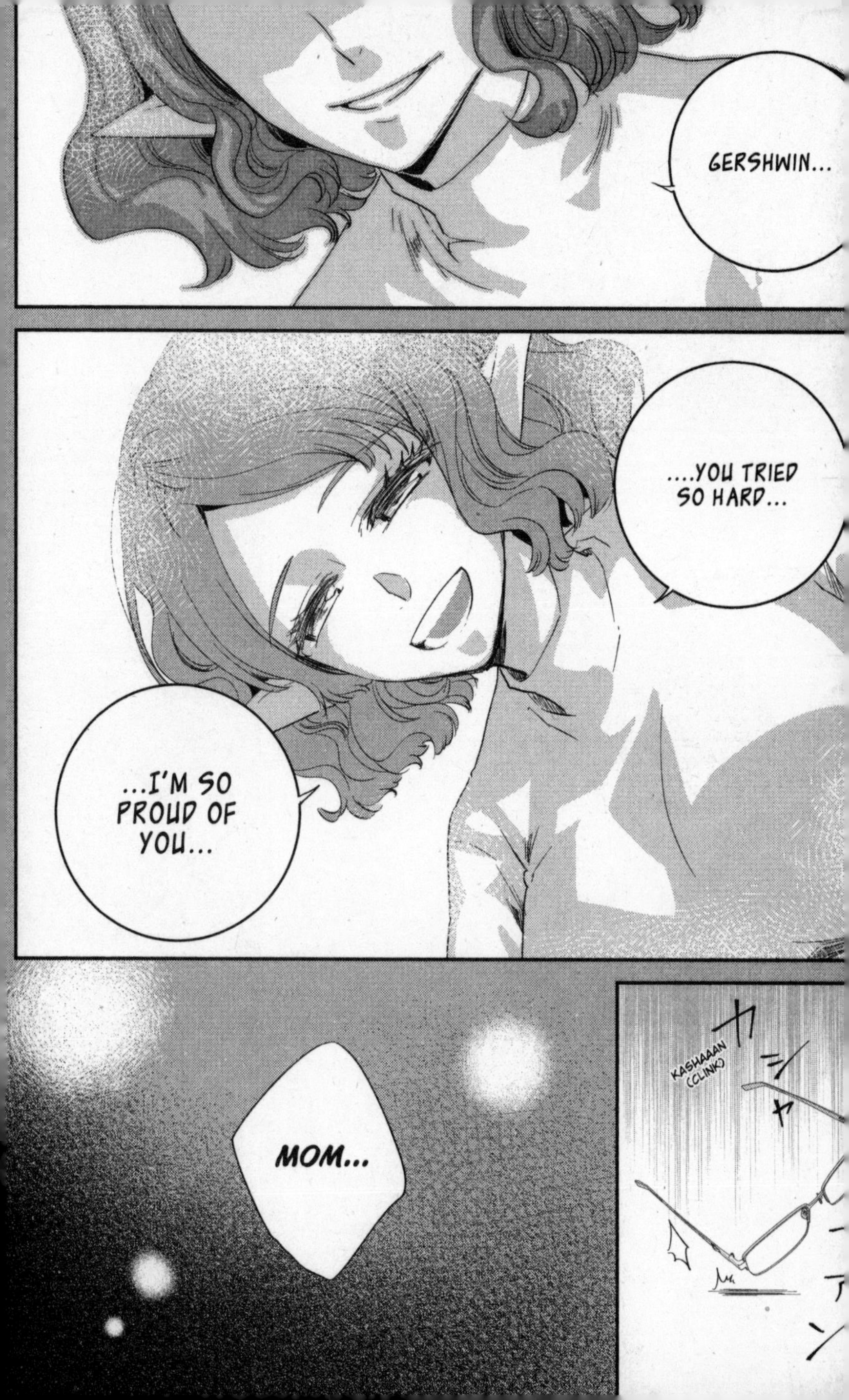
GERSHWIN...
....YOU TRIED SO HARD...
...I'M SO PROUD OF YOU...
KASHAAAN (CLINK)
MOM...

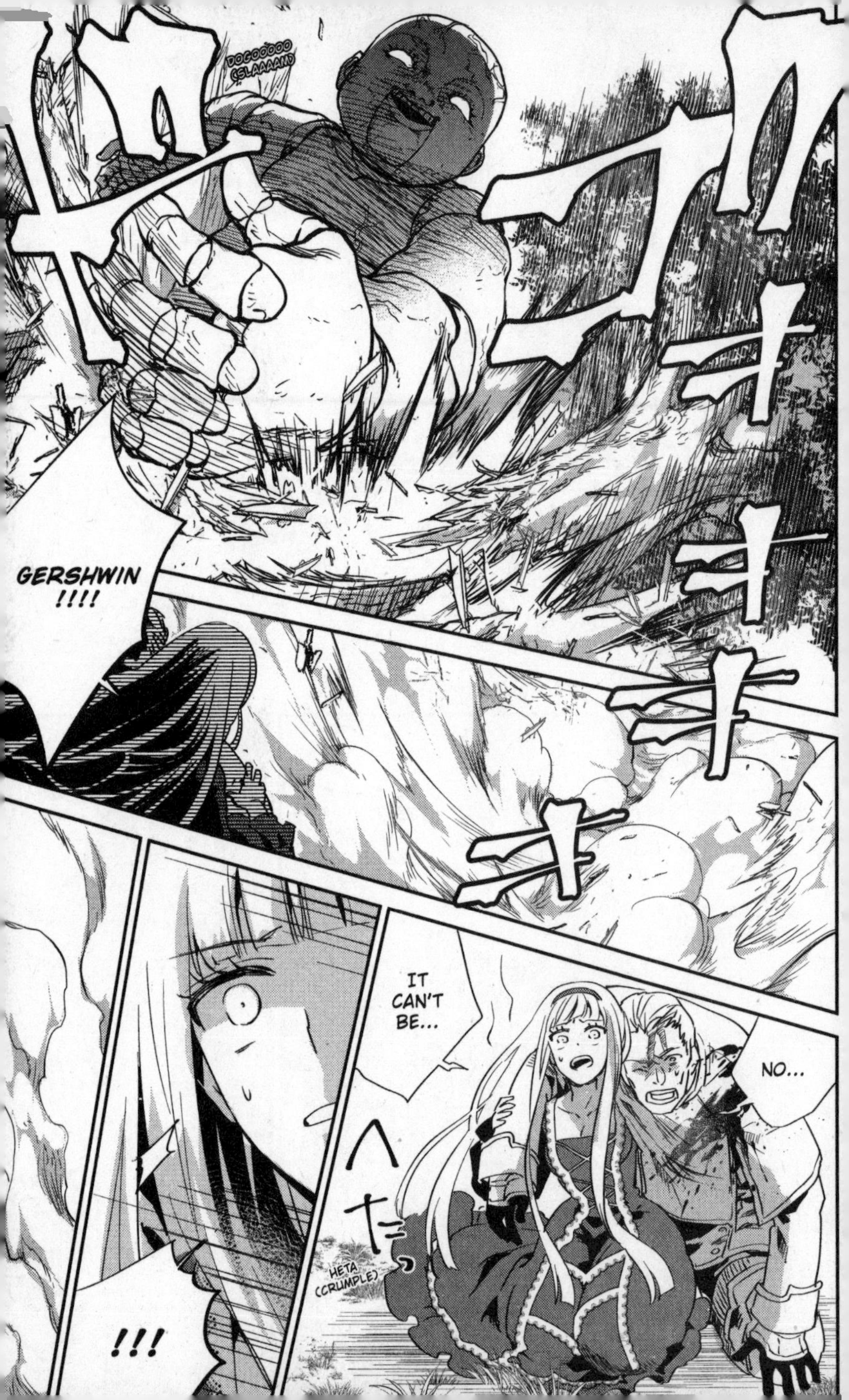
DOGOOOOO
(SLAAAAM)
GERSHWIN
!!!!
NO...
IT CAN'T BE...
HETA
(CRUMPLE)
!!!

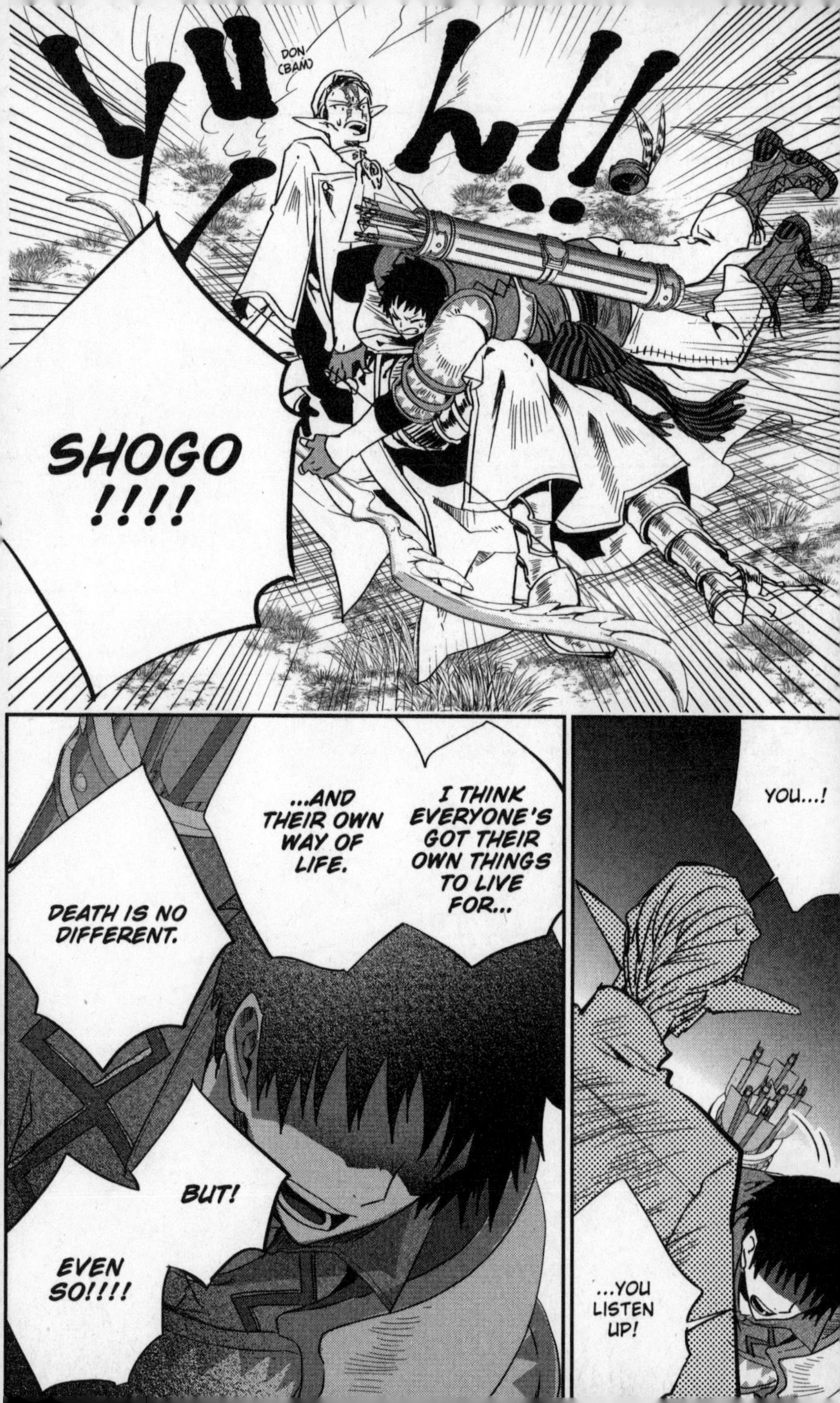
DON (BAM)
SHOGO !!!!
YOU...!
...YOU LISTEN UP!
I THINK EVERYONE'S GOT THEIR OWN THINGS TO LIVE FOR...
...AND THEIR OWN WAY OF LIFE.
DEATH IS NO DIFFERENT.
BUT!
EVEN SO!!!!

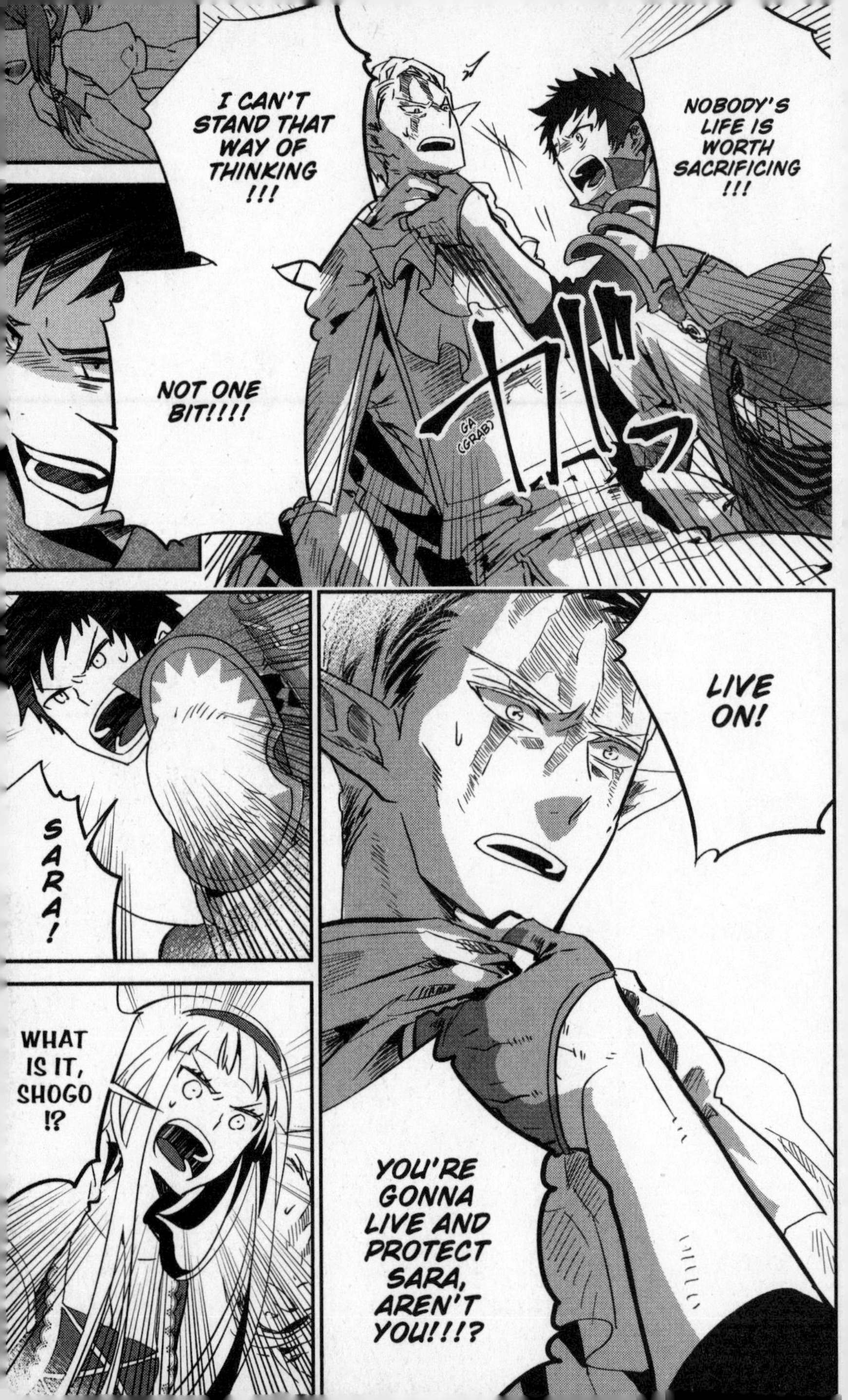
NOBODY'S LIFE IS WORTH SACRIFICING !!!
I CAN'T STAND THAT WAY OF THINKING !!!
GA (GRAB)
NOT ONE BIT!!!!
LIVE ON!
YOU'RE GONNA LIVE AND PROTECT SARA, AREN'T YOU!!!?
SARA!
WHAT IS IT, SHOGO !?

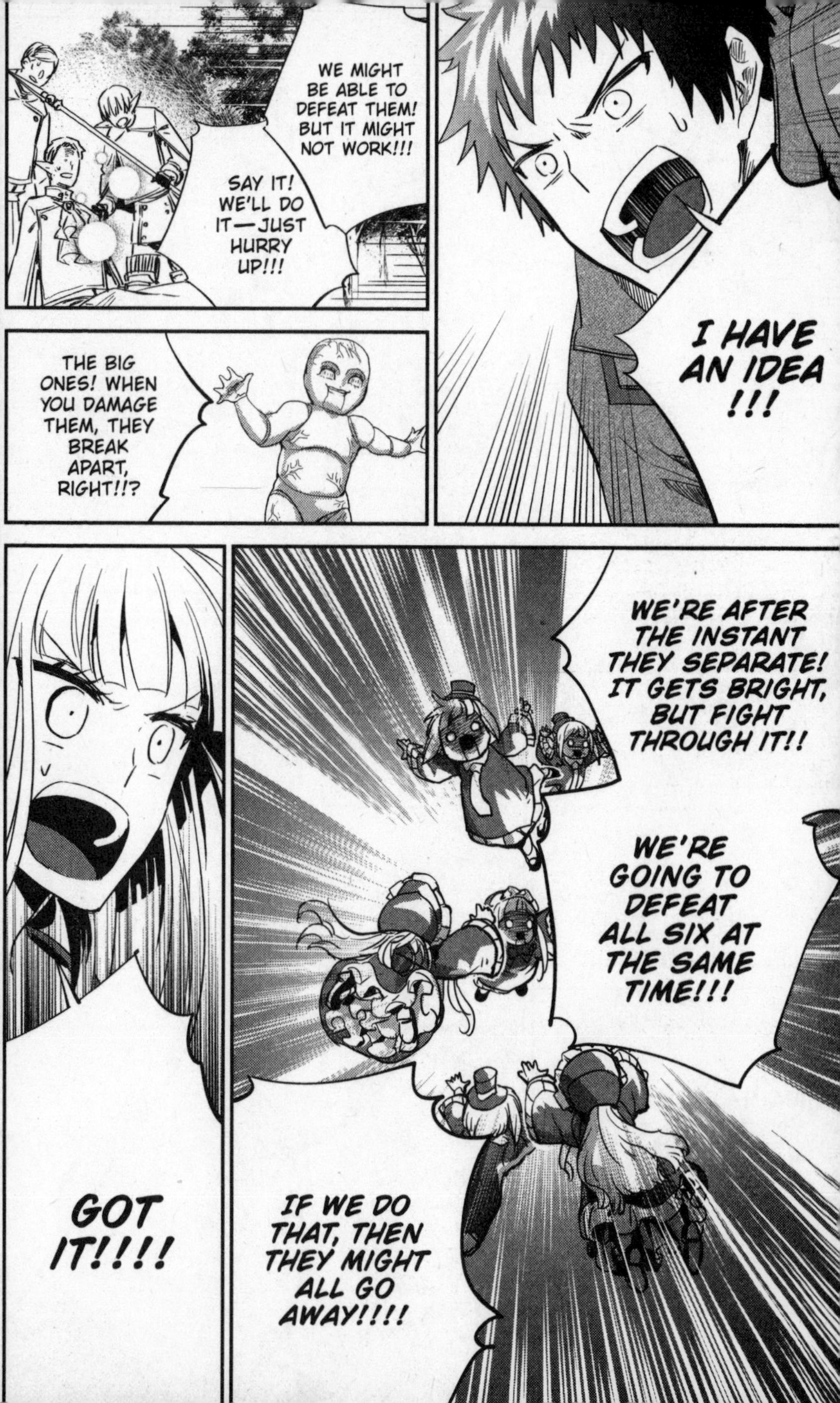
I HAVE AN IDEA!!!
WE MIGHT BE ABLE TO DEFEAT THEM! BUT IT MIGHT NOT WORK!!!
SAY IT! WE'LL DO IT—JUST HURRY UP!!!
THE BIG ONES! WHEN YOU DAMAGE THEM, THEY BREAK APART, RIGHT!!?
WE'RE AFTER THE INSTANT THEY SEPARATE! IT GETS BRIGHT, BUT FIGHT THROUGH IT!!
WE'RE GOING TO DEFEAT ALL SIX AT THE SAME TIME!!!
IF WE DO THAT, THEN THEY MIGHT ALL GO AWAY!!!!
GOT IT!!!!

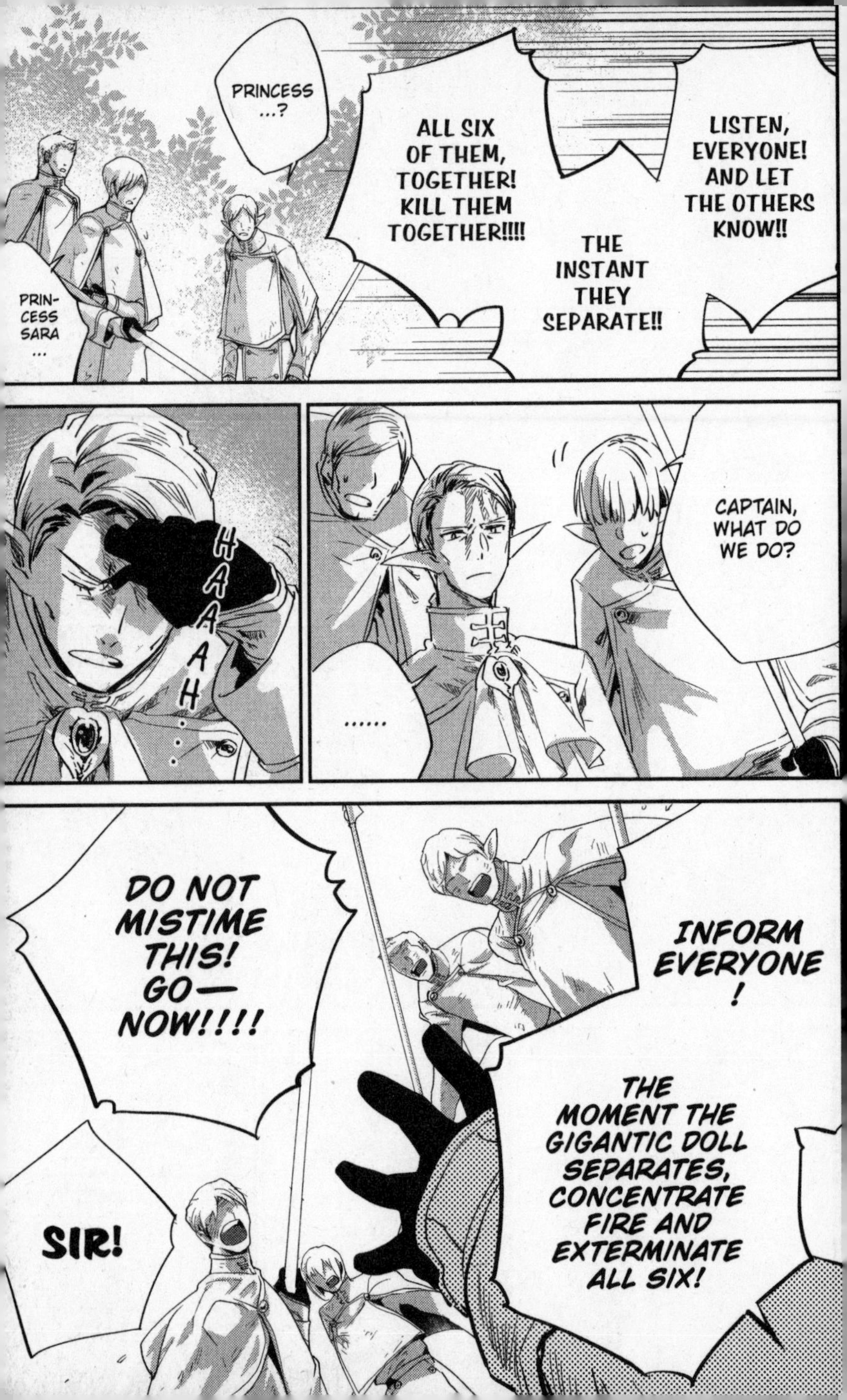
LISTEN, EVERYONE! AND LET THE OTHERS KNOW!!
THE INSTANT THEY SEPARATE!!
ALL SIX OF THEM, TOGETHER! KILL THEM TOGETHER!!!!
PRINCESS ...?
PRIN-CESS SARA ...
CAPTAIN, WHAT DO WE DO?
......
HAAAAH...
THE MOMENT THE GIGANTIC DOLL SEPARATES, CONCENTRATE FIRE AND EXTERMINATE ALL SIX!
INFORM EVERYONE !
DO NOT MISTIME THIS! GO— NOW!!!!
SIR!

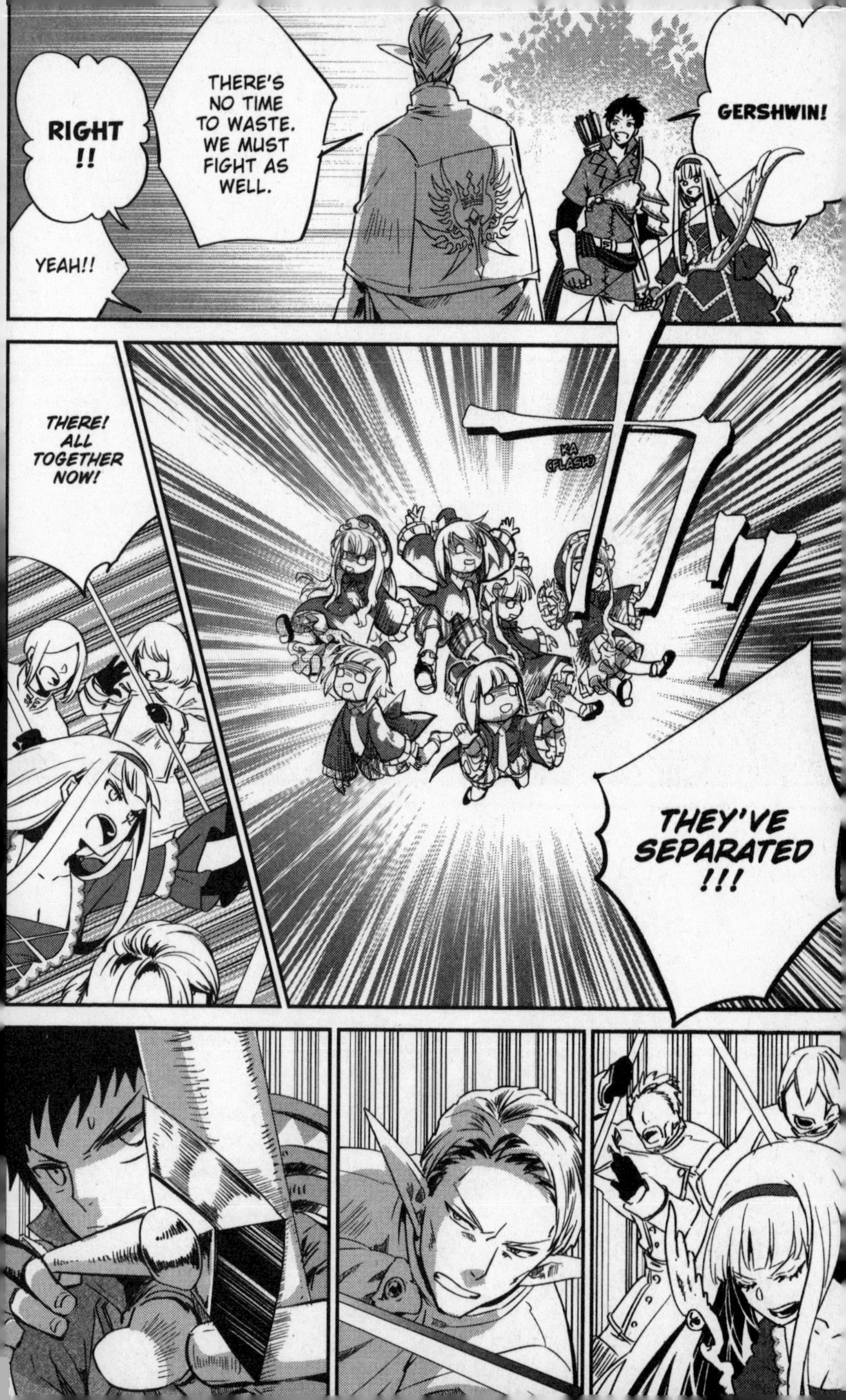
GERSHWIN!
THERE'S NO TIME TO WASTE. WE MUST FIGHT AS WELL.
RIGHT!!
YEAH!!
KA (FLASH)
THEY'VE SEPARATED!!!
THERE! ALL TOGETHER NOW!

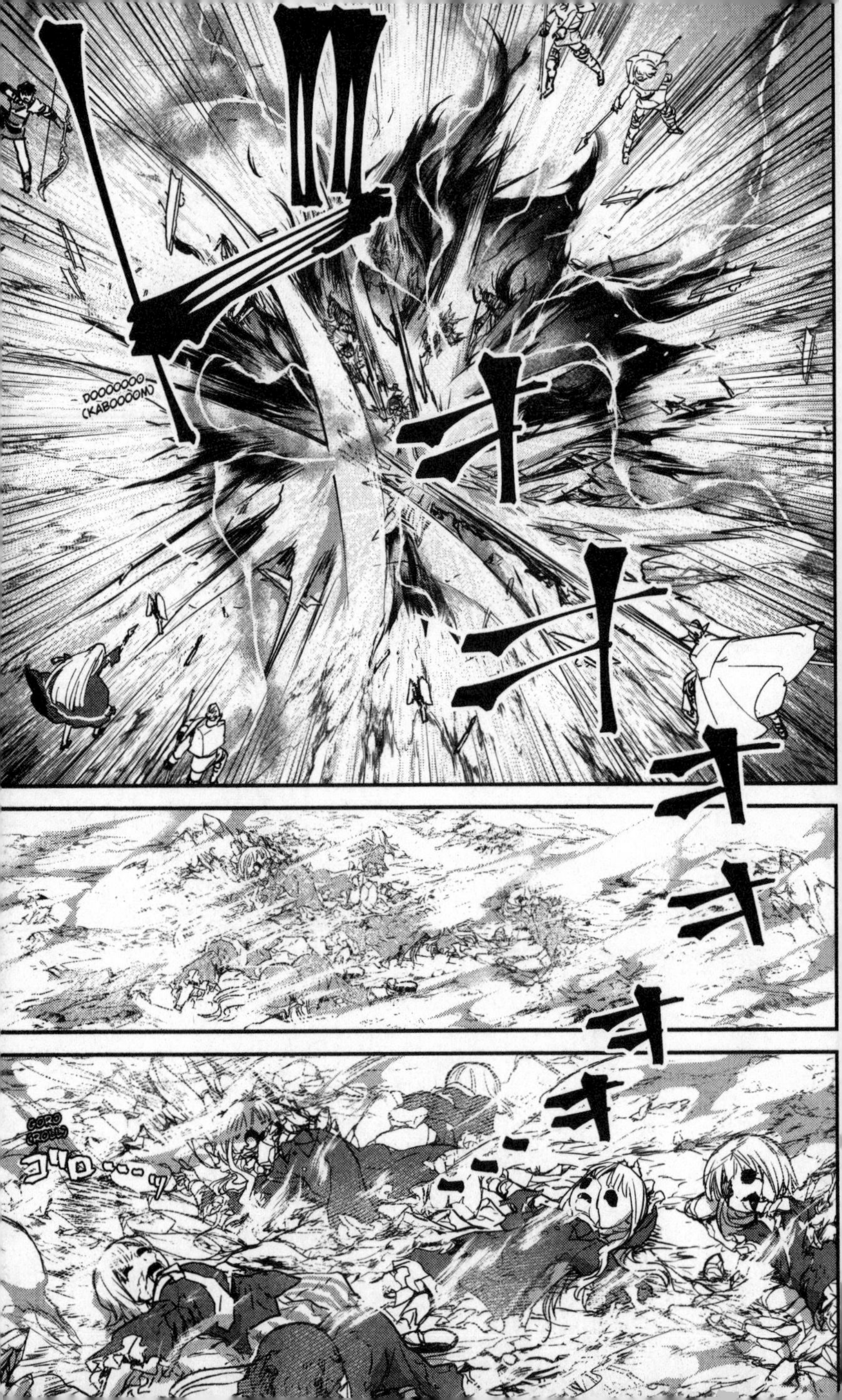
DOOOOOOO
(KABOOOOM)
GORO
(ROLL)

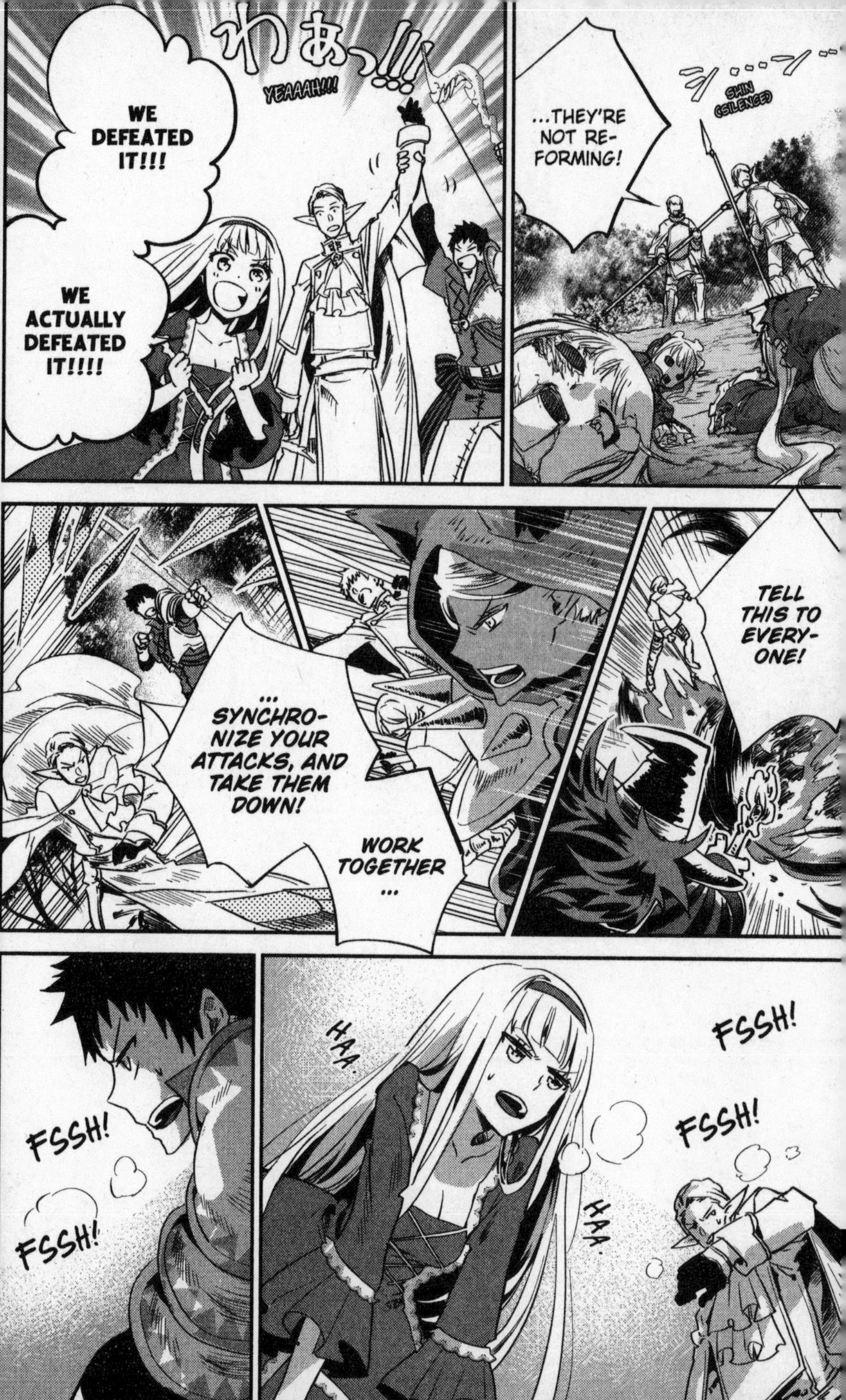
シーン
SHIN (SILENCED)
...THEY'RE NOT RE-FORMING!
わあっ!!!
YEAAAH!!!
WE DEFEATED IT!!!
WE ACTUALLY DEFEATED IT!!!!
TELL THIS TO EVERY-ONE!
WORK TOGETHER...
...SYNCHRO-NIZE YOUR ATTACKS, AND TAKE THEM DOWN!
FSSH!
FSSH!
HAA
HAA
FSSH!
FSSH!

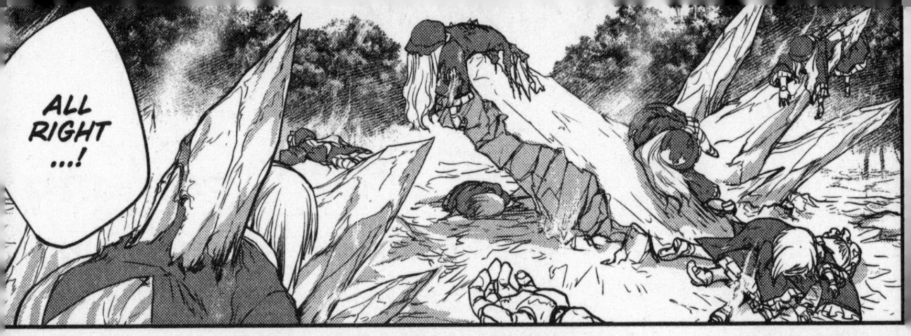
ALL RIGHT ...!
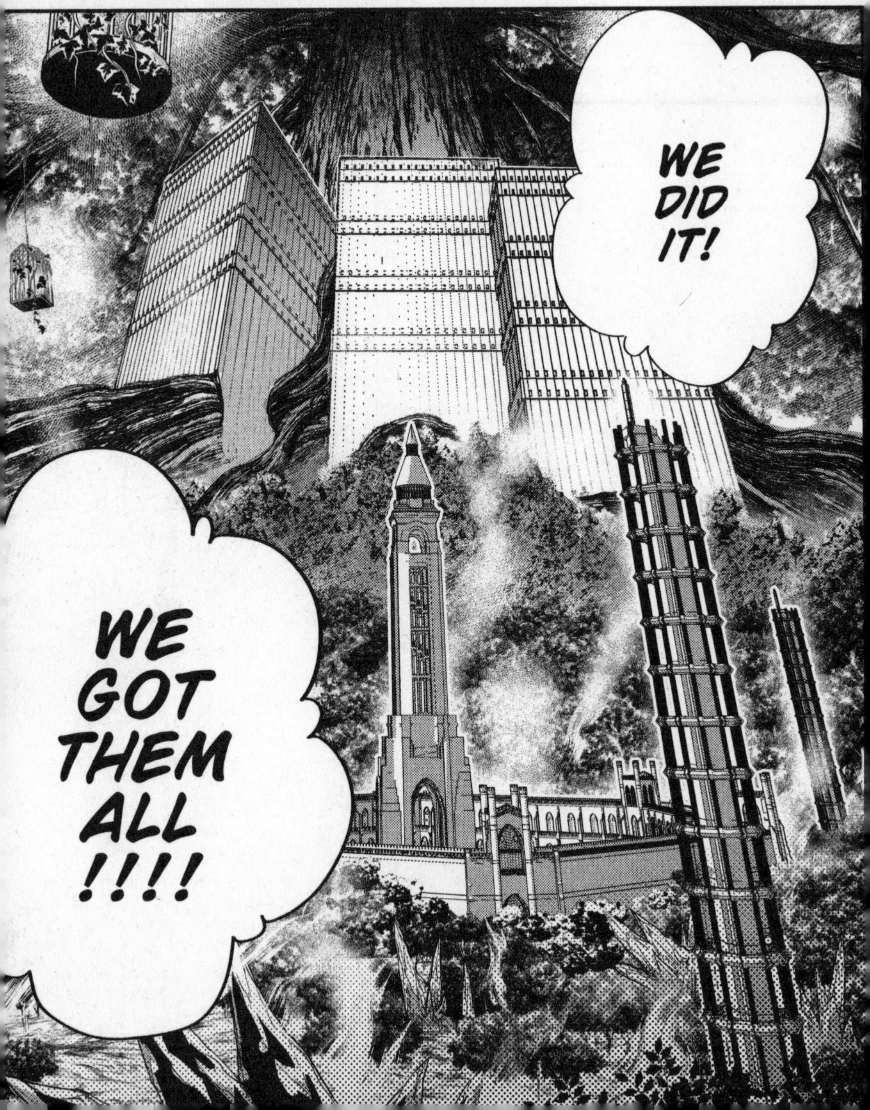
WE DID IT!
WE GOT THEM ALL !!!!

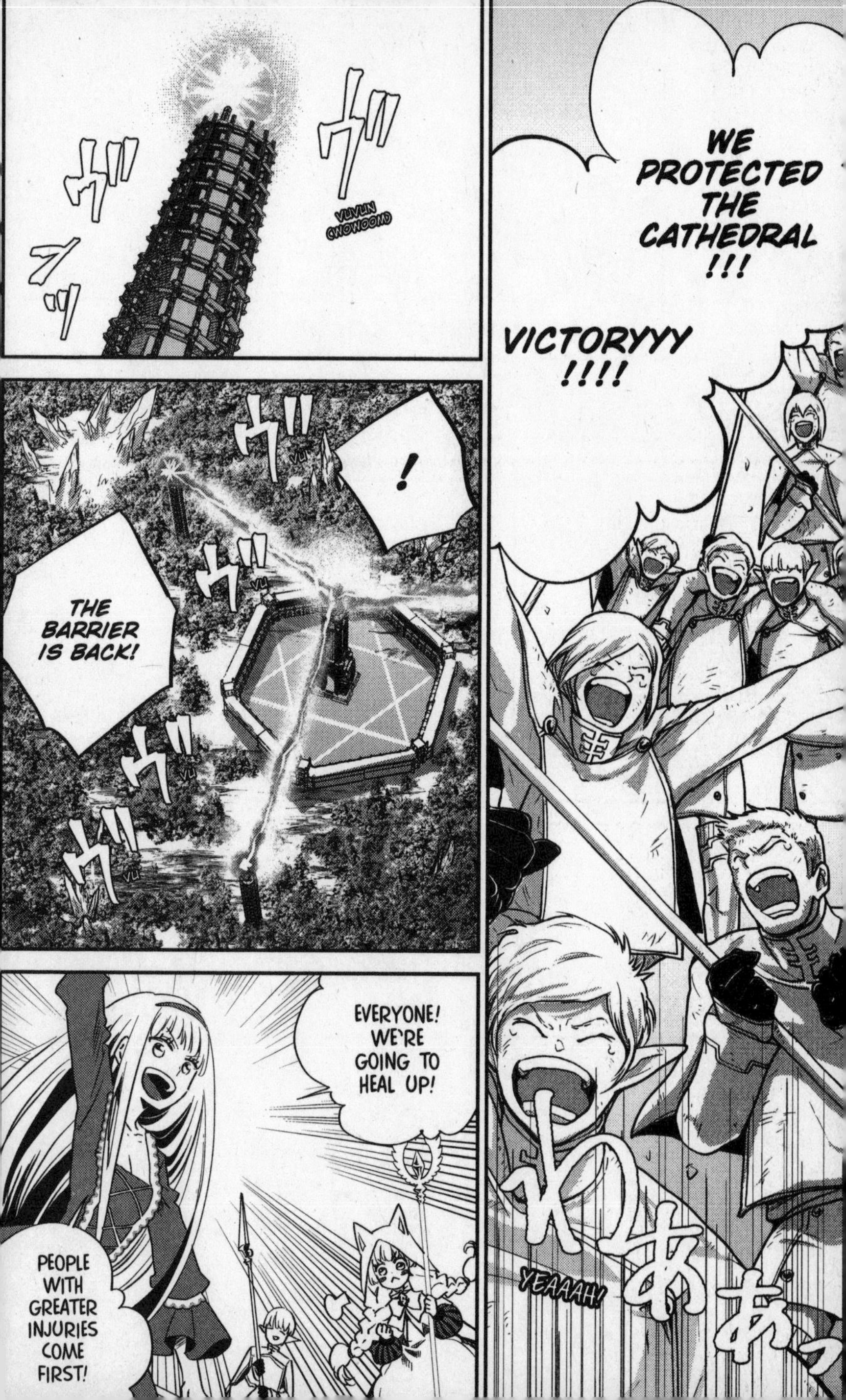
WE PROTECTED THE CATHEDRAL !!!
VICTORYYY !!!!
YEAAAH!
VUVUN (NOWOOM)
!
THE BARRIER IS BACK!
VU
VU
VU
VU
EVERYONE! WE'RE GOING TO HEAL UP!
PEOPLE WITH GREATER INJURIES COME FIRST!

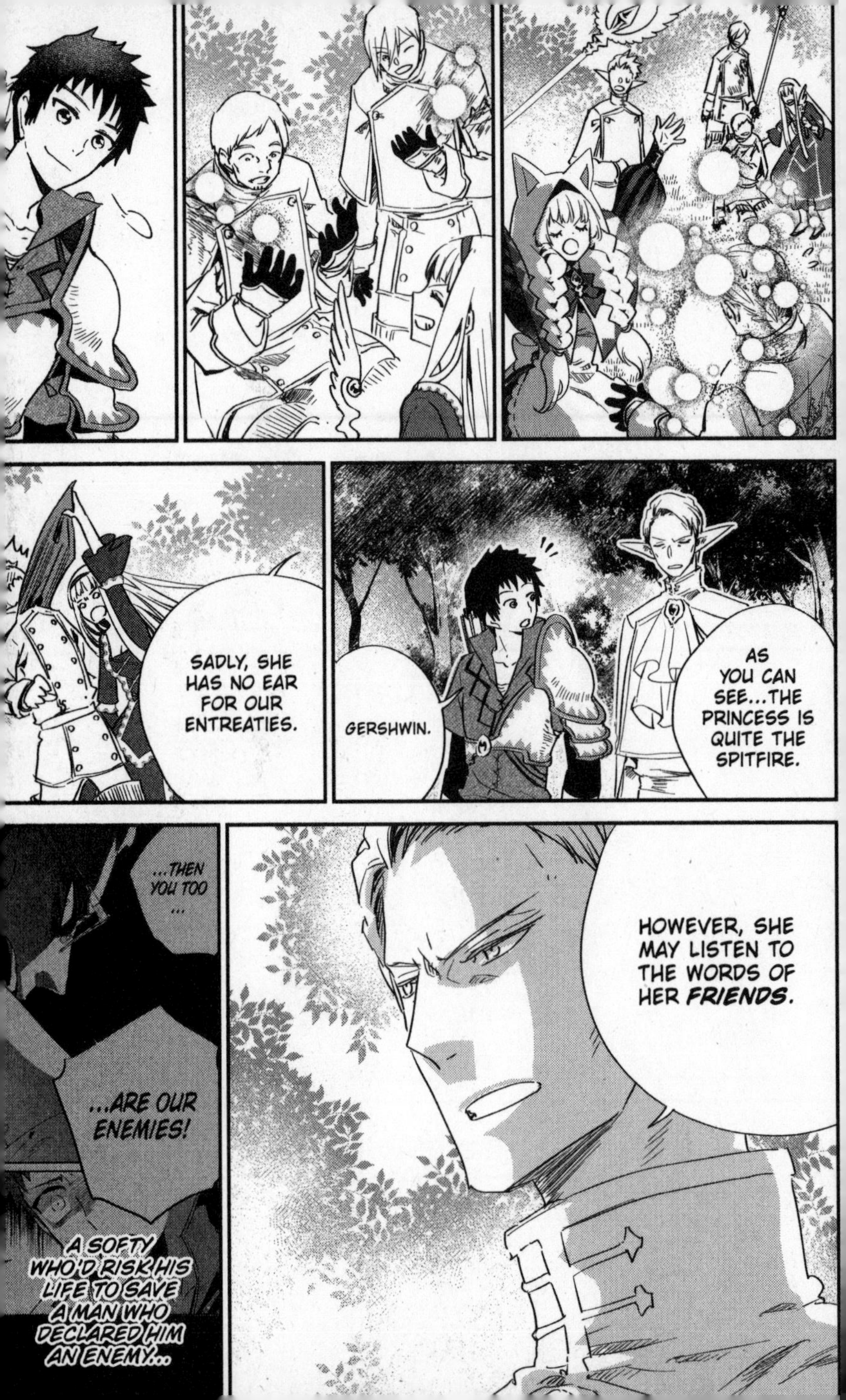
AS YOU CAN SEE...THE PRINCESS IS QUITE THE SPITFIRE.
GERSHWIN.
SADLY, SHE HAS NO EAR FOR OUR ENTREATIES.
HOWEVER, SHE MAY LISTEN TO THE WORDS OF HER FRIENDS.
...THEN YOU TOO ...
...ARE OUR ENEMIES!
A SOFTY WHO'D RISK HIS LIFE TO SAVE A MAN WHO DECLARED HIM AN ENEMY...

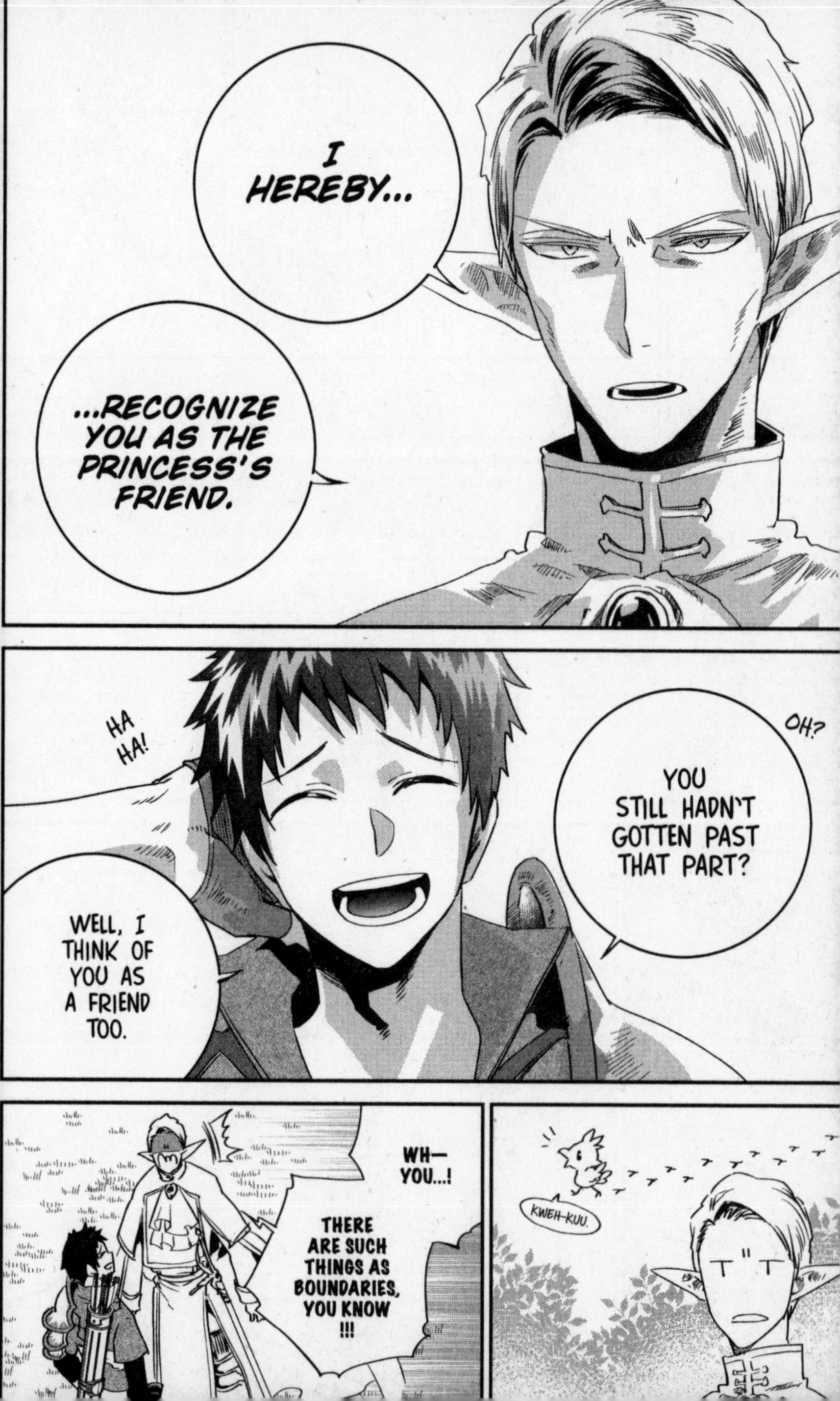
I HEREBY...
...RECOGNIZE YOU AS THE PRINCESS'S FRIEND.
OH?
YOU STILL HADN'T GOTTEN PAST THAT PART?
HA HA!
WELL, I THINK OF YOU AS A FRIEND TOO.
KWEH-KUU.
WH— YOU...!
THERE ARE SUCH THINGS AS BOUNDARIES, YOU KNOW!!!

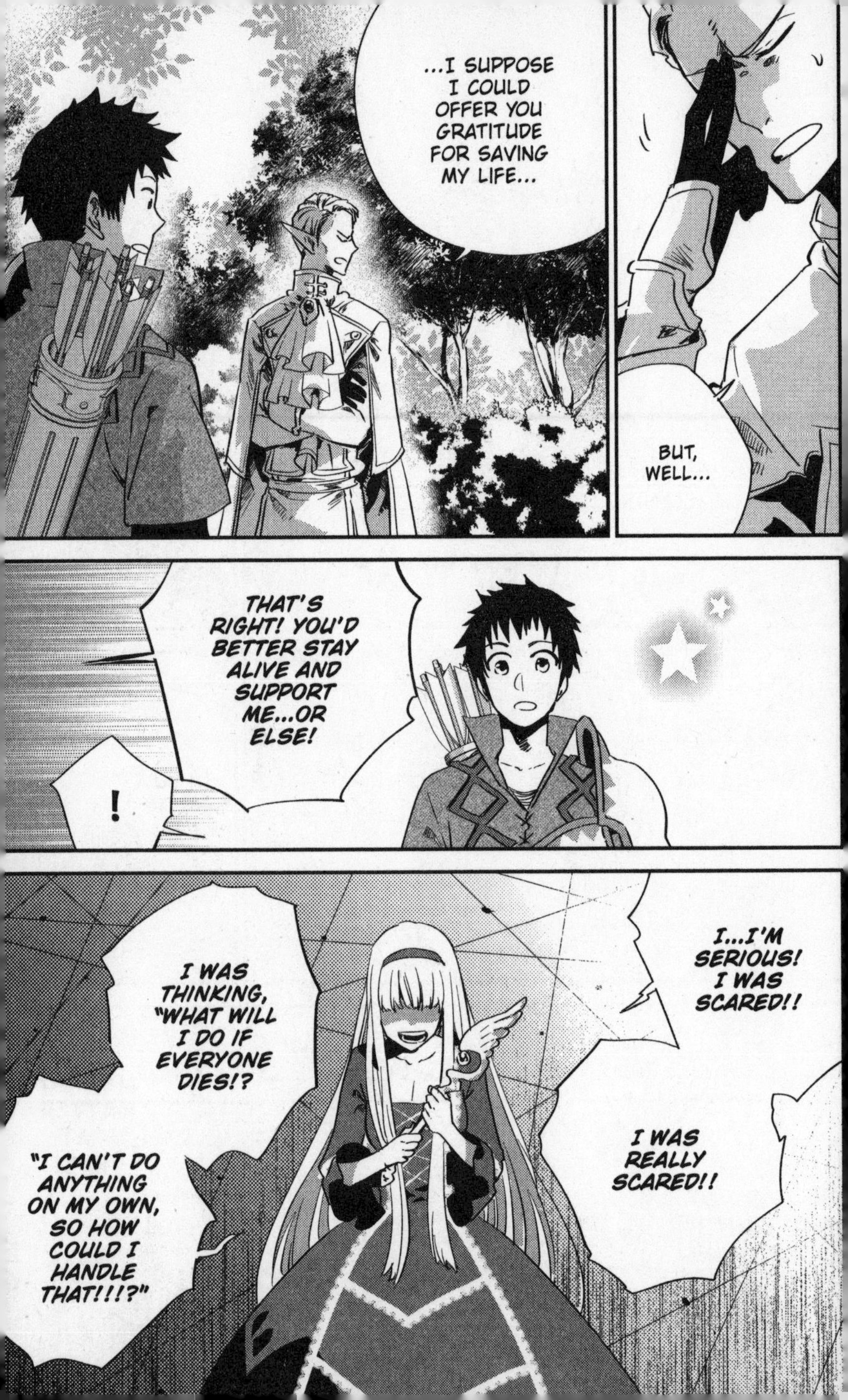
BUT, WELL...
...I SUPPOSE I COULD OFFER YOU GRATITUDE FOR SAVING MY LIFE...
THAT'S RIGHT! YOU'D BETTER STAY ALIVE AND SUPPORT ME...OR ELSE!
!
I...I'M SERIOUS! I WAS SCARED!!
I WAS REALLY SCARED!!
I WAS THINKING, "WHAT WILL I DO IF EVERYONE DIES!?
"I CAN'T DO ANYTHING ON MY OWN, SO HOW COULD I HANDLE THAT!!!?"

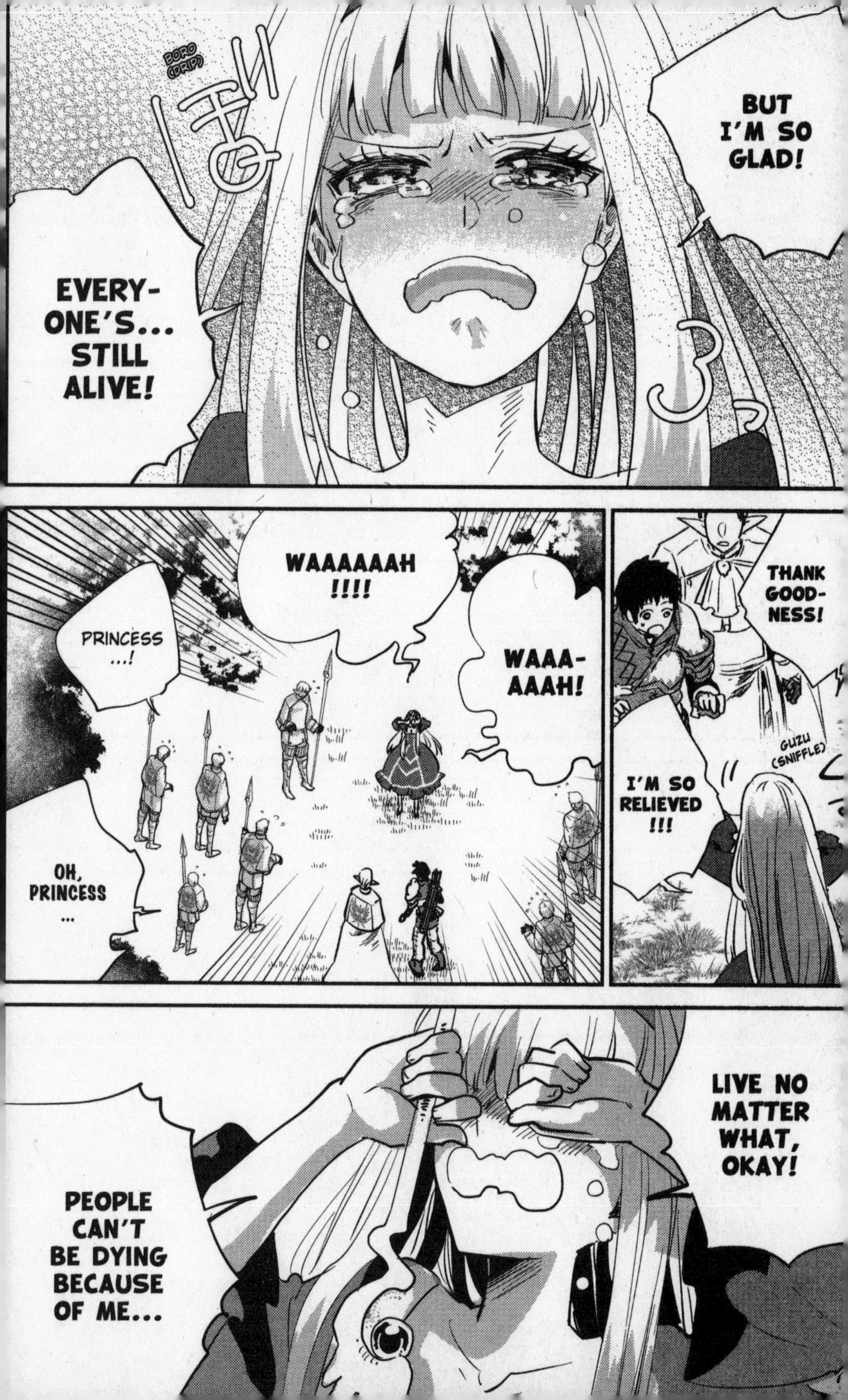
BUT I'M SO GLAD!
BORO (DRIP)
EVERY-ONE'S... STILL ALIVE!
THANK GOOD-NESS!
GUZU (SNIFFLE)
I'M SO RELIEVED!!!
WAAA-AAAH!
WAAAAAAH!!!!
PRINCESS...!
OH, PRINCESS...
LIVE NO MATTER WHAT, OKAY!
PEOPLE CAN'T BE DYING BECAUSE OF ME...

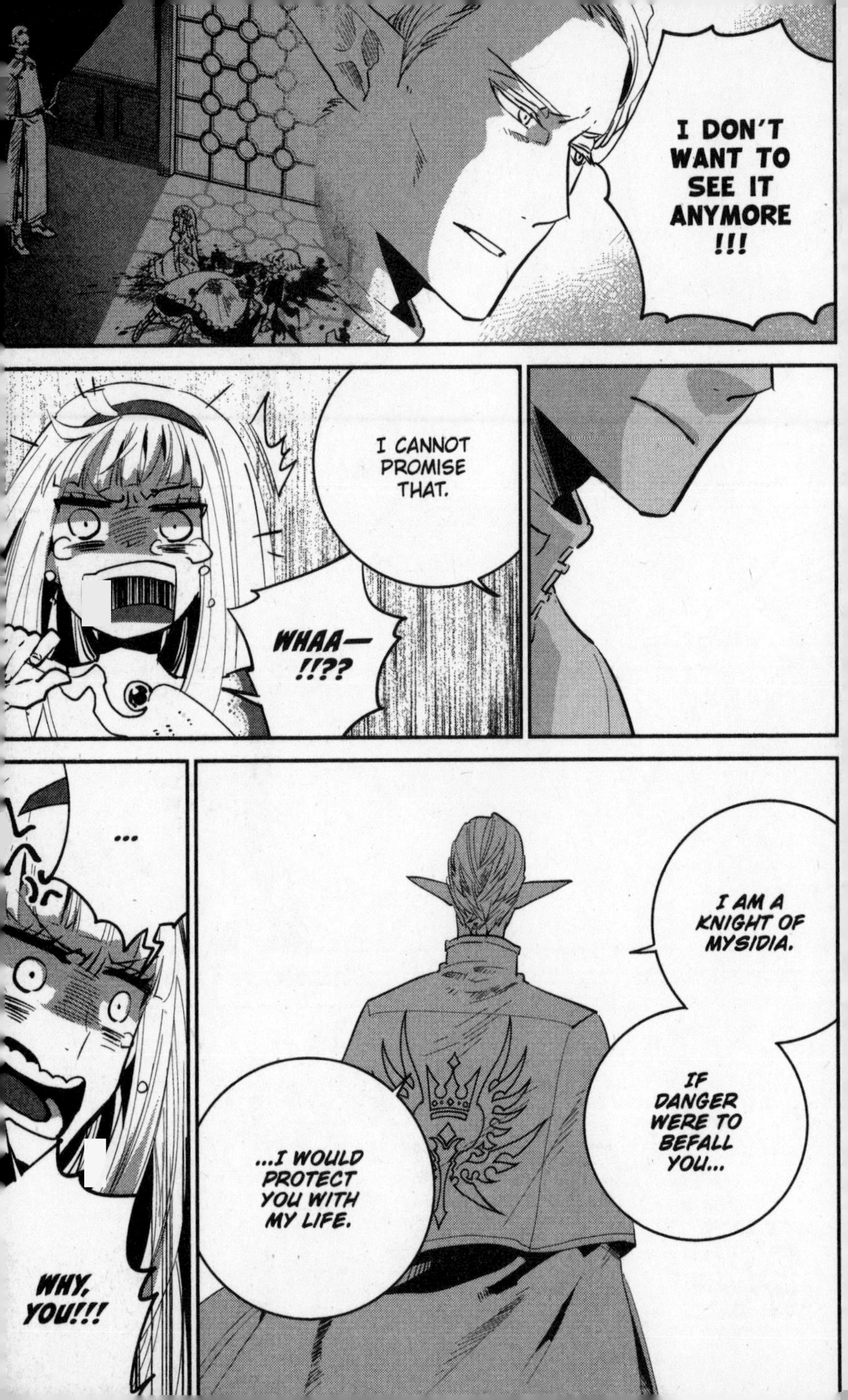
I DON'T WANT TO SEE IT ANYMORE !!!
I CANNOT PROMISE THAT.
WHAA— !!??
I AM A KNIGHT OF MYSIDIA.
IF DANGER WERE TO BEFALL YOU...
...I WOULD PROTECT YOU WITH MY LIFE.
...
WHY, YOU!!!

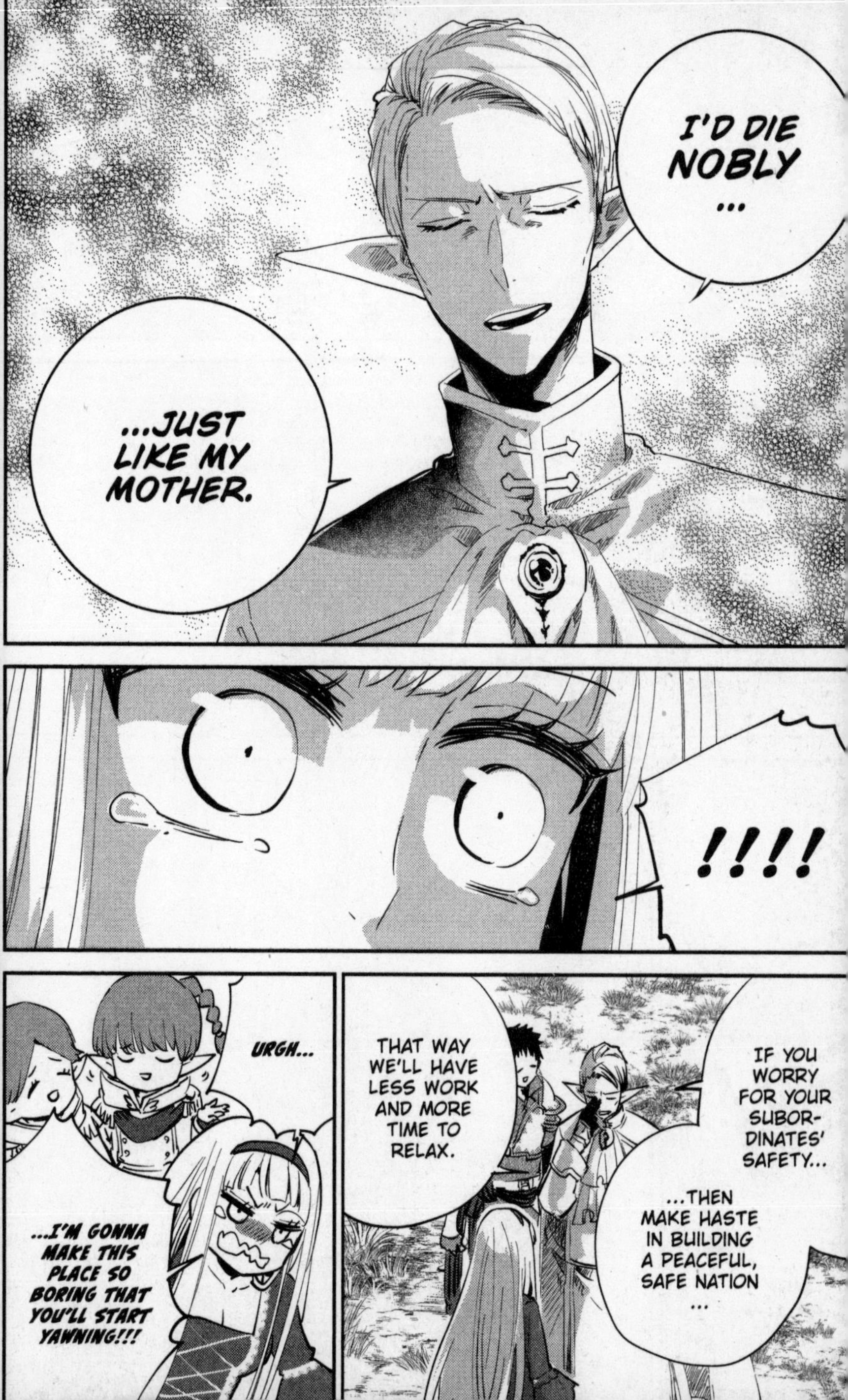
I'D DIE NOBLY ...
...JUST LIKE MY MOTHER.
!!!!
IF YOU WORRY FOR YOUR SUBOR-DINATES' SAFETY...
...THEN MAKE HASTE IN BUILDING A PEACEFUL, SAFE NATION ...
THAT WAY WE'LL HAVE LESS WORK AND MORE TIME TO RELAX.
URGH...
...I'M GONNA MAKE THIS PLACE SO BORING THAT YOU'LL START YAWNING!!!

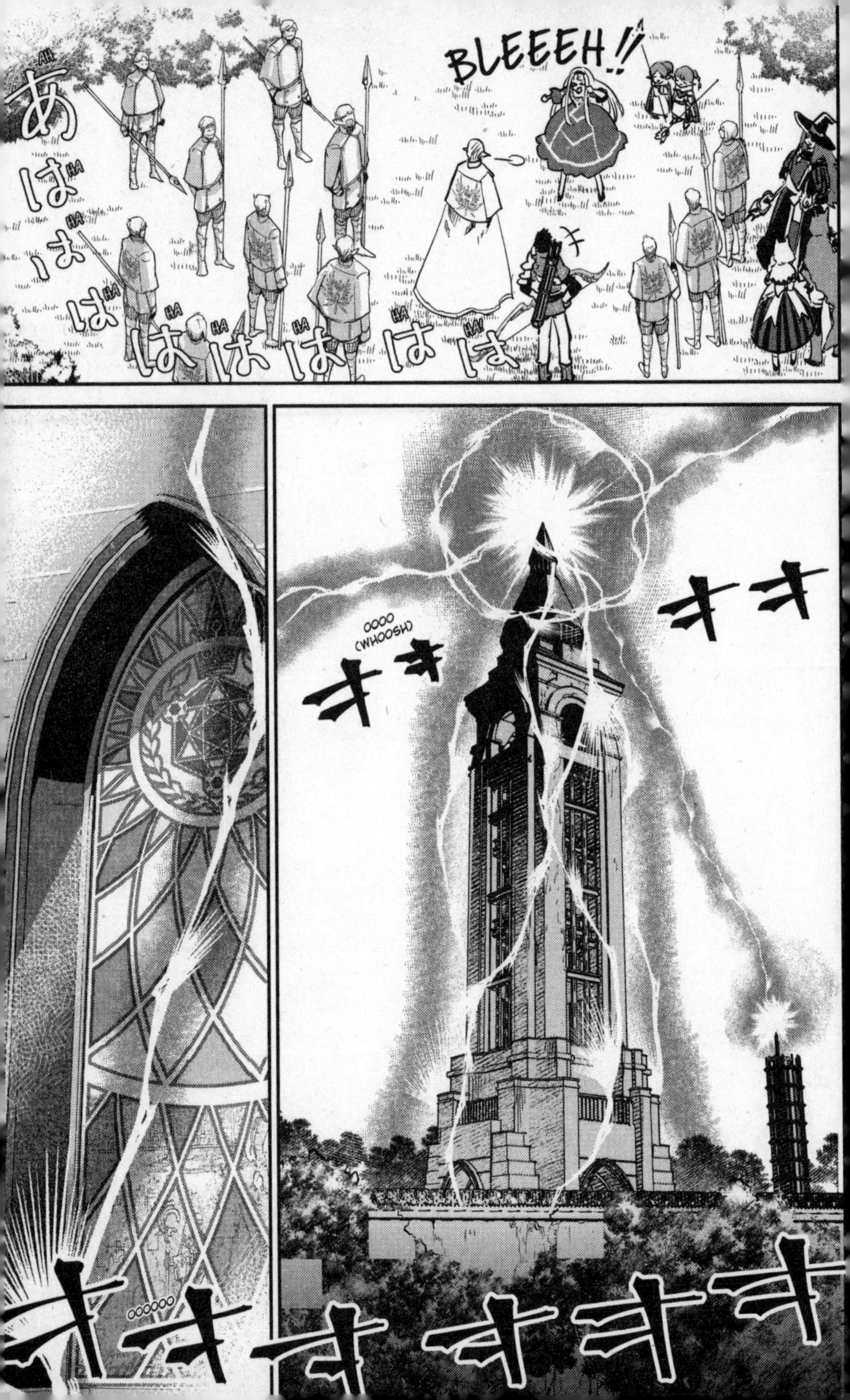
BLEEEH!!
キ
あ AH
は HA
は HA
は HA
は HA
は HA
は HA
は HA
は HA!
オオ
OOOO (WHOOSH)
オオ
オオオオオ
OOOOOO
オオ

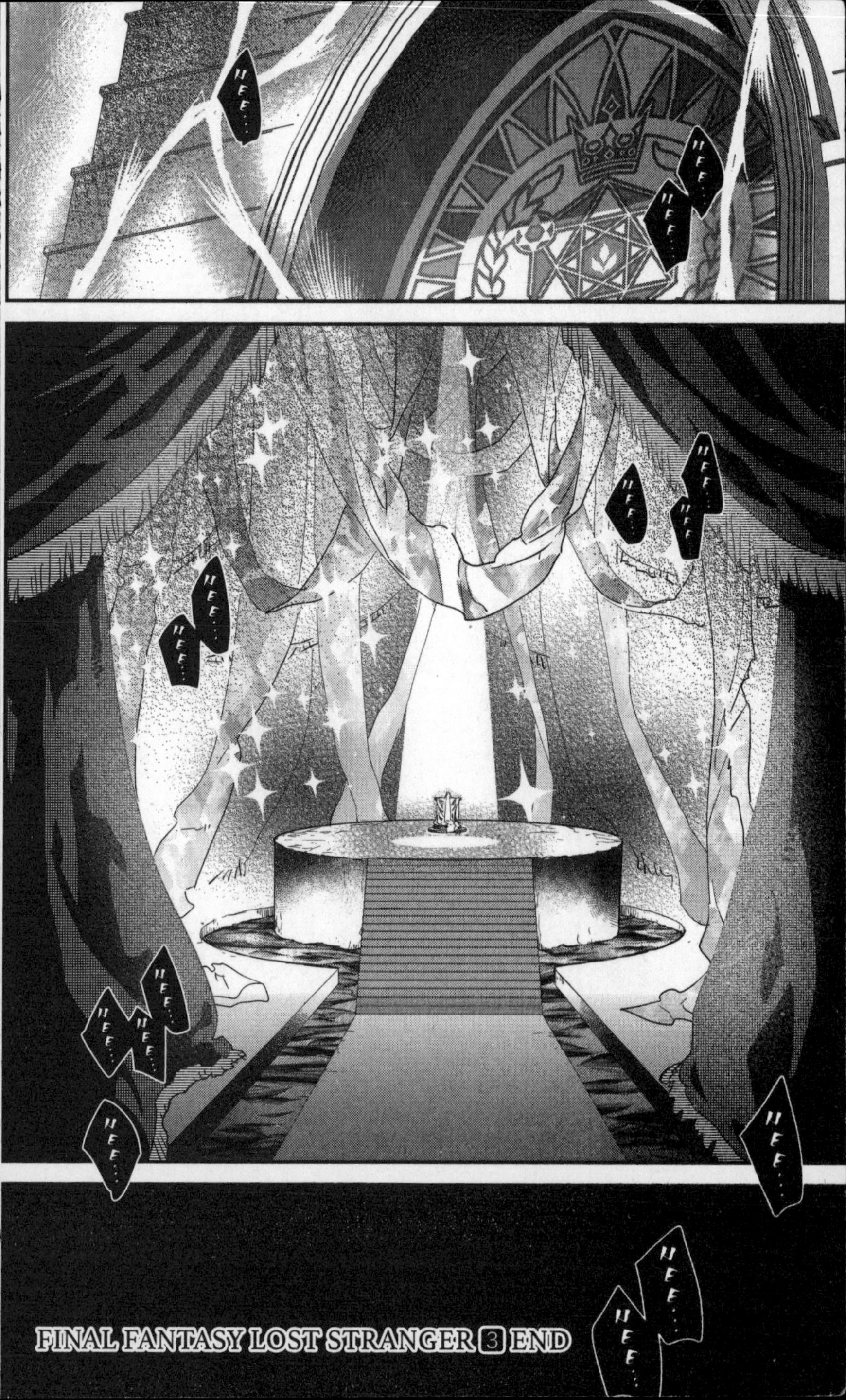
HEE...
HEE...
HEE...
HEE...
HEE...
HEE...
HEE...
HEE...
HEE...
HEE...
HEE...
HEE...
HEE...
HEE...
HEE...
HEE...
FINAL FANTASY LOST STRANGER 3 END

TRANSLATION
NOTES

COMMON HONORIFICS

no honorific: Indicates familiarity or closeness; if used without permission or reason, addressing someone in this manner would constitute an insult.

-san: The Japanese equivalent of Mr./Mrs./Miss. If a situation calls for politeness, this is the fail-safe honorific.

-kun: Used most often when referring to boys, this indicates affection or familiarity. Occasionally used by older men among their peers, but it may also be used by anyone referring to a person of lower standing.

-chan: An affectionate honorific indicating familiarity used mostly in reference to girls; also used in reference to cute persons or animals of either gender.

-sensei: A respectful term for teachers, artists, or high-level professionals.

Onii-chan: An affectionate term used for older brothers or brother figures.

-◊- PAGE 4
The Japanese title of this chapter translates to "To the End of the Abyss", but it's also the name of the FF10 track "Beyond the Darkness".

-◊- PAGE 9
In FF14, your job is defined by the weapon you're wielding, so no weapon means no job and no spells.

-◊- PAGE 39
The Japanese title of this chapter translates to "Messenger of Destruction", but it's also the name of the FF9 track "The Darkness of Eternity".

-◊- PAGE 71
The Japanese title of this chapter translates to "Sprouting", but it's also the name of the FF10 track "Movement in Green".

-◊- PAGE 121
The Japanese title of this chapter translates to "Someday, Surely", but it's also the name of the FF5 track "The Day Will Come".

-◊- PAGE 159
The Japanese title of this chapter translates to "Dancing Doll", but it's also the name of the FF4 track "Dancing Calcabrina".

FINAL FANTASY

LOST STRANGER

Story: Hazuki Minase　　Art: Itsuki Kameya

VOLUME 3

Translation: Melody Pan　Lettering: Bianca Pistillo

FINAL FANTASY LOST STRANGER Volume 3 ©2019 Hazuki Minase, Itsuki Kameya/SQUARE ENIX CO., LTD. ©2019 SQUARE ENIX CO., LTD. All Rights Reserved. First published in Japan in 2019 by SQUARE ENIX CO., LTD. English translation rights arranged with SQUARE ENIX CO., LTD. and Yen Press, LLC through Tuttle-Mori Agency, Inc., Tokyo.

· English translation © 2019 by SQUARE ENIX CO., LTD.

Yen Press
150 West 30th Street, 19th Floor
New York, NY 10001

Visit us at yenpress.com
facebook.com/yenpress
twitter.com/yenpress
yenpress.tumblr.com
instagram.com/yenpress

First Yen Press Edition: August 2019
The chapters in this volume were originally published as ebooks by Yen Press.

Yen Press is an imprint of Yen Press, LLC.
The Yen Press name and logo are trademarks of Yen Press, LLC.

The publisher is not responsible for websites (or their content) that are not owned by the publisher.

Library of Congress Control Number: 2018948073

ISBNs: 978-1-9753-8498-2 (paperback)
978-1-9753-8499-9 (ebook)

10 9 8 7 6 5 4 3 2 1

WOR

Printed in the United States of America